Critical Essays on
Theodore Dreiser

Critical Essays on Theodore Dreiser

Donald Pizer

G. K. Hall & Co. • Boston, Massachusetts

Library of Congress Cataloging in Publication Data
Main entry under title:

Critical essays on Theodore Dreiser.

  (Critical essays on American literature)
  Includes index.
  1. Dreiser, Theodore, 1871-1945—Criticism and
interpretation—Collected works. I. Pizer, Donald.
II. Series.
PS3507.R55Z576   813'.52   80-29495
ISBN 0-8161-8257-4

This publication is printed on permanent/durable acid-free paper

CRITICAL ESSAYS ON AMERICAN LITERATURE

This series seeks to collect the most important previously published criticism on writers and topics in American literature, along with, in various volumes, original essays, interviews, bibliographies, letters, manuscript sections, and other materials brought to public attention for the first time. Professor Pizer has assembled in this volume a distinguished collection of reviews and essays on Theodore Dreiser written by such important American writers as Sherwood Anderson and Robert Penn Warren and such leading Dreiser scholars as Ellen Moers, F. O. Matthiessen, Charles C. Walcutt, and Richard Lehan, among others. We are confident that this book will make a permanent and significant contribution to American literary scholarship.

James Nagel, GENERAL EDITOR

Northeastern University

For Robert H. Elias and Neda Westlake
And in memory of Ellen Moers

CONTENTS

INTRODUCTION

It is possible to distinguish three distinctive though overlapping phases in the criticism of Theodore Dreiser and his work. The first centered on the validity of Dreiserian naturalism as an adequate rendering of American life. This phase began with the reviews of *Sister Carrie* in 1900 and peaked during the years following the publication of *The "Genius"* in 1915, when the forces of "decency" led by Stuart P. Sherman and those of "freedom" led by H. L. Mencken engaged in a bitter debate which was focused on Dreiser and his fiction. The publication of *An American Tragedy* in 1925 caused a decline in this specific argumentative use of Dreiser. The great acclaim accorded the novel (including a laudatory review by Sherman) and the possibility that Dreiser might become the first American to win the Nobel Prize for literature tended to legitimatize Dreiser as a major American author.

The second phase of Dreiser criticism began in the 1930s. The emphasis now was less on the social and ethical acceptability of his fiction and more on the contradictions and inconsistencies in his philosophical and political ideas, whether these ideas were expressed in his novels or elsewhere. This period of Dreiser criticism, like the first, reached a climax in a debate when Dreiser's death in 1946 stimulated a number of conflicting evaluations of his work and career. Among these, Robert H. Elias in his biography and F. O. Matthiessen in his critical study argued for Dreiser's greatness, while Lionel Trilling, in a famous essay on Dreiser in *The Liberal Imagination*, denied him permanent significance.

The third or scholarly phase of Dreiser criticism began in the 1940s with Elias's biography and Charles C. Walcutt's *PMLA* essay on the three stages of Dreiser's naturalism, but it was launched fully only in the late 1950s with the publication of Elias's three-volume edition of Dreiser's letters, Walcutt's expanded version of his essay in his *American Literary Naturalism*, and Alfred Kazin and Charles Shapiro's collection of Dreiser criticism in *The Stature of Theodore Dreiser*. Although scholarly criticism from the mid-1950s until the present still has sought to confront basic issues in the interpretation of Dreiser's work—both his work as a whole and his major novels in particular—it also has attempted to provide a factual base of knowledge about Dreiser's life, writing, and thought as an aid to interpretation.

From the first, discussion of Dreiser and his fiction often has served as a vehicle for cultural and literary polemics. Few American writers have occasioned as much criticism which reveals more about its moment than about its ostensible subject. From the appearance of *Sister Carrie* to the present, an opportunity to examine Dreiser also has meant an opportunity to press the claims of a particular view of American life and a specific concept about the nature of fiction. To read the criticism of Dreiser is to receive an education in the ways in which art and society interact when an artist devotes most of his career to attacking the prevailing assumptions of his society.

During Dreiser's early career, such defenders of his work as Harris M. Lyon, William Marion Reedy, Edgar Lee Masters, Sherwood Anderson, Randolph Bourne, and above all H. L. Mencken not merely were praising a writer whose novels moved them. They also were seeking to cast Dreiser in the symbolic role of the trailblazer whose willingness to ignore or openly challenge the conventional beliefs and genteel codes of American life had opened a way for others. "The feet of Dreiser," Anderson wrote, are "making a path for us." If Dreiser's feet were "heavy" and "brutal," as Anderson went on to note, it was because he had mountains of resistance to scale. If his work appeared to lack beauty, it was because the concept of beauty had degenerated into a belief in mere surface grace and polish. And if his ideas were often tedious or obscure, it was because he was fumbling honestly for truths which men had so long refused to acknowledge. In short, Dreiser's defects were the virtues of a pathfinder and iconoclast. To those who opposed Dreiser—and these included the great majority of journalistic reviewers and most academic critics—the issue also was joined on the question of "brutality"—or, more specifically, the amorality and sexuality of the first two volumes of the Cowperwood trilogy (published in 1912 and 1914) and of The "Genius." To Stuart Sherman in 1915 and later to such New Humanists as Paul Elmer More and Robert Shafer, Dreiser was not the pure voice of truth but rather the howl of atavistic animalism. Men often may be selfish and bestial, they agreed, but they also argued that civilization was man's effort to control these aspects of his animal past through reason and will, and that literature should represent the possibility and desirability of this effort. (It is of interest to note that this attack on Dreiser's "barbarism" reached its shrillest level during World War I, when critics such as Sherman frequently alluded to Dreiser's German ancestry.)

By the mid–1930s, with the critical acceptance of writers far more sensationally explicit than Dreiser in their material and themes—writers such as John Dos Passos, James T. Farrell, and William Faulkner—it appeared that Dreiser's struggle for recognition had been won. But instead during this decade Dreiser became the focus of two additional critical movements with widespread cultural significance. Although writers and critics sympathetic to Dreiser such as Farrell and later Matthiessen and Kazin would continue to praise him for having achieved a powerful blend of social realism and authorial compassion, it became far more common to attack Dreiser (as did Trilling in his 1950 essay on "Reality in America") both for his idea of reality and for his mode of depicting it.

Trilling's essay indirectly expresses a widely shared revulsion by formerly radical critics of the 1930s toward writers whose work and thought had been preempted by the Communist Party during the decade. Dreiser was perhaps the principal example of a major literary figure of this kind. During the 1930s and early 1940s he could be counted upon to endorse almost every policy decision of the party, from its adoption of the Scottsboro and Mooney cases as left-wing causes to its support of the Soviet Union during the Russian-Finnish War. When Dreiser died not only an unrepentant camp follower but also an actual party member (in a symbolic act, Dreiser had joined the party a few months before his death) he became a prime target for those critics who themselves had been party sympathizers during the early 1930s but who had rejected the leadership and ideology of the party as the decade progressed. And since it was Dreiser's intellect which was suspect in his continued support of Communism, what better way to demonstrate Dreiser's vacuity than to point out the inadequacies of the ideas in his fiction?

Another literary movement indirectly reflected in Trilling's essay which adversely affected Dreiser's reputation for almost two decades was the New Criticism. To many academic critics bred upon the great attention to form and structure in the close reading of Jamesian intricacies and post-Jamesian experimentation, Dreiser's awkwardness and massiveness seemed the antithesis of the art of fiction. Thus, with Dreiser in disfavor as both thinker and artist—to say nothing of the confusion created by the mystic element in his two posthumous novels—it is no wonder that during the 1940s and 1950s, as Irving Howe recalls, his work was "a symbol of everything a superior intelligence was supposed to avoid."

Although the Trilling–Matthiessen dispute over Dreiser's "power" (Is it a left-wing myth, or does it in truth reside in his fiction?) still occasionally surfaces (for example, as in Charles T. Samuels's attack on Robert Penn Warren's praise of *An American Tragedy*), much of the significant critical writing about Dreiser since the mid-1950s has shifted from the use of him as a cultural symbol to a close examination of his career and work. Robert Elias's edition of Dreiser's letters and W. A. Swanberg's lengthy biography provided a solid base of fact about Dreiser's life, and since the early 1960s the availability of Dreiser's literary estate at the University of Pennsylvania (a magnificent collection of Dreiser's manuscripts and correspondence) has provided an equally important basis for the detailed study of the genesis of his work. A number of scholars—for example, Ellen Moers, Richard Lehan, Philip Gerber, and Donald Pizer—have since the early 1960s written full-length studies of Dreiser which are based in large part upon material in the Dreiser Collection.

By the mid-1960s, some of the older strains in Dreiser criticism had died out. No longer was it necessary to defend or attack his subjects or ideas because of their challenge to contemporary conventions. But other issues of long-standing controversy in the discussion of Dreiser's work continued to attract much attention, which suggests that they have become the permanent center of Dreiser criticism. One of these is Dreiser's naturalism—or, to put it another way, what is naturalism, and how is Dreiser a naturalist? The question appears simple, and many early critics treated it as such. Naturalism was Darwinian materialistic determinism in theme and crude massiveness in technique, and Dreiser was a prime example of both. But most critics who have written since the seminal essay by Eliseo Vivas in 1938 have recognized that many different strains make up the distinctive fictional voice which is Dreiser's, and that some of these strains—his mysticism and transcendentalism, or his prophetic tone—are antithetical to the amoral objectivity of a conventionally conceived naturalist. It is now increasingly clear that Dreiser's tragic view of life and his power as a novelist are not the products of a naturalist who somehow transcends the limitations of his literary mode but rather must reside in a redefined conception of that mode. In short, though critics still engage the problems of defining naturalism as a major American literary movement and explaining Dreiser as our principal naturalist, they now incline toward an acceptance of the complexities and ambivalences of both the movement and Dreiser.

Dreiser criticism is also still concerned with the related problem of his verbal ineptness. Even Mencken, the most persistent of Dreiser's early champions, could not ignore this aspect of Dreiser's fiction, and of course it was one of the major reasons for the New Critics' contempt for Dreiser's work. However, more recently a number of critics (Ellen Moers and William L. Phillips, for example) have discovered considerable subtlety and even "finesse" in Dreiser's prose style, while still others (notably Julian Markels, David Weimer, and Robert Penn Warren) have argued that the novel as a form creates its effect as much through symbolic constructs as through language, and that Dreiser's success with such constructs explains his success as a novelist.

A good deal of the best criticism of Dreiser has continued also to examine the question of his preoccupation with our lives as Americans. To these readers Dreiser is not merely a documentary social realist in the manner of turn-of-the-century muckrakers or 1930s proletarian novelists. He is rather a profound observer of the underlying myths and emotional realities of the American experience. They find that Dreiser's rendering of our lives as an inconclusive mixture of hope and despair and of beauty and degradation constitutes a major source of his permanent power. Criticism of Dreiser thus has rejected the old conventional judgments about him as a doctrinaire naturalist, as an inept novelist, and as a superficial social realist and now seeks to discover the springs of his permanence in the complex actualities of his fiction.

It might be helpful to note the principles of selection which have guided me in the choice of material for this volume. My emphasis has been on critical essays which deal mainly with Dreiser's fiction. For most readers, Dreiser is preeminently a novelist. In addition, there has been little of importance written about his other forms of expression, though discussion of these forms does occasionally play a significant role in the criticism of his novels, as in the essay by Roger Asselineau. Studies which are primarily biographical, historical, or bibliographical have also been slighted. Of course, such scholarship is extremely valuable but it is also limited in its general interest. I have tried to choose the best criticism of Dreiser's fiction, including the work of critics who shed light on his writing even while attacking it, but I also have included a few examples of Dreiser criticism at its most biased and obtuse in order to suggest the nature of this criticism. However, I have not attempted to represent the full extent of Dreiser "negative" criticism from the reviews of *Sister Carrie* to the posthumous surveys of his career. Most of this is journalistic criticism, and repetitiously and superficially echoes such familiar notes as Dreiser's suspect philosophy, weak prose, and excessive documentation. Nevertheless, I have sought to include in this volume the best of Mencken's reviews of Dreiser's fiction, reviews which in their argumentative vigor and critical incisiveness represent literary journalism at its best. The reader interested in a full sampling (over 700 pages) of reviews of Dreiser's work should consult Jack Salzman's *Theodore Dreiser: The Critical Reception* (New York: David Lewis, 1972). A listing of all Dreiser criticism (including reviews) through 1973 is contained in Donald Pizer, Richard W. Dowell, and Frederic Rusch's *Theodore Dreiser: A Primary and Secondary Bibliography* (Boston: G. K. Hall, 1975). And Robert H. Elias offers an interpretive survey of Dreiser criticism in his "Theodore Dreiser," *Sixteen Modern American Authors*, ed. Jackson Bryer (Durham, N.C.: Duke University Press, 1973).

I have thought it best to divide the selections into general essays which deal with Dreiser's work and thought as a whole and specific essays which concentrate on a single novel. In this way users of the volume can be guided by the table of contents to sections of the book which pertain to their special interests. However, since many of the general essays also include substantial commentary on particular novels, and since some of the specific essays contain discussion of other novels by Dreiser besides the novel of principal interest, the reader is advised to consult the index for a complete record of comments on a specific novel in this volume.

I have sought to reprint complete essays and chapters rather than excerpts. When this has not been possible, omissions have been noted by a line of asterisks in the text. (All ellipses are the authors'.)

GENERAL ESSAYS

Theodore the Poet

As a boy, Theodore, you sat for long hours
On the shore of the turbid Spoon
With deep-set eye staring at the door of the craw-
    fish's burrow,
Waiting for him to appear, pushing ahead,
First his waving antennae, like straws of hay,
And soon his body, colored like soap stone,
Gemmed with eyes of jet.
And you wondered in a trance of thought
What he knew, what he desired, and why he lived
    at all.
But later your vision watched for men and women
Hiding in burrows of fate amid great cities,
Looking for the souls of them to come out,
So that you could see
How they lived, and for what,
And why they kept crawling so busily
Along the sandy way where water fails
As the summer wanes.

*Reprinted from *The Spoon River Anthology* (New York: Macmillan, 1915), p. 36; reprinted
by permission of Mrs. Edgar Lee Masters.

The Naturalism of Mr. Dreiser

Stuart P. Sherman*

The layman who listens reverently to the reviewers discussing the new novels and to the novelists discussing themselves can hardly escape persuasion that a great change has rather recently taken place in the spirit of the age, in the literature which reflects it, and in the criticism which judges it. The nature of the supposed revolution may be briefly summarized.

The elder generation was in love with illusions, and looked at truth through a glass darkly and timorously. The artist, tongue-tied by authority and trammelled by aesthetic and moral conventions, selected, suppressed, and rearranged the data of experience and observation. The critic, "morally subsidized," regularly professed his disdain for a work of art in which no light glimmered above "the good and the beautiful."

The present age is fearless and is freeing itself from illusions. Now, for the first time in history, men are facing unabashed the facts of life. "Death or life," we cry, "give us only reality!" Now, for the first time in the history of English literature, fiction is become a flawless mirror held up to the living world. Rejecting nothing, altering nothing, it presents to us—let us take our terms from the bright lexicon of the reviewer—a "transcript," a "cross-section," a "slice," a "photographic" or "cinematographic" reproduction of life. The critic who keeps pace with the movement no longer asks whether the artist has created beauty or glorified goodness, but merely whether he has told the truth.

Mr. Dreiser, in his latest novel, describes a canvas by a painter of this austere modern school: "Raw reds, raw greens, dirty gray paving stones—such faces! Why, this thing fairly shouted its facts. It seemed to say: 'I'm dirty, I am commonplace, I am grim, I am shabby, but I am life.' And there was no apologizing for anything in it, no glossing anything over. Bang! Smash! Crack! came the facts one after another, with a bitter, brutal insistence on their so-ness." If you do not like what is in the picture, you are to be crushed by the retort that perhaps you do not like what

*Reprinted from *Nation*, 101 (December 2, 1915), 648–50. When reprinted by Sherman in his *On Contemporary Literature* (New York: Holt, 1917), the essay was entitled "The Barbaric Naturalism of Theodore Dreiser." Copyright © 1915 The Nation Associates; reprinted by permission.

is in life. Perhaps you have not the courage to confront reality. Perhaps you had better read the chromatic fairy-tales with the children. Men of sterner stuff exclaim, like the critic in this novel, "Thank God for a realist!"

Mr. Dreiser is a novelist of the new school, for whom we have been invited off and on these fourteen years to thank God—a form of speech, by the way, which crept into the language before the dawn of modern realism. He has performed with words what his hero performed with paint. He has presented the facts of life "one after another with a bitter, brutal insistence on their so-ness," which marks him as a "man of the hour," a "portent"—the successor of Mr. Howells and Mr. James. In the case of a realist, biographical details are always relevant. Mr. Dreiser was born of German-American parents in Terre Haute, Indiana, in 1871. He was educated in the Indiana public schools and at the State University. He was engaged in newspaper work in Chicago, St. Louis, New York and elsewhere, from 1892 to 1910. He has laid reality bare for us in five novels published as follows: "Sister Carrie," 1901; "Jennie Gerhardt," 1911; "The Financier," 1912; "The Titan," 1914; and "The Genius," 1915. These five works constitute a singularly homogeneous mass of fiction. I do not find any moral value in them, nor any memorable beauty—of their truth I shall speak later; but I am greatly impressed by them as serious representatives of a new note in American literature, coming from that "ethnic" element of our mixed population which, as we are assured by competent authorities, is to redeem us from Puritanism and insure our artistic salvation. They abundantly illustrate, furthermore, the methods and intentions of our recent courageous, veracious realism. Before we thank God for it, let us consider a little more closely what is offered us.

I

The first step towards the definition of Mr. Dreiser's special contribution is to blow away the dust with which the exponents of the new realism seek to becloud the perceptions of our "reverent layman." In their main pretensions, there are large elements of conscious and unconscious sham.

It should clear the air to say that courage in facing and veracity in reporting the facts of life are no more characteristic of Theodore Dreiser than of John Bunyan. These moral traits are not the peculiar marks of the new school; they are marks common to every great movement of literature within the memory of man. Each literary generation detaching itself from its predecessor—whether it has called its own movement Classical or Romantic or what not—has revolted in the interest of what it took to be a more adequate representation of reality. No one who is not drunken with the egotism of the hour, no one who has penetrated with sober senses into the spirit of any historical period anterior to his own, will fall into the indecency of declaring his own age preëminent in the desire to see and to tell the truth. The real distinction between one generation and another is in the thing which each takes for its master truth—in the thing which each recognizes as the essential reality for it. The difference between Bunyan and Dreiser is in the order of facts which each reports.

It seems necessary also to declare at periodic intervals that there is no such thing as a "cross-section" or "slice" or "photograph" of life in art—least of all in the realistic novel. The use of these catchwords is but a clever hypnotizing pass of the artist, employed to win the assent of the reader to the reality of the show, and, in some cases, to evade moral responsibility for any questionable features of the exhibition. A realistic novel no more than any other kind of a novel can escape being a composition, involving preconception, imagination, and divination. Yet, hearing one of our new realists expound his doctrine, you might suppose that writing a novel was a process analogous to photographing wild animals in their habitat by trap and flashlight. He, if you will believe him, does not invite his subjects, nor group them, nor compose their features, nor furnish their setting. He but exposes the sensitized plate of his mind. The pomp of life goes by, and springs the trap. The picture, of course, does not teach nor preach nor moralize. It simply re-presents. The only serious objection to this figurative explanation of the artistic process is the utter dissimilarity between the blank impartial photographic plate, commemorating everything that confronts it, and the crowded inveterately selective human mind, which, like a magnet, snatches the facts of life that are subject to its influence out of their casual order and redisposes them in a pattern of its own.

In the case of any specified novelist, the facts chosen and the pattern assumed by them are determined by his central theory or "philosophy of life"; and this is precisely criticism's justification for inquiring into the adequacy of any novelist's general ideas. In vain, the new realist throws up his hands with protestations of innocence, and cries: "Search me. I carry no concealed weapons. I run life into no preconceived mould. I have no philosophy. My business is only to observe, like a man of science, and to record what I have seen." He cannot observe without a theory, nor record his observations without betraying it to any critical eye.

As it happens, the man of science who most profoundly influenced the development of the new realistic novel—Charles Darwin—more candid than the writers of "scientific" fiction—frankly declared that he could not observe without a theory. When he had tentatively formulated a general law, and had begun definitely to look for evidence of its operation, then first the substantiating facts leaped abundantly into his vision. His "Origin of Species" has the unity of a work of art, because the recorded observations support a thesis. The French novelists who in the last century developed the novel of contemporary life learned as much, perhaps, from Darwin's art as from his science. Balzac emphasized the relation between man and his social *milieu*; the Goncourts emphasized the importance of extensive collection of "human documents"; Zola emphasized the value of scientific hypotheses. He deliberately adopted the materialistic philosophy of the period as his guide in observation and as his unifying principle in composition. His theory of the causes of social phenomena, which was derived largely from medical treatises, operated like a powerful magnet among the chaotic facts of life, rejecting some, selecting others, and redisposing them in the pattern of the *roman naturaliste*. Judicious French critics said: "My dear man," or words to that effect, "your representations of life are inadequate. This which you are offering us with so earnest an air is not reality. It is your own private nightmare." When they had exposed his theory, they had condemned his art.

Let us, then, dismiss Mr. Dreiser's untenable claims to superior courage and veracity of intention, the photographic transcript, and the unbiassed service of truth; and let us seek for his definition in his general theory of life, in the order of facts which he records, and in the pattern of his representations.

II.

The impressive unity of effect produced by Mr. Dreiser's five novels is due to the fact that they are all illustrations of a crude and naïvely simple naturalistic philosophy, such as we find in the mouths of exponents of the new *Real-Politik*. Each book, with its bewildering masses of detail, is a ferocious argument in behalf of a few brutal generalizations. To the eye cleared of illusions it appears that the ordered life which we call civilization does not really exist except on paper. In reality our so-called society is a jungle in which the struggle for existence continues, and must continue, on terms substantially unaltered by legal, moral, or social conventions. The central truth about man is that he is an animal amenable to no law but the law of his own temperament, doing as he desires, subject only to the limitations of his power. The male of the species is characterized by cupidity, pugnacity, and a simian inclination for the other sex. The female is a soft, vain, pleasure-seeking creature, devoted to personal adornment, and quite helplessly susceptible to the flattery of the male. In the struggles which arise in the jungle through the conflicting appetites of its denizens, the victory goes to the animal most physically fit and mentally ruthless, unless the weaklings, resisting absorption, combine against him and crush him by sheer force of numbers.

The idea that civilization is a sham Mr. Dreiser sometimes sets forth explicitly, and sometimes he conveys it by the process known among journalists as "coloring the news." When Sister Carrie yields to the seductive drummer, Drouet, Mr. Dreiser judicially weighs the advantages and disadvantages attendant on the condition of being a well-kept mistress.

When the institution of marriage is brushed aside by the heroine of "The Financier," he comments "editorially" as follows: "Before Christianity was man, and after it will also be. A metaphysical idealism will always tell him that it is better to preserve a cleanly balance, and the storms of circumstance will teach him a noble stoicism. Beyond this there is nothing which can reasonably be imposed upon the conscience of man." A little later in the same book he says: "Is there no law outside of the subtle will and the power to achieve? If not, it is surely high time that we knew it—one and all. We might then agree to do as we do; but there would be no silly illusion as to divine regulation." His own answer to the question, his own valuation of regulation, both divine and human, may be found in the innumerable contemptuous epithets which fall from his pen whenever he has occasion to mention any power set up against the urge of instinct and the indefinite expansion of desire. Righteousness is always "legal"; conventions are always "current"; routine is always "dull"; respectability is always "unctuous"; an institution for transforming schoolgirls into young ladies is presided over by "owl-like conventionalists"; families in which parents are faithful to each other lead an "apple-pie order of existence"; a man who yields to his impulses yet condemns himself for yielding is a "rag-bag moralistic ass." Jennie Gerhardt, by a facile surrender of her chastity, shows that *she could not be readily corrupted by the world's selfish lessons* on how to preserve oneself from the evil to come." Surely, this is "coloring the news."

By similar devices Mr. Dreiser drives home the great truth that man is essentially an animal, impelled by temperament, instinct, physics, chemistry—anything you please that is irrational and uncontrollable. Sometimes he writes an "editorial" paragraph in which the laws of human life are explained by reference to the behavior of certain protozoa or by reference to a squid and a lobster fighting in an aquarium. His heroes and heroines have "cat-like eyes," "feline grace," "sinuous strides," eyes and jaws which vary "from those of the tiger, lynx, and bear to those of the fox, the tolerant mastiff, and the surly bulldog." One hero and his mistress are said to "have run together temperamentally like two leopards." The lady in question, admiring the large rapacity of her mate, exclaims playfully: "Oh, you big tiger! You great, big lion! Boo!" Courtship as presented in these novels is after the manner of beasts in the jungle. Mr. Dreiser's leonine men but circle once or twice about their prey, and spring, and pounce; and the struggle is over. A pure-minded serving-maid, who is suddenly held up in the hall by a "hairy, axiomatic" guest and "masterfully" kissed upon the lips, may for an instant be "horrified, stunned, *like a bird in the grasp of a cat*." But we are always assured that "through it all something tremendously vital and insistent" will be speaking to her, and that in the end she will not resist the urge of the *élan vital*. I recall no one of all the dozens of obliging women in these books who makes any effective resistance when summoned to capitulate. "The *psychology of the human animal*, when confronted by these tangles, these ripping tides of the heart," says the author of "The Titan," "has little to do with so-called reason or logic." No; as he informs us elsewhere with endless iteration, it is a question of chemistry. It is the "chemistry of her being" which rouses to blazing the ordinarily dormant forces of Eugene Witla's sympathies in "The Genius." If Stephanie Platow is disloyal to her married lover in "The Titan," "let no one quarrel" with her. Reason: "She was an unstable chemical compound."

Such is the Dreiserian philosophy.

III.

By thus eliminating distinctively human motives and making animal instincts the supreme factors in human life, Mr. Dreiser reduces the problem of the novelist to the lowest possible terms. I find myself unable to go with those who admire the powerful reality of his art while deploring the puerility of his philosophy. His philosophy quite excludes him from the field in which a great realist must work. He has deliberately rejected the novelist's supreme task—understanding and presenting the development of character; he has chosen only to illustrate the unrestricted flow of temperament. He has evaded the enterprise of representing human conduct; he has confined himself to a representation of animal behavior. He demands for the demonstration of his theory a moral vacuum from which the obligations of parenthood, marriage, chivalry, and citizenship have been quite withdrawn or locked in a twilight sleep. At each critical moment in his narrative, where a realist like George Eliot or Thackeray or Trollope or Meredith would be asking how a given individual would feel, think, and act under the manifold combined stresses of organized society, Mr. Dreiser sinks supinely back upon the law of the jungle or mutters his mystical gibberish about an alteration of the chemical formula.

The possibility of making the unvarying victoriousness of jungle-motive plausible depends directly upon the suppression of the evidence of other motives. In this work of suppression Mr. Dreiser simplifies American life almost beyond recognition. Whether it is because he comes from Indiana, or whether it is because he steadily envisages the human animal, I cannot say; I can only note that he never speaks of his men and women as "educated" or "brought up." Whatever their social status, they are invariably "raised." Raising human stock in America evidently includes feeding and clothing it, but does not include the inculcation of even the most elementary moral ideas. Hence Mr. Dreiser's field seems curiously outside American society. Yet he repeatedly informs us that his persons are typical of the American middle class, and three of the leading figures, to judge from their names—Carrie Meeber, Jennie Gerhardt, and Eugene Witla—are of our most highly "cultured" race. Frank Cowperwood, the hero of two novels, is a hawk of finance and a rake almost from the cradle; but of the powers which presided over his cradle we know nothing save that his father was a competent official in a Philadelphia bank. What, if anything, Carrie Meeber's typical American parents taught her about the conduct of life is suppressed, for we meet the girl in a train to Chicago, on which she falls to the first drummer who accosts her. Eugene Witla emerges in his teens from the bosom of a typical middle-class American family—with a knowledge of the game called "post office," takes the train for Chicago, and without hesitation enters upon his long career of seduction. Jennie Gerhardt, of course, succumbs to the first man who puts his arm around her; but, in certain respects, her case is exceptional.

In the novel "Jennie Gerhardt" Mr. Dreiser ventures a disastrous experiment at making the jungle-motive plausible without suppressing the evidence of other motives. He provides the girl with pious Lutheran parents, of fallen fortune, but alleged to be of sterling character, who "raise" her with the utmost strictness. He even admits that the family were church-goers, and he outlines the doctrine preached by Pastor Wundt: right conduct in marriage and absolute innocence before that state, essentials of Christian living; no salvation for a daughter who failed to keep her chastity unstained or for the parents who permitted her to fall; Hell yawning for all such; God angry with sinners every day. "Gerhardt and his wife, and also Jennie," says Mr. Dreiser, "accepted the doctrines of their church without reserve." Twenty pages later Jennie is represented as yielding her virtue in pure gratitude to a man of fifty, Senator Brander, who has let her do his laundry and in other ways has been kind to her and to her family. The Senator suddenly dies; Jennie expects to become a mother; Father Gerhardt is broken-hearted, and the family moves from Columbus to Cleveland. This first episode is not incredibly presented as a momentary triumph of emotional impulse over training—as an "accident." The incredible appears when Mr. Dreiser insists that an accident of this sort to a girl brought up *under the conditions stated* is not necessarily followed by any sense of sin or shame or regret. Upon this simple pious Lutheran he imposes his own naturalistic philosophy, and, in analyzing her psychology before the birth of her illegitimate child, pretends that she looks forward to the event "without a murmur," with "serene, unfaltering courage," "the marvel of life holding her in trance," with "joy and satisfaction," seeing in her state "the immense possibilities of racial fulfilment." This juggling is probably expected to prepare us for her instantaneous assent, perhaps a year later, when a healthy, magnetic manufacturer, who has seen her perhaps a dozen times, claps his paw upon her and says, "You belong to me," and in a perfectly cold-blooded interview proposes the terms on which he will set her up in New York as his mistress. Jennie, who is a fond mother and a dutiful daughter, goes to her pious Lutheran mother and talks the whole matter over with her quite candidly. The mother hesitates—not on Jennie's account, gentle reader, but because she will be obliged to deceive old Gerhardt; "the difficulty of telling this lie was very great for Mrs. Gerhardt"! But she acquiesces at last. "I'll help you out with it," she concludes—"with a little sigh." The unreality of the whole transaction shrieks.

Mr. Dreiser's stubborn insistence upon the jungle-motive results in a dreary monotony in the form and substance of his novels. Interested only in the description of animal behavior, he constructs his plot in such a way as to exhibit the persistence of two or three elementary instincts through every kind of situation. He finds, for example, a subject in the career of an American captain of industry, thinly disguised under the name of Frank Cowperwood. He has just two things to tell us about Cowperwood: that he has a rapacious appetite for money, and that he has a rapacious appetite for women. In "The Financier" he "documents" those two truths about Cowperwood in seventy-four chapters in each one of which he shows us how his hero made money or how he captivated women in Philadelphia. Not satisfied with the demonstration, he returns to the same theses in "The Titan," and shows us in sixty-two chapters how the same hero made money and captivated women in Chicago and New York. He promises us a third volume, in which we shall no doubt learn in a work of sixty or seventy chapters—a sort of huge club-sandwich composed of slices of business alternating with erotic episodes—how Frank Cowperwood made money and captivated women in London. Meanwhile Mr. Dreiser has turned aside from his great "trilogy of desire" to give us "The Genius," in which the hero, Witla, alleged to be a great realistic painter, exhibits in 101 chapters, similarly "sandwiched" together, an appetite for women and money indistinguishable from that of Cowperwood. Read one of these novels, and you have read them all. What the hero is in the first chapter, he remains in the hundred-and-first or the hundred-and-thirty-sixth. He acquires naught from his experience but sensations. In the sum of his experiences there is nothing of the impressive mass and coherence of activities bound together by principles and integrated in character, for all his days have been but as isolated beads loosely strung on the thread of his desire. And so after the production of the hundredth document in the case of Frank Cowperwood, one is ready to cry with fatigue: "Hold! Enough! We believe you. Yes, it is very clear that Frank Cowperwood had a rapacious appetite for women and for money."

If at this point you stop and inquire why Mr. Dreiser goes to such great lengths to establish so little, you find yourself once more confronting the jungle-motive. Mr. Dreiser, with a problem similar to De Foe's in "The Apparition of Mrs. Veal," has availed himself of De Foe's method for creating the illusion of reality. The essence of the problem and of the method for both these authors is the certification of the unreal by the irrelevant. If you wish to make acceptable to your reader the incredible notion that Mrs. Veal's ghost appeared to Mrs. Bargrave, divert his incredulity from the precise point at issue by telling him all sorts of detailed credible things about the poverty of Mrs. Veal's early life, the sobriety of her brother, her father's neglect, and the bad temper of Mrs. Bargrave's husband. If you wish to make acceptable to your reader the incredible notion that Aileen Butler's first breach of the seventh article in the decalogue was "a happy event," taking place "much as a marriage might have," divert his incredulity by describing with the technical accuracy of a fashion magazine not merely the gown that she wore on the night of Cowperwood's reception, but also with equal detail the half-dozen other gowns that she thought she might wear, but did not. If you have been for three years editor-in-chief of the Butterick Publications, you can probably perform this feat with unimpeachable verisimilitude; and having acquired credit for expert knowledge in matters of dress and millinery, you can now and then emit unchallenged a bit of philosophy such as "Life cannot be put in any one mould, and the attempt may as well be abandoned at once. . . . Besides, whether we will or no, theory or no theory, the large basic facts of chemistry and physics remain." None the less, if you expect to gain credence for the notion that your hero can have any woman in Chicago or New York that he puts his paw upon, you had probably better lead up to it by a detailed account of the street-railway system in those cities. It will necessitate the loading of your pages with a tremendous baggage of irrelevant detail. It will not sound much like art. It will sound more like one of Lincoln Steffens's special articles. But it will produce an overwhelming impression of reality, which the reader will carry with him into the next chapter where you are laying bare the "chemistry" of the human animal.

IV.

It would make for clearness in our discussions of contemporary fiction if we withheld the title of "realist" from a writer like Mr. Dreiser, and called him, as Zola called himself, a "naturalist." While asserting that all great art in every period intends a representation of reality, I have tried to indicate the basis for a working distinction between the realistic novel and the naturalistic novel of the present day. Both are representations of the life of man in contemporary or nearly contemporary society, and both are presumably composed of materials within the experience and observation of the author. But a realistic novel is a representation based upon a theory of human conduct. If the theory of human conduct is adequate, the representation constitutes an addition to literature and to social history. A naturalistic novel is a representation based upon a theory of animal behavior. Since a theory of animal behavior can never be an adequate basis for a representation of the life of man in contemporary society, such a representation is an artistic blunder. When half the world attempts to assert such a theory, the other half rises in battle. And so one turns with relief from Mr. Dreiser's novels to the morning papers.

Dreiser

Sherwood Anderson*

Heavy, heavy, hangs over thy head.
Fine, or Superfine.

Theodore Dreiser is old—he is very, very old. I do not know how many years he has lived, perhaps thirty, perhaps fifty, but he is very old. Something gray and bleak and hurtful that has been in the world almost forever is personified in him.

When Dreiser is gone we shall write books, many of them. In the books we write there will be all of the qualities Dreiser lacks. We shall have a sense of humor, and everyone knows Dreiser has no sense of humor. More than that we shall have grace, lightness of touch, dreams of beauty bursting through the husks of life.

Oh, we who follow him shall have many things that Dreiser does not have. That is a part of the wonder and the beauty of Dreiser, the things that others will have because of Dreiser.

When he was editor of *The Delineator*, Dreiser went one day, with a woman friend, to visit an orphans' aslyum. The woman told me the story of that afternoon in the big, gray building with Dreiser, heavy and lumpy and old, sitting on a platform and watching the children—the terrible children—all in their little uniforms, trooping in.

"The tears ran down his cheeks and he shook his head," the woman said. That is a good picture of Dreiser. He is old and he does not know what to do with life, so he just tells about it as he sees it, simply and honestly. The tears run down his cheeks and he shakes his head.

Heavy, heavy, the feet of Theodore. How easy to pick his books to pieces, to laugh at him. Thump, thump, thump, here he comes, Dreiser, heavy and old.

The feet of Dreiser are making a path for us, the brutal heavy feet. They are tramping through the wilderness, making a path. Presently the path will be a street, with great arches overhead and delicately carved

---

*Reprinted from *Little Review*, 3 (April, 1916), 5. Anderson reprinted the sketch as the "Introduction" to his *Horses and Men* (New York: Huebsch, 1923), pp. xi–xii. Reprinted by permission of Harold Ober Associates; copyright © 1923 by Sherwood Anderson, renewed 1950 by Eleanor Copenhaver Anderson.

spires piercing the sky. Along the street will run children, shouting "Look at me"—forgetting the heavy feet of Dreiser.

The men who follow Dreiser will have much to do. Their road is long. But because of Dreiser, we, in America, will never have to face the road through the wilderness, the road that Dreiser faced.

> Heavy, heavy, hangs over thy head.
> Fine or superfine.

The Art of Theodore Dreiser

Randolph Bourne*

Theodore Dreiser has had the good fortune to evoke a peculiar quality of pugnacious interest among the younger American *intelligentsia* such
as has been the lot of almost nobody else writing to-day unless it be Miss
Amy Lowell. We do not usually take literature seriously enough to quarrel over it. Or else we take it so seriously that we urbanely avoid squab-
bles. Certainly there are none of the vendettas that rage in a culture like
that of France. But Mr. Dreiser seems to have made himself, particularly
since the suppression of "The 'Genius,' " a veritable issue. Interesting and
surprising are the reactions to him. Edgar Lee Masters makes him a "soul-
enrapt demi-urge, walking the earth, stalking life"; Harris Merton Lyon
saw in him a "seer of inscrutable mien"; Arthur Davison Ficke sees him as
master of a passing throng of figures, "labored with immortal illusion, the
terrible and beautiful, cruel and wonder-laden illusion of life"; Mr.
Powys makes him an epic philosopher of the "lifetide"; H. L. Mencken
puts him ahead of Conrad, with "an agnosticism that has almost passed
beyond curiosity." On the other hand, an unhappy critic in the "Nation"
last year gave Mr. Dreiser his place for all time in a neat antithesis between the realism that was based on a theory of human conduct and the
naturalism that reduced life to a mere animal behavior. For Dreiser this
last special hell was reserved, and the jungle-like and simian activities of
his characters rather exhaustively outlined. At the time this antithesis
looked silly. With the appearance of Mr. Dreiser's latest book, "A Hoosier
Holiday," it becomes nonsensical. For that wise and delightful book
reveals him as a very human critic of very common human life, romantically sensual and poetically realistic, with an artist's vision and a thick,
warm feeling for American life.

This book gives the clue to Mr. Dreiser, to his insatiable curiosity
about people, about their sexual inclinations, about their dreams, about
the homely qualities that make them American. His memories give a picture of the floundering young American that is so typical as to be almost
epic. No one has ever pictured this lower middle-class American life so

*Reprinted from *Dial*, 62 (June 14, 1917), 507–509. The essay was initially republished in
Bourne's *History of a Literary Radical and Other Essays* (New York: Huebsch, 1920),
195–204.

winningly, because no one has had the necessary literary ski!l with the lack of self-consciousness. Mr. Dreiser is often sentimental, but it is a sentimentality that captivates you with its candor. You are seeing this vacuous, wistful, spiritually rootless, middle-Western life through the eyes of a naïve but very wise boy. Mr. Dreiser seems queer only because he has carried along his youthful attitude in unbroken continuity. He is fascinated with sex because youth is usually obsessed with sex. He puzzles about the universe because youth usually puzzles. He thrills to crudity and violence because sensitive youth usually recoils from the savagery of the industrial world. Imagine incorrigible, sensuous youth endowed with the brooding skepticism of the philosopher who feels the vanity of life, and you have the paradox of Mr. Dreiser. For these two attitudes in him support rather than oppose each other. His spiritual evolution was out of a pious, ascetic atmosphere into intellectual and personal freedom. He seems to have found himself without losing himself. Of how many American writers can this be said? And for this much shall be forgiven him,—his slovenliness of style, his lack of nuances, his apathy to the finer shades of beauty, his weakness for the mystical and the vague. Mr. Dreiser suggests the over-sensitive temperament that protects itself by an admiration for crudity and cruelty. His latest book reveals the boyhood shyness and timidity of this Don Juan of novelists. Mr. Dreiser is complicated, but he is complicated in a very understandable American way, the product of the uncouth forces of small-town life and the vast disorganization of the wider American world. As he reveals himself, it is a revelation of a certain broad level of the American soul.

Mr. Dreiser seems uncommon only because he is more naïve than most of us. It is not so much that he swarms his pages with sexful figures as that he rescues sex for the scheme of personal life. He feels a holy mission to slay the American literary superstition that men and women are not sensual beings. But he does not brush this fact in the sniggering way of the popular magazines. He takes it very seriously, so much so that some of his novels become caricatures of desire. It is, however, a misfortune that it has been Brieux and Freud and not native Theodore Dreiser who soaked the sexual imagination of the younger American *intelligentsia*. It would have been far healthier to have absorbed Mr. Dreiser's literary treatment of sex than to have gone hysterical over its pathology. Sex has little significance unless it is treated in personally artistic, novelistic terms. The American tradition had tabooed the treatment of those infinite gradations and complexities of love that fill the literary imagination of a sensitive people. When curiosity got too strong and reticence was repealed in America, we had no means of articulating ourselves except in a deplorable pseudo-scientific jargon that has no more to do with the relevance of sex than the chemical composition of orange paint has to do with the artist's vision. Dreiser has done a real service to the American imagination in despising the underworld and going gravely to the business of picturing sex as it is lived in the personal relations of bungling, wistful, or masterful men and women. He seemed strange and rowdy only because he made sex human, and American tradition had never made it human. It had only made it either sacred or vulgar, and when these categories no longer worked, we fell under the dubious and perverting magic of the psycho-analysts.

In spite of his looseness of literary gait and heaviness of style Dreiser seems a sincere groper after beauty. It is natural enough that this should so largely be the beauty of sex. For where would a sensitive boy, brought up in Indiana and in the big American cities, get beauty expressed for him except in women? What does mid-Western America offer to the starving except its personal beauty? A few landscapes, an occasional picture in a museum, a book of verse perhaps! Would not all the rest be one long, flaunting offense of ugliness and depression? "The 'Genius,' " instead of being that mass of pornographic horror which the Vice Societies repute it to be, is the story of a groping artist whose love of beauty runs obsessingly upon the charm of girlhood. Through different social planes, through business and manual labor and the feverish world of artists, he pursues this lure. Dreiser is refreshing in his air of the moral democrat, who sees life impassively, neither praising nor blaming, at the same time that he realizes how much more terrible and beautiful and incalculable life is than any of us are willing to admit. It may be all *apologia*, but it comes with the grave air of a mind that wants us to understand just how it all happened. "Sister Carrie" will always retain the fresh charm of a spontaneous working-out of mediocre, and yet elemental and significant, lives. A good novelist catches hold of the thread of human desire. Dreiser does this, and that is why his admirers forgive him so many faults.

If you like to speculate about personal and literary qualities that are specifically American, Dreiser should be as interesting as any one now writing in America. This becomes clearer as he writes more about his youth. His hopelessly unorientated, half-educated, boyhood is so typical of the uncritical and careless society in which wistful American talent has had to grope. He had to be spiritually a self-made man, work out a philosophy of life, discover his own sincerity. Talent in America outside of the ruling class flowers very late, because it takes so long to find its bearings. It has had almost to create its own soil, before it could put in its roots and grow. It is born shivering into an inhospitable and irrelevant group. It has to find its own kind of people and piece together its links of comprehension. It is a gruelling and tedious task, but those who come through it contribute, like Vachel Lindsay, creative work that is both novel and indigenous. The process can be more easily traced in Dreiser than in almost anybody else. "A Hoosier Holiday" not only traces the personal process, but it gives the social background. The common life, as seen throughout the countryside, is touched off quizzically, and yet sympathetically, with an artist's vision. Dreiser sees the American masses in their commonness and at their pleasure as brisk, rather vacuous people, a little pathetic in their innocence of the possibilities of life and their optimistic trustfulness. He sees them ruled by great barons of industry, and yet unconscious of their serfdom. He seems to love this countryside, and he makes you love it.

Dreiser loves, too, the ugly violent bursts of American industry,—the flaming steel-mills and gaunt lakesides. "The Titan" and 'The Financier" are unattractive novels, but the are human documents of the brawn of a passing American era. Those stenographic conversations, webs of financial intrigue, bare bones of enterprise, insult our artistic sense. There is too much raw beef, and yet it all has the taste and smell of the primitive business-jungle it deals with. These crude and greedy captains of finance with their wars and their amours had to be given some kind of literary embodiment, and Dreiser has hammered a sort of raw epic out of their lives.

It is not only his feeling for these themes of crude power and sex and the American common life that make Dreiser interesting. His emphases are those of a new America which is latently expressive and which must develop its art before we shall really have become articulate. For Dreiser is a true hyphenate, a product of that conglomerate Americanism that springs from other roots than the English tradition. Do we realize how rare it is to find a talent that is thoroughly American and wholly un-English? Culturally we have somehow suppressed the hyphenate. Only recently has he forced his way through the unofficial literary censorship. The *vers-librists* teem with him, but Dreiser is almost the first to achieve a largeness of utterance. His outlook, it is true, flouts the American canons of optimism and redemption, but these were never anything but conventions. There stirs in Dreiser's books a new American quality. It is not at all German. It is an authentic attempt to make something artistic out of the chaotic materials that lie around us in American life. Dreiser interests because we can watch him grope and feel his clumsiness. He has the artist's vision without the sureness of the artist's technique. That is one of the tragedies of America. But his faults are those of his material and of uncouth bulk, and not of shoddiness. He expresses an America that is in process of forming. The interest he evokes is part of the eager interest we feel in that growth.

The Dreiser Bugaboo

H. L. Mencken*

Dr. William Lyon Phelps, the Lampson professor of English at Yale, opens his chapter on Mark Twain in his "Essays on Modern Novelists" with a humorous account of the critical imbecility which pursued Mark in his own country down to his last years. The favorite national critics of that era (and it extended to 1895, at the least) were wholly anaesthetic to the fact that he was a great artist. They admitted him, somewhat grudgingly, a certain low dexterity as a clown, but that he was an imaginative writer of the first rank, or even of the fifth rank, was something that, in their insanest moments, never so much as occurred to them. Phelps cites, in particular, an ass named Professor Richardson, whose "American Literature," it appears, "is still a standard work" and "a deservedly high authority"—apparently in colleges. In the 1892 edition of this *magnum opus*, Mark is dismissed with less than four lines, and ranked below Irving, Holmes and Lowell—nay, actually below Artemus Ward, Josh Billings and Petroleum V. Nasby! The thing is fabulous, fantastic—but nevertheless true. Lacking the "higher artistic or moral purpose of the greater humorists" (*exempli gratia*, Rabelais, Molière, Aristophanes!), Mark is put off by this Prof. Balderdash as a laborious buffon . . . But stay! Do not laugh yet! Phelps himself, indignant at the stupidity, now proceeds to prove that Mark was really a great moralist, and more, a great optimist . . . Turn to "The Mysterious Stranger" and "What is Man?"! . . .

College professors, alas, never learn anything. The identical pedagogue who achieved this nonsense about old Mark in 1910 now seeks to dispose of Theodore Dreiser in the precise manner of Richardson. That is to say, he essays to finish him by putting him into Coventry, by loftily passing him over. "Do not speak of him," said Kingsley of Heine; "he was a wicked man." Search the latest volume of the Phelps revelation, "The Advance of the English Novel," and you will find that Dreiser is not once mentioned in it. The late O. Henry is hailed as a genius who will have "abiding fame"; Henry Sydnor Harrison is hymned as "more than a clever novelist," nay, "a valuable ally of the angels" (the right-thinker complex!

*Reprinted from *Seven Arts*, 2 (August, 1917), 507–17. Reprinted by AMS Press, Inc. New York.

art as a form of snuffling!), and an obscure Pagliaccio named Charles D. Stewart is brought forward as "the American novelist most worthy to fill the particular vacancy caused by the death of Mark Twain"—but Dreiser is not even listed in the index. And where Phelps leads with his baton of birch most of the other drovers of rah-rah boys follow. I turn, for example, to "An Introduction to American Literature," by Henry S. Pancoast, A. M., L. H. D., dated 1912. There are kind words for Richard Harding Davis, for Amélie Rives, and even for Will N. Harben, but not a syllable for Dreiser. Again, there is "A History of American Literature," by Reuben Post Halleck, A.M., LL.D., dated 1911. Lew Wallace, Marietta Holley, Owen Wister and Augusta Evans Wilson have their hearings, but not Dreiser. Yet again, there is "A History of American Literature Since 1870," by Prof. Fred. Lewis Pattee, instructor in "the English language and literature" somewhere in Pennsylvania. Fred has praises for Marion Crawford, Margaret Deland and F. Hopkinson Smith, and polite bows for Richard Harding Davis and Robert W. Chambers, but from end to end of his fat tome I am unable to find the slightest mention of Dreiser.

So much for one group of heroes of the new Dunciad. That it includes most of the acknowledged heavyweights of the craft—the Babbitts, Mores, Brownells and so on—goes without saying; as Van Wyck Brooks has pointed out in *The Seven Arts*, these magnificoes are austerely above any consideration of the literature that is in being. The other group, more courageous and more honest, proceeds by direct attack; Dreiser is to be disposed of by a moral *attentat*. Its leaders are two more professors, Stuart P. Sherman and H. W. Boynton, and in its ranks march the lady critics of the newspapers with much shrill, falsetto clamor. Sherman is the only one of them who shows any intelligible reasoning. Boynton, as always, is a mere parroter of conventional phrases, and the objections of the ladies fade imperceptibly into a pious indignation which is indistinguishable from that of the professioanl suppressors of vice.

What, then, is Sherman's complaint? In brief, that Dreiser is a liar when he calls himself a realist; that he is actually a naturalist, and hence accursed. That "he has evaded the enterprise of representing human conduct, and confined himself to a representation of animal behavior." That he "imposes his own naturalistic philosophy" upon his characters, making them do what they ought not to do, and think what they ought not to think. That he "has just two things to tell us about Frank Cowperwood: that he has a rapacious appetite for money, and a rapacious appetite for women." That this alleged "theory of animal behavior" is not only incorrect, but immoral, and that "when one half the world attempts to assert it, the other half rises in battle."[1]

Only a glance is needed show the vacuity of all this irate flubdub. Dreiser, in point of fact, is scarcely more the realist or the naturalist, in any true sense, than H. G. Wells or the later George Moore, nor has he ever announced himself in either the one character or the other—if there be, in fact, any difference between them that anyone save a pigeon-holing pedagogue can discern. He is really something quite different, and, in his moments, something far more stately. His aim is not merely to record, but to translate and understand; the thing he exposes is not the empty event and act, but the endless mystery out of which it springs; his pictures have a passionate compassion in them that it is hard to separate from poetry. If this sense of the universal and inexplicable tragedy, if this vision of life as a seeking without a finding, if this adept summoning up of moving images, is mistaken by college professors for the empty, meticulous nastiness of Zola in "Pot-Bouille"—in Nietzsche's phrase, for "the delight to stink"—then surely the folly of college professors, as vast as it seems, has been underestimated. What is the fact? The fact is that Dreiser's attitude of mind, his manner of reaction to the phenomena he represents, the whole of his alleged "naturalistic philosophy," stems directly, not from Zola, Flaubert, Augier and the younger Dumas, but from the Greeks. In the midst of democratic cocksureness and Christian sentimentalism, of doctrinaire shallowness and professorial smugness, he stands for a point of view which at least has something honest and courageous about it; here, at all events, he is a realist. Let him put a motto to his books, and it might be:

> O ye deathward-going tribes of men!
> What do your lives mean except that they go to
>   nothingness?

If you protest against that as too harsh for Christians and college professors, right-thinkers and forward-lookers, then you protest against "Oedipus Rex."

As for the animal behavior prattle of the learned headmaster, it reveals on the one hand only the academic fondness for seizing upon high-sounding but empty phrases and using them to alarm the populace, and on the other hand, only the academic incapacity for observing facts correctly and reporting them honestly. The truth is, of course, that the behavior of such men as Cowperwood and Eugene Witla and of such women as Carrie Meeber and Jennie Gerhardt, as Dreiser describes it, is no more merely animal than the behavior of such acknowledged and undoubted human beings as Dr. Woodrow Wilson and Dr. Jane Addams. The whole point of the story of Witla, to take the example which seems to concern the horrified watchmen most, is this: that his life is a bitter conflict between the animal in him and the aspiring soul, between the flesh and the spirit, between what is weak in him and what is strong, between what is base and what is noble, Moreover, the good, in the end, gets its hooks into the bad: as we part from Witla he is actually bathed in the tears of remorse, and resolved to be a correct and godfearing man. And what have we in "The Financier" and "The Titan"? A conflict, in the ego

of Cowperwood, between aspiration and ambition, between the passion
for beauty and the passion for power. Is either passion animal? To ask the
question is to answer it.

I single out Dr. Sherman, not because his pompous syllogisms have
any plausibility in fact or logic, but simply because he may well stand as
archetype of the booming, indignant corrupter of criteria, the moralist
turned critic. A glance at his paean to Arnold Bennett[2] at once reveals the
true gravamen of his objection to Dreiser. What offends him is not
actually Dreiser's shortcomings as an artist, but Dreiser's shortcomings as
a Christian and an American. In Bennett's volumes of pseudo-phil-
osophy—*e.g*, "The Plain Man and His Wife" and "The Feast of St.
Friend"—he finds the intellectual victuals that are to his taste. Here we
have a sweet commingling of virtuous conformity and complacent optimism, of sonorous platitude and easy certainty—here, in brief, we have
the philosophy of the English middle classes—and here, by the same
token, we have the sort of guff that the half-educated of our own country
can understand. It is the calm, superior numskullery that was Victorian;
it is by Samuel Smiles out of Hannah More. The offense of Dreiser is that
he has disdained this revelation and gone back to the Greeks. Lo, he reads
poetry into "the appetite for women"—he rejects the Pauline doctrine
that all love is below the diaphragm! He thinks of Ulysses, not as a mere
heretic and criminal, but as a great artist. He sees the life of man, not as a
simple theorem in Calvinism, but as a vast adventure, an enchantment, a
mystery. It is no wonder that respectable schoolteachers are against
him. . . .

The comstockian attack upon "The 'Genius' " seems to have sprung
out of the same muddled sense of Dreiser's essential hostility to all that is
safe and regular—of the danger in him to that mellowed Methodism
which has become the national ethic. The book, in a way, was a direct
challenge, for though it came to an end upon a note which even a
Methodist might hear as sweet, there were provocations in detail. Dreiser,
in fact, allowed his scorn to make off with his taste—and *es ist nichts
fürchtlicher als Einbildungskraft ohne Geschmack*. The Comstocks arose
to the bait a bit slowly, but none the less surely. Going through the
volume with the terrible industry of a Sunday-school boy dredging up
pearls of smut from the Old Testament, they achieved a list of no less than
89 alleged floutings of the code—75 described as lewd and 14 as profane.
An inspection of these specifications affords mirth of a rare and lofty
variety; nothing could more cruelly expose the inner chambers of the
moral mind. When young Witla, fastening his best girl's skate, is so overcome by the carnality of youth that he hugs her, it is set down as lewd. On
page 51, having become an art student, he is fired by "a great, warm-
tinted nude of Bouguereau"—lewd again. On page 70 he begins to draw
from the figure, and his instructor cautions him that the female breast is

round, not square—more lewdness. On page 151 he kisses his girl on mouth and neck and she cautions him: "Be careful! Mamma may come in"—still more. On page 161, having got rid of mamma, she yields "herself to him gladly, joyously" and he is greatly shocked when she argues that an artist (she is by way of being a singer) had better not marry—lewdness doubly damned. On page 245 he and his bride, being ignorant, neglect the principles laid down by Dr. Sylvanus Stall in his great works on sex hygiene—lewdness most horrible! But there is no need to proceed further. Every kiss, hug and tickle of the chin in the chronicle is laboriously snouted out, empanelled, exhibited. Every hint that Witla is no vestal, that he indulges his unchristian fleshliness, that he burns in the manner of I. Corinithians, VII, 9, is uncovered to the moral inquisition.

On the side of profanity there is a less ardent pursuit of evidence, chiefly, I daresay, because their unearthing is less stimulating. (Besides, there is no law prohibiting profanity in books: the whole inquiry here is but so much *lagniappe*.) On page 408, describing a character called Daniel C. Summerfield, Dreiser says that the fellow is "very much given to swearing, more as a matter of habit than of foul intention," and then goes on to explain somewhat lamely that "no picture of him would be complete without the interpolation of his various expressions." They turn out to be *God damn* and *Jesus Christ*—three of the latter and five or six of the former. All go down; the pure in heart must be shielded from the knowledge of them. (But what of the immoral French? They call the English *Goddams*.) Also, three plain *damns*, eight *hells*, one *my God*, five *by Gods*, one *go to the devil*, one *God Almighty* and one plain *God*. Altogether, 31 specimens are listed. "The 'Genius' " runs to 350,000 words. The profanity thus works out to somewhat less than one word in 10,000. . . . Alas, the Comstockian proboscis, feeling for such offendings, is not as alert as when uncovering more savoury delicacies. On page 191 I find an overlooked *by God*. On page 372 there are *Oh, God, God curses her*, and *God strike her dead*. On page 373 there are *Ah, God, Oh, God*, and three other invocations of God. On page 617 there is *God help me*. On page 720 there is *as God is my judge*. On page 723 there is *I'm no damned good* . . . . But I begin to blush.

When the Comstock Society began proceedings against "The 'Genius,' " a group of English novelists, including Arnold Bennett, H. G. Wells, W. L. George and Hugh Walpole, cabled an indignant caveat. This bestirred the Authors' League of America to activity, and its executive committee issued a minute denouncing the business. Later a protest of American *literati* was circulated, and more than 400 signed, including such highly respectable authors as Winston Churchill, Percy Mackaye, Booth Tarkington and James Lane Allen, and such critics as Lawrence Gilman, Clayton Hamilton and James Huneker, and the editors of such journals as the *Century*, the *Atlantic Monthly* and the *New*

Republic. Among my literary lumber is all the correspondence relating to this protest, not forgetting the letters of those who refused to sign, and some day I hope to publish it, that posterity may not lose the joy of an extremely diverting episode. Meanwhile, the case moves with stately dignity through the interminable corridors of jurisprudence, and the bulk of the briefs and exhibits that it throws off begins to rival the staggering bulk of "The 'Genius' " itself.

In all this, of course, there is a certain savoury grotesquerie; the exposure of the Puritan mind makes life, for the moment, more agreeable. The danger of the combined comstockian professorial attack, to Dreiser as artist, is not that it will make a *muss*-Presbyterian of him, but that it will convert him into a professional revolutionary, spouting stale perunas for all the sorrows of the world. Here Greenwich Village pulls as Chautauqua pushes; already, indeed, the passionate skepticism that was his original philosophy begins to show signs of being contaminated by various so-called "radical" purposes. The danger is not one to be sniffed in. Dreiser, after all, is an American like the rest of us, and to be an American is to be burdened by an ethical prepossession, to lean toward causes and remedies. Go through "The 'Genius' " or "A Hoosier Holiday" carefully, and you will find disquieting indications of what might be called a democratic trend in thinking—that is, a trend toward short cuts, easy answers, glittering theories. He is bemused, off and on, by all the various poppycock of the age, from Christian Science to spiritism, and from the latest guesses in eschatology and epistemology to *art pour l'art*. A true American, he lacks a solid culture, and so he yields a bit to every wind that blows, to the inevitable damage of his representation of the eternal mystery that is man.

Joseph Conrad, starting out from the same wondering agnostism, holds to it far more resolutely, and it is easy to see why. Conrad is, by birth and training, an aristocrat. He has the gift of emotional detachment. The lures of facile doctrine do not move him. In his irony there is a disdain which plays about even the ironist himself. Dreiser is a product of far different forces and traditions, and is capable of no such escapement. Struggle as he may to rid himself of the current superstitions, he can never quite achieve deliverance from the believing attitude of mind—the heritage of the Indiana hinterland. One half of the man's brain, so to speak, wars with the other half. He is intelligent, he is thoughtful, he is a sound artist—but always there come moments when a dead hand falls upon him, and he is once more the Indiana peasant, snuffing absurdly over imbecile sentimentalities; giving a grave ear to quackeries, snorting and eye-rolling with the best of them. One generation spans too short a time to free the soul of man. Nietzsche, to the end of his days, remained a Prussian pastor's son, and hence two-thirds a Puritan; he erected his war upon holiness, toward the end, into a sort of holy war. Kipling, the grandson of a Methodist preacher, reveals the tin-pot evangelist with increasing clarity as youth and its ribaldries pass away and he falls back upon his fundamentals. And that other English novelist who springs from the servants' hall—let us not be surprised or blame him if he sometimes writes like a bounder.

As for Dreiser, as I hint politely, he is still, for all his achievement, in the transition stage between Christian Endeavor and civilization; between Warsaw, Indiana, and the Socratic grove; between being a good American and being a free man; and so he sometimes vacillates perilously between a moral sentimentalism and a somewhat extravagant revolt. "The 'Genius,' " on the one hand, is almost a tract for rectitude, a Warning to the Young; its motto might be *Scheut die Dirnen!* And on the other hand, it is full of a laborious truculence that can be explained only by imagining the author as heroically determined to prove that he is a plain-spoken fellow and his own man, let the chips fall where they may. So, in spots, in "The Financier" and "The Titan," both of them far better books. There is an almost moral frenzy to expose and riddle what passes for morality among the stupid. The isolation of irony is never reached; the man is still a bit evangelical; his ideas are still novelties to him; he is as solemnly absurd in some of his floutings of the Code American as he is in his respect for Bouguereau, or in his flirtings with New Thought, or in his naïve belief in the importance of novel-writing. . . .

But his books remain, particularly his earlier books—and not all the ranting of the outraged orthodox will ever wipe them out. They were done in the stage of wonder, before self-consciousness began to creep in and corrupt it. The view of life that got into "Sister Carrie," the first of them, was not the product of a deliberate thinking out of Carrie's problem. It simply got itself there by the force of the artistic passion behind it; its coherent statement had to wait for other and more reflective days. This complete rejection of ethical plan and purpose, this manifestation of what Nietzsche used to call moral innocence, is what brought up the guardians of the national tradition at the gallop, and created the Dreiser bugaboo of today. All the rubber-stamp formulae of American fiction were thrown overboard in these earlier books; instead of reducing the inexplicable to the obvious, they lifted the obvious to the inexplicable; one could find in them no orderly chain of causes and effects, of rewards and punishments; they represented life as a phenomenon at once terrible and unintelligible, like a stroke of lightning. The prevailing criticism applied the moral litmus. They were not "good"; *ergo*, they were "evil."

The peril that Dreiser stands in is here. He may begin to act, if he is not careful, according to the costume forced on him. Unable to combat the orthodox valuation of his place and aim, he may seek a spiritual refuge in embracing it, and so arrange himself with the tripe-sellers of heterodoxy, and cry wares that differ from the other stock only in the bald fact that they are different. . . . Such a fall would grieve the judicious, of whom I have the honor to be one.

Notes

1. *Nation*, 101 (Dec. 2, 1915), 648–50.
2. New York *Evening Post*, Dec. 31, 1915.

Modern Currents

Paul Elmer More*

* * * * * * *

Theodore Dreiser was born in Terre Haute in 1871. His father, a German, was by the son's account a poor feckless creature, a "religionist" of the maudlin sentimental sort, who passed his later days going the round of the Roman Catholic churches of Chicago, whither he had taken his family. At an early age the boy Theodore was travelling the streets of Chicago selling shabby goods for an "easy-payment instalment house," from which occupation he broke away after stealing twenty-five dollars. The fear of detection and punishment, he says, made him "very cautious." In his twenty-second year he got a small job on a struggling newspaper, owned and controlled by a ward politician. In 1892 he moved to St. Louis, where for a while he had the advantage of reporting under "Little Mac," an editor of outstanding ability and in those days of almost incredible repute throughout the South-Western States. Here I am able to check up Mr. Dreiser's narrative in part, for he came to the city of my birth just when I was leaving it, and I can testify to his account of its streets and institutions, and to his characterization of some of its well-known citizens, as truthful and extraordinarily vivid. From St. Louis he soon drifted eastward, and ended in New York, the Mecca of all our writing men, to whom Chicago is a kind of halfway house. Lean years still lay before him; but his stories began to attract attention, and his *American Tragedy*, a novel spun out through two long volumes, has captured the heedless reading mob and has been acclaimed a masterpiece by reputable reviewers here and abroad.

For my own part I regard his autobiography, despite or possibly because of its shameless "exhibitionism," as more significant than any of his novels, as perhaps, with Sherwood Anderson's similar *Story Teller's Story*, the most significant thing that has come out of our school of realism. I may be prejudiced in its favour by the fact that the autobiography, though the events of Mr. Dreiser's life were different enough from my own, recalls so vividly the intellectual and sentimental atmosphere of the America in which my youth was passed, and which is

*Reprinted from *The Demon of the Absolute* (Princeton: Princeton University Press, 1928), pp. 64–69. Copyright 1928 © 1956 by Princeton University Press. Reprinted by permission.

rapidly disappearing. But, apart from such accidental reasons, it is notable that the *Book About Myself* has the telling straightforward style and method natural to a trained reporter, whereas the English of Mr. Dreiser, when, as sometimes in his novels, he tries to be literary, is of the mongrel sort to be expected from a miscegenation of the gutter and the psychological laboratory. Certainly for those interested in such matters the springs of American realism are laid bare in these autobiographical records with startling frankness. Take a boy of humble origin in a Mid-Western town some forty years ago. The only breath of immaterial things to reach him would be through religion, in the case of Mr. Dreiser a perfectly uncritical catholicism, but with most of the others a thin poverty-stricken Protestantism from which all ritual and symbolism had dropped and every appeal to the imagination had exuded. Art and letters would be about as remote from him as from the Bushmen of Africa. Intellectually and aesthetically and emotionally he is starved. Suppose then that such a lad, with no schooling to speak of or with a degree from some lonely hungry "college," is carried to the bustling conceited Chicago of those days, and, aspiring to write, gets a job on a sensation-mongering newspaper. Of knowledge of life in its larger aspects he has brought nothing, and in the new school of experience he is pretty well confined to the police courts, the morgue, scenes of crime and calamity, sodden streets where unsavoury news may be picked up, homes which scandal has made public property. We need not guess at the colours the world would assume in the eyes of such a youth, for Mr. Dreiser has described his own reactions with sufficient energy. He began his work "still sniffing about the Sermon on the Mount and the Beatitudes, expecting ordinary human flesh and blood to do and be those things"; he discovered that most of the people among whom he was now thrown "looked upon life as a fierce, grim struggle in which no quarter was either given or taken, and in which all men laid traps, lied, squandered, erred through illusion," or, more succinctly in the words of one of his admired and imitated friends, "life is a God-damned stinking, treacherous game."

Meanwhile our young aspirant to fame and wealth, being endowed with no ordinary brain, begins to read. Translations of Balzac and Zola fall into his hands, and he learns that the society of Paris, the *ville lumière*, is playing a game very much like that which he sees about him, only on a more magnificent scale and with vastly greater opportunities. And he learns, or thinks he learns, that the high art of letters is to develop the sort of realism he is acquiring as a reporter. Later he dips into the works of Huxley and Tyndall and Spencer, and finds his "gravest fears as to the unsolvable disorder and brutality of life eternally verified" by authorities who were then supposed by the uneducated or the scientifically educated to have uttered the last word on the mysteries of the universe, the last word *eternally verified*. "Up to this time," he observes rather innocently, "there had been in me a blazing and unchecked desire to get on and the feeling that in doing so we did get somewhere; now in its place was the definite conviction that spiritually one got nowhere, that there was no hereafter, that one lived and had his being because one had to, and that it was of no importance. Of one's ideals, struggles, deprivations, sorrows and joys, it could only be said that they were chemic compulsions, something which for some inexplicable but unimportant reason responded to and resulted from the hope of pleasure and the fear of pain. Man was a mechanism, undevised and uncreated, and a badly and carelessly driven one at that."

Add to this education a spark of genius, an eye to note and record the panorama of the streets, a nervous system highly sensitive to the moods of those about him, and you have the realism of which *An American Tragedy* is the most notable achievement. In his drawing of characters from the lower strata of life and from the gilded haunts of Broadway Mr. Dreiser shows an easy competence. In particular the hero of this tale, from his suppressed childhood in the home of ignorant wandering evangelists, through his career as bell-boy in a hotel, and employee in a factory, ending in trial and conviction for the murder of his mistress, is portrayed with a masterly understanding of the devious ways of a weak untutored nature. But when the author passes to the doings of conventional society, even to the account of a game of tennis, he displays a ludicrous ignorance and awkwardness. The same sort of contrast is seen in other fields. At one moment the tone of comment is callous and cynical, befitting his acquired theory of life's unsolvable disorder and brutality; and then there will break through the native note of sentimentality that pervaded the atmosphere he breathed in the rural Mid-West of his childhood. Just as he himself remains, as he says, "a poetic melancholic, crossed with a vivid materialistic lust of life." In one place religion is only "religionism," a contemptible yet hated deception; and then again the spell laid on his early years reasserts itself, and at the end of the story you might suppose that his deepest sympathy was with the self-sacrificing minister of the Gospel who befriends the condemned murderer, and with the poor mother on whose face was written the "fighting faith in the wisdom and mercy of the definite overruling and watchful and merciful power" of God.

I lay down Mr. Dreiser's novel with a feeling that it is an American tragedy in a sense never intended by him when he chose that title. If only he knew the finer aspects of life as he knows its shabby underside; if only his imagination had been trained in the larger tradition of literature instead of getting its bent from the police court and the dregs of science; if only religion had appeared to him in other garb than the travesty of superstition and faded fanaticism; if only he had had a chance, he might possibly have produced that fabulous thing, the great American novel. As it is he has brought forth a *monstrum informe cui lumen ademptum.*

* * * * * * * *

Dreiser, an Inconsistent Mechanist

Eliseo Vivas*

I

It has become the fashion among the youngest intellectuals to dismiss Dreiser in a lofty and condescending manner. The man, we are informed, is essentially confused. Hence he is not worth reading. He is passé. All the more so since, lacking style, he cannot even be superficially enjoyed. Of course if style is defined in terms of cadence and euphony, in terms of choice of the impeccable image and the inevitable word, Dreiser has no style. But if style is more than this, then he cannot be denied style. For he has architectonic genius. In his lumbering, slow, painful, clumsy way he builds up a story. And when the story is built, the manner fits the matter even to clichés and all. Again, there is no doubt that in an important sense Dreiser is a confused man. But to dismiss him without further qualification is to ignore his depth and his range.

Dreiser's philosophy may be naïve, as his critics have so often pointed out, but it should not be forgotten that naïve is a very relative term. In comparison with the views of professional philosophers his ideas are no doubt unacceptable. But they are not foolish or unworthy of consideration. They were held, and not in an essentially different form, by some of the best minds of the last half of the nineteenth century; and essentially in the very form in which he holds them, they are still held by some thinkers whom we can not easily dismiss. But even if we could be sure that these ideas deserve no consideration whatever as systematic philosophy, it cannot be denied that their essential insight, that life has no transcending meaning that we can discover, is still valid and held by the very best of our modern minds. In any case, whether naïve or not, Dreiser's philosophy is still of high importance, for if he is not a philosopher he is certainly a novelist. As a novelist we can ignore him, but we cannot dismiss him. He has a deep sense of the dramatic movement of human life and a knowledge of its dark urges and baffled quality. He also has a wide range

*Reprinted from *Ethics*, 48 (July, 1938), 498–508. Republished by Vivas in his *Creation and Discovery* (New York: Noonday, 1955), pp. 3–13. Reprinted by permission of the University of Chicago Press.

of vision and a deep sense of the relation of man to the cosmos. He is not only an American novelist but a universal novelist in a very literal sense of the word. The mystery of the universe, the puzzle of destiny, haunts him; and he, more than any of his contemporaries, has responded to the need to relate the haunting sense of puzzlement and mystery to the human drama. No other American novelist of his generation has so persistently endeavored to look at men under the form of eternity. It is then the surest sign of immaturity and naïveté to dismiss Dreiser on the counts of being naïve and lacking style. His prose is indeed fussy, his language a string of clichés; his thought is indeed naïve in many respects. But his prose is the man; his architectonic is superb; and his vision is turned towards horizons the existence of which novelists seldom suspect. But if all these claims can be asserted consistently the need arises to explain how a man guided by a naïve and unacceptable philosophy can be said to occupy the position he does—can be said to have the depth of insight he possesses.

II

Early in his youth Dreiser read and accepted the then popular materialistic mechanism. The picture of the world which Dreiser gained from his youthful reading must have been grasped by him with a deep sense of relief. He hated for deep personal reasons anything remotely allied with religion. Mechanism had the sanction of science. And the theory of evolution, with its emphasis on the ruthlessness of the struggle for survival, was merely an extension on a larger scale of what he himself had observed in Indiana, in Chicago, and in New York. He was untrained in the ways of rigorous analysis; and the materialism he accepted on affective rather than logical grounds was reduced by him to the notion of "chemisms," a word which has no doubt on him a strong and subtle emotive power. Through "chemism" he thinks he explains adequately all phenomena, organic no less than inorganic. Life is chemism, personality is chemism, the emotions are chemisms. There can really be no difference between the urge of the lower animals, human sex desire, and any sentiment that we have agreed to call higher. The animal in the darkness of the forest, Casanova, Dante, and Petrarch, as well as the Marquis de Sade or an Indiana young couple on a swing under an apple tree—they are all examples of chemism, and are fundamentally but the same thing. On his conception of chemism Dreiser grounds an individualistic philosophy. He tells us, not in these terms but to the same effect, that society is a mechanical addition of atomic individuals, each an independent package of force, each a self-contained monad, each determined somehow by chemic forces, each pushing or yielding, as it comes into contact with forces larger or smaller than its own. Thus society is but an additive compounding of mechanical forces, dynamically seeking a harmony which is constantly disrupted by the addition of new forces or by the disappearance of old ones. The individuals who additively make up society have each their own urges and their own strength. One seeks power, one peace, one the realization of an artist, the other security. Each encounters obstacles which baffle him or meets with helping currents which aid him toward his goal. The strong ones forge ahead, and the weak ones submit and are the tools of their betters. This is Darwinism at its starkest. When powerful individuals like Cowperwood appear, they disrupt the previously struck balance. The giants who have already arrived, and whose power is threatened by the appearance of a new one, gang up against the newcomer, use the pigmies for their purposes, the conflict quickens, and at the end, whatever the result, a new balance is struck.

In such a pitiless Darwinian world, where might is ultimate lord, he tells us that it is not morality but the appearance of it that counts. The hearty acceptance of ethical principles puts a handicap on the individual in the struggle. But pretense is a useful and invaluable aid. Society is a masked ball—that beauty, dancing so gaily with that man, is an old woman, has false teeth, suffers from arteriosclerosis, and has a bad breath in the morning; and the gallant leading her may be a beggar, or a horse thief, or a rat catcher, or a clever rogue, so cleverly disguised that he can deceive even himself. There you can see a great idealist preaching democracy and the supreme worth of each human personality; everybody wonders at his kindness and admires his gentleness. But we are all easily deceived. He is really a small man with a mean soul; he preaches equality because he hates and fears excellence; and he is a mirror of kindness because he achieves through it the sense of power which big-souled men achieve directly and frankly. He hates selfishness, because it interferes with his own selfishness; and hates self-assertion, because he can not tolerate his claims being crossed. He hates men who are arrogant, and loves modest men. But if we only look we can see he is himself the very essence of arrogance. And so with the others. Society is a masked ball. But there is one crime for which there is no forgiveness, no absolution—no man must appear in public without a mask. And a crime still greater, no man must ever tear a mask from another and leave him uncovered.

But this is not the whole picture, for Dreiser tells us that human society is made up of a number of subsocieties arranged hierarchically in terms of power and wealth, and in each one of these subdivisions the same pattern repeats itself. Within each group there are honors to be gained, privileges to be conquered, and relative ease and security to be enjoyed. And in each one, low or high, these are come by in the same way—through cunning, pitilessness, and luck.

In such a pitiless Darwinian world what can morality really mean? Morality is a technique of control, a means of keeping in check those men whose powerful and strong drives would wreck the balance struck by the group; it is in short a conspiracy of some of the masters and the slaves to keep the parvenu from running amuck. But of course truly strong men disregard the mythical sanctions which may deceive the weak but cannot deceive them. And for that reason no moral code ever fits the facts. One of his characters, obviously speaking for Dreiser himself—for he has expressed the same idea in the first person—was "always thinking in his private conscience that life was somehow bigger and subtler, and darker than any given theory or order of living." And for this reason, "life is to be learned from life, and the professional moralist is at best but the manufacturer of shoddy wares." These wares, shoddy and gratuitous for the strong, have another purpose—they are the sole consolation of the weak and the oppressed. And they may even have an aesthetic value, like the ephemeral rainbows one often catches sight of on the spray over an angry wave; but, like them, though they may be beautiful, they are utterly ineffective for controlling the danger of the sea.

In such a world, what meaning can life have? None of course. In a world which is the product of blind forces, in a world of chemic determinations and mechanical resolutions, how can one expect that life have meaning?

> Privately his mind was a maelstrom of contradictions and doubts, feelings and emotions. Always of a philosophic turn of mind, this peculiar faculty of reasoning deeply and feeling emotionally were now turned upon himself and his own condition and, as in all such cases where we peer too closely into the subtleties of creation, confusion was the result . . . . the world knew nothing. Neither in religion, philosophy nor science was there any answer to the riddle of existence. Above and below the little scintillating plane of man's thought was—what? Beyond the optic strength of the greatest telescope—far out upon the dim horizon of space—were clouds of stars. What were they doing out there? Who governed them? When were their sidereal motions calculated? He figured life as a grim dark mystery, a sad semi-conscious activity turning aimlessly in the dark. No one knew anything. God knew nothing—least of all himself. Malevolence, life living on death, plain violence—these were the chief characteristics of existence. If one failed in strength in any way, if life were not kind in its bestowal of gifts, if one were not born to fortune's pampering care—the rest was misery. In the days of his strength and prosperity the spectacle of existence had been sad enough: in the hours of threatened delay and defeat it seemed terrible. . . . . (In the end, what one has, is death.) The abyss of death! When he looked into that after all of life and hope, how it shocked him, how it hurt! Here was life and happiness and love in health—there was death and nothingness—aeons and aeons of nothingness. . . . .

His own life, a life of arduous labor and the most scrupulous artistic sincerity, has no more meaning than that of anyone else. And this is what he says of it in the *Bookman*, September, 1928, in a statement of his beliefs:

> I can make no comment on my work or my life that holds either interest or import for me. Nor can I imagine any explanation or interpretation of any life, my own included, that would be either true—or important, if true. Life is to me too much a welter and play of inscrutable forces to permit, in my case at least, any significant comment. One may paint for one's own entertainment, and that of others—perhaps. As I see him the utterly infinitesimal individual weaves among the mysteries a floss-like and wholly meaningless course—if course it be. In short I catch no meaning from all I have seen, and pass quite as I came, confused and dismayed.

III

In its most important details this is the picture of man and the universe which Dreiser seems to believe he has discovered in his experiences and expressed in his novels. But fortunately for his greatness as a novelist, his explicit intellectual vision of the world is not point by point congruous with his vision as a novelist. And the philosophy which he has given us in essays and intercalated in the form of editorial comments in the movement of his dramas is not always true to the record. For there is more to his own concrete dramatic picture of men and society than he finds room for in his mechanistic philosophy. And if we miss this more, we miss, I am afraid, what is truly significant in Dreiser. His mechanism is indeed inadequate, but his dramatic vision of the world is fully ripe and mature. His characters are alive and real, moving and acting and brooding with all the urge and hesitation, passion and fear, doubts and contradictions, of fully real human beings. Few contemporary novelists have built up characters as solid, as three dimensional, as fully bodied, as Dreiser. And the reason why he has succeeded where others have failed is that in spite of his mechanism, few novelists respond to human beings as sensitively as he does. He admires or pities all kinds of men—the forceful money-makers; the weak ones who are born to fail and suffer; the brilliant women who walk in and conquer; the respectable men and the disreputable ones; the masters and the slaves; the happy ones and the victims of meaningless forces who are condemned to live a life of pain, frustration, and denial.

Dreiser not only responds to human beings in a very immediate and sympathetic manner, but what is more important, he understands them. And his understanding goes far beyond the chemisms through which he thinks he explains them. For what does it mean to understand a man? Does it not mean to discover some order, some underlying direction, some permanent tendency by reference to which we as observers are able to organize what we know of him, and to decide what is important or relevant and what is not? And this is the reason why we read Dreiser and read him with profit, because in spite of his chemisms, and in spite of his poor taste in words and phrases, in spite of his fuzzy prose, and his addiction to unimportant realistic detail—which is never really as unimportant as we in our impatience think it is—we discover in his books insights about human beings we did not have before.

But what is most important of all, his dramatic picture of society and of morality do not corroborate the theories which he has put forth, and which have caused such violent reaction from conservative critics. His picture of men is not a picture of the hard atomic entities which his individualistic mechanism tells him they are. Nor does he really see society as a mere collection of atomic individuals. His characters are often a-social forces, working for ends destructive of the social equilibrium. But never completely so. Nor is society a mechanical addition of forces. Cowperwood, his reckless Robber Baron, is propelled by a strong will directed to the conquest of power and reckless of the claims of society in its search for satisfaction. But even Cowperwood is not utterly destructive, and his genius, in the pursuit of its own arbitrary ends, has a constructive side to it in quite an objective social sense. Nor is that will utterly arbitrary, nor is he utterly free and a-moral. Less so is Kalvin, a powerful but respectable and conservative business man, and Witla, the genius. We need not go any farther. The personalities and characters of his big men as well as of his small are socially determined, and this in turn means really that it is society that furnishes the shark-man with the precise mold through which his power expresses itself and sets the limits to how far that will shall express itself unchallenged. We do not need to read this into his picture of society; it is there for us to see. Some of his Titans may even be utterly devoid, as he thinks, of ordinary human ties; this is never entirely the case, but grant it. Still in any case these Titans are what they are only in terms of the forces that shaped them, and thus it is that only in the society in which they are reared could they find the necessary outward resistance in terms of which their will can express itself. Grant this, and one has to grant that the ties one has with society are integral and internal and the relations that exist not external to the individuals which make up society. Thus from his own picture he could have seen that society is an organic pattern and as such makes the individual possible as the individual makes it possible. Morality then is not a club with which the individual is struck down and kept in line. It is, properly conceived, the molds in which the activities of individuals express themselves. There can be no matter without form, no activity without style. And the morality of any society is but the style or manner in which the individuals which are organic parts of it act.

Thus conceived, morality is larger than the codes through which men say they rule their actions, and life larger than any of its codes and rules, as Dreiser claims. But it cannot be larger than the forms and manners in which it expresses itself. "Life is larger than morality," only if morality is a set of rules, a code, which is fixed once for all and is too rigid to give way. And of course the moralist's wares are then shoddy wares. But it is coextensive with living if it is conceived as the manner life finds in which to express itself and through which it channels its forces. The mechanistic, atomistic conception of society and the belief that the individual is prior to it in both a logical and existential sense make this notion of morality incomprehensible. But a more acceptable conception of society would urge as part of it the dependences, the interconnections, and the often deep bonds which underly many of the stresses under normal circumstances, and even under abnormal ones. Even in overt conflict interdependences exist and rules of behavior obtain. Men never can live in utter and complete chaos. There are laws of war as well as of peace. Men simply have to trust others and depend on them mutually; nor are we free, even the least sentimental of us, from loyalties and sympathies and deep-rooted interests. Factors such as these, bonds, ties, forces, deep interconnections, are always found. And they make up society as much as the will of the strong and the yielding of the weak. And they do so as much in Dreiser's pictures as they do in actuality.

Why does he not see this? The phenomenon is common. It is simply a failure to readjust theory to facts. Dreiser does not find the moral code in which he was brought up by a narrow and intense father anywhere operative in the world into which, ill equipped but sensitive, he was thrust. But emotionally he has never ceased to demand that morality be what he was taught it was—a rigid code, where idealism is always unmistakably good, and selfishness distinctly an unalloyed evil. His characters are capable of pity and courage and idealism as often as of ruthlessness and strength and indifference to their fellows. But a man's idealism must needs adjust itself to other forces, is but a need among many, and needs be intelligent and enlightened; nor is there guaranty that it will be even then unconditionally successful.

Essentially the same considerations apply to Dreiser's discovery that life has no meaning. Nowhere in the cold ranges of the sky and in the wonders of submicroscopic space can we find a direction, a purpose, to guide us and give our activity an assurance of transcending significance. Hence his perplexity, his sense of futility, his monotonous refrain regarding the vanity of effort in such a sorry world. But would he think that life was without meaning if it were not for the fact that though he is a mechanist, he insists nevertheless on a transcendent meaning? His characters and his own life never lacked drive, never lacked purpose, never lacked meaning. One of his characters finds the meaning to his activity in success, another finds it in power, another in love, and one in dedication to a Benevolent Deity. Dreiser himself, an artist, finds it in the sincere and uncompromising expression of his vision of life. What meaning can it have besides that? Obviously what has happened to Dreiser is that he never outgrew his childhood training, and though intellectually he knows better, emotionally he still hankers for transcendent support. He *knows*, that is, that the universe is a purposeless affair, but he never learned a lesson Spinoza might have taught him, namely that it couldn't but be, since purpose and therefore value, are relative human affairs.What are they then? Where do they spring from? From within, of course, from drives and wants and needs. Given an organism which has urges and seeks their satisfaction in a social environment, and value and purpose appear, at the level of intelligence, in terms of plans, directions, and campaigns.

Dreiser is a bigger and more faithful artist than his philosophy permits him to be. As editor, he is always telling us that the picture he paints is meaningless. But within his novels his men and women always find life has a driving significance which overpowers them. Sometimes the meaning it has is sinister; sometimes pathetic; sometimes tragic. But meaning it always has. And if life's meaning is sometimes sad or tragic, in Dreiser we find, in his enormous pity and in his sympathy, a vision of life not altogether impossible to realize in which some at least of the darkness he records could be eliminated.

Reality in America

Lionel Trilling*

*   *   *   *   *   *   *

Parrington lies twenty years behind us, and in the intervening time there has developed a body of opinion which is aware of his inadequacies and of the inadequacies of his coadjutors and disciples, who make up what might be called the literary academicism of liberalism. Yet Parrington still stands at the center of American thought about American culture because, as I say, he expresses the chronic American belief that there exists an opposition between reality and mind and that one must enlist oneself in the party of reality.

II

This belief in the incompatibility of mind and reality is exemplified by the doctrinaire indulgence which liberal intellectuals have always displayed toward Theodore Dreiser, an indulgence which becomes the worthier of remark when it is contrasted with the liberal severity toward Henry James. Dreiser and James: with that juxtaposition we are immediately at the dark and bloody crossroads where literature and politics meet. One does not go there gladly, but nowadays it is not exactly a matter of free choice whether one does or does not go. As for the particular juxtaposition itself, it is inevitable and it has at the present moment far more significance than the juxtaposition which once used to be made between James and Whitman. It is not hard to contrive factitious oppositions between James and Whitman, but the real difference between them is the difference between the moral mind, with its awareness of tragedy, irony, and multitudinous distinctions, and the transcendental mind, with its passionate sense of the oneness of multiplicity. James and Whitman are unlike not in quality but in kind, and in their very opposition they serve to complement each other. But the difference between James and Dreiser is not of kind, for both men addressed themselves to virtually the same social

* Reprinted from *The Liberal Imagination* (New York: Viking, 1950), pp. 7–21. The portion of Trilling's essay on Dreiser appeared originally in the *Nation*, 162 (April 20, 1946), 466–72. Reprinted by permission of Charles Scribner's Sons. Copyright © 1946, 1950 by Lionel Trilling.

and moral fact. The difference here is one of quality, and perhaps nothing is more typical of American liberalism than the way it has responded to the respective qualities of the two men.

Few critics, I suppose, no matter what their political disposition, have ever been wholly blind to James's great gifts, or even to the grandiose moral intention of these gifts. And few critics have ever been wholly blind to Dreiser's great faults. But by liberal critics James is traditionally put to the ultimate question: of what use, of what actual political use, are his gifts and their intention? Granted that James was devoted to an extraordinary moral perceptiveness, granted too that moral perceptiveness has something to do with politics and the social life, of what possible practical value in our world of impending disaster can James's work be? And James's style, his characters, his subjects, and even his own social origin and the manner of his personal life are adduced to show that his work cannot endure the question. To James no quarter is given by American criticism in its political and liberal aspect. But in the same degree that liberal criticism is moved by political considerations to treat James with severity, it treats Dreiser with the most sympathetic indulgence. Dreiser's literary faults, it gives us to understand, are essentially social and political virtues. It is Parrington who established the formula for the liberal criticism of Dreiser by calling him a "peasant": when Dreiser thinks stupidly, it is because he has the slow stubbornness of a peasant; when he writes badly, it is because he is impatient of the sterile literary gentility of the bourgeoisie. It is as if wit and flexibility of mind, and perception, and knowledge were to be equated with aristocracy and political reaction, while dullness and stupidity must naturally suggest a virtuous democracy, as in the old plays.

The liberal judgment of Dreiser and James goes back of politics, goes back to the cultural assumptions that make politics. We are still haunted by a kind of political fear of the intellect which Tocqueville observed in us more than a century ago. American intellectuals, when they are being consciously American or political, are remarkably quick to suggest that an art which is marked by perception and knowledge, although all very well in its way, can never get us through gross dangers and difficulties. And their misgivings become the more intense when intellect works in art as it ideally should, when its processes are vivacious and interesting and brilliant. It is then that we like to confront it with the gross dangers and difficulties and to challenge it to save us at once from disaster. When intellect in art is awkward or dull we do not put it to the test of ultimate or immediate practicality. No liberal critic asks the question of Dreiser whether *his* moral preoccupations are going to be useful in confronting the disasters that threaten us. And it is a judgment on the proper nature of mind, rather than any actual political meaning that might be drawn from the works of the two men, which accounts for the unequal justice they have received from the progressive critics. If it could be conclusively demonstrated—by, say, documents in James's handwriting—that James explicitly intended his books to be understood as pleas for co-operatives, labor unions, better housing, and more equitable taxation, the American critic in his liberal and progressive character would still be worried by James because his work shows so many of the electric qualities of mind. And if something like the opposite were proved of Dreiser, it would be brushed aside—as his doctrinaire anti-Semitism has in fact been brushed aside—because his books have the awkwardness, the chaos, the heaviness which we associate with "reality." In the American metaphysic, reality is always material reality, hard, resistant, unformed, impenetrable, and unpleasant. And that mind is alone felt to be trustworthy which most resembles this reality by most nearly reproducing the sensations it affords.

In *The Rise of American Civilization*, Professor Beard uses a significant phrase when, in the course of an ironic account of James's career, he implies that we have the clue to the irrelevance of that career when we know that James was "a whole generation removed from the odors of the shop." Of a piece with this, and in itself even more significant, is the comment which Granville Hicks makes in *The Great Tradition* when he deals with James's stories about artists and remarks that such artists as James portrays, so concerned for their art and their integrity in art, do not really exist: "After all, who has ever known such artists? Where are the Hugh Verekers, the Mark Ambients, the Neil Paradays, the Overts, Limberts, Dencombes, Delavoys?" This question, as Mr. Hicks admits, had occurred to James himself, but what answer had James given to it? "If the life about us for the last thirty years refused warrant for these examples," he said in the preface to volume xii of the New York Edition, "then so much the worse for that life. . . . There are decencies that in the name of the general self-respect we must take for granted, there's a rudimentary intellectual honor to which we must, in the interest of civilization, at least pretend." And to this Mr. Hicks, shocked beyond argument, makes this reply, which would be astonishing had we not heard it before: "But this is the purest romanticism, this writing about what ought to be rather than what is!"

The "odors of the shop" are real, and to those who breathe them they guarantee a sense of vitality from which James is debarred. The idea of intellectual honor is not real, and to that chimera James was devoted. He betrayed the reality of what is in the interests of what ought to be. Dare we trust him? The question, we remember, is asked by men who themselves have elaborate transactions with what ought to be. Professor Beard spoke in the name of growing, developing, and improving America. Mr. Hicks, when he wrote *The Great Tradition*, was in general sympathy with a nominally radical movement. But James's own transaction with what ought to be is suspect because it is carried on through what I have called the electrical qualities of mind, through a complex and rapid imagination and with a kind of authoritative immediacy. Mr. Hicks

knows that Dreiser is "clumsy" and "stupid" and "bewildered" and
"crude in his statement of materialistic monism"; he knows that Dreiser in
his personal life—which is in point because James's personal life is always
supposed to be so much in point—was not quite emancipated from "his
boyhood longing for crass material success," showing "again and again a
desire for the ostentatious luxury of the successful business man." But
Dreiser is to be accepted and forgiven because his faults are the sad,
lovable, honorable faults of reality itself, or of America itself—huge, in-
choate, struggling toward expression, caught between the dream of raw
power and the dream of morality.

"The liability in what Santayana called the genteel tradition was due
to its being the product of mind apart from experience. Dreiser gave us
the stuff of our common experience, not as it was hoped to be by any
idealizing theorist, but as it actually was in its crudity." The author of this
statement certainly cannot be accused of any lack of feeling for mind as
Henry James represents it; nor can Mr. Matthiessen be thought of as a
follower of Parrington—indeed, in the preface to *American Renaissance*
he has framed one of the sharpest and most cogent criticisms of Parrington's method. Yet Mr. Matthiessen, writing in the *New York Times Book
Review* about Dreiser's posthumous novel, *The Bulwark*, accepts the
liberal cliché which opposes crude experience to mind and establishes
Dreiser's value by implying that the mind which Dreiser's crude experience is presumed to confront and refute is the mind of gentility.

This implied amalgamation of mind with gentility is the rationale of
the long indulgence of Dreiser, which is extended even to the style of his
prose. Everyone is aware that Dreiser's prose style is full of roughness and
ungainliness, and the critics who admire Dreiser tell us it does not matter.
Of course it does not matter. No reader with a right sense of style would
suppose that it does matter, and he might even find it a virtue. But it has
been taken for granted that the ungainliness of Dreiser's style is the only
possible objection to be made to it, and that whoever finds in it any fault
at all wants a prettified genteel style (and is objecting to the ungainliness
of reality itself). For instance, Edwin Berry Burgum, in a leaflet on
Dreiser put out by the Book Find Club, tells us that Dreiser was one of
those who used—or, as Mr. Burgum says, utilized—"the diction of the
Middle West, pretty much as it was spoken, rich in colloquialism and
frank in the simplicity and directness of the pioneer tradition," and that
this diction took the place of "the literary English, formal and bookish, of
New England provincialism that was closer to the aristocratic spirit of the
mother country than to the tang of everyday life in the new West." This is
mere fantasy. Hawthorne, Thoreau, and Emerson were for the most part
remarkably colloquial—they wrote, that is, much as they spoke; their
prose was specifically American in quality, and, except for occasional
lapses, quite direct and simple. It is Dreiser who lacks the sense of colloquial diction—that of the Middle West or any other. If we are to talk of

bookishness, it is Dreiser who is bookish; he is precisely literary in the bad sense; he is full of flowers of rhetoric and shines with paste gems; at hundreds of points his diction is not only genteel but fancy. It is he who speaks of "a scene more distingué than this," or of a woman "artistic in form and feature," or of a man who, although "strong, reserved, aggressive, with an air of wealth and experience, was *soi-disant* and not particularly eager to stay at home." Colloquialism held no real charm for him and his natural tendency is always toward the "fine:"

> . . . . Moralists come and go; religionists fulminate and declare the pronouncements of God as to this; but Aphrodite still reigns. Embowered in the festal depths of the spring, set above her altars of porphyry, chalcedony, ivory and gold, see her smile the smile that is at once the texture and essence of delight, the glory and despair of the world! Dream on, oh Buddha, asleep on your lotus leaf, of an undisturbed Nirvana! Sweat, oh Jesus, your last agonizing drops over an unregenerate world! In the forests of Pan still ring the cries of the worshippers of Aphrodite! From her altars the incense of adoration ever rises! And see, the new red grapes dripping where votive hands new-press them!

Charles Jackson, the novelist, telling us in the same leaflet that Dreiser's style does not matter, remarks on how much still comes to us when we have lost by translation the stylistic brilliance of Thomas Mann or the Russians or Balzac. He is in part right. And he is right too when he says that a certain kind of conscious, supervised artistry is not appropriate to the novel of large dimensions. Yet the fact is that the great novelists have usually written very good prose, and what comes through even a bad translation is exactly the power of mind that made the well-hung sentence of the original text. In literature style is so little the mere clothing of thought—need it be insisted on at this late date?—that we may say that from the earth of the novelist's prose spring his characters, his ideas, and even his story itself.[1]

To the extent that Dreiser's style is defensible, his thought is also defensible. That is, when he thinks like a novelist, he is worth following—when by means of his rough and ungainly but no doubt cumulatively effective style he creates rough, ungainly, but effective characters and events. But when he thinks like, as we say, a philosopher, he is likely to be not only foolish but vulgar. He thinks as the modern crowd thinks when it decides to think: religion and morality are nonsense, "religionists" and moralists are fakes, tradition is a fraud, what is man but matter and impulses, mysterious "chemisms," what value has life anyway? "What, cooking, eating, coition, job holding, growing, aging, losing, winning, in so changeful and passing a scene as this, important? Bunk! It is some form of titillating illusion with about as much import to the superior forces that bring it all about as the functions and gyrations of a fly. No more. And maybe less." Thus Dreiser at sixty. And yet there is for him always the vulgarly saving suspicion that maybe, when all is said and done, there is Something Behind It All. It is much to the point of his intellectual vulgarity that Dreiser's anti-Semitism was not merely a social prejudice but an idea, a way of dealing with difficulties.

No one, I suppose, has ever represented Dreiser as a masterly intellect. It is even commonplace to say that his ideas are inconsistent or inadequate. But once that admission has been make, his ideas are hustled out of sight while his "reality" and great brooding pity are spoken of. (His pity is to be questioned: pity is to be judged by kind, not amount, and Dreiser's pity—*Jennie Gerhardt* provides the only exception—is either destructive of its object or it is self-pity.) Why has no liberal critic ever brought Dreiser's ideas to the bar of political practicality, asking what use is to be made of Dreiser's dim, awkward speculation, of his self-justification, of his lust for "beauty" and "sex" and "living" and "life itself," and of the showy nihilism which always seems to him so grand a gesture in the direction of profundity? We live, understandably enough, with the sense of urgency; our clock, like Baudelaire's, has had the hands removed and bears the legend, "It is later than you think." But with us it is always a little too late for mind, yet never too late for honest stupidity; always a little too late for understanding, never too late for righteous, bewildered wrath; always too late for thought, never too late for naïve moralizing. We seem to like to condemn our finest but not our worst qualities by pitting them against the exigency of time.

But sometimes time is not quite so exigent as to justify all our own exigency, and in the case of Dreiser time has allowed his deficiencies to reach their logical, and fatal, conclusion. In *The Bulwark* Dreiser's characteristic ideas come full circle, and the simple, didactic life history of Solon Barnes, a Quaker business man, affirms a simple Christian faith, and a kind of practical mysticism, and the virtues of self-abnegation and self-restraint, and the belief in and submission to the hidden purposes of higher powers, those "superior forces that bring it all about"—once, in Dreiser's opinion, so brutally indifferent, now somehow benign. This is not the first occasion on which Dreiser has shown a tenderness toward religion and a responsiveness to mysticism. *Jennie Gerhardt* and the figure of the Reverend Duncan McMillan in *An American Tragedy* are forecasts of the avowals of *The Bulwark*, and Dreiser's lively interest in power of any sort led him to take account of the power implicit in the cruder forms of mystical performance. Yet these rifts in his nearly monolithic materialism cannot quite prepare us for the blank pietism of *The Bulwark*, not after we have remembered how salient in Dreiser's work has been the long surly rage against the "religionists" and the "moralists," the men who have presumed to believe that life can be given any law at all and who have dared to suppose that will or mind or faith can shape the savage and beautiful entity that Dreiser liked to call "life itself." Now for

Dreiser the law may indeed be given, and it is wholly simple—the safe conduct of the personal life requires only that we follow the Inner Light according to the regimen of the Society of Friends, or according to some other godly rule. And now the smiling Aphrodite set above her altars of porphyry, chalcedony, ivory, and gold is quite forgotten, and we are told that the sad joy of cosmic acceptance goes hand in hand with sexual abstinence.

Dreiser's mood of "acceptance" in the last years of his life is not, as a personal experience, to be submitted to the tests of intellectual validity. It consists of a sensation of cosmic understanding, of an overarching sense of unity with the world in its apparent evil as well as in its obvious good. It is no more to be quarreled with, or reasoned with, than love itself—indeed, it is a kind of love, not so much of the world as of oneself in the world. Perhaps it is either the cessation of desire or the perfect balance of desires. It is what used often to be meant by "peace," and up through the nineteenth century a good many people understood its meaning. If it was Dreiser's own emotion at the end of his life, who would not be happy that he had achieved it? I am not even sure that our civilization would not be the better for more of us knowing and desiring this emotion of grave felicity. Yet granting the personal validity of the emotion, Dreiser's exposition of it fails, and is, moreover, offensive. Mr. Matthiessen has warned us of the attack that will be made on the doctrine of *The Bulwark* by "those who believe that any renewal of Christianity marks a new 'failure of nerve.' " But Dreiser's religious avowal is not a failure of nerve—it is a failure of mind and heart. We have only to set his book beside any work in which mind and heart are made to serve religion to know this at once. Ivan Karamazov's giving back his ticket of admission to the "harmony" of the universe suggests that *The Bulwark* is not morally adequate, for we dare not, as its hero does, blandly "accept" the suffering of others; and the Book of Job tells us that it does not include enough in its exploration of the problem of evil, and is not stern enough. I have said that Dreiser's religious affirmation was offensive; the offense lies in the vulgar ease of its formulation, as well as in the comfortable untroubled way in which Dreiser moved from nihilism to pietism.[2]

The Bulwark is the fruit of Dreiser's old age, but if we speak of it as a failure of thought and feeling, we cannot suppose that with age Dreiser weakened in mind and heart. The weakness was always there. And in a sense it is not Dreiser who failed but a whole way of dealing with ideas, a way in which we have all been in some degree involved. Our liberal, progressive culture tolerated Dreiser's vulgar materialism with its huge negation, its simple cry of "Bunk!," feeling that perhaps it was not quite intellectually adequate but certainly very *strong*, certainly very *real*. And now, almost as a natural consequence, it has been given, and is not unwilling to take, Dreiser's pietistic religion in all its inadequacy.

Dreiser, of course, was firmer than the intellectual culture that accepted him. He *meant* his ideas, at least so far as a man can mean ideas who is incapable of following them to their consequences. But we, when it came to his ideas, talked about his great brooding pity and shrugged the ideas off. We are still doing it. Robert Elias, the biographer of Dreiser, tells us that "it is part of the logic of [Dreiser's] life that he should have completed *The Bulwark* at the same time that he joined the Communists." Just what kind of logic this is we learn from Mr. Elias's further statement. "When he supported left-wing movements and finally, last year, joined the Communist Party, he did so not because he had examined the details of the party line and found them satisfactory, but because he agreed with a general program that represented a means for establishing his cherished goal of greater equality among men." Whether or not Dreiser was following the logic of his own life, he was certainly following the logic of the liberal criticism that accepted him so undiscriminatingly as one of the great, significant expressions of its spirit. This is the liberal criticism, in the direct line of Parrington, which establishes the social responsibility of the writer and then goes on to say that, apart from his duty of resembling reality as much as possible, he is not really responsible for anything, not even for his ideas. The scope of reality being what it is, ideas are held to be mere "details," and, what is more, to be details which, if attended to, have the effect of diminishing reality. But ideals are different from ideas; in the liberal criticism which descends from Parrington ideals consort happily with reality and they urge us to deal impatiently with ideas—a "cherished goal" forbids that we stop to consider how we reach it, or if we may not destroy it in trying to reach it in the wrong way.

Notes

1. The latest defense of Dreiser's style, that in the chapter on Dreiser in the *Literary History of the United States*, is worth noting: "Forgetful of the integrity and power of Dreiser's whole work, many critics have been distracted into a condemnation of his style. He was, like Twain and Whitman, an organic artist; he wrote what he knew—what he was. His many colloquialisms were part of the coinage of his time, and his sentimental and romantic passages were written in the language of the educational system and the popular literature of his formative years. In his style, as in his material, he was a child of his time, of his class. Self-educated, a type or model of the artist of plebeian origin in America, his language, like his subject matter, is not marked by internal inconsistencies." No doubt Dreiser was an organic artist in the sense that he wrote what he knew and what he was, but so, I suppose, is every artist; the question for criticism comes down to *what* he knew and *what* he was. That he was a child of his time and class is also true, but this can be said of everyone without exception; the question for criticism is how he transcended the imposed limitations of his time and class. As for the defense made on the ground of his particular class, it can only be said that liberal thought has come to a strange pass when it assumes that a plebeian origin is accountable for a writer's faults through all his intellectual life.

2. This ease and comfortableness seem to mark contemporary religious conversions.

Religion nowadays has the appearance of what the ideal modern house has been called, "a machine for living," and seemingly one makes up one's mind to acquire and use it not with spiritual struggle but only with a growing sense of its practicability and convenience. Compare *The Seven Storey Mountain*, which Monsignor Sheen calls "a twentieth-century form of the *Confessions* of St. Augustine," with the old, the as it were original, *Confessions* of St. Augustine.

The Stature of
Theodore Dreiser

Alfred Kazin*

> "The impression is simply one of truth, and therein lies at once
> the strength and the horror of it."
>
> —The Newark *Sunday News* on
> *Sister Carrie*, September 1, 1901.

At a time when the one quality which so many American writers
have in common is their utter harmlessness, Dreiser makes painful
reading. The others you can take up without being involved in the least.
They are "literature"—beautiful, stylish literature. You are left free to
think not of the book you are reading but of the author, and not even of
the whole man behind the author, but just of his cleverness, his sensibility, his style. Dreiser gets under your skin and you can't wait to get him
out again: he stupefies with reality:

> Carrie looked about her, very much disturbed and quite sure
> that she did not want to work here. Aside from making her un-
> comfortable by sidelong glances, no one paid her the least at-
> tention. She waited until the whole department was aware of
> her presence. Then some word was sent around, and a
> foreman, in an apron and shirt sleeves, the latter rolled up to
> his shoulders, approached.
> "Do you want to see me?" he asked.
> "Do you need any help?" said Carrie, already learning
> directness of address.
> "Do you know how to stitch caps?" he returned.
> "No, sir," she replied.
> "Have you had any experience at this kind of work?" he in-
> quired.
> She answered that she had not.
> "Well," said the foreman, scratching his ear meditatively,
> "we do need a stitcher. We like experienced help, though.
> We've hardly got time to break people in." He paused and

* Reprinted from *The Stature of Theodore Dreiser*, ed. Alfred Kazin and Charles Shapiro
(Bloomington: Indiana University Press, 1955), pp. 4–12. Reprinted by permission of Indiana
University Press.

looked away out of the window. "We might, though, put you at finishing," he concluded reflectively.

"How much do you pay a week?" ventured Carrie, emboldened by a certain softness in the man's manner and his simplicity of address.

"Three and a half," he answered.

"Oh," she was about to exclaim, but she checked herself and allowed her thoughts to die without expression.

"We're not exactly in need of anybody," he went on vaguely, looking her over as one would a package.

The city had laid miles and miles of streets and sewers through regions where, perhaps, one solitary house stood out alone—a pioneer of the populous ways to be. There were regions open to the sweeping winds and rain, which were as yet lighted throughout the night with long, blinking lines of gas-lamps, fluttering in the wind. Narrow board walks extended out, passing here a house, and there a store, at far intervals, eventually ending on the open prairie.

"He said that if you married me you would only get ten thousand a year. That if you didn't and still lived with me you would get nothing at all. If you would leave me, or if I would leave you, you would get all of a million and a half. Don't you think you had better leave me now?"

These are isolated passages—the first two from *Sister Carrie*, the third from *Jennie Gerhardt*—and normally it would be as unkind to pick passages from Dreiser as it would be to quote for themselves those frustrated mental exchanges that Henry James's characters hold with each other. For Dreiser works in such detail that you never really feel the force of any until you see the whole structure, while James is preoccupied with an inner meditation that his own characters always seem to be interrupting. But even in these bits from Dreiser there is an overwhelming impression that puzzles and troubles us because we cannot trace it to its source. "One doesn't see how it's made," a French critic once complained about some book he was reviewing. That is the trouble we always have with Dreiser. Carrie measuring herself against the immensity of Chicago, that wonderful night scene in which we see a generation just off the farms and out of the small towns confronting the modern city for the first time; the scene in which Hurstwood comes on Carrie sitting in the dark; Jennie Gerhardt's growing solitude even after the birth of her child; Clyde Griffiths and Roberta Alden walking around the haunted lakes when he is searching for one where he can kill her—one doesn't see the man writing this. We are too absorbed. Something is happening that tastes of fear, of the bottom loneliness of human existence, that just barely breaks into speech from the depths of our own souls; the planet itself seems to creak under our feet, and there are long lines of people bitterly walking to work in the morning dark, thinking only of how they can break through the iron circle of their frustration. Every line hurts. It hurts because you never get free enough of anything to ask what a character or a situation "really" means; it hurts because Dreiser is not trying to prove anything by it or to change what he sees; it hurts even when you are trying to tell yourself that all this happened in another time, that we are cleverer about life than Dreiser was. It hurts because it is all too much like reality to be "art."

It is because we have all identified Dreiser's work with reality that, for more than half a century now, he has been for us not a writer like other writers, but a whole chapter of American life. From the very beginning, as one can see in reading over the reviews of *Sister Carrie*, Dreiser was accepted as a whole new class, a tendency, a disturbing movement in American life, an eruption from below. The very words he used, the dreaminess of his prose, the stilted but grim mater-of-fact of his method, which betrayed all the envy and wonder with which he looked at the great world outside—all this seemed to say that it was not art he worked with but *knowledge*, some new and secret knowledge. It was this that the reviewers instantly felt, that shocked the Doubledays so deeply, that explains the extraordinary bitterness toward Dreiser from the first—and that excited Frank Norris, the publisher's reader (Dreiser looked amazingly like the new, "primitive" types that Norris was getting into his own fiction). Dreiser was the man from outside, the man from below, who wrote with the terrible literalness of a child. It is this that is so clearly expressed in Frank Doubleday's efforts to kill the book, in the fact that most literary and general magazines in the country did not review the book at all, that even some newspapers reviewed the book a year late, and that the tone of these early reviews is plainly that of people trying to accustom themselves to an unpleasant shock.

Sister Carrie did not have a bad press; it had a frightened press, with many of the reviewers plainly impressed, but startled by the concentrated truthfulness of the book. The St. Louis *Mirror* complained that "the author writes with a startling directness. At times this directness seems to be the frankness of a vast unsophistication. . . . The scenes of the book are laid always among a sort of people that is numerous but seldom treated in a serious novel." The general reaction was that of the Newark *Sunday News*, almost a year after the book had been published. "Told with an unsparing realism and detail, it has all the interest of fact. . . . The possibility of it all is horrible: an appalling arraignment of human society. And there is no word of preachment; there are scarcely any philosophic reflections or deductions expressed. The impression is simply one of truth, and therein lies at once the strength and the horror of it."

This was the new note of the book, the unrelieved seriousness of it—but a seriousness so native, so unself-conscious, that Dreiser undoubtedly saw nothing odd about his vaguely "poetic" and questioning chapter titles, which were his efforts to frame his own knowledge, to fit it into a traditional system of thought, though he could not question any of his knowledge itself. Writing *Sister Carrie*, David Brion Davis comments, "was something like translating the Golden Plates." For Carrie was Dreiser's own sister, and he wrote without any desire to shock, without any knowledge that he could. Compare this with so "naturalistic" a book as Hardy's *Tess of the d'Urbervilles*, where the style is itself constantly commenting on the characters, and where the very old-fashioned turn of the prose, in all its complex urbanity, is an effort to interpret the story, to accommodate it to the author's own tradition of thought. Dreiser *could* not comment; so deeply had he identified himself with the story that there was no place left in it for him to comment *from*. And such efforts as he made to comment, in the oddly invertebrate chapter titles, were like gasps in the face of a reality from which he could not turn away. The book was exactly like a dream that Dreiser had lived through and which, in fact, after the failure of *Sister Carrie*, he was to live again, up to the very brink of Hurstwood's suicide.

It was this knowledge, this exclusive knowledge, this *kann nicht anders*, this absence of alternatives, that led people to resent Dreiser, and at the same time stunned the young writers of the period into instant recognition of his symbolic value to them. We never know how much has been missing from our lives until a true writer comes along. Everything which had been waiting for them in the gap between the generations, everything which Henry James said would belong to an "American Balzac"—that world of industrial capitalism which, James confessed, had been a "closed book" to him from his youth—everything free of "literature" and so free to become literature, now became identified with this "clumsy" and "stupid" ex-newspaperman whose book moved the new writers all the more deeply because they could not see where Dreiser's genius came from. To the young writers of the early twentieth century, Dreiser became, in Mencken's phrase, the Hindenburg of the novel—the great beast who pushed American life forward for them, who went on, blindly, unchangeably, trampling down the lies of gentility and Victorianism, of Puritanism and academicism. Dreiser was the primitive, the man from the abyss, the stranger who had grown up outside the Anglo-Saxon middle-class Protestant morality and so had no need to accept its sanctions. In Sherwood Anderson's phrase, he could be honored with "an apology for crudity"; and in fact the legend that *Sister Carrie* had been suppressed by the publisher's wife was now so dear to the hearts of the rising generation that Mrs. Doubleday became a classic character, the Carrie Nation of the American liberal epos, her ax forever lifted against "the truth of American life." So even writers like Van Wyck Brooks, who had not shared in the bitterness of Dreiser's early years, and who as socialists disapproved of his despair, now defended him as a matter of course—he cleared the way; in the phrase that was to be repeated with increasing meaninglessness through the years, he "liberated the American novel."

Dreiser now embodied the whole struggle of the new American literature. The "elderly virgins of the newspapers," as Mencken called them, never ceased to point out his deficiencies; the conservative academicians and New Humanists, the old fogeys and the young fogeys—all found in Dreiser everything new, brutal and alien they feared in American life. Gertrude Atherton was to say during the first World War that Dreiser represented the "Alpine School of Literature"—"Not a real American could be found among them with a magnifying glass"; Mary Austin was to notice that "our Baltic and Slavic stock will have another way than the English of experiencing love, and possibly a more limited way. . . . All of Theodore Dreiser's people love like the peasants in a novel by Bojer or Knut Hamsun. His women have a cowlike complaisance such as can be found only in people who have lived for generations close to the soil"; Stuart Sherman, in his famous article of 1915 on "The Barbaric Naturalism of Theodore Dreiser," made it clear that Dreiser, "coming from that 'ethnic' element of our mixed population," was thus unable to understand the higher beauty of the American spirit.

So Dreiser stood in no-man's-land, pushed ahead like a dumb ox by one camp, attacked by the other. Everything about him made him a polemical figure; his scandals, miseries, and confusions were as well-known as his books. The "liberals," the "modernists," defended books like *The "Genius"* because "it told the truth"—and how delighted they must have been when John S. Sumner tried to get the book banned in 1915 and anybody who *was* anybody (including Ezra Pound, John Reed and David Belasco) rushed to its defense. To the English novelists of the period (and *Sister Carrie* owed its sudden fame to the edition Heinemann brought out in London) he was like a powerhouse they envied amid the Georgian doldrums of literary London. How much of that fighting period comes back to you now when you discover Arnold Bennett with his feverish trips to America identifying all the raw, rich, teeming opportunities of American life with Dreiser, or listen to Ford Madox Ford—"Damn it all, it *is* fun to see that poor old language, that vehicle for conveying moderated thoughts, having the guts kicked out of it, like a deflated football, over all the fields of the boundless Middle West." While Mencken, in Dreiser's name, slew William Lyon Phelps in his thousands, the young English discovered that Dreiser was the friend of art. Each side in the controversy used Dreiser, and each, in its own way, was embarrassed. How many times did the young Turks have to swallow Dreiser's bad books, to explain away his faults, and how clear it is from reading Paul Elmer More (who was a deeper critic than his opponents and would have been almost a great one if he had not always tried to arm himself against American life) that he was always more moved by Dreiser's cosmic doubts than he could confess. More settled the problem, as he settled every writer he feared, by studying the man's "philosophy"—where he could show up Dreiser to his heart's content, and, in a prose that could not have been more removed from the actualities of the subject, prove that he had disposed forever of this intellectual upstart.

This pattern remained to the end—Dreiser was the great personifier. When he went to Russia, even the title of the book he wrote had to begin with Dreiser rather than with Russia; when Sinclair Lewis praised Dreiser in his Nobel Prize speech, he did so with all the enthusiasm of a Congressman trying for the farm vote; when Dreiser delivered himself of some remarks about Jews, the *Nation* was not so much indignant as bewildered that this son of the common people could express such illiberal sentiments; when he spoke against England at the beginning of the Second World War, there was a similar outcry that Dreiser was letting the masses down. It is typical of Dreiser's symbolic importance that a writer now so isolated as James T. Farrell has been able to find support for his own work only in Dreiser's example; that the word *plebeian* has always been used either to blacken Dreiser or to favor him; that Eisenstein suffered so long to make a film of *An American Tragedy* that would be the ultimate exposure of American capitalism. When Dreiser joined the Communists, his act was greeted as everything but what it really was—the lonely and confused effort of an individual to identify himself with a group that had taken him up in his decline; when he died in 1945, in the heyday of American-Soviet friendship, one left-wing poet announced that Dreiser's faults had always been those of America anyway, that he was simply America writ large—"Much as we wish he had been surer, wiser, we cannot change the fact. The man was great in a way Americans uniquely understand who know the uneven contours of their land, its storms, its droughts, its huge and turbulent Mississippi, where his youth was spent." Even Dreiser's sad posthumous novels, *The Bulwark*, and *The Stoic*, each of which centers around a dying old man, were written about with forced enthusiasm, as if the people attacking them were afraid of being called reactionary, while those who honestly liked them reported that they were *surprisingly* good. And how F. O. Matthiessen suffered all through the last year of his life to do justice to Dreiser as if that would fulfill an *obligation* to the cause of "progressivism" in America.

But soon after the war all this changed—Dreiser was now simply an embarrassment. The reaction against him was only partly literary, for much of it was founded on an understandable horror of the fraudulent "radicals" who had been exploiting Dreiser before his death. And thanks not a little to the cozy prosperity of a permanent war economy, America, it seemed, no longer required the spirit of protest with which Dreiser had been identified. The writers were now in the universities, and they all wrote about writing. No longer hoary sons of toil, a whole intelligentsia, post-Communist, post-Marxist, which could not look at Alger Hiss in the dock without shuddering at how near they had come to his fate, now tended to find their new ideology in the good old middle-class virtues. A new genteel tradition had come in. Writing in America had suddenly become very conscious that literature is made with words, and that these words should look nice on the page. It became a period when fine writing was everything, when every anonymous smoothie on *Time* could write cleaner prose about God's alliance with America than poor old Dreiser could find for anything, when even the *Senior Scholastic*, a magazine intended for high-school students, complained of Dreiser that "some of the writing would shock an English class." It is of this period, in which we live, that Saul Bellow has noted in his tribute to Dreiser: "I think that the insistence on neatness and correctness is one of the signs of a modern nervousness and irritability. When has clumsiness in composition been felt as so annoying, so enraging? The 'good' writing of the *New Yorker* is such that one experiences a furious anxiety, in reading it, about errors and lapses from taste; finally what emerges is a terrible hunger for conformity and uniformity. The smoothness of the surface and its high polish must not be marred. One has a similar anxiety in reading a novelist like Hemingway and comes to feel that in the end Hemingway wants to be praised for the offenses he does not commit. He is dependable; he never names certain emotions or ideas, and he takes pride in that—it is a form of honor. In it, really, there is submissiveness, acceptance of restriction."

The most important expression of the reaction against Dreiser is Lionel Trilling's "Reality in America." This essay expresses for a great many people in America just now their impatience with the insurgency that dominated our famously realistic fiction up to the war, and not since Paul Elmer More's essay of 1920 has anyone with so much critical insight made out so brilliant a case against Dreiser; not since William Dean Howells supported Stephen Crane's *Maggie* and not *Sister Carrie* has anyone contrasted so sharply those notorious faults of style and slovenly habits of thought which our liberal criticism has always treated as "essentially social and political virtues" with the wonderful play of mind and fertility of resource one finds in Henry James. Never has the case against the persistent identification of Dreiser with "reality" in America—coarse, heavy, external reality—been put with so much intellectual passion. For Mr. Trilling is writing against the decay of a liberal movement ruined largely by its flirtation with totalitarianism, by its disregard of human complexity and its fear of intellect. No one who has followed the extent to which our liberal critics have always acknowledged that Dreiser *is* a bad thinker—and have excused it on the grounds that the poor man at least "told the truth about American life"—can help but share Mr. Trilling's impatience with what has recently passed in this country for liberal "imagination."

But may it not be suggested that Henry James as a cultural hero serves us as badly as Dreiser once did? What happens whenever we convert a writer into a symbol is that we lose the writer himself in all his indefeasible singularity, his particular inimitable genius. A literature that modeled itself on Dreiser would be unbearable; a literature that saw all its virtues of literature in Henry James would be preposterous. If one thing is clear about our addiction to Henry James just now, it is that most of our new writing has nothing in common with James whatever. For James's essential quality is his intellectual appetite—"all life belongs to you"—his unending inner meditation, and not the air of detachment which so misleads us whenever we encounter it on the surface of the society James wrote about—the only society he knew, and one he despaired of precisely because it was never what it seemed. Just now, however, a certain genteel uninvolvement is dear to us, while Dreiser's bread lines and street-car strikes, his suffering inarticulate characters, his Chicago, his "commonness"—are that bad dream from which we have all awakened. As Dreiser's faults were once acclaimed as the virtues of the common man, so now we are ashamed of him because he brings up everything we should like to leave behind us.

There is no "common man"—though behind the stereotype (how *this* executioner waits!) stand those who may yet prepare all too common a fate for us all. Literary people, as a class, can get so far away from the experience of other classes that they tend to see them only symbolically. Dreiser as "common man" once served a purpose; now he serves another. The basic mistake of all the liberal critics was to think that he could ever see this world as something to be ameliorated. They misjudged the source of Dreiser's strength. This is the point that David Brion Davis documents so well in his study of what Dreiser and the early naturalists really believed.[1] For as Mr. Davis shows, these writers and painters were "naturalists" only in the stark sense that the world had suddenly come down to them divested of its supernatural sanctions. They were actually obsessed with the transcendental possibilities of this "real" world; like Whitman, they gloried in the beauty of the iron city. In their comtemplative acceptance of this world, in their indifference to social reform, in their awe before life itself, they were actually not in the tradition of political "liberalism" but in that deeper American strain of metaphysical wonder which leads from the early pietists through Whitman to the first painters of the modern city.

This gift of contemplativeness, of wonder, of reverence, even, is at the center of Dreiser's world—who can forget the image of the rocking chair in *Sister Carrie*, where from *this* cradle endlessly rocking man stares forever at a world he is not too weak but too bemused to change? And it is this lack of smartness, this puzzled lovingness for the substance of all our mystery, that explains why we do not know what to *do* with Dreiser today. For Dreiser is in a very old, a very difficult, a very lonely American tradition. It is no longer "transcendentalist," but always it seeks to transcend. This does not mean that Dreiser's philosophy is valuable in itself, or that his excursions into philosophy and science—fields for which he was certainly not well equipped—have to be excused. It does mean that the vision is always in Dreiser's work, and makes it possible. Just as the strength of his work is that he got into it those large rhythms of wonder, of curiosity, of amazement before the power of the universe that give such largeness to his characters and such unconscious majesty to life itself, so the weakness and instability of his work is that he could become almost too passive before the great thing he saw out there, always larger than man himself. The truth is, as Eliseo Vivas says in his essay,[2] that Dreiser is "not only an American novelist but a universal novelist, in the very literal sense of the word. The mystery of the universe, the puzzle of destiny, haunts him, and he, more than any other of his contemporaries, has responded to the need to relate the haunting sense of puzzlement and mystery to the human drama. No other American novelist of his generation has so persistently endeavored to look at men under the aspect of eternity. It is no . . . paradox, therefore, that . . . while Dreiser tries to demonstrate that man's efforts are vain and empty, by responding to the need to face the problem of destiny, he draws our attention to dimensions of human existence, awareness of which is not encouraged by current philosophical fashions. . . ." To understand how this gets into Dreiser's work one must look not back of it but into it for that sense of "reality" which he thirsted for—that whole reality, up to the very shores of light, that made him cry out in *Jennie Gerhardt*: "We turn our faces away from the creation of life as if that were the last thing that man should dare to interest himself in, openly."

This is what makes Dreiser so painful—in his "atheism," his cosmology; this is what dismays us in our sensible culture, just as it bothered a generation that could never understand Dreiser's special bitterness against orthodox religion, against the churches; this is what drove Dreiser to look for God in the laboratories, to write essays on "My Creator." He may have been a "naturalist," but he was certainly not a materialist. What sticks in our throats is that Dreiser is outside the agreed boundaries of our concern, that he does not accept our "society" as the whole of reality, that he may crave after its fleshpots, but does not believe that getting along is the ultimate reach of man's effort. For we live in a time when traditionalists and "progressives" and ex-progressives alike are agreed that the man not to be trusted is the man who does not fit in, who has no "position," who dares to be distracted—when this great going machine, this prig's paradise in which we live just now, is the best of all possible worlds.

Dreiser committed the one sin that a writer can commit in our society—he would not accept this society itself as wholly real. And it is here, I think, that we can get perspective on his famous awkwardness. For what counts most with a writer is that his reach should be felt as well as his grasp, that words should be his means, not his ends. It is this that

Malcolm Cowley noticed when he wrote that "there are moments when Dreiser's awkwardness in handling words contributes to the force of his novels, since he seems to be groping in them for something on a deeper level than language." This is what finally disturbs us about Dreiser in a period when fine writing is like a mirror that gives back our superficiality. Dreiser hurts because he is always looking to the source; to that which broke off into the mysterious halves of man's existence; to that which is behind language and sustains it; to that which is not ourselves but gives life to our words.

Notes

1. David Brion Davis, "Dreiser and Naturalism Revisited," *The Stature of Theodore Dreiser*, ed. Alfred Kazin and Charles Shapiro (Bloomington, 1955). (Ed. Note.)

2. Eliseo Vivas, "Dreiser, an Inconsistent Mechanist," *Ethics*, 48 (July, 1938), 498–508; republished in *The Stature of Theodore Dreiser*. (Ed. Note.)

Theodore Dreiser:
The Wonder and
Terror of Life

Charles C. Walcutt*

*　*　*　*　*　*　*　*

My thesis is that naturalism is the offspring of transcendentalism. American transcendentalism asserts the unity of Spirit and Nature and affirms that intuition (by which the mind discovers its affiliation with Spirit) and scientific investigation (by which it masters Nature, the symbol of Spirit) are equally rewarding and valid approaches to reality. When this mainstream of transcendentalism divides, as it does toward the end of the nineteenth century, it produces two rivers of thought. One, the approach to Spirit through intuition, nourishes idealism, progressivism, and social radicalism. The other, the approach to Nature through science, plunges into the dark canyon of mechanistic determinism. The one is rebellious, the other pessimistic; the one ardent, the other fatal; the one acknowledges will, the other denies it. Thus "naturalism," flowing in both streams, is partly defying Nature and partly submitting to it; and it is in this area of tension that my investigation lies, its immediate subject being the forms which the novel assumes as one stream or the other, and sometimes both, flow through it. The problem, as will appear, is an epitome of the central problem of twentieth-century thought.

*　*　*　*　*　*　*　*

Theodore Dreiser (1871–1945) drank his inspiration from both branches of the divided stream. He has been described as a pessimist, a socialist, a communist; he has been said to embody the antithesis of American transcendentalism; he has himself acknowledged beliefs in the meaninglessness of life, in the moral autonomy of the superman, in the ultimate value and dignity of the individual. In his later works he has placed mind above matter. And even while he was writing his early books

* Reprinted from *American Literary Naturalism, A Divided Stream* (Minneapolis: University of Minnesota Press, 1956), pp. vii–viii, 180–221. An earlier version of the essay appeared in *PMLA*, 55 (March, 1940), 261–89, under the title "The Three Stages of Theodore Dreiser's Naturalism." Reprinted by permission of the University of Minnesota Press and Charles C. Walcutt.

he believed in a mystical Cosmic Consciousness that one would hardly have suspected from reading those books. His mixture of despair and idealism, of wonder and fear, of pity and guilt, of chemistry and intuition has given us the most moving and powerful novels of the naturalistic tradition. Examined chronologically, they reveal naturalistic ideas struggling to find a structure by which the novel could move without turning upon crucial ethical choices. They also reveal a continuous *ethical* questioning of tradition, dogma, received morality, and social "justice." Thus they always contain the antithesis of their materialistic premises. Between the poles of this tension is Dreiser's "naturalism." It moves, during his literary career, through phases of objectivity, resignation, and protest toward the groping affirmation of spirit that presides over and, oddly, defeats his final work.

Psychologically, Dreiser is himself a divided stream of pity and guilt, of wonder and terror, of objectivity and responsibility. He observes a world without meaning, yet he also responds to a compelling need to believe. Misery in any form moved the young Dreiser to tears. Of his brother, to whom he does not appear to have been especially close, he wrote: "A——— always seemed more or less thwarted in his ambitions, and whenever I saw him I felt sad, because, like so many millions of others in this grinding world, he had never had a real chance. Life is so casual, and luck comes to many who sleep and flies from those who try."[1] And one sees that to him his brother was a symbol of all human sorrow and thwarted potentiality.

Elsewhere he remarked: "I was never tired of looking at the hot, hungry, weary slums."[2] "I was honestly and sympathetically interested in the horrible deprivations inflicted upon others, their weaknesses of mind and body, afflictions of all sizes and sorts, the way so often they blundered or were driven by internal chemic fires."[3] Again, he was so moved by these words in a letter from a girl he had abandoned that he used them almost verbatim in *The "Genius"* more than twenty years later: "I stood by the window last night and looked out on the street. The moon was shining and those dead trees over the way were waving in the wind. I saw the moon on that little pool of water over in the field. It looked like silver. Oh, Theo, I wish I were dead."[4]

Throughout *A Book about Myself* one of the dominant notes is Dreiser's wondering sympathy for the pain which life inflicts in the form of hunger, weariness, and uncertainty on those whom poverty and suffering have already rendered inarticulate. He was ever "sensitive to the brevity of life and what one may do in a given span."[5] In Pittsburgh he was curious about the captains of industry, but "It was the underdog that always interested me more than the upper one, his needs, his woes, his simplicities."[6] "Indeed," he writes, "I could never think of the work being done in any factory or institution without passing from that work to the lives behind it, the separate and distinct dramas of their individual lives."[7] A less sensitive and sympathetic man would have either fled from such painful sights or, if flight were impossible, developed a cynical indifference and saved his pity for more gratifying exercise. He had, furthermore, experienced no little of the poverty for which he pitied others. His autobiography is full of the poignancy of his hungry craving for comfort, travel, finery, and the leisure to know sophisticated men and glamorous women.

Dreiser's repeated references in his early books to the "chemical compound which is youth," the "chemic force" within the mind, "the chemic formula which works to reproduce the species," show that he believed in a sort of mechanistic psychology. He did not pretend to comprehend the workings of the mind, but he was, *apparently*, sure that there is nothing transcendental in it. This real but as yet unexplained phenomenon of human thought and vitality he deprived of some of its mystery by naming it "chemic." The notion that mental activity is a chemical reaction is not, of course, a full explanation of that activity, and nowhere does Dreiser suggest that it does constitute such a full explanation. He still recognized some wonderful mystery, some all-important force, which gives life its wonder and terror and meaning. Again and again in his autobiography he broods over the impermanence of life and his conviction that only living is of absolute value:

> I could see the tiny sands of my little life's hourglass sifting down, and what was I achieving? Soon the strength of time, the love time, the gay time, of color and romance, would be gone, and if I had not spent it fully, joyously, richly what would there be left for me, then? The joys of a mythical heaven or hereafter played no part in my calculations. When one was dead one was dead for all time. Hence the reason for the heartbreak over failure here and now; the awful tragedy of a love lost, a youth never properly enjoyed. Think of living and yet not living in so thrashing a world as this, the best of one's hours passing unused or not properly used. Think of seeing this tinkling phantasmagoria of pain and pleasure, beauty and all its sweets, go by, and yet being compelled to be a bystander, a mere onlooker, enhungered but never satisfied![8]

This yearning is everywhere in his books; it is a part of his temperament which we must feel in order to understand the peculiar qualities that he brought to his writing. As a materialist, then, he recognized that man is not in control of his destiny:

> Most of these young men [reporters] looked upon life as a fierce, grim struggle in which no quarter was either given or taken, and in which all men laid traps, lied, squandered, erred

through illusion; a conclusion with which I now most heartily
agree.[9]

In this connection the account he gives of his first acquaintance with the
works of Herbert Spencer, in about 1893, is worthy of extended quotation:

At this time I had the fortune to discover Huxley and Tyndall and Herbert Spencer, whose introductory volume to his
Synthetic Philosophy (First Principles) quite blew me, intellectually, to bits. Hitherto, until I had read Huxley, I had some
lingering filaments of Catholicism trailing about me, faith in
the existence of Christ, the soundness of his moral and
sociologic deductions, the brotherhood of man. But on reading
Science and Hebrew Tradition and *Science and Christian
Tradition*, and finding both Old and New Testaments to be not
compendiums of revealed truth but mere records of religious
experiences, and very erroneous ones at that, and then taking
up First Principles and discovering that all I deemed substantial—man's place in nature, his importance in the universe,
this, too, too solid earth, man's very identity save as an infinitesimal speck of energy or a "suspended equation" drawn
or blown here and there by larger forces in which he moved
quite unconsciously as an atom—all questioned and dissolved
into other and less understandable things, I was completely
thrown down in my conceptions or non-conceptions of life.
Up to this time there had been in me a blazing and unchecked desire to get on and the feeling that in doing so we did
get somewhere; now in its place was the definite conviction
that spiritually one got nowhere, and there was no hereafter,
that one lived and had his being because one had to, and that it
was of no importance. Of one's ideals, struggles, deprivations,
sorrows and joys, it could only be said that there were chemic
compulsions, something which for some inexplicable but
unimportant reason responded to and resulted from the hope
of pleasure and the fear of pain. Man was a mechanism,
undevised and uncreated, and a badly and carelessly driven
one at that.
I fear that I cannot make you feel how these things came
upon me in the course of a few weeks' reading and left me
numb, my gravest fears as to the unsolvable disorder and
brutality of life eternally verified. . . . There was of course
this other [note the dichotomy] matter of necessity, internal
chemical compulsion, to which I had to respond whether I
would or no. I was daily facing a round of duties which now
more than ever verified all that I had suspected and that these
books proved. With a gloomy eye I began to watch how the
chemical—and their children, the mechanical—forces operated through man and outside him, and this under my very

eyes . . . and when I read Spencer I could only sigh. All I could think of was that since nature would not or could not do anything for man, he must, if he could, do something for himself; and of this I saw no prospect, he being a product of these selfsame accidental, indifferent and bitterly cruel forces.[10]

Science did not appeal to Dreiser. He had had so much experience with human misery that it did not seem to him possible to achieve any reasoned explanation of the riddle of life. On the contrary he was endlessly impressed by the instances he saw of life's steady and purposeless flux: "What a queer, haphazard, disconnected thing this living was!" ". . . life is haphazard and casual and cruel; to some lavish, to others niggardly." "But as I wandered about I realized . . . that life was a baseless, shifting thing, its seeming ties uncertain and unstable and that that which one day we held dear was tomorrow gone, to come no more." "The tangle of life, its unfairness and indifference to the moods and longings of any individual, swept over me once more weighing me down far beyond the power of expression."[11] This wonder at the ceaseless, confusing flux of life is elaborated in his book of "philosophy," the very title of which—*Hey Rub-a-Dub-Dub; A Book of the Mystery and Terror and Wonder of Life*—is an expression of his characteristic attitude toward cosmic forces:

> But these [justice, truth, etc.] have been assumed, in an absolute and not a relative sense, to be attributes of a Supreme Being who is all-just, all-truthful, all-merciful, all-tender, rather than as mechanic or, if one accepts the created theory of life, as an intelligently and yet not moralistically worked-out system of minor arrangements, reciprocations and minute equations, which have little to do with the aspects and movements of much larger forces of which as yet we know nothing and which at first glance hinder rather than aid the intellect in perceiving the ultimate possibilities of the governing force in any direction. Indeed the rough balance or equation everywhere seen and struck between element and element, impulse and impulse . . . really indicates nothing more than this rough approximation to equation in everything—force with matter, element with element—as an offset to incomprehensible and, to mortal minds, even horrible and ghastly extremes and disorders; nothing more. For in face of all the schemes and contrivances whereby man may live in harmony with his neighbor there is the contrary fact that all these schemes are constantly being interfered with by contrary forces, delays, mistaken notions, dreams which produce inharmony. This can mean nothing if not an inherent impulse in Nature that makes for change and so rearrangement, regardless of any existing harmonies or balances, plus the curious impulse in man and Nature (inertia?) which seems to wish to avoid change.[12]

The combination of his observations with his philosophy could produce only moral and ethical agnosticism; and indeed if his autobiography is to be relied upon Dreiser had lost faith in conventional moral codes long before he had come upon the writings of Spencer. We find him declaring that

> The world, as I see it now, has trussed itself up too helplessly with too many strings of convention, religion, dogma. . . . Is it everybody's business to get married and accept all the dictates of conventional society—that is, bear and rear children according to a given social or religious theory? . . . And, furthermore, I am inclined to suspect that the monogamous standard to which the world has been tethered much too harshly for a thousand years or more now is entirely wrong. I do not believe that it is Nature's only or ultimate way of continuing or preserving itself. Nor am I inclined to accept the belief that it produces the highest type of citizen.[13]

And not only did he distrust the unthinking Christian repression of sex—he was concerned with the importance of the sexual urge in normal human life and with the impossibility of giving an authentic or rounded picture of human activity without taking full cognizance of its ubiquitous pressure and stimulation:

> While it is true that some of the minor professors of psychoanalysis are offering what they are pleased to term the "sublimation of the holophilic (or sex) impulse" into more "useful," or, at any rate, more agreeable fields of effort via suppression or restraint, this in my judgment is little more than a sop, and an obvious one, to the moralists. What is actually true is that via sex gratification—or perhaps better, its ardent and often defeated pursuit—comes most or all that is most distinguished in art, letters and our social economy and progress generally. It may be and usually is "displaced," "referred," "transferred," "substituted by," "identified with" desires for wealth, preferment, distinction and what not, but underneath each and every one of such successes must primarily be written a deep and abiding craving for women, or some one woman, in whom the sex desires of any one person for the time being are centered. "Love" or "lust" (and the one is but an intellectual sublimation of the other) moves the seeker in every field of effort.[14]

A warm, boundless human sympathy; a tremendous vital lust for life with a conviction that man is the end and measure of all things in a world which is nevertheless without purpose or standards; moral, ethical, and religious agnosticism; contact with the scientific thought of the late nineteenth century which emphasized the power and scope of mechanical laws over human desires; belief in a chemical-mechanistic explanation of the human machine; plus a constant yearning for faith—these are the elements which Dreiser brought to the writing of his novels. Determinism as a working hypothesis did not attract him because he was more interested in the mystery and terror and wonder of life itself than in tracing those forces which might account for and so dispel the mystery.[15]

By knowing Dreiser's life and character one avoids the pitfall of assuming that his naturalism is derived primarily from other writers. Of literary "influences" it is sufficient to indicate that Dreiser had been urged to read Zola[16] but had not read him when he wrote *Sister Carrie*,[17] although he had been considerably impressed by a Zolaesque novel composed by one of his friends on a Chicago newspaper.[18] On the other hand, he had devoured Balzac as early as 1893–1894.[19] If literary influences were to be pursued, they would obviously point toward realism; but our concern here is to analyze the form which the naturalistic impulse received in his novels, rather than to search out the exact sources of that impulse in his reading.

Dreiser's "naturalism" found expression in four distinct stages. Different ideas about the body of theory just presented appear in succeeding novels and give them different significant forms—until we come to his last novels, where the predominance of materialistic, non-teleological theory has gone, and in its place appears a solid affirmation of tradition and moral restraint as the values capable of resisting the deteriorating effects of modern society.

In the first stage Dreiser was expounding his conviction of the essential purposelessness of life and attacking the conventional ethical codes which to him seemed to hold men to standards of conduct that had no rational basis in fact, while they condemned others without regard to what Dreiser thought might be the real merits of their situations. The first half of this program—expounding the purposelessness of life—is the backbone of his first novel, *Sister Carrie*, published in 1900. Through a queer juxtaposition of incidents, and with only small regard for the worthiness of their impulses, one character achieves fame and comfort while another loses his wealth, social position, pride, and finally his life.

Into this novel Dreiser has brought all the vivid reality of his own experience with the dreary, beaten, downtrodden life of those who have no money, no background, no sophistication, and no especial talent. With a deep compassion that never assumes the right to pass moral judgment upon the actions of his characters, he shows Carrie Meeber coming to Chicago from the country, drearily passing from one ill-paid and health-breaking job to another, and at length, jobless and depressed by the thought of having to return defeated to the country, setting up housekeeping with Drouet, a "drummer" whom she had met on the train as she first entered the city.

At this crucial instance begins Carrie's rise in the world. As a "fallen woman" she is in no wise judged; and even more astonishing, Drouet is shown to be flashy, crude, essentially shallow, but nevertheless at the antipodes from villainy. He is goodhearted and generous; in fact he has every intention of marrying Carrie. With this social and financial advance over the miserable narrowness that characterized the home life of the sister with whom she had been living, Carrie begins to recognize class differences, to long for "better" things, even to sense Drouet's limitations. Drouet's friend Hurstwood represents the next higher level of culture and wealth. He is manager of a prosperous saloon, he owns a fine house, and his family is eagerly climbing the social ladder. When he meets Carrie he falls desperately in love with her and, in what almost amounts to an abduction, abandons his family, steals $10,000 from his employers, and flees with her through Canada and into New York.

From this point the fall of Hurstwood and the rise of Carrie are depicted in antiphonal relationship. Hurstwood's degeneration is a remarkable representation of the meaningless, almost unmotivated sort of tragedy that art had, until then, conspired to ignore. His wife's grasping jealousy and pettiness impel him toward Carrie, and his being seen with her gives his wife grounds for a divorce action. It is by the merest chance that he finds the safe open on the very night when he had planned to disappear. His theft of the money results from a frantic impulse which he is too weak to resist. When he tries to return the cash to the safe, he finds that the lock has clicked shut. So the theft is consummated by an accident. He is later forced to return the money, but he never recovers his self-esteem. In New York he takes a half interest in a second-rate saloon and after a time loses his investment. Then he dawdles, first looking for jobs, finally sitting in hotels instead of looking; at length he stays home, reading newspapers endlessly and hoarding the little money he has left. The change in his character from an affluent good-fellow to a seedy miser is convincing and pathetic.

> Some men never recognize the turning in the tide of their abilities. It is only in chance cases, where a fortune or a state of success is wrested from them, that the lack of ability to do as they did formerly becomes apparent. Hurstwood, set down under new conditions, was in a position to see that he was no longer young.[20]

Carrie stays with him as long as she can; but when she gets a place in a stage chorus she leaves him in order to room with a girl who is dancing in the same chorus. Hurstwood goes down and down—to poverty, destitution, begging, starvation, and finally suicide.

Carrie, on the other hand, rises rapidly from the moment she leaves Hurstwood. She graduates from the chorus to a minor role:

> Evidently the part was not intended to take precedence as Miss Madenda [Carrie] is not often on the stage, but the au-

dience, with the characteristic perversity of such bodies, selected for itself. The little Quakeress was marked for a favourite the moment she appeared, and thereafter easily held attention and applause. The vagaries of fortune are indeed curious.

The last sentence of this newspaper account of Carrie's first step forward on the stage emphasizes the major theme of the book—how curious are the vagaries of fortune. As Hurstwood is drawing nearer to his sordid death, Carrie climbs rapidly until she is earning what is to her an unheard-of salary, living in one of the finest hotels in the city, and receiving proposals and attentions from men as far superior to Hurstwood at his best as he had been to the flashy Drouet. "Even had Hurstwood returned in his original beauty and glory, he could not now have allured her." The books ends on a note of uncertainty. Carrie is not to be thought of as having attained any final goal. She is still longing and wondering, "an illustration of the devious ways by which one who feels, rather than reasons, may be led in the pursuit of beauty. Though often disillusioned, she was still waiting for that halcyon day when she should be led forth among dreams become real."

Shocking to contemporary readers—or reviewers, for there were few readers at first—was the amoral attitude from which *Sister Carrie* was written.[21] Nowhere is a moral pointed. There is no inevitable punishment for transgression, no suggestion that there ought to be. In one passage Dreiser even appeals to nature as against conventional moral standards and intimates that the only evil in what is ordinarily considered sinful comes from the codes which call it evil, because they introduce elements of guilt and hypocrisy into conduct:

> He [Drouet] could not help what he was going to do. He could not see clearly enough to wish to do differently. He was drawn by his innate desire to act the old pursuing part. He would need to delight himself with Carrie as surely as he would need to eat his heavy breakfast. He might suffer the least rudimentary twinge of conscience in whatever he did, and *in just so far he was evil and sinning*. But whatever twinges of conscience he might have would be rudimentary . . .[22]

What is perfectly natural or spontaneous is good: the brooding mind makes it sin. Conventional morals may thus be rigid and unrealistic; but they do reflect a reality that transcends (while it includes) simple mechanism. This is what the transcendentalist called spirit. Dreiser's feeling for this transcendental reality appears clearly in the following passage, where morals are not denied even though conventional morality has been rejected:

> For all the liberal analysis of Spencer and our modern naturalistic philosophers, we have but an infantile perception

of morals. There is more in the subject than mere conformity to
a law of evolution. It is yet deeper than conformity to things of
earth alone. It is more involved than we, as yet, perceive.
Answer, first, why the heart thrills; explain wherefore some
plaintive note goes wandering about the world, undying; make
clear the rose's subtle alchemy evolving its ruddy lamp in light
and rain. In the essence of these facts lie the first principles of
morals.[23]

Dreiser has been shown to distrust the concept of purpose or ethical design
in the universe; yet such passages as that just quoted betray him in the
characteristically naturalistic action of substituting the compelling, vital
mystery of Nature for the failing God of orthodox religion.

Here the transcendental roots thrust boldly up, showing that the apparent line separating the spiritual tree from the natural earth is only apparent: the tree of spirit grows from the earth. Yet the confidence that
nature reveals spirit and design is not as strong with Dreiser, who has
come to see the impossibility of reducing all phenomena to orderly laws,
as it was with those earlier devotees of science who transferred their
religious zeal directly to Nature, never doubting that the answers to all
men's problems were to be found by patient searching through her
spacious domain. For them Nature was perfect meaning; for Dreiser the
Design is perpetually tantalizing and elusive.

A consciously scientific use of detail appears when Dreiser brings
chemical physiology to the explanation of Hurstwood's mental condition
as he is beginning his final downward plunge:

Constant comparison between his old state and his new
showed a balance for the worse, which produced a constant
state of gloom or, at least, depression. Now, it has been shown
experimentally that a constantly subdued frame of mind produces certain poisons in the blood, called katastates, just as virtuous feelings of pleasure and delight produce helpful
chemicals called anastates. The poisons generated by remorse
inveigh against the system, and eventually produce marked
physical deterioration. To these Hurstwood was subject.[24]

This, in small compass, is a clear-cut instance of the influence of science
upon Dreiser's method: he is approaching his problem with a new set of
instruments. The chemical explanation of mental conditions is of a piece
with the amoral outlook and the change of focus away from ethical plot-
conflict toward the dispassionate *observation* of life. This latter problem
brings one to the heart of what is new in the form of *Sister Carrie*.

Structurally the novel consists of the two life cycles which are opposed to each other in studied balance. What *Sister Carrie* exhibits that is
most characteristically naturalistic is the complete absence of ethical plot-
complication. The movement of the novel does not depend upon acts of
will by the central figures. There is no suspense waiting to be resolved by

a decision which will be judged in terms of absolute ethical standards. The movement is the movement of life—skillfully selected and represented by the artist, to be sure, but still a movement which has little resemblance to the typical plot that begins with a choice or a crucial action and ends with the satisfaction of the forces and the passions set in motion by that choice. The difference is fundamental. The novels of such writers as Thackeray and Trollope have complication, climax, and denouement in every instance. *Sister Carrie* has no such movement. There is no suspense created because the art of the novelist is directed by an entirely different motive. Dreiser is not manipulating a portion of life; he is observing it. It is the quality of the lives represented that moves the reader, not the excitement of what the characters do. Here Dreiser reflects the impressionism of Crane and strikes a note that we hear later in the work of Sherwood Anderson, where a very different sort of writer has in a different way presented the qualities of experience instead of choices and results. Having deprived his novel of the conventional structure, Dreiser supplies the two cycles—Carrie's rise and Hurstwood's descent. These two cycles embody the principle of change which Dreiser finds fundamental to all life and all natural process. In a naïve mechanist's novel they would pretend to embody social laws. Not so with Dreiser.

Dreiser is primarily a novelist, a student of humanity, and only incidentally a philosopher. Human values are never subordinated to philosophical implications. *Sister Carrie* is more important as a story than for the ideas it contains. The reader is interested in Carrie as a person who faces problems comparable to his own; and if the reader is not to be offended by the course of the story, the successes and failures of the characters must in some way answer to the reader's notion of their worth as human beings. Because of this fact, ethical standards can hardly be eliminated from any novel. Carrie's rise, even though accidental and not, by conventional standards, "deserved," is welcome because she is an appealing character; and Hurstwood's degeneration, distressing though it may be, is not unbearably offensive because Hurstwood has qualities which cause him to lose some of the reader's sympathy. The philosopher in Dreiser makes concessions to the novelist because his heart is in league with humanity. This is another way of saying that what happens in a piece of fiction must be probable, and probability includes the satisfaction, to some degree, of the moral sense. Hardy's *Return of the Native* appears to turn upon the cruelest coincidences, and yet each character in it experiences a morally probable fate. So with Dreiser. One cannot write stories in which, just as the crisis is approaching, the villain is killed by a falling meteor. Such things occur in life, but they cannot in novels, which in their design and organization depict a truth free from the outrageous accidents of actuality. With these reservations, which return us to the fact that the novelist cares more for human suffering than for demonstrating the principle of cosmic indifference, we may return to the assertion that

Sister Carrie is organized to depict the essential purposelessness of life. The plot structure of conventional fiction is abandoned for the new organization that answers to Dreiser's view of life.

But though he recognized the operation of external force he is not, in *Sister Carrie*, concerned with an experimental demonstration of the nature of that operation. Rather he is concerned with the pathos of human life and with the constant inscrutable change that attends it. We come, in the last analysis, to a matter of emphasis: one may study the way external forces operate upon man, attempting to lay bare the secrets of their action; or one may see life through the eyes of the objects of these forces, with the wonder and terror of the changes unexplained. Dreiser does a little of both: he shows clearly enough how Hurstwood and Carrie change as they do; but mostly he is concerned with bringing out the shifting, uncertain, mysterious nature of life as it appears when being acted upon by forces which it cannot fathom and which—most terrible truth—have no purpose that can be related to the purposes of men.

Dreiser believes in a determinism which destroys or modifies the moral view of conduct. He is, further, impressed by the inscrutability of fortune, the lack of meaning and purpose in the action of external force. Between these two smothering convictions flourishes his affirmation—his belief in the vitality and importance of life. It is upon the latter that one's attention is directed in *Sister Carrie*. The inscrutable variations of fortune serve chiefly to underline the positive quality of living. Throughout the book it is this quality of life—shifting, elusive, unaccountable—that holds our attention, rather than the spectacle of carefully analyzed forces operating under "experimental" conditions. Dreiser's affirmation of the human spirit is in the transcendental tradition.[25]

The generalizations applied to *Sister Carrie* are also true of *Jennie Gerhardt* (1911). The difference between the two books which is of importance to this study is a difference of emphasis. In *Sister Carrie* conventional ethical codes are assumed to be invalid or at least impractical for evaluating life as it is, while the story is largely pointed toward demonstrating the unpredictable purposelessness of all things. In *Jennie Gerhardt* this emphasis is reversed. Ceaseless and unintentioned change has become an accepted hypothesis with Dreiser, while the story is devoted to a consideration of the moral and ethical standards according to which society (supposedly) operates. The previous assumption that they are unreal here becomes the point at issue, the substance of Dreiser's thesis. He shows how the life of a "kept woman" is blighted by society's treatment of what it considers her immorality. The criticism is pointed by the heroine's being a rich and lovely character (which illustrates again the contention that Dreiser is primarily a novelist, in league with humanity), and the effect of the story is to show how utterly inadequate are standard Christian ethics for the judgment or guidance of conduct in a world that does not, as Dreiser sees it, correspond to the notion of reality upon which that ethical code is based.

Jennie Gerhardt is the daughter of a stupidly devout German glass blower. She is one of a large family which lives in the poor district of Columbus, Ohio, at a bare subsistence level. She is not a semi-moron (as one critic has said) but a girl rich and direct in feeling—the sort of person whose feelings take the place of thoughts:

> There are natures born to the inheritance of flesh that come without understanding, and that go again without seeming to have wondered why. Life, so long as they endure it, is a true wonderland, a thing of infinite beauty, which could they but wander into it wonderingly, would be heaven enough. . . . From her earliest youth goodness and mercy had molded her every impulse.[26]

At the hotel where she scrubs floors, Senator Brander is impressed by her beauty, decides to marry her, and presently seduces her.

The Senator dies suddenly, before he is able to carry out his intention of marrying Jennie, leaving her pregnant. After the child is born, the disgraced family moves to Cleveland where Jennie presently meets the man who is to be the center of her thoughts for the rest of her life. Lester Kane comes from a wealthy Cincinnati family of carriage makers. He is generous, forceful, direct, and the slightest bit coarse-grained. In spite of his wealth and good breeding, the reader is made to feel that he is, emotionally, less beautifully constructed than Jennie, though he is capable of appreciating her fine nature and is, indeed, worlds beyond her culturally. Most of the book is devoted to their changing relations. He keeps her in various apartments, supplying her liberally with money, always half intending to marry her but never quite making up his mind to disturb the comfortable *status quo*. Jennie's most pressing concern, after her love for Lester, is to keep her little girl near her without having Lester, whom she has foolishly kept in ignorance, learn of the child's existence. She is happy in her love for him and in being able to help her impoverished family with money. Lester's discovery of the child precipitates a crisis, and he thinks of leaving her. But he has become so attached to her goodness that he cannot bear the thought of separation. When his family discovers the connection and tries to break it off he defiantly installs Jennie in a large house in Chicago, and a period of precarious happiness follows.

Then forces conspire to take Lester away from her. His father dies, leaving Lester's inheritance contingent upon his abandoning Jennie. His family brings all its persuasive force to bear. And, to sweep aside the last hesitation, Lester is attracted by a cultivated and wealthy widow who is deeply in love with him. As always, Jennie is wholly unselfish in wanting Lester to do what is best for himself—and it is he who is uncertain which way to turn, drawn at once by loyalty to Jennie, fascination for Mrs. Gerald, the desire to retain his accustomed wealth and to be active in his father's business, and the influences exerted by his family and the polite society which wants him to become finally "respectable."

But he did not want to do this. The thought was painful to him—objectionable in every way. Jennie was growing in mental acumen. She was beginning to see things quite as clearly as he did. She was not a cheap, ambitious, climbing creature. She was a big woman and a good one. It would be a shame to throw her down, and besides she was good-looking. . . . It is an exceptional thing to find beauty, youth, compatibility, intelligence, your own point of view—softened and charmingly emotionalized—in another.

The reader cannot entirely blame Lester when he finally gives Jennie up, for he understands the many subtle pressures—which Dreiser so fully presents—that condition his exercise of volition. Lester could choose readily enough if he knew exactly what he wanted. What makes the influence of external forces credible is the wealth of careful documentation that Dreiser presents so that the reader may actually see all the influences that work upon Lester and paralyze his will. Social ostracism and the loss of a large part of his independent fortune, which makes his need for a share in his father's estate more pressing, finally turn the balance against Jennie—though it is she who urges him to go.

At a subsequent meeting he tries to explain his feelings:

"I was just as happy with you as I ever will be. It isn't myself that's important in this transaction apparently; the individual doesn't count much in the situation. . . . All of us are more or less pawns. We're moved about like chessmen by circumstances over which we have no control. . . .

"After all, life is more or less of a farce," he went on a little bitterly. "It's a silly show. The best we can do is to hold our personality intact. It doesn't appear that integrity has much to do with it."[27]

Stricken with a fatal illness, he calls her to his deathbed, where he tells her,

"I haven't been satisfied with the way we parted. It wasn't the right thing, after all. I haven't been any happier. I'm sorry. I wish now, for my own peace of mind, that I hadn't done it. . . . It wasn't right. The thing wasn't worked out right from the start; but that wasn't your fault. I'm sorry. I wanted to tell you that. I'm glad I'm here to do it."

The story ends with Jennie at the station for a last glimpse of the coffin. Nowhere has Dreiser matched the pathos of these closing lines:

Before her was stretching a vista of lonely years down which she was steadily gazing. Now what? She was not so old yet. There were those two orphan children to raise. They would marry and leave after a while, and then what? Days and days in endless reiteration, and then—?

A novel with a "kept woman" for its central figure was somewhat unusual in 1911, but when that kept woman is presented as good and admirable, as possessing positive virtues which raise her quite above the general run of socially minded people, then we recognize a novel in which conventional values are challenged, in which the approach that is taken to the problem of man in society is not an ordinary one.

This approach constitutes the philosophy. As in *Sister Carrie*, it can be stated as belief in determinism accompanied by a conviction that the appointed course of events has neither purpose nor an order that is accessible to man's intellect. What strikes the reader again and again is the unreasonable way in which events pile up to direct the lives of the characters. Luck is more important than careful planning, and "goodness" does not necessarily appeal to the unknown or nonexistent controllers of destiny. The evidence shows that a thousand circumstances enfold man in their invisible garment of steel; no one is capable of seeing the pattern according to which the garment is woven; one only feels the pressures which check or direct him in particular movements. Conventional moral standards constitute one part of this garment; they control Jennie's life and prevent her from achieving happiness.

The same kind of thinking is extended to Dreiser's idea of the human will. He recognizes will as a function of what he might call personality. His people act from apparently autonomous impulses. Jennie's goodness, for example, he regards as something which need not and indeed cannot be accounted for. But at the same time, by the approach outlined in the preceding pages, Dreiser shows that the will is not free to operate independently, that it has not the power to bring its impulses to fulfillment. Thus instead of attempting to go behind the will and identify the components of its apparently free volitions, he follows these impulses into the world and shows us precisely why and how they are thwarted by social and economic forces. We might say that he admits free will with reference to volition but denies it with reference to action. One can wish freely, but one cannot freely carry out one's wishes.

In a world so envisaged, good intentions do not necessarily bear good results. Nor is what is conventionally called evil punished. Hence standard ethics are discredited because they do not represent a realistic interpretation of social relations. They do not constitute the genuine forces which make for social cohesion and regulate the conduct of civilized man. It would be useless to blame someone for conditions beyond his control. This assumption is fundamental in *Jennie Gerhardt*. As the hero says, "The best we can do is to hold our personality intact." Jennie's goodness is valued more highly than the society which destroys her chance for happiness. Dreiser does not show that there may be extenuating circumstances to pardon the sinfulness of the "fallen woman." He denies that she is sinful; he deplores the moral codes which, failing to restrain her first slip, inflict a consciousness of guilt upon her ever after; he considers her good and beautiful, and the reader is led to conclude that Lester Kane was foolish (or very unlucky) not to have married her. These conclusions show that Dreiser believes in a spiritual truth which exists above the flux and error of actuality. He does not account for it, but he affirms its presence in Jennie and he deplores through his novel the social conditions which blight its growth and free expression.

All these abstract notions depend for their conviction upon the emotional weight which Dreiser is able to attach to the personality of Jennie. That he succeeds with his message is due to his success in making of her a rich and lovely woman, a creature who is all good and whose simple heart is capable of endless devotion. Jennie is undoubtedly his richest creation. The reader's sympathies are entirely with her. Her sufferings are so real that the reader is not aware of an auctorial "message," for he reaches the conclusions here described through his emotional response to the events of the story. This point is important, for it shows that the pathos of Jennie's life is the outstanding fact of the novel, the fact upon which depend any ideas that the reader may gather. As a work of art *Jennie Gerhardt* is highly successsful, the ideas upon which it is based serve first of all to create a certain aesthetic effect and do not obtrude themselves in the way of that effect. It is too bad that Jennie should suffer, and the system is to be deplored for making her suffer, but that is not tantamount to saying that the institution of marriage, for example, should be rejected. It would indeed detract from the pathos of Jennie's situation if the author were crusading for change. The conditions which crush her must, for the purposes of the novel, be regarded as unchangeable.

In the second stage of his development Dreiser added the idea of the superman to the two main ideas which I have described. When one had found that life was meaningless and morals absurdly inadequate, the next step was to conclude that the only good lay in exercising one's will to power. The philosophy of the superman was conveniently available to enable Dreiser to take this step; and he wrote four novels about the activities of supermen in the modern business world. Nietzsche's philosophy saw in the superman the only hope for the betterment of mankind. Dreiser may have known this aspect of Nietzsche's thought, he may even have begun *The Financier* with the intention of demonstrating some such idea, but his study of the activities of one of the Robber Barons of the late nineteenth century seems finally to have drawn him away from the notion that the financial superman was an indispensable agent in the development of a capitalistic society.

Dreiser's "Trilogy of Desire," composed of *The Financier* (1912), *The Titan* (1914), and *The Stoic* (1947), represents his effort to set forth the life of a modern financial superman. Although written from the point of view of the superman and begun as a celebration rather than an indictment of him, these novels virtually accomplish Jack London's avowed but unfulfilled purpose in writing *The Sea-Wolf*—to show that "the super-man cannot be successful in modern life . . . he acts like an irritant in the social body."[28] This cannot be called Dreiser's purpose, however, for he never arrived at that degree of conviction which would permit him to organize a portion of the social scene and write about it as if he had thought his way through to a final conclusion about its meaning. It is the planlessness and inconclusiveness of life that interested Dreiser. On the other hand, nearly all critics have ceased accusing him of being merely a patient recorder who copied his books tediously from newspaper records. The organizing hand of the artist is always present, but its purpose is not to reduce the complexity of life to a prettily simplified pattern that answers all one's questions about cause and effect, design and purpose.

The Financier and *The Titan* contain perhaps the greatest mass of documentation to be found in any American novels in the naturalistic tradition. They are records of an epoch of American life. The career of Charles T. Yerkes, traction magnate of Philadelphia and Chicago, supplied Dreiser with the materials for his two books. Yerkes is transformed into Frank Algernon Cowperwood, and the novels record his economic and amorous affairs in minutest detail. *The Financier* takes Cowperwood from boyhood up to the panic of 1873. A "superman" devoid of ethical restraints, he goes from business to business, gaining control of the Philadelphia street-railway network, and buying cooperation from the politicians. He becomes a millionaire and is laying plans to make a billion when the Chicago fire of 1871 causes a panic which wipes out his fortune. Because he seduced the daughter of the political boss, he is at this time abandoned by those in control and made a scapegoat to appease an indignant populace. After thirteen months in prison he is pardoned just in time to regain his fortune by selling short in the panic of 1873. Here ends *The Financier*.

The Titan is longer and more detailed. It tells how Cowperwood moves to Chicago and, through bribes and cleverness, gains a number of franchises for the distribution of suburban gas. After this coup he launches into a long fight to gain control of all the Chicago street railways. The novel presents the great struggle in all its complexity, showing how banks, local politicians, legislators, governors, and newspapers are drawn into the vortex of the conflict—and how Cowperwood is finally defeated in his efforts to buy or control the entire state legislature and obtain from them a fifty-year franchise on Chicago street-railway transportation. The details of these transactions are given so fully that the reader is convinced of their authenticity: he comes from the books feeling that he has seen the whole picture, presented more minutely—and far more effectively—than it could have been presented in the best historical or economic treatise available. The facts are all there, vividly realized and brought to life. And since the affairs of Cowperwood are part and parcel of this vast economic complex, the recording of its intricacies is documentation in the closest naturalistic tradition. It is as intimately united with the story as the documentation of Zola's *L'Assommoir* or *Germinal*. It is setting, condition, and material for the novel; none of it is extraneous, none gratuitous, because it is all a part of Cowperwood's career.

Intermingled with Cowperwood's business dealings throughout the two novels are his amorous intrigues and domestic difficulties. One critic described *The Titan* as a "huge club-sandwich composed of slices of business alternating with erotic episodes,"[29] and the description is an apt one, although it gives less attention than it might to the close relationship between the two sides of Cowperwood's life that Dreiser is continually bringing out. Cowperwood's amorous escapades round out his "business" personality; they also cause violent repercussions in his various business transactions, for the women he knows quite naturally are connected with the men with whom he deals in the world of politics and finance.

It has been shown in the discussion of both *Sister Carrie* and *Jennie Gerhardt* that Dreiser's determinism is determinism *after the fact*. That is, he does not pretend to go behind an act of so-called will and show all the conditions and pressures of which it is composed. He does not pretend to set down a perfect chain of causal relationships that account for the fiction known as free will; but, admitting its existence, he does show how in its actions it is swayed and guided by "deterministic" forces beyond it—so that in effect it is relatively helpless.[30]

In *The Financier* and *The Titan* there is the same attitude toward man and society, but the situation is greatly altered by a change in one of the factors of the problem. That factor of course is Frank Algernon Cowperwood. Instead of being relatively weak like Carrie, Hurstwood, Jennie, and Lester Kane, Cowperwood is endowed with tremendous energy and ability. He is born to conquer, and he knows it. At the age of eighteen he receives a five-hundred-dollar Christmas bonus from the grain brokers to whom he has been apprenticed without salary to learn the business. Already he is indispensable—and perfectly confident:

> On his way home that evening he speculated as to the nature of this business. He knew he wasn't going to stay there long, even in spite of this gift and promise of salary. They were grateful, of course; but why shouldn't they be? He was efficient, he knew that; under him things moved smoothly. It never occurred to him that he belonged in the realm of clerkdom. Those people were the kind of beings who ought to work for him, and who would. There was nothing savage in his attitude, no rage against fate, no dark fear of failure.[31]

He is selfish because his own concerns are paramount with him. In another paragraph his nature is carefully described:

> Cowperwood was innately and primarily an egoist and in-tellectual, though blended strongly therewith was a humane

and democratic spirit. We think of egoism and intellectualism as closely confined to the arts. Finance is an art. And it presents the operations of the subtlest of the intellectuals and of the egoists. Cowperwood was a financier. Instead of dwelling on the works of nature, its beauty and subtlety, to his material disadvantage, he found a happy mean, owing to the swiftness of his intellectual operations, whereby he could, intellectually and emotionally, rejoice in the beauty of life without interfering with his perpetual material and financial calculations. And when it came to women and morals, which involved so much relating to beauty, happiness, a sense of distinction and variety in living, he was but now beginning to suspect for himself at least that apart from maintaining organized society in its present form there was no basis for this one-life, one-love idea.[32]

Toward the end of *The Titan* he is still strong: "he seemed a kind of superman, and yet also a bad boy—handsome, powerful, hopeful . . . impelled by some blazing internal force which harried him on and on.[33] He is the apotheosis of individualism, the man who moves the mass, which "only moves forward because of the services of the exceptional individual." He answers to the wish "that the significant individual will always appear and will always do what his instincts tell him to do."[34]

At the end of *The Financier* Cowperwood has asserted himself stupendously, made and lost a great fortune, complicated the life of every banker and politician in Philadelphia, and yet, like Jennie and Lester Kane and Hurstwood, has been swept back and forth by environing forces more powerful than even his intelligence and resolution. Being a larger figure, he moves in a more elaborate complex of forces; but the forces elude his foresight and generalship and temporarily strip him of freedom and fortune.

At the end of the great struggle related in *The Titan*, when Cowperwood is temporarily defeated by the enmity his power has evoked (a situation which is a better example than London could produce of how the financial superman "acts like an irritant in the social body"), Dreiser expatiates upon the spectacle of his superman's career:

Rushing like a great comet to the zenith, his path a blazing trail, Cowperwood did for the hour illuminate the terrors and wonders of individuality. But for him also the eternal equation—the pathos of the discovery that even giants are but pygmies, and that an ultimate balance must be struck. Of the strange, tortured, terrified, reflection of those who, caught in his wake, were swept from the normal and the commonplace, what shall we say? Legislators by the hundreds were hounded from politics into their graves; a half-hundred aldermen of various councils who were driven grumbling or whining into the limbo of the dull, the useless, the commonplace.

These sentences repeat the philosophy outlined earlier in connection with *Sister Carrie* and *Jennie Gerhardt*. The action of the books involves the same wondering uncertainty, the same vision of life as purposeless and unpredictable, the same denial of ethical codes, the same recognition of external pressures which determine the courses of our lives. What distinguishes *The Financier* and *The Titan* from the two previous novels is, as we have seen, the different weight given in them to the human factor in Dreiser's equation of change. Cowperwood is a greater force than Dreiser's earlier characters, but his position in the cosmos is essentially the same.

In conclusion we may consider the ethical import of these books. Hearing about them, one's reaction is that Dreiser must have composed them as an indictment of the business methods of the Robber Barons—to show that they were social menaces who should have been extirpated. Doubtless some such conclusion comes to the reader after he has finished the novels; but so long as he is reading them Cowperwood is the hero. His morals may not be held up as exemplary for American society, but his intelligence and energy make him the center of attention and concern. The reader sees the struggle through Cowperwood's eyes; he cannot avoid lending his sympathy to the owner of those eyes. He is attracted, as people always are in reality, to a man with the personal force to affect the lives of thousands of people. Further than this, Dreiser is frequently at pains to cast doubt upon the judgments which condemn Cowperwood. Early in *The Financier*, young Cowperwood gets his first lesson in the law of tooth and fang by watching a lobster devour a squid that is placed in a tank with him in a store window. The same novel ends with a parable about the black grouper, a fish which survives by virtue of its ability to change color and so deceive enemy and prey alike. We are asked,

> What would you say was the intention of the overruling, intelligent, constructive force which gives to Mycteroperca this ability? To fit it to be truthful? To permit it to present an unvarying appearance which all honest life-seeking fish may know? Or would you say that subtlety, chicanery, trickery, were here at work? An implement of illusion one might readily suspect it to be, a living lie, a creature whose business it is to appear what it is not, to simulate that with which it has nothing in common, to get its living by great subtlety, the power of its enemies to forefend against which is little. The indictment is fair.
>
> Would you say, in the face of this, that a beatific, beneficent, creative overruling power never wills that which is either tricky or deceptive?

The conclusion is that Christian ethics are illusory, that people should not be blamed for disobeying a code which, if followed, would render them unfit to survive. Indeed, he found, as Burton Rascoe writes, "an epic quality in the rise of individuals to merciless and remorseless power through the adaptation of their combative instincts to the peculiar conditions of the American struggle for existence."[35] In the same spirit Dreiser interpolates a disquisition on monogamy, his point being that Christian moral standards do not answer human needs.[36] Again, he questions the idea of divine guidance and the relation of man to nature:

> How shall I explain these subtleties of temperament and desire? Life has to deal with them at every turn. They will not down, and the large, placid movements of nature outside of man's little organisms would indicate that she is not greatly concerned. We see much punishment in the form of jails, diseases, failure, and wrecks; but we also see that the old tendency is not visibly lessened. Is there no law outside of the subtle will and power of the individual to achieve? If not, it is surely high time that we knew it—one and all. We might then agree to do as we do; but there would be no silly illusions as to divine regulation.[37]

It does not follow from this denial of conventional ethics that a Cowperwood is a boon to society. He may "move the mass," but Dreiser's own story shows that he does not move it to any good end. There is no paradox here. The point is that Dreiser is thinking in terms of the individual without sufficiently considering his social function. He is condemning "Divine Law" without apparently realizing that it often corresponds to natural law. Cowperwood cannot reasonably be condemned to hell-fire for following his natural bent, and it is natural for him to strive for power; but his social value is another matter. Dreiser denies a beneficent guiding Purpose, and so removes moral blame; but he does not investigate the social function of Cowperwood. If he did, he would unquestionably recognize society's need to restrain such individuals. And he has done so since then.

The "Genius" (1915) is cut from the same block as The Financier and The Titan. Both in form and thesis it resembles those novels so closely that an extended analysis of it is unnecessary. Eugene Witla, the hero of The "Genius," is a superman like Cowperwood. He is an artist rather than a financier, but otherwise he is much the same sort of person. Like Cowperwood, again, he is set loose in the turbulence of modern life and permitted to exercise his superior cunning and resourcefulness untrammeled by moral restraints or inhibiting consideration for others. Like Cowperwood he has his successes and his failures, the forces which thwart his intentions frequently being the combination of weaker people who unite in defiance of his superman self-assertion. And again, Witla's amours occupy a large portion of the story, represent the superabundance of his artistic "genius," and are responsible for several of his misfortunes. Like The Financier and The Titan, The "Genius" consists of a loosely connected sequence of events related by chronology and by the fact that Eugene Witla participates in them all. The book, furthermore, ends upon a note of wonder and uncertainty which we have found to be characteristic of Dreiser's attitude toward life at this stage. And finally, the superman hero is the center of reference and attention throughout the story. His effect upon society is not considered, for Dreiser is still brooding over the place of the individual in his meaningless cosmos. *The "Genius"* is probably also the most personal of Dreiser's books. Revelation replaces theory to a considerable degree.

The third stage in Dreiser's naturalism is marked by his conversion to socialism. Here the ideas that signalized his first stage remain, but instead of advocating individual anarchy, as he tended to do under the aegis of Nietzsche, he has come to believe that something can be accomplished toward the amelioration of social evils if men will unite in a concerted attack upon those evils. *An American Tragedy* (1925) is founded upon this point of view, although we must remember that this, like Dreiser's other novels, is first of all a human story.

An American Tragedy recounts the life of Clyde Griffiths. He is first seen in Kansas City, the child of itinerant street preachers, singing on a corner with them. He becomes a bellhop in a large hotel and there acquires a longing for the luxuries which his family cannot provide. He soon goes to Chicago where, still working as a bellhop, he meets his rich uncle Samuel, a collar manufacturer in Lycurgus, New York. The uncle later has Clyde come to Lycurgus and starts him at the bottom of his business, with every opportunity to work his way to the top. But Clyde is not accepted socially by his wealthy relatives until the fascinating Sondra Finchley takes him up—out of spite—and introduces him to the highest social set of Lycurgus. In the meantime Cylde had been sharing his loneliness with Roberta Alden, a simple country girl who was working under him in the factory. Now when he sees a promising future before him, he learns that Roberta is pregnant. In desperation, after weeks of torturing worry, he plans to take her boating in the country and "accidentally" drown her. At the final moment he lacks courage to overturn the boat, but chance—or the situation produced by the two personalities in their particular relation—completes the design in another way: seeing his despairing and horrified expression, Roberta comes toward him in the boat. He strikes out desperately to fend her off and unintentionally hits her with a camera. The boat capsizes, striking Roberta as she falls into the water, and Clyde refrains from saving her.[38]

The rest of the story is devoted to the apprehension, trial, conviction, and execution of Clyde for the murder of Roberta. As the passage referred to above indicates, Clyde himself is not perfectly sure whether or not he is guilty. Before Roberta arose and came toward him in the rowboat, he had certainly decided that he would not commit the crime he had planned. On the other hand, he instituted the expedition with murder in his heart—a fact which exerted great influence upon the final decision of the jury. The prosecution brings dozens of witnesses and traces Clyde's movements minutely. Clyde's only defense is his last-minute change of heart, for which there is no evidence and which is easily counterbalanced by the absolute proof of his murderous intentions.

The peculiar way in which the "murder" of Roberta occurred is one of the most important facts in the novel. Clyde's inability to commit the deed in cold blood is indicative of his general weakness of will. But when some kind of chance (which might be described by an omniscient psychologist as the inevitable reaction of Roberta to Clyde's horrified expression) enters the action and the boat is capsized, Clyde is given a shock which enables him to allow her to drown. The effect of this careful decription of the incident is to show that Clyde is not the master of his fate, that only under particular conditions is he able to "choose" the "evil" course that he desires to carry out. He does not really "choose" to abandon Roberta; it would be more accurate to say that he is conditioned by his weeks of planning so that when the situation enables him to overcome his scruples (equally the product of long training) he is carried along by the impetus of this conditioning to commit the act he has planned. Thus from an objective point of view one can hardly blame Clyde for an action in which he was largely a weak and helpless participant. Clyde did not willfully produce the dilemma which called forth his attempt to resolve it. His craving for wealth and social position can be understood—like his complementary lack of ethical standards—in the light of his upbringing. His weakness is contemptible to some readers, but Dreiser certainly does not condemn it. Clyde has a certain power of choice, to be sure, which Dreiser does not reduce to its ultimate chemical constituents as the first naïve naturalists thought they might finally be able to do; but that power of choice, though accepted as a factor in the problem, is shown to be conditioned by the many forces among which it exists. Jennie Gerhardt and Lester Kane had "wills" that were impotent, because of external pressures, to fulfill their desires. The same generalization holds for Clyde. In both books Dreiser's attitude toward the relation between personal will and conditioning pressures is the same, and that attitude has been sufficiently described in the preceding pages.

In *An American Tragedy*, however, there is a difference of emphasis which is intimately associated with the structure of the novel. To begin with, Clyde is doubtless the weakest of Dreiser's heroes; he has least of the inexplicable inner drive which makes a commanding personality. He begins, further, with a pitifully meager background and a narrow view of life. He is no Cowperwood or Witla superman—he has not even the charm of Carrie or Jennie. And as the novel proceeds there is so careful an attention to detail and so complete a delineation of the various experiences which add to Clyde's miserable store of ideas and ideals that the reader seems to be gaining a full insight into the forces which account for Clyde's personality.

This statement involves a good deal of oversimplification—for indeed Clyde has a certain amount of personality from the beginning which is never explained as the product of any known forces. It is, further, only a literary convention which permits the novelist to appear to be presenting all the facts of a situation. Dreiser, to be sure, presents more documentation perhaps than any other novelist has ever gathered about a comparable problem; and so the illusion of completeness achieved is less "illusory" than in any other novel which seeks to create the same illusion. The effect on the reader is to make him understand the Clyde who commits the crime in terms of the growth through which Dreiser has conducted him in the first half of the novel. Clyde is more fully accounted for by the nature of his environment than any other character of Dreiser's. The characters in *Sister Carrie* and *Jennie Gerhardt* begin, so to speak, in mid-career; they enter the story with attributes the sources of which Dreiser has not time to explore. Only a suggestion of their previous experiences is recorded, and the reader has no feeling that he has seen their minds grow or watched the important influences which have molded their personalities. They have, further, more of that charm or individuality which creates the impression of free will and ethical independence. Thus we illustrate the truism that only with simple characters—who usually live under sordid conditions—can the naturalistic method succeed in appearing to present the external pressures which control the characters' lives and account for what they are as well as what they do. It is because of the simplicity of Clyde's character and the narrowness of his initial outlook that Dreiser is able to go so much further behind the phenomenon of his will and explain its constituents.

This is a striking difference between the naturalism of *An American Tragedy* and that of Dreiser's earlier novels. But even so it is a difference only in degree, for Dreiser still gazes at the wonder and mystery and terror of life and is unable to find purpose or organization in its ceaseless ebb and flow. His American tragedy contains so much detail that one is aware of the hundreds of independent pressures, working at odds or in complete indifference to each other, that produce the simplest event. The reader is impressed with the futility of trying either to control or to comprehend any event in all of its ramifications. Dreiser, to repeat, pretends to explain Clyde's character more fully in terms of heredity and especially milieu than he has done before—but he is still bound to the conviction that the changes of fate are too inscrutable ever to be finally revealed by man.

Having offered these generalizations, I must hasten to qualify them in another respect. *An American Tragedy* differs greatly in structure from the earlier novels. In all of them we have discerned a formlessness which seemed to answer to Dreiser's conception of reality. Carrie was left in mid-career with a question. Lester and Jennie were buffeted about, but not through any sharply articulated dramatic sequence of events. Cowperwood and Witla, likewise, moved through a long series of incidents which were not integrated into a single action. The structure of

The "Genius" and *The Titan* is Dreiser's assertion that real life is not made up of beautifully organized patterns but of ceaseless fluctuations about a norm which is hidden or even nonexistent. *An American Tragedy*, however, is completely unified by the fact that every event in the novel is related to the central crisis of Roberta's murder.

Book One presents Clyde's early years and his development. Book Two deals with his life in Lycurgus, his affair with Roberta, and the complications brought about by his love for Sondra Finchley—ending with murder. Book Three contains the apprehension, trial, and execution of Clyde. What would have been a tawdry and wandering life is given meaning and centrality by the great event of the murder. By making the last two books of the novel specifically the story of the murder Dreiser is able to have his action single and unified. Doubtless this unity is characteristic of tragedy, which can occur even in a naturalist's world and give a principle of organization to what might otherwise be a dreary, meaningless, and tangled life. This change in structure, then, arises from a change in the content of the novel, not from a change in Dreiser's ideas.

There is, on the other hand, a difference between the philosophy of *An American Tragedy* and that of the earlier novels which justifies the assertion that it marks a third distinct stage in Dreiser's naturalism. In *The Financier*, *The Titan*, and *The "Genius"* he saw life through the eyes of a superman, to whom it appeared as a welter of forces among which he must try somehow to work out his individual salvation. The damage to society in the career of a Cowperwood may be discovered in the books; but the purpose of those books is not to dwell upon the social evil of his career. Similarly Eugene Witla's career is seen as an individual's struggle, without particular social implications. In Clyde Griffith's progress, on the contrary, social implications abound. Dreiser had been converted to socialism since writing *The "Genius"*; his American tragedy is a tragedy brought about by the society in which we live. That society is responsible, as the immediate cause, for Clyde's actions. This social consciousness marks the third stage of Dreiser's naturalism. This is not to say that *An American Tragedy* is an indictment of our social order. It is first of all a work of art, the tragedy of Clyde Griffiths, a picture of a life that is tragic because the protagonist is at once responsible (as any human being feels another to be) and helpless (as the philosopher views events). Clyde's tragedy is a tragedy that depends upon the American social system. It shows the unfortunate effects of that system more, for example, than did the defeat of Cowperwood at the end of *The Titan*. In the latter instance a "superman" was battling the opposition aroused by his will to power. In Clyde's case the whole of the American social order, in its normal activity, is brought into the picture.

An American Tragedy is naturalistic because normal social pressures make Clyde's downfall inevitable. The reader's being led to wonder about the rightness of the social order is, like his doubts about the social value of

Cowperwood, an activity subsequent to the aesthetic experience of the tragedy itself. Dreiser the artist deals with things as they are. Dreiser the socialist demonstrates the evils of our society in a way that may lead the reader sometime to think about correcting them. But this socialistic purpose—if it may be called a purpose—does not become part of the movement of the novel; it does not contaminate the tragedy; it does not, in short, prevent Dreiser from being, still, a naturalist.

I have deferred discussion of *The Stoic* because, although it completes the "Trilogy of Desire," taking up Cowperwood's career after the Chicago debacle, it was not published until 1947, thirty-three years after *The Titan*. Dreiser had most of the book written shortly after publication of *The Titan*, but he kept it by him because he could not, apparently, work out a satisfactory conclusion. In the meantime he wrote new sorts of novels which took him into new spheres of thought where it became increasingly difficult to carry through the implications of ideas which were still growing while he wrote the two earlier volumes.

The opening chapters discover Cowperwood taking stock after his expulsion from the Chicago scene. Love and business as usual are interwoven, on this occasion when Berenice Fleming, whom he has supported through her adolescence and who is now in the bloom of young womanhood, gives herself to him and persuades him also to undertake a new and grander venture in the world of finance. Renewed by the consummation of his love for Berenice, the most charming and talented woman he has known, he lays plans to invade the traction business of London; and this project creates the problems which occupy the reader through the volume. In the first place, Cowperwood must somehow dispose of Aileen, his wife, whose uncontrollable jealousy will lead her to create a scandal if she learns that Berenice has traveled to England and is to be established in a country house where, passing as Cowperwood's ward, she will by her poise and beauty help him into the select circles without whose support it is impossible for a foreigner to break into the world of British finance. To this end he employs an indigent American socialite named Tollifer who pursues Aileen, takes her to Paris, introduces her into a circle of aristocratic waifs and strays, and altogether gives her the happiest days she has known for more than a decade. Meanwhile Cowperwood makes his usual startling impression on British financiers and aristocrats and very soon has set in motion a gigantic scheme to unify and modernize the London Underground system.

Complications appear by virtue, as usual, of the impingement of sex upon business. Lord Stane, who is to launch Cowperwood socially as well as bring his large Underground holdings into the financial pool, falls in love with Berenice. On a money-raising trip to America, Cowperwood enters a brief but intense affair with a young dancer, which gets into the papers. When Aileen reads of this she sends the clipping to Berenice whose relation to Cowperwood she believes to be innocent. Presently Aileen learns why Tollifer has been taking such good care of her and she returns to New York in a fury, threatening to expose Cowperwood in a scandal that will ruin his British operations. But now, when the elements of a highly dramatic involvement are set before us, the story comes to an abrupt and inconclusive ending: Cowperwood dies of Bright's disease.

Following his death, his fortune of some $12,000,000 is quickly eaten away by taxes, litigation, assessments, litigation, and more litigation. His great house and art collection are auctioned off to pay claims. There is no money to build the hospital he had arranged to leave to the city of New York, Aileen is put out of her house, forced to take an absurdly small settlement, and dies of pneumonia without ever adjusting herself to the uncertainties of living in the shadow of continual litigation. We hear nothing of what happens to the great London Underground unification. Cowperwood is treated somewhat unkindly by the press, as his enormous fortune and influence evaporate when he is no longer present to maintain them. If he has been a "superman," he has made no permanent impression on society, and his material contribution of street railway systems will not provide alms for oblivion. Any larger significance of his demise is lost because Dreiser devotes most of his attention to the sordid vanity of Aileen, who deserts Cowperwood on his deathbed when she learns that Berenice is seeing him.

But most striking and extraordinary of culminations is the turning of Berenice to Yogi in the concluding chapters. Here the divided stream of American transcendentalism does astonishing things. Wandering in a chaos of pure materialistic flux, Dreiser allows his heroine in these closing chapters to leap to pure spirit, to Brahma, and to the contemplation and realization of Divine Love. And Dreiser too seems to make this leap, because it appears beyond any question that Berenice carries his thought and conviction. She is the most sensitive and intelligent of his characters; she is the only one who makes significant discoveries about the folly and selfishness of even the most cultivated materialistic life; her four years of study with a Guru in India are presented with what I can read only as utter seriousness on the part of the author. This leap of Dreiser's from pure matter to pure Spirit invites various speculations and comments. The philosophical abysses of Brahmanism, with its concepts of unknowable mysteries and endless cosmic cycles of repetition, are psychologically not unrelated to the abysses of purposeless flux which terrify the devoted materialist. Nor has it ever been possible to say that Dreiser denied the existence of mysteries. Always in league with humanity, he from his earliest book presented the mazes of the human quest as pathetic and compelling. He sought through his love of man to express the sense of an ideal pattern for which he had sought vainly in nature.

Viewed in artistic terms, however, Dreiser's conclusion of *The Stoic* must be considered grotesque. Berenice is too utterly brilliant and dazzling to be quite real. Her love of fine things, her absorption with herself, her whimsical intelligence, and her courageous defiance of convention in becoming Cowperwood's mistress—these are too many traits to fuse into a convincing personality. In India she ascends through all the levels of Yogi to a direct experience of the supreme Reality—a level from which it is hardly probable that she would return to New York, make the amazing discovery that there is poverty there just as in India, and so devote herself to building and working in the hospital that Cowperwood had planned. The birth of a social consciousness comes naïvely twinned to the discovery of Brahma.

Another false start occurs when Berenice finds herself drawn by the culture and charm of Lord Stane. He seems to have the background that Cowperwood lacks. His interests, too, are much broader. And Cowperwood, after swearing his undying love for Berenice, has just been revealed as having a new love affair in New York. But nothing comes of this potential conflict (a favorite in American fiction, by the way), for Berenice decides that Cowperwood's attraction is irresistible. We see her at one moment shrewdly calculating a liaison of vengeance but at the next giving in to pure passion and fascination. After Berenice returns from India to discover that Cowperwood's fortune has vanished into the pockets of lawyers, she "was filled with sorrow as she inwardly viewed the wreckage of all of his plans." Now Cowperwood's plans were largely predaceous and materialistic. After her years of study with the Guru, Berenice would have known that Cowperwood's desire to perpetuate his name by leaving a hospital was not to be confused with the charity which suffereth all. Yet this is what she appears to do. These are all indications of Dreiser's failure to adapt his materials into an effective pattern. Too many ideas wander about the borders of his action without actually being drawn into it.

What finally identifies the structural weakness of this book is Dreiser's failure to manage the problem of *scale*. He begins by describing financial transactions with an attention to detail that would have carried the volume to 600 pages, but these are abandoned without remorse in the midst of the barest beginnings of the great London venture. The love entanglements, likewise, are given here and there chapters of such minute detail that they create the expectation of an exhaustive presentation; but these turn out to be only samples of a whole that does not take shape. The point of view shifts loosely from person to person at least a dozen times during the story. Minds are invaded and then abandoned with little regard for the values of a controlled point of view. We have no sense of exhaustive documentation, of the patient methodical accumulation of all the facts needed to understand a great personal and social condition. The tired and grainy fragments of the story fall apart. The architectonics of naturalism have disappeared. Instead of liberating Dreiser's talent, naturalism left him with a cumbersome technique which he could not use for his newer ideas.

An example of this weakness is the fact that although Cowperwood is, in the title, called a stoic, there is no indication in the book that he is one. He has changed only physiologically, age making it somewhat more difficult for him to be consumed with zeal for an enterprise. But his restless seeking cannot be considered stoical. He comments on the new venture:

> "There's a lot of nonsense to all this, you know. . . . Here we are, you and I, both of us getting along in years, and now running around on this new job, which, whether we do it or not, can't mean so much to either of us. For we're not going to be here so much longer . . . neither of us can do much more than eat a little, drink a little, play about a little longer, that's all. What astonishes me is that we can get so excited over it."[39]

Some time later he speculates with wonder and resignation on morality and human motives:

> Was any man noble? Had there ever been such a thing as an indubitably noble soul? He was scarcely prepared to believe it. Men killed to live—all of them—and wallowed in lust in order to reproduce themselves. In fact, wars, vanities, pretenses, cruelties, greeds, lusts, murder, spelled their true history, with only the weak running to a mythical saviour or god for aid. And the strong using this belief in a god to further the conquest of the weak.

A page later he muses on "the mystery and meaninglessness of human activity." Cowperwood has not changed except that he has tired somewhat and therefore occasionally questions the hustle and striving of life. After he is stricken with his fatal illness we are told almost nothing of his thoughts, even though he lives for several months.

If Dreiser's novel appears wooden, it is because the mixture of new ideas and old is grotesque; the style and the techniques of characterization have not accommodated the new ideas. His characters are introduced and described formally—background, occupation, financial status, followed by a few words of generalization about personality or character. For example:

> Also present were Lord and Lady Bosvike, both young and smart and very popular. They were clever at all sports, enjoyed gambling and the races, and were valuable in any gathering because of their enthusiasm and gaiety. Secretly they laughed at Ettinge and his wife, though at the same time they valued their position and deliberately set themselves out to be agreeable to them.

This writing has not made use of modern techniques of characterization or modern concepts of personality. It illustrates rather Dreiser's consistent use of the formal Victorian categories, like honesty, diligence, and piety. This made *The Stoic* seem old fashioned in 1947; the startling "newness" of early naturalism was not one of its characteristics. Where the newness does appear is in Dreiser's treatment of love. This is anything but Victorian, for to him love is dependent upon all the social, financial, and personal forces that operate at any moment. It is a tension of lust, ambition, vanity, insecurity, and hate; an alteration in any of these elements will unbalance the tension and set it moving toward a new relationship. Dreiser is not able to exhibit this idea dramatically, but it appears again and again in the thoughts of his characters. Anyone making a new acquaintance of the opposite sex wonders what it would be like to be in love with him and adds up the various financial and social complications. Even in their moments of passion, lovers are busy assessing the *status* of their relation, for nothing is permanent and every action initiates irreversible changes. This fragment of the old Dreiser struggles rather feebly in *The Stoic* with Yogi, traces of socialism, and the writer's weariness. The return to spirit, although it completes the broken arc of the transcendental tradition, does not furnish here a pattern for coherent fiction.

Dreiser's final novel, although published only a year before *The Stoic*, was conceived many years earlier and most of it was written long before *The Stoic* was begun. In its published form *The Bulwark* (1946) appears to represent a transitional stage between the materialism of his earlier work and the Brahmanism which appears in the closing pages of *The Stoic*. It deals with three generations of Quakers in Pennsylvania. They go from piety to prosperity to perdition. The protagonist is Solon, of the middle generation, who gets rich, clings to the Inner Light, but sees his children drawn away into various forms of vice and vanity because they cannot resist the material attractions of fine clothes and automobiles or the physical attractions of sex.

The novel has a double theme. Sociologically, it shows that the control exercised by a religion of simplicity like Quakerism is powerless against the lures of American materialism. Within Solon it shows the same conflict: Solon contributes to the downfall of his children because he thinks he can serve both God and Mammon. By serving Mammon he makes a lot of money, which opens up the world of ostentation and vice to his children. If they had all lived in poverty, they would not have been tempted. Yet, paradoxically, it is Solon's Quaker background that makes him sober, industrious, and trustworthy—so that he can rise to affluence as a banker. (I do not know what to say about the unquestioned fact that there have been and still are many Quaker families where wealth and simplicity do go together without difficulty, even through several generations. They do not appear in the argument of *The Bulwark*.)

The Bulwark does not reveal the mixture and confusion of socialism and Yogi that appear in *The Stoic*. When Solon becomes a successful banker, rich enough to give his children the luxuries they crave, it is not suggested that he is exploiting the poor or living on the unearned increment of usury. His rise is presented as the reward of diligence and devotion. It appears in time that he has erred in believing that the moral sobriety of Quakerism could carry him through financial maneuvers unscathed; but his error is, depending upon how one regards it, either a fatal error that was inescapable under the circumstances or the error of judgment of a man who could not foresee where his commercial involvements would take him. Any Marxian analysis of his experience must be supplied by the reader. The frivolous outlooks of his children are not attributed to the class struggle but are presented *sub specie aeternitatis*; here, he seems to say, are children growing up with false human values—values that do not call for the good of which these children are capable. Their lives are wasted in ostentation and frivolity.

The early Dreiser would have stressed the idea that they were not responsible for their standards; he would have implied that any standards were relative and therefore questionable. In 1946 he hurried past these old and easy assumptions to consider what values are good and where they can be found. The Inner Light of Quakerism is not said to be the perfect guide, but it is a guide which made the old people strong and which sustained Solon until he meddled with such powerful gods as Mammon and Moloch. Although Quakerism is not contrasted with Buddhism or Yogi or Platonism, it is clearly presented as a way which made strong Americans; and its strength lies in its qualities of tradition and myth. These compel belief, fidelity, and discipline—without which it would appear that man is not capable of leading a coherent life. The whole book asserts that man must be guided—that is, man in modern America—by powerful attachments to an Authority that he accepts on faith. The rigid morality of Quakerism dampens spontaneity and snubs impulse. To the early Dreiser such repression was bad. Now it is good, for it is a discipline that strengthens the will and quickens the spirit. Dreiser has turned from materialistic monism to Christian dualism, from impulse to control, from nature to spirit, from iconoclasm to traditionalism, from flux to myth.

This is the first novel in which Dreiser has been confronted with the problem of advancing four or five separate actions, instead of concentrating on one person, as in his early novels, and the result is not fortunate. It is, to begin with, difficult for a writer of Dreiser's diffuseness to deal with the birth, early education, adolescence, and "end" of five children and their parents in fewer than 400 pages. He has performed this task as it were through the small end of a telescope: occasional incidents are dramatized, but most are recounted hastily, in a bewildering succession of two- and three-page chapters. Characters are developed only to be dropped; some live and die without ever coming to life; others are introduced, forgotten, and then embarrassingly revived for a new occasion.

This failure of form reveals a literary artistry that could not keep pace with changing times. In the historical context of 1900, a straight-line presentation of one incident after another was striking and powerful. Given a prevailing notion of form in the novel, the denial of it becomes a form. The movement of Dreiser's early novels had such a form. But without the foil of that-from-which-it-revolts the same work would be either chaotic or commonplace. Here the latter is true, for there is, in this matter, a dialectic at work; whereas in 1900 Dreiser expressed a powerful antithesis, in 1946 the same kind of form is irrelevant because several new syntheses have nullified the tension in which it formerly participated. Nor, in view of the confusion of its plots, can we say that *The Bulwark* is as well constructed as *Sister Carrie*. Today it will be asked, with genuine bewilderment, whether *The Bulwark* is naturalistic. The question would not have been asked in 1900, when it would have struck the pious reader that here was a shockingly detached presentation of moral issues: a boy who strays into vice because he has been repressed at home, who commits suicide rather than bear the shame of having been in jail, who has, in fine, not been equipped to judge wisely and so is not judged by the author. To the world of 1900 this would have seemed an attack upon the very concept of moral responsibility. Today it is old-fashioned.

As I have already said, Dreiser's greatness as a novelist cannot be accounted for by his naturalism. His greatness is in his insight, his sympathy, and his tragic view of life. Although *The Bulwark* reveals major shifts in his beliefs, and although it is very clumsily contrived, it could still have all the power and greatness of *Jennie Gerhardt* or *An American Tragedy* if Dreiser had succeeded, to use James's term, in "rendering" his idea. I would not suggest that *The Bulwark* fails because Dreiser abandoned some of his old theories. Not at all. Much the same view of life is there. Dreiser has always been seeking solid foundations for social and personal order. His characters have always been bewildered because the world was too complicated and they were not equipped to understand it. Sister Carrie seeks a meaning in her experience which she cannot find. Solon Barnes has a meaning but he cannot live by it, and at the end of the book he is not unlike Carrie in wondering why events have happened as they have.

Thus the fourth stage of Dreiser's naturalism is not naturalism, after all, and it is indeed most instructive to see how easily the style, the method, and the attitudes of the early Dreiser are entirely converted in these final novels to the uses of Authority and Spirit. Having brooded long and sadly over the materialist's world, he turns away from it at the end without greatly changing his tone.

Notes

1. *A Book about Myself* (New York, 1922), p. 253. The title has since been changed to *Newspaper Days*.

2. *Ibid.*, p. 210.

3. *Ibid.*, p. 140.

4. *Ibid.*, p. 127. In *The "Genius"* (New York, 1923), p. 104, he wrote: "I stood by the window last night and looked out on the street. The moon was shining and those dead trees were waving in the wind. I saw the moon on that pool of water over in the field. It looked like silver. Oh, Eugene, I wish I were dead." It should be remarked that a good deal of *The "Genius"* is autobiographical.

5. *A Book about Myself*, p. 451.

6. *Ibid.*, p. 370.

7. *Ibid.*, pp. 369–370.

8. *Ibid.*, p. 198.

9. *Ibid.*, p. 70. This was in 1891–1892; though written in 1922 it reflects ideas which Dreiser seems to have held steadily from about 1892 on.

10. *Ibid.*, pp. 457–459.

11. *Ibid.*, pp. 375, 141, 263, and 344.

12. *Hey Rub-a-Dub-Dub* (New York, 1919), pp. 157–158. Dreiser's wide and sympathetic vision of life, his willingness to see and think about its sordid side, make one respect him for failing to arrive at a categorial explanation for the meaning of it all. If the philosopher must withdraw into an ivory tower in order to round out his system, the man who deals with the whole moving pathos of life-as-it-is should not be without some admiration. The practice among academic critics of disposing of Dreiser as a "peasant" or a "journalist" who could not think things through is based, if it has a base, upon ignorance of his personal experience.

13. *A Book about Myself*, p. 326.

14. *Hey Rub-a-Dub-Dub*, p. 134. This book was written in 1919 and consequently shows evidence of familiarity with the Freudian approach to sex. It may be remarked, however, that Dreiser's attitude toward problems of sex is substantially the same in all his novels from 1900 to 1925.

15. Joseph W. Beach supports this interpretation of Dreiser's thought: "If I suggest a possible inspiration from the French naturalists, it is because his work is strongly colored by the terminology and deterministic assumptions of nineteenth-century science, which were so strong an element in Zola and his group. But it may have been direct from science, rather than from literature, that Dreiser took his disposition to regard human behavior as one manifestation of animal behavior in general, or even—to use his more frequently recurring term—as a chemical phenomenon." (*Twentieth Century Novel*, pp. 325–326.)

16. One Wandell, a city editor, "was always calling upon me to imitate Zola's vivid description of the drab and gross and the horrible if I could, assuming that I had read him, which I had not." (*A Book about Myself*, p. 207.) Again: "Be careful how you write that now. All the facts you know, just as far as they will carry you. . . . Write it strong, clear, definite. Get in all the touches of local color you can. And remember Zola and Balzac, my boy, remember Zola and Balzac. Bare facts are what are needed in cases like this, with lots of color as to the scenery or atmosphere, the room, the other people, the street, and all that." (*Ibid.*, p. 211.)

17. "It is interesting that Dreiser, who is often alleged to have derived from Zola, says here that he never read him, not until after his own first novel, *Sister Carrie*. But in Wandell's presence he dared not admit it." (Dorothy Dudley, *Forgotten Frontiers: Dreiser and the Land of the Free* (New York, 1932), p. 95.)

18. "Hazard had . . . written a novel entitled *Theo*, which was plainly a bog-fire kindled by those blazing French suns, Zola and Balzac. The scene was laid in Paris . . . and had much of the atmosphere of Zola's *Nana*, plus the delicious idealism of Balzac's *The Great Man from the Provinces* . . . It seemed intensely beautiful to me at the time, this book, with its frank pictures of raw, greedy, sensual human nature, and its open pictures of self-

indulgence and vice." (*A Book about Myself*, p. 126.) This work "was the opening wedge for me into the realm of realism . . . the book made a great impression on me!" (*Ibid.*, pp. 131–133.) Unfortunately *Theo* was never published.

19. "For a period of four or five months I ate, slept, dreamed, lived him and his characters and his views and his city. I cannot imagine a greater joy and inspiration than I had in Balzac these Spring and Summer days in Pittsburgh." (*Ibid.*, p. 412.)

20. *Sister Carrie* (New York, 1900; ed. 1917), p. 362. There is no collected edition of Dreiser's writings.

21. American reviewers were also offended by its treatment of lives which they deemed too sordid for genteel readers. See Dudley, *Forgotten Frontiers*, p. 186.

22. *Sister Carrie*, p. 85. The italics are mine.

23. *Ibid.*, p. 101.

24. *Ibid.*, p. 362.

25. The gap between Dreiser's work and the experimental novel of Zola is a wide one, for Dreiser does not make even a pretense of controlling his conditions and discovering truths about the nature of human psychology and physiology. Just where Zola, for example, would theoretically put most emphasis—i.e., on the extraction of laws about human nature—Dreiser is most uncertain and most sure that no certainty can be attained. To him such laws would be fruitless for the very reason that external conditions cannot ever be controlled—a fact of which all his experience had convinced him.

26. *Jennie Gerhardt* (New York, 1911; ed. 1926), pp. 15–16.

27. *Ibid.*, pp. 400–401. This passage is notable as the most explicit statement of belief in the novel. It comes from Lester, but it represents Dreiser's own attitude because it is virtually the thesis of his novel.

28. Quoted in Charmian London, *The Book of Jack London*, 2 vols. (New York, 1921), II, 57.

29. Stuart P. Sherman, *On Contemporary Literature* (New York, 1917), p. 98.

30. Dreiser comments as follows upon the "meaning" of life: "I can make no comment on my work or my life that holds either interest or import for me. Nor can I imagine any explanation or interpretation of any life, my own included, that would be either true—or important, if true. Life is to me too much a welter and play of inscrutable forces to permit, in my case at least, any significant comment. One may paint for one's own entertainment, and that of others—perhaps. As I see him the utterly infinitesimal individual weaves among the mysteries a floss-like and wholly meaningless course—if course it be. In short I catch no meaning from all I have seen, and pass quite as I came, confused and dismayed." ("Statements of Belief," *Bookman*, 68 (September 1928), 25.)

31. *The Financier* (New York, 1912; ed. London, 1927), p. 35.

32. *Ibid.*, p. 140.

33. *The Titan* (New York, 1914; ed. London, 1928), p. 461.

34. *Hey Rub-a-Dub-Dub*, p. 89. These ideas, expressed in 1919, show Dreiser touched by the Nietzschean philosophy; they precede his conversion to socialism. Mr. Hartwick, however, goes on to insist that they prove Dreiser to have admired and condoned the behavior of Cowperwood as valuable to society. This cannot be entirely true, for the course of the novels does not show Cowperwood to have been socially useful. The ethical implications are considered further below.

35. *Theodore Dreiser* (New York, 1925), p. 78.

36. *The Financier*, pp. 152–153. "That the modern home is the most beautiful of schemes, when based upon mutual sympathy and understanding between two, need not be questioned. And yet this fact should not necessarily carry with it a condemnation of all love

not so fortunate as to find so happy a denouement. Life cannot be put in any mould, and the attempt might as well be abandoned at once."

37. *Ibid.*, p. 137.

38. *An American Tragedy*, 2 vols. (New York, 1925), II, 78–80.

39. *The Stoic* (New York, 1947), p. 113.

Theodore Dreiser's Transcendentalism

Roger Asselineau*

Historians of literature unanimously regard Theodore Dreiser as a naturalistic novelist. This, however, is a very hasty conclusion. If astronomers also judged by appearances, they would maintain that the moon is nothing but a flat disk hanging in the sky or a hemisphere unaccountably cut off from its other half. Dreiser, like the moon, is composed of two hemispheres, one which meets the eye, his naturalism; the other which generally remains in the dark and which only a few bold critics like Alfred Kazin, F. O. Matthiessen and Charles Walcutt, have ventured to explore[1], namely his transcendentalism. At first sight, the two notions may seem incompatible. Yet, Dreiser somehow managed to reconcile them. Like a true transcendentalist he was indifferent to contradictions and cared little for logic[2]. He felt that, since life was made up of contraries, he had the right to include them side by side in his mind.

> There are those, he wrote in *A Traveler at Forty*, who still think that life is something which can be put into a mold and adjusted to a theory, but I am not one of them. I cannot view life or human nature save as an expression of contraries—in fact I think that is what life is. I know there can be no sense of heat without cold; no fulness without emptiness; no force without resistance; no anything, in short, without its contrary.[3]

Consequently he saw no inconsistency in describing psychological and social phenomena from a materialistic standpoint with the detachment—and sometimes the jargon—of a scientist, while at the same time expressing the wonder of a child or poet before the mystery of life. He constantly swung between these two extreme positions and the amplitude of the oscillation increased to such an extent in the last few months of his life that he was eventually both a fervent religionist and a member of the communist party. But he did not mind being in uncertainties. He confessed it in *A History of Myself*: "Chronically nebulous, doubt-

*Reprinted from *English Studies Today: Second Series*, ed. G. A. Bonnard (Bern: Francke Verlag, 1961), 233–43. Reprinted by permission of Francke Verlag and Roger Asselineau.

ing, uncertain, I stared and stared at everything, only wondering, not solving." So, on his own admission, he never reached any intellectual certainty. His mind restlessly groped for some transcendent reality beyond material appearances, for something which the meshes of scientific laws failed to catch—in short, he was a transcendentalist first and foremost.

Dreiser's transcendentalism is most forcibly expressed in a much neglected collection of poems in free verse which he very fittingly entitled *Moods*[4]. According to his own testimony it was "written between 1914 and 1926"[5] and he kept revising and enlarging it for another ten years, which shows how much he prized it. In his own words, it "represents in the first instance a fair summary of [his] philosophy in mood form, and in the second, an elaborated presentation of it"[6]. It is "lyrical philosophy and possibly the firt conscious attempt to express an individual philosophy lyrically . . ."[7] Thus, in *Wood Note*, he concludes a brief sketch with lines which suggest a mysterious spiritual presence in the woods and the unreality of matter:

> Of what vast deep is this the echo?
> Of what old dreams the answer? (*Moods*, p. 17)

God, for the poet of *Moods*, is present in all things and in the humblest of men:

> God
> To my astonishment
> Is shining my shoes.
> He has taken the form,
> In part,
> Of an Italian shoe black
> Who is eager to earn a dime . . .
> Reading a newspaper
> To learn of Himself
> I presume . . .
> Getting drunk,
> Eating a ham sandwich
> In order to maintain His strength.
> A most varied
> Restless
> Changeful
> Moody
> God . . . (pp. 91–92)[8]

In his lyrical moods, Dreiser mystically identifies himself with this changeful God and, like Proteus, in the poem which bears this name, becomes in turn:

> Birds flying in the air over a river,
> And children playing in a meadow beside it,
> A stream that turns an ancient wheel

> Under great trees,
> And cattle in the water
> Below the trees,
> And sun, and shade,
> And warmth, and grass,
> And myself
> And not myself
> Dreaming in the grass . . . (p.7)

But, strangely enough, this keen perception of an underlying mystery in all things is again and again spoilt, so to speak, by a disquieting sense of the purposelessness and meaninglessness of the world, in *The Passing Freight* for instance in which the disillusioned poet dejectedly meditates on the passage of a train:

> Out of the mystery
> And meaninglessness of things
> And into it again;
> A train bearing cotton
> With thunder and smoke
> And a flare of fire,
> Yet bearing that
> Which is nothing more than an idea;
> That has come out of the darkness of chemistry
> And will soon return into it . . .
> And I, myself,
> Who view it
> And admire—
> Out of the mystery
> And meaninglessness of things
> And into them again. (pp. 54–55)

In the same way, in *Ephemeron*, instead of buoyantly singing his self like Whitman he bitterly complains, like Clyde Griffiths, of being "betrayed",

> But not by the thousand impossible Gods
> Of mine [i.e. man's] own invention
> To whom I have yearningly
> And hopelessly prayed,
> But by mine own lacks
> And insufficiencies
> That are not of my creating.
> Ask me not whose. (p. 58)

And he resignedly concludes in a fit of depression:

> Too tired—
> And indifferent
> To be a part of that
> That has no meaning—
> Is not that the ultimate

>And is not that
>A justification
>And
>The greater wisdom? (p. 311)

At such times we seem to be a very long way indeed from Emerson's boundless optimism. Dreiser's position is then almost that of an agnostic. We are reminded of the sceptical utterances with which he had sprinkled A *Traveler at Forty*:

>For myself, I accept now no creeds. I do not know what truth is, what beauty is, what love is, what hope is. I do not believe any one absolutely and I do not doubt any one absolutely . . . I indict nature here and now . . . as being aimless, pointless, unfair, unjust. I see in the whole thing no scheme, but an accidental one—no justice save accidental justice (pp. 4, 42)

But such statements expressed only "moods", to take up his own word. They corresponded to only one facet of his thought. Emerson too did not always yield himself to "the perfect whole"[9] and had to admit that "our torment is Unbelief, the Uncertainty as to what we ought to do; the distrust of the value of what we do, and the distrust that the Necessity (which we all at last believe in) is fair and beneficent"[10]. But, like Emerson, Dreiser succeeded in transcending his doubts—even though he never entirely discarded them,—and in some of his *Moods* he prays "the hidden God", "the substance of suns, and flowers, rats and kings" (p. 197), and worships with the fervour of a true transcendentalist:

>Yet I must pray,—
>Pray.
>And do.
>I lift up my hands.
>I kneel.
>I seek in heart
>Because I must,—
>Must. (p. 178)
>Honor that spirit in man
>That, in the face of shame
>And failure,
>Still dreams of better things.
>Give honor unto him
>Who, in the midst of doubt . . .
>Still, still can dream
>And still build temples—
>Not to Christ,
>Or Buddha,
>But to Beauty—
>The human will to loveliness. (p. 154)

> Beauty,
> Its worship,
> Shall never die. (p. 327)

Like the transcendentalists, what Dreiser means by beauty is not plastic beauty, but the mysterious presence behind appearances of something wonderful which escapes his senses. His apprehension of beauty is in fact a mystical intuition, a form of religious worship:

> Behind this seeming substance
> Of reality . . .
> Picturing something
> Seeking something
> The image of our dreams. (p. 306)

What he keeps seeking and wondering at is the enigmatic force which carries all things forward irresistibly towards an unknown destination. He ultimately equates reality with Life. In *Protoplast*, he represents the world as

> A substance that is not flesh
> Or thought
> Or reality
> But the likeness,
> The wish,
> The dream, mayhap,
> Of something that is eternal,
> But will not rest
> Or stay
> In any form. (p. 249)

He worships life in all its forms—life "as it is," to take the words which he himself used to define his realism (and this incidentally shows that there was after all no fundamental incompatibility between his transcendentalism and his naturalism). He felt a "Creative Force" at work in the world, "the amazing Creative force which has brought 'humanity' along with its entire environment into being"[11]. According to him, "man is not really and truly living and thinking, but, on the contrary, is being lived and thought by that which has produced him. Apart from it . . . he has no existence"[12] In 1940, writing to Miss Dorothy Payne Davis, who had maintained in a Master's thesis submitted to Loyola University of the South that he believed "in God and the immortality of the soul even though [he called] it the unintelligible," he affirmed:

> All things to me are emanations and evolutions of cosmic forces and cosmic laws. Buddha and Mary Baker Eddy affirmed an *over* or *one* universal soul, itself *being* and so *containing* all wisdom and all creative power. Modern science sees no other answer than this, but it is not willing to affirm it . . . As for the human soul—my scientific as well as my

philosophic studies compel me to feel that there can be but one
primary creative force or soul, the discoverable physical as
well as chemical laws of which appear to be obeyed by all matter and energy—or matter-energy. I think of all creatures or
'creations' as material or energy constructions and so
manifestations of whatsoever force it is that occupies space and
expresses itself as matter or energy—or matter-energy. (*Letters* . . ., iii. pp. 886–889.)

Emerson's "oversoul" thus becomes identified with energy as conceived by modern physicists:

> Energy,
> Color,
> Form,
> Tone,
> Mingle and make 'Life.' (p. 127)

Therefore, in Whitman's own words, "the smallest sprout shows
there is really no death" (*Song of Myself*, section 6, l. 28):

> My span is brief
> But my world-flower,—
> It blooms
> Forever. (p.170)

"There is in my judgment no death," he declared more explicitly in *A
Traveler at Forty*, "the universe is composed of life; but nevertheless, I
cannot see any continuous life for any individual." (p.448)

As with transcendentalists, this dynamic vitalism leads up to a wish
to live rather than expiate[13], to self-reliance and the exaltation of individualism. Dreiser did not believe in original sin or the innate corruption of man any more than Emerson. All his characters are men of good
will. True, they are eminently fallible, but they are not really responsible
for their lapses since they are caught in a tangle of biological and social
forces which, to a large extent, determine their behaviour. For Dreiser
there is no such thing as "sin":

> Come now—
> The thing which you call sin
> Is still not sin to me,
> Or you. (pp. 18–19)

And he curses conscience, that troublesome interrupter, that "whis-
pering, pushing thing," that "damned equation/Between the weak and
strong, The wise and foolish" (*Ibid*). On the contrary, he glorifies instincts and the desire for pleasure and, above all, exalts the "divine af-
flatus" of love which "gives color, force and beauty" to those who are
lightened by its touch[14]. He celebrates what he calls "the rich upwelling
force of life and love"[15] Like Whitman, he likes "big, raw, crude, hungry

men who are eager for gain—for self-glorification"[16]. He hoped for more "great individuals among women as well as among men"[17]. Like Emerson, he believed in "representative men":

> The world is always struggling to express itself . . . Most people are not capable of voicing their feelings. They depend upon others. That is what genius is for. One man expresses their desire for them in music; another one in poetry; another one in a play . . . As harps in the wind [they voice] in their moods all the ebb and flow of the ideal (*Sister Carrie*, pp. 537, 555).

His Cowperwood is such a man—"a kind of superman . . . impelled by some blazing internal force which hurried him on and on," a "significant individual" doing "what his instincts tell him to do," "rushing like a great comet to the zenith" and illuminating "the terrors and wonders of individuality"[18]. *The Financier* and *The Titan* constitute an apotheosis of individualism. Dreiser himself once declared in an interview that he was too "intense an individualist" to believe in socialism[19]. As a matter of fact, he was such a self-reliant individualist that he proudly entitled one of his travel-books *Dreiser Looks at Russia*, as if he had been Emerson's "transparent eyeball" at the centre of the universe.

All these resemblances between transcendentalism and Dreiser's philosophy were not accidental. In his youth, Dreiser read Emerson's works with passion. In 1940, when Edgar Lee Masters sent him a copy of his Emerson book, *The Living Thoughts of Emerson*, Dreiser wrote to him enthusiastically:

> . . . it's been so long that I looked into Emerson that I sat down and read the most of it and found it fascinating. As a matter of fact I find these condensations . . . have the value of fresh creative writing—an entirely new work. For so much that is prolix and not absolutely essential is done away with and you have the sense of something brisk, highly integrated and of tremendous as well as delightful import. At least this is true of your Emerson volume. (*Letters* . . ., iii, pp.873–874)

In another letter of the same period he quoted a stanza of "Emerson's interpretive [sic] *Brahma*" (*Ibid.*, p.887) for he was as vitally interested as Emerson in Oriental mysticism. In *The Titan*, he even made Berenice Fleming, the heroine, study with a Guru in India for four years and sound the philosophical abysses of Brahmanism. He was also an admirer of Thoreau. He had compiled a book entitled *Thoreau's Living Thoughts* for the same series in which Edgar Lee Masters's condensation of Emerson appeared, and he wrote of it: "I felt . . . that I had gotten together a body of real thought most valuable to me if no other" (*Ibid.*, p. 874). He was even acquainted with the teachings of Elias Hicks, the Quaker heretic, whom Whitman had heard preach when a child and respected so much[20]. Dreiser declared that Elias Hicks's creed constituted "the most reasonable of religions"[21].

So transcendentalism undeniably exerted an influence on his thought. But its importance should not be exaggerated. There was a sort of pre-established harmony between the transcendentalists and himself. Their writings merely encouraged him to preserve and develop, instead of suppressing or repressing, the mystical tendencies of his temperament. Even as a child he was an exceptionally sensitive lover of nature endowed with a keen sense of wonder which he never lost. In *Dawn* he describes himself as a

> child of three or four and standing at a gate looking up a road and wondering if the sky actually came down to the street as it seemed to . . . or . . . sitting of an evening watching the trees, the sky, the setting sun, and feeling an intense emotional stir of beauty, so wonderful, so strange, so new, that I recall it even now as if it had been a moving and appealing strain of music.[22]

He also notes in the same book that, when a little older, though he soon realized "the futility of prayer," he nevertheless staunchly believed that "there must be a land somewhere to which I belonged and where I could fly" (p.60).

This innate sense of the mystery and beauty of the world, which his transcendentalism no doubt re-inforced, illuminated not only his poems, but also his so-called naturalistic novels. It glows even in *An American Tragedy* which is probably the most prosaic of his books. Instead of describing "life as it is," he often looks at it through the wondering eyes of Clyde Griffiths who stares at the rich and their dwellings and feels "like looking through the gates of Paradise" (p.57). Reality often gives place to dreams, dreams of beauty and wealth and pleasure. The novel was at first to be entitled *Mirages*[23], an unexpected title for a naturalistic study, but a fitting one for this strange story in which the material world at times becomes something unsubstantial:

> To be sure, there was Roberta over there, but by now she had faded to a shadow or thought really, a form of illusion more vaporous than real . . . she was very insubstantial . . . (p.528)

Dreiser's sense of wonder is so intense that it occasionally enables him to clothe with beauty the most commonplace and even the most vulgar sights:

> . . . there would gather on her upper lip and chin and forehead little beads of perspiration which . . . like jewels . . . only seemed to enhance her charm." (p.278)

Moreover, Dreiser constantly suggests intangible things (there are at least three cases of telepathy in *An American Tragedy*) and, generally speaking, we feel him haunted by the mystery of the universe, the wonder of life and the terror of death, by what he calls "the beauty of the days—of the sun and rain—of work, love, energy, desire." (p.864)

As to the characters—at least the major ones—they are essentially forces which move forward and come into conflict with other forces, but they have no idiosyncrasies, no minor traits. They are never sharply individualized. They remind the reader of Mayakowsky's "clouds in trousers," for their clothes are carefully described, but, though they have bodies full of appetites and desires, they have no faces. Dreiser's point of view is not psychological, but social *and* metaphysical. He is not interested in his characters as individuals, but as social types *and* as manifestations of the central life force which flows through all things, as parts of the "oversoul."

Besides, most of these characters constantly aspire to something beyond the workaday world in which they are caught. They crave for a fuller life, for beauty, for some ideal which they are unable to define, but in whose existence they firmly believe. In *Sister Carrie* in particular Dreiser again and again suggests "that constant drag to something better" which Carrie feels so strongly (p.114), but it is not particular to her, it is a universal feeling, according to Dreiser. He makes her face "representative of all desire" and warns us that "her look was something which represented the world's longing." (p.337) She is a transcendentalist poet in her own silent way when she rocks in her chair and dreams:

> Sitting alone, she was now an illustration of the devious ways by which one who feels, rather than reasons, may be led in the pursuit of beauty . . . Oh, Carrie, Carrie! Oh, blind strivings of the human heart! Onward, onward, it saith, and where beauty leads, there it follows. (p.557)

In short, to use his own words, she yields to "the lure of the spirit"[24].

Dreiser's transcendentalism also accounts for the images which at times unexpectedly bloom in the drabbest realistic passages. They are never very remarkable, or original, but they are meant to suggest the wonder of life and the craving of the characters for some unattainable and undefinable ideal. In the same way, the chapter headings in *Sister Carrie* transmute the prosaic contents of the various chapters into something rich and strange—though they are for the most part borrowed from such operas as "Sinbad the Sailor" and "Ali Baba and the Forty Thieves" which Dreiser saw in Chicago. They metamorphose everyday reality into something mysterious and suggest the existence of another world beyond mere appearances.

Dreiser, thus, instead of minutely and objectively describing the more or less sordid background of his characters, again and again allows himself to be carried away by his imagination—and his imagination is not mere fancy, but that poetic faculty which Coleridge in his *Biographia Literaria* defined as "an esemplastic power." It adds, "the gleam,/The light that never was, on sea or land, The consecration, and the Poet's dream," as Wordsworth said[25]. And Dreiser was perfectly aware of it. He even used the same words as Wordsworth, not only in one of his *Moods*, where he referred to

> The high suggestion of a world that never was
> On earth or sea (p.296)

but also in *Dawn* where he warns us that "The City of which [he is] now about to write [namely Chicago] never was on land or sea," for even "if it appears to have the outlines of reality, they are but shadow to the glory that was in [his] own mind" (p. 156).

Thanks to the intervention of this quasi-mystical faculty, when we read Dreiser's novels, we are again and again reminded of the cosmic context of his characters' lives. His books are not mere naturalistic studies of social conditions; we are never allowed to forget the presence of an infinite and mysterious universe in the background. Carrie, for instance, is made to look "at the blue sky overhead with more realisation of its charm than had ever come to her before" (p.20). She sits "looking out upon the night and streets in silent wonder" (p.15). To her, as

> to a child . . . the approach to a great city for the first time is a wonderful thing. Particularly if it be evening—that mystic period between the glare and gloom of the world when life is changing from one sphere or condition to another. Ah, the promise of the night. (p.9)

And, on another occasion, "she tripped along, the clear sky pouring liquid blue into her soul. Oh, blessed are the children of endeavour in this, that they try and are hopeful," Dreiser adds, "and blessed also are they who, knowing, smile and approve" (p.188). There is no trace of a Marxist interpretation of American society in all this. In such passages, Dreiser merely wants to convey his sense of the totality and oneness of the world. This form of cosmic imagination must have been inborn in him, but he may also have deliberately cultivated it. For, in *An American Tragedy*, the Reverend McMillan prescribes the following spiritual exercise to Clyde Griffiths:

> You have a Bible . . . Open to St. John. Read it all—over and over. Think and pray—and think on all the things about you—the moon, the stars, the sun, the trees, the sea—your own beating heart, your body and strength . . . (p.840)

Now this recommendation strangely resembles the following note which has been found among Whitman's papers:

> First of all prepare for study by the following self-teaching

exercises. Abstract yourself from this book; realize where you are at present located, the point you stand that is now to you the centre of all. Look up overhead, think of space stretching out, think of all the unnumbered orbs wheeling safely there, invisible to us by day, some visible by night . . . Spend some minutes faithfully in this exercise . . .[26]

So it seems that, in order to reach a state of grace, Dreiser practised the same kind of spiritual exercises as the poet who sang himself and the cosmos.

Thus, Dreiser was a poet and in several respects a belated transcendentalist in his naturalistic novels as well as in his poems. True, his transcendentalism co-existed with lurking doubts that prevented him from giving any dogmatic content to his intuitions and with a tenacious pessimism that made it impossible for him to ignore social and other evils, but, nevertheless, he spontaneously sensed beneath this world of appearances another inward world which he kept wondering at and whose universal presence conferred beauty and mystery on the most banal and insignificant sights. Without this poetical power his works would be nothing but dull naturalistic descriptions of American society, whereas, thanks to it, he has, however massively, sung himself and celebrated—or pitied—himself in the guise of various characters ("Sister Carrie, Cowperwood, Clyde Griffiths, c'est moi," he might have exclaimed), and, at the same time, he sang and celebrated man and the presence in man of the irresistible creative force at work in the world. His transcendentalism is therefore the true source of his greatness.

Notes

1. Cf. Alfred Kazin's chapter on Dreiser in *On Native Grounds* and his introduction to *The Stature of Theodore Dreiser*, ed. by A. Kazin and Charles Shapiro, Indiana University Press, 1955. The latter book contains a fine essay by Charles Child Walcutt on *Theodore Dreiser and the Divided Stream* (pp. 246–269). Cf. also the chapter on *Dreiser's Philosophy* in F. O. Matthiessen's *Dreiser*, New York, 1951.

2. Cf. Emerson's statement in *Self-Reliance*: "Suppose you should contradict yourself; what then?", which Whitman echoed in the famous lines:

"Do I contradict myself?
Very well then, I contradict myself . . ." *Song of Myself*, section 51.

3. *A Traveler at Forty*, New York, 1914, p.34.

4. The first edition, to which we are henceforward going to refer, was limited to 550 copies and published in New York in 1926. A second edition, enlarged and illustrated, came out in 1928 and a third one, further revised and enlarged, in 1935.

5. Cf. a letter to H. L. Mencken dated March 8, 1943, in *Letters of Theodore Dreiser, A Selection*, ed. by Robert H. Elias, University of Pennsylvania Press, 1959, iii, p. 979.

6. Letter to Richard L. Simon, Feb. 5, 1935, *Ibid.*, ii, p. 722.

7. Letter to Miss Ish-Kishor, Feb. 14, 1935, *Ibid.*, p. 728.

8. This poem is entitled *All in All*, a title which recalls Emerson's *Each in All*.

9. Cf. last line of *Each in All*.

10. Essay on *The Times*.

11. In a letter to Mencken quoted by Elias, *Theodore Dreiser, Apostle of Nature*, New York, 1949, p. 279.

12. *The Myth of Individuality* in *American Mercury*, xxxi, 1934, p. 341.

13. "I do not wish to expiate but to live." Emerson, *Self-Reliance*.

14. *Sister Carrie*, Modern Library Ed., p. 179.

15. *An American Tragedy*, Modern Library Ed., p. 327.

16. *A Traveler at Forty*, p. 778.

17. Quoted by Elias in *Theodore Dreiser*, p. 169.

18. Quoted by C. C. Walcutt in *The Stature of Theodore Dreiser*, p. 259.

19. *New York Evening Post*, Jan. 11, 1927.

20. Cf. his essay on Elias Hicks in *Specimen Days*.

21. *Boston Evening Transcript*, Jan. 29, 1927.

22. *Dawn*, New York, 1931, pp. 16–17.

23. A passage in book I, Chap. iv (p. 38), still recalls this early title: "Decidedly this simple and yet idyllic compound of the commonplace had all the luster and wonder of a spiritual transfiguration, the true mirage of the lost and thirsting and seeking victim of the desert."

24. Title of Chap. xx. Initially Dreiser thought of entitling the book "The Flesh and the Spirit," a true transcendentalist title.

25. *Peele Castle*, 1. 14–16.

26. Quoted in my essay on "Whitman's Fundamental Aesthetics" in *Walt Whitman Abroad*, ed. by Gay W. Allen, Syracuse University Press, 1955, p. 97.

The Imagery of Dreiser's Novels

by William L. Phillips*

The fiction of Theodore Dreiser has often been praised for its fidelity to the facts of ordinary experience, its massive accumulation and arrangement of incidents, and its criticism of bourgeois America. It has seldom been praised as skillful writing, however; and with almost the sole exception of F. O. Matthiessen, critics have dismissed Dreiser as a poor manipulator of the language, whose effects are achieved in spite of his style. It is usually suggested, furthermore, that beyond a recurring use of clothing as symbols, Dreiser had no awareness of the resources of image and metaphor. It is said that his efforts at comparison were likely to be hackneyed and incredibly jumbled, as in a passage in *The Financier* about men who fade into poverty: "They were compelled by some devilish accident of birth or lack of force or resourcefulness to stew in their own juice of wretchedness, or to shuffle off this mortal coil—which under other circumstances had such glittering possibilities—*via* the rope, the knife, the bullet, or the cup of poison."[1]

Nevertheless, a close reading of Dreiser's novels reveals complex patterns of imagery, sometimes the result, apparently, of conscious manipulation and sometimes of an unconscious compulsion to say things in a particular way, a way which occasionally runs counter to the overt content of the novel. These patterns have the effect of drawing into a larger context the figurative clichés which are ineffective or even painful when they stand alone, and they contribute to the ultimately rich effect of Dreiser's novels, which often puzzles a reader who has been disturbed by the ineptitude of individual passages. Nor are the image patterns drawn from the chemical-physical conception of life which Dreiser preached in a number of essays. One may find allusions to "chemic conditions," "magnetic impulses," and "electric glances" if he searches for them; but they are rare compared to the extensive manipulation of a more conventional literary imagery drawn from three traditional sources—water (the sea, the lake, the stream), animal life, and tales of magic. This traditional imagery provides the moral undercurrent which the reader often senses in

*Reprinted from *PMLA*, 78 (December, 1963), 572–85. Reprinted by permission of the Modern Language Association of America.

Dreiser's novels in spite of his frequent protests that he never judged or condemned.

This study will examine the dominant image patterns of five novels, *Sister Carrie, The Financier, The Titan, An American Tragedy,* and *The Bulwark;* demonstrate by extensive quotation the ways in which Dreiser's imagery enriches the total effect of the novels and helps to discriminate individual incidents and characters; and point out the ways in which Dreiser's use of his major groups of images shifted with his changing philosophical preoccupations and the changing intentions of his novels.

II

The largest and most obvious group of images in *Sister Carrie* is that clustering around the sea, which was for the early Dreiser the symbol of modern urban life. This image is introduced at the end of the first chapter when Carrie's situation is summarized: She is "alone, away from home, rushing into a great sea of life and endeavor . . . a lone figure in a tossing, thoughtless sea."[2] The hydrography is soon laid out: "the entire metropolitan centre possessed a high and mighty air calculated . . . to make the gulf between poverty and success seem both wide and deep" (p. 16). The most terrifying quality of Dreiser's society-sea, however, is not the width of the gulf between poverty and success, but the suggestions that those who attempt a crossing are without power to advance or to remain anchored, that each traveller makes more perilous the plight of another, and that the port of success constantly shifts.

The powerless travellers in this sea *drift* (the word is repeated at least a dozen times in the novel) on the tide; we are told that Carrie "felt the flow of the tide of effort and interest—felt her own helplessness without quite realizing the wisp on the tide that she was" (p. 26). Indeed, one survives in this sea only if he does not have too acute an idea of his condition of helplessness. Drouet clowns his way through the novel, "assured that he was alluring all, that affection followed tenderly in his wake" (p. 114), although Carrie seems "ever capable of getting herself into the tide of changes where she would be easily borne along" (p. 278). Whether or not Dreiser consciously intended the pun on Carrie's name, it is clear that he conceives of her as *carried* along by the sea, not moving by the exertions of her will. Hurstwood, on the other hand, is destroyed by his nagging awareness that in taking the money from the safe of Fitzgerald and Moy he has cut himself off from security. In Chicago, Hurstwood strikes Carrie as one who easily controls the life around him: his apparent solidity and strength draw her to him. It soon appears that "in an ocean like New York," however, he is only "an inconspicuous drop" (p. 265); there he finally becomes a derelict, one "of the class which simply floats and drifts, every wave of people washing up one, as breakers do driftwood upon a stormy shore," and he ends as a nameless corpse carried to his grave on "a slow, black boat setting out from the pier at Twenty-seventh Street" (pp. 440, 453).

Not only is life in general characterized by the ceaseless motion and the relentless tides of the sea; individuals in their desires for a secure harbor make perilous the condition of others. Hurstwood, forty, and weary of a marriage which had lost all its meaning, is attracted by Carrie's youth and grace; Carrie, by his promise of a new security. Yet, when they first meet alone in her parlor, his gaze makes her weak and in-secure; "The little shop-girl was getting into deep water. She was letting her few supports float away from her."[3] When Hurstwood first proposes that she leave Drouet, Carrie feels "a wave of feeling sweep over her" (p. 137). Later when Hurstwood urges her more strongly, the scene again is filled with water images: "[Hurstwood] wanted to plunge in and ex-postulate with her. . . . He looked at her steadily for a moment, slowing his pace and fixing her with his eye. She felt the flood of feeling. 'How about me?' he asked. This confused Carrie considerably, for she realized the floodgates were open . . . 'I don't know,' returned Carrie, still il-logically drifting and finding nothing at which to catch. . . . What should she do? She went on thinking this, answering vaguely, languishing affectionately, and altogether drifting, until she was on a borderless sea of speculation. . . . He turned on her such a storm of feeling that she was overwhelmed."[4]

If the figure of life as a turbulent sea is the commonest metaphor in *Sister Carrie*, the comparison of life to a world of struggling animals is also important. In a passage often quoted, and often seen as related to the interest in animal evolution among the literary naturalists of the 1890's, the comparison is made explicit; "Our civilization is still in a middle stage, scarcely beast, in that it is no longer wholly guided by instinct; scarcely human, in that it is not yet wholly guided by reason. . . . We see man far removed from the lairs of the jungles. . . . He is becoming too wise to hearken always to instincts and desires; he is still too weak to always prevail against them. As a beast, the forces of life aligned him with them; as a man, he has not yet wholly learned to align himself with the forces. In this intermediate stage he wavers. . ." (pp. 70–71). Incidental animal imagery runs through the novel, although the animals specified are as often domestic as wild. Carrie fears the coming of winter, like "the sparrow on the wire, the cat in the doorway, the draw horse tugging his weary load"; poverty hangs around her "like a hungry dog at her heels" (pp. 87–88, 57). Mrs. Hurstwood is "a pythoness in humour" who, "animal-like," turns on her husband, and scents his disaffection "as animals do danger, afar off" (pp. 197–198, 188). Fitzgerald and Moy's restaurant is an "insect-drawing, insect-infected rose of pleasure" (p. 46). Drouet is "the old butterfly" (p. 448). Lola Osborne, the chorus girl, clings "with her soft little claws to Carrie" in "a sort of pussy-like way" (p. 388). Hurstwood begins his involvement with Carrie by "merely spinning those gossamer threads of thought which, like the spider's, he hoped would lay hold somewhere" (p. 99); when he is presented with $10,000 in an open safe, he wavers between his desire for the money and a fear comparable to "the animal's instinctive recoil at evil" (p. 238); and when he arrives in swarming New York, "the sea was already full of whales. A common fish must needs disappear wholly from view—remain unseen. In other words, Hurstwood was nothing" (pp. 99, 238, 265). New York is not only an ocean; it is an animal world where angry strikers surround Hurstwood "like a small swarm of bees," as contrasted to the "hive of peculiarly listless and indifferent individuals" in the theater where Carrie searches for work (pp. 380, 341–342); where hungry men wait at a mission door "like cattle" and oppose Hurstwood with an "animal feeling of opposition" (pp. 440–441) when he moves to the head of a bread line, and where the face of a starving derelict may be "as white as drained veal" (p. 449) and men only look "sheepish . . . when they fall" (p. 447).

Out of context, such a word as "sheepish" may seem no longer to evoke any sense of the animal from which it derives; yet in the context of Hurstwood's decline the worn figure is refurbished. In addition to the truly functional animal imagery in the novel, there are many animal clichés: "a snail's pace" (p. 10), "moths . . . in the light of the flame" (pp. 45, 60), "the grapeless fox" (p. 107), "the fly in the spider's net" (p. 113), "birds of fine feather" (pp. 90, 173, 255) and "money-feathers" (p. 275), thoughts "upon eagles' wings" (p. 177), and "a dog's life" (p. 382). Even such common comparisons as these, the staple of the journalism of the 1890's, tend to regain some luster when they are embedded in the total texture of the imagery: after it occurs to Hurstwood that he is leading "a dog's life" his condemnation of others who oppose him as "the little cur!" (p. 382), "God damned dog!" (p. 446), and "damned old cur" (p. 446) has an ironic force. Although sometimes Dreiser clumsily piles together unrelated conventional figures seemingly aiming at decoration and achieving only imprecision, as in the quotation in the first paragraph of this article, he often effectively combines sea and animal imagery. An example occurs in the final scene of the book, as Hurstwood waits in the snow among a crowd of derelicts to enter the Bowery lodginghouse where he expects to commit suicide. The men "looked at [the closed door] as dumb brutes look, as dogs paw and whine and study the knob. . . . Then the door opened. It was push and jam for a minute, with grim, beast silence to prove its quality, and then it melted inward, like logs floating, and disappeared. There were wet hats and wet shoulders, a cold, shrunken, disgruntled mass, pouring in between bleak walls" (pp. 450–451).

Life is a sea; life is a jungle; reality is outside, wet, cold, snarling, swarming, and dark (much of the action takes place at night, and time is marked off by the passing of winters). What is inside, dry, warm, comforting, and light, is only illusion, an *Arabian Nights* tale which man invents to keep himself from suicide, "a door to an Aladdin's cave . . .

delights which were not . . . lights of joy that never were on land or sea"
(p. 411). Someone has remarked that the characteristic stance for
Dreiser's characters is that of the outsider looking in upon comfort and
luxury. More specifically, in the early novels it is that of the outsider
gazing into Aladdin's cave, which he imagines holds the life of delight.
The pathos of Carrie's struggles arises from the contrast between the
delights which she envisages from outside her various caverns and the
disappointment which she inevitably feels once she is inside and the genie
proves inadequate: "she encountered a great wholesale shoe company,
through the broad plate windows of which she saw an enclosed executive
department, hidden by frosted glass. Without this enclosure, but just
within the street entrance, sat a grey-haired gentleman at a small table,
with a large open ledger before him. . . . 'Well, young lady,' observed
the old gentleman, looking at her somewhat kindly, 'what is it you wish?'
'I am, that is, do you—I mean, do you need any help?' she stammered.
'Not just at present,' he answered smiling. 'Not just at present' " (p. 19).

Her escape from the factory chambers is only to the chambers of
Drouet, however; under his protection she is "safe in a halcyon harbour"
(p. 86), and within his rooms she sits in her rocking-chair, endlessly rocking, in an ironic likeness to the sea she thinks she has escaped. Beyond
Drouet's chambers are others more promising for Carrie. There are the
mansions on Lake Shore Drive, which Carrie subconsciously connects
with Hurstwood: "Such childish fancies as she had had of fairy palaces
and kingly quarters now came back. She imagined that across these richly
carved entranceways, where the globed and crystalled lamps shone upon
panelled doors set with stained and designed panes of glass, was . . .
happiness" (p. 107). Most compelling for Carrie is "the fascinating make-
believe of the moment"—the theater; for her a role in a hackneyed melodrama in an Elks' Club is "A Glimpse Through the Gateway." The
theater and "all the nameless paraphernalia of disguise . . . took her by
the hand kindly, as one who says, 'My dear, come in.' It opened for her as
if for its own. . . . She had come upon it as one who stumbles upon a
secret passage, and, behold, she was in the chamber of diamonds and
delight!" (p. 158). Ironically, Drouet is the "witless Aladdin" who opens
for Carrie these chambers more exciting than his own. Although Carrie
escapes from poverty through the theater, she finally recognizes, in a
chapter which Dreiser titles "And This Is Not Elfland," that still "the door
to life's perfect enjoyment was not open" (p. 413), and Bob Ames soon appears to "unlock the door to a new desire" (p. 437), the career in serious
drama which Carrie ponders at the close of the novel as she sits in her
rocking chair, dreaming by a window.[5]

Hurstwood's career, as has been often remarked, traces a descending
line contrasting to Carrie's ascent; in terms of the sea and chamber imagery, while Carrie begins as "a lone figure in a tossing, thoughtless sea"
(p. 11) and ends in "comfortable chambers at the Waldorf" (p. 447),
Hurstwood begins in the illusory elegance of Fitzgerald and Moy's "bub-

bling, chattering, glittering chamber" (p. 45) and ends as a corpse in the sea. The rooms which he inhabits become progressively more depressing until he reaches the dingy room in which he commits suicide, in a pathetic parody of Aladdin's lamp: "A small gas-jet furnished sufficient light for so rueful a corner. . . . He arose and turned the gas out, standing calmly in the blackness, hidden from view. After a few moments . . . he turned the gas on again but applied no match. Even then he stood there, hidden wholly in that kindness which is night, while the uprising fumes filled the room. When the odour reached his nostrils, he quit his attitude and fumbled for the bed. 'What's the use?' he said, weakly, as he stretched himself to rest."[6]

III

Sister Carrie established the basic opposition of image groups upon which Dreiser was later to play extensive variations—the indifferent sea and the animal world, which exist as uncomfortable fact, and the appealing harbour-chambers of illusion, magic, and the supernatural, in which man seeks comfort, love, and beauty.[7] However different in some respects Carrie Meeber and Frank Cowperwood may be, the alternatives open to them are essentially the same: struggling in a sea-jungle or retreating to an illusory harbor-chamber.

In the first two novels of the Cowperwood series, *The Financier* and *The Titan*,[8] the animal becomes dominant and the sea imagery secondary. From the earliest reviews of *The Financier* to the present, critics have taken the incident in Chapter One in which young Frank Cowperwood watches the battle of a lobster and a squid as pointing an important, if obvious, parallel to the fiercely competitive philosophy which the young man takes as his guide to life. In literary histories of the period, this incident has frequently been quoted to show Dreiser's acceptance of the Darwinian struggle as a fundamental principle of life.[9] The attention paid it, however, has diverted attention from the very extensive and varied animal imagery in the remainder of the novel, and in its immediate sequel, *The Titan*. In *The Financier*, one finds metaphors drawn from sea animals: seahorse, squid, lobster, fish, oyster, clam, herring, Black Grouper, and jellyfish; from among predatory land animals: wildcat, bear, leopard, tiger, lion, fox, wolf, and beaver; and many others: bird, partridge, hawk, gull, pigeon, chicken, duck, drake, dog, puppy, New-foundland, collie, hound, cattle, bull, pig, horse, sheep, lamb, snake, cat, rat, mouse, insect, spider, moth, bee, fly, and worm. In *The Titan*, half of these recur, augmented by another thirty: eel, barnacle, sponge, walrus, clam, shark, octopus; lynx, rhinoceros, hyena, ferret, gray wolf; eagle, owl, ostrich, buzzard, goose, rooster; mastiff, bulldog, terrier; cow, ox, swine, donkey, ass; pussy, kitten; chameleon, butterfly, wasp, and scorpion.[10]

Dreiser's theme is forced home: however civilized and ordinary the activities of businessmen and politicians may seem to be on the surface, they have at bottom the ferocity and the irrationality of animal life. Near the end of *The Titan*, in describing the Illinois legislature, Dreiser makes clear his theme, as well as his fictional method: "The surface might appear commonplace—ordinary men of the state of Illinois going here and there . . . yet a jungle-like complexity was present, a dark, rank growth of horrific but avid life—life at the full, life knife in hand, life blazing with courage and dripping at the jaws with hunger" (*T*, p. 516). He is aided by the dead metaphors of animal life which are a part of business and political talk: "wildcat banks," "bulls" and "bears" of the market, a "stalking horse," "small-fry politicians," "one-horse banks," "watch-dogs" of treasuries, "political sharks," and politicians "waiting to get their noses in the trough" (*F*, pp. 34, 41, 350, 453, et passim; *T*, pp. 366, 421, 514, 534). The conversations of Cowperwood and his associates are full of commonplace animal comparisons like "It's a case of dog eat dog in this game."[11] Dreiser develops and extends this traditional similarity with fresh, precise variations. Traders on the stock exchange are "like a lot of gulls or stormy petrels, hanging on the lee of the wind, hungry and anxious to snap up any unwary fish" (*F*, p. 43); and at Chicago's Union Club the luncheon table is ringed by "eyes and jaws which varied from those of the tiger, lynx, and bear to those of the fox, the tolerant mastiff, and the surly bulldog."[12] As each character enters Cowperwood's career, Dreiser sketches his appearance, very often in animal terms: Warden Desmas has "even-edged, savage-looking teeth, which showed the least bit in a slightly wolfish way when he smiled" (*F*, p. 444). Occasionally, through carelessness or unrestrained enthusiasm for the method, he makes a character a multi-animal: Laughlin "had a thick growth of upstanding hair looking not unlike a rooster's comb . . . [and] a slightly aquiline nose. . . . His eyes were as clear and sharp as those of a lynx. . . . His one companion was a small spaniel, simple and affectionate, a she dog, Jennie by name, with whom he slept" (*T*, p. 23). Often, however, the comparisons are apt and ingenious: the first Mrs. Cowperwood's mind is described as "oyster-like in its functioning, or, perhaps better, clam-like, [with] its little siphon of thought-processes forced up or down into the mighty ocean of fact and circumstance" (*F*, pp. 244–245).

Dreiser forces the reader's attention to the animal-man comparison not only by beginning *The Financier* with the lobster-squid battle but also by ending it with a little sermon about *Mycteroperca Bonaci*, the Black Grouper, a huge fish capable of simulating its surroundings by controlling its pigmentation. Because it has been created "tricky and deceptive" to "all honest life-seeking fish," it suggests to Dreiser that "the constructive genius of nature . . . is not beatific," and that Man's "feet are in the trap of circumstance; his eyes are on an illusion" (*F*, pp. 501–502). This treatise, "Concerning *Mycteroperca Bonaci*," is an awkward addition to the novel, an attempt to foreshadow the disillusionment yet to come to

Cowperwood, even though he leaves the novel full of "youth and wealth and a notable vigor of body" (*F*, p. 499). As in a similar essay at the end of *The Titan* ("In Retrospect"), Dreiser here seems to recognize that he has not adequately objectified his argument that Cowperwood, in spite of his dreams of power and beauty and his intense animal energy, is doomed to disillusionment and failure at last. Dreiser has created a Cowperwood on such a grand scale that he dwarfs the puny men who surround him, just as F. Scott Fitzgerald drew Gatsby so large in comparison to the Tom Buchanans that the reader may not sufficiently understand Gatsby's serious flaws.

Bound to the Charles Yerkes story as he was, Dreiser could, through the major incidents, only show Cowperwood with temporary defeats at the conclusions of *The Financier* and *The Titan*. He relies upon his manipulation of the animal imagery, however, to imply the ambiguity of Cowperwood's character, his position, and his ultimate success; for Cowperwood, like the Black Grouper, takes on a variety of appearances. To the business rivals who hate him, he is "a ravening wolf," "slippery as an eel," with "the heart of a hyena and the friendliness of a scorpion"; and when Dreiser pictures him as fighting his lonely battles with his competitors, he calls him "a wolf prowling under glittering, bitter stars in the night, . . . looking down into the humble folds of simple men" and "a canny wolf prowling in a forest of trees of his own creation" (*F*, pp. 380, 495; *T*, 220, 286, 398). Although even Cowperwood's business rivals must admire his courage and speak of him as "A very lion of a man. . . . A man with the heart of a Numidian lion" (*T*, pp. 437), in the Philadelphia prison where he spends more than a year his most savage activity is trapping the rats that infest his cell (*F*, pp. 436 ff.).

In his numerous love affairs, Cowperwood's fortunes are no more stable, and their instability suggested in shifting animal metaphors. When Cowperwood first meets Aileen, she reminds him of "a high-stepping horse without a check-rein" (*F*, p. 89). A man like Cowperwood who "could not endure poor horse-flesh" (*T*, p. 19) might be expected to tire of Aileen as she ages; "You'd like to turn me off like an old horse," she charges (*T*, p. 503), and she is right. But ironically Cowperwood soon finds in Berenice Fleming another "likely filly [with] the signs and lineaments of the future winner of a Derby . . . the air, the grace, the lineage, the blood . . . and she appealed to him . . . as no other woman before had ever done" (*T*, p. 358). Berenice herself, however, is an ambiguous animal; she has "cat-like eyes," moves with "cat-like grace," can affect the languid air of "a chilly cat," and catches fish with her hands; but when she catches a young baby sparrow she insists to Cowperwood that the mother bird will not mind because " 'She knows I am not a cat,' . . . The word 'cat' had a sharp, sweet sound in her mouth" (*T*, pp. 351, 361, 394, 396, 550.)[13]

Although animal imagery is more fully exploited in the Cowperwood novels than in *Sister Carrie,* the imagery of the stormy sea and the tossing ship are also continued strongly. Life is a "mighty ocean of fact and circumstance" (*F*, p. 245) where "there is no tracing to the ultimate sources all the winds of influence that play upon a given barque—all the breaths of chance that fill or desert our bellies or our sagging sails" (*T*, p. 188), for "the impediments that can arise to baffle a great and swelling career are strange and various. In some instances all the crosswaves of life must be cut by the strong swimmer. With other personalities there is a chance, or force, that happily allies itself with them; or they quite unconsciously ally themselves with it, and find that there is a tide that bears them on" (*T*, p. 251). This tide, however, which seemed to carry the will-less Carrie Meeber through her life, now begins in the Cowperwood books to be attached in Dreiser's mind to a transcendental vision of ultimate order, foreshadowing his preoccupation with the mystical experience in *The Bulwark.* Nature itself displays an "instinct" toward wholeness and order, to be perceived "in the drifting of sea-wood to the Sargasso Sea, in the geometric interrelation of air-bubbles on the surface of still water . . . as though the physical substance of life—this apparition of form which the eye detects and calls real—were shot through with some vast sublety that loves order, that is order" (*F*, pp. 363–364). Dreiser's language takes on the confidence of the early Emerson when he extends this instinct toward order to the individual: "The atoms of our so-called *being*, in spite of our so-called *reason*—the dreams of a mood—know where to go and what to do. They represent an order, a wisdom, a willing that is not of us" (*F*, p. 364). Although Cowperwood doubts "the existence of a kindly, over-ruling Providence" because of "the unheralded storms out of clear skies—financial, social, anything you choose—that so often brought ruin and disaster to so many" (*F*, p. 226), he fails to recognize that his activities are responsible for at least some of "the ruffled surface of the angry sea that he had blown to fury" (*T*, p. 548), and that these activities are themselves the means by which "God, or the life force" maintains itself as "an equation." "In the end a balance is invariably struck wherein the mass subdues the individual or the individual the mass—for the time being. For behold, the sea is ever dancing or raging . . . without variation how could the balance be maintained?" (*T*, p. 551).

The animal imagery and the sea imagery are occasionally combined in passages which, although individually distracting and ineffective, demonstrate the connection in Dreiser's mind between the animal world and the sea. He speaks of a "storm of wildcat money which was floating about" and a jury of "assorted social fry which the dragnets of the court, cast into the ocean of the city, bring to the surface" (*F*, pp. 2, 330). Cowperwood's "curiously leonine glare which went over [Aileen] like a dash of cold water" (*T*, p. 109) indicates the fading of his love for her, which was "to leave her high and dry on land, as a fish out of its native element, to take all the wind out of her sails—almost to kill her" (*T*. pp.

109, 145). These well-worn metaphors suggest again the base of popular figurative language, here particularly the language of business, upon which Dreiser built his imagery. Cowperwood and his associates "float" schemes, and when there is trouble, they "trim sails" or "shorten sail" (T, pp. 41, 103, 400). But the humble origins of Dreiser's imagery are not so important as the great numbers of variations which he plays upon them. His unfortunate attachment to such words as "trig" and "chemic" have often been noticed by his critics, but the word of which he is fondest in the Cowperwood novels is neither of these: it is "storm." On the level of diction at least, *The Financier* and *The Titan* are as stormy as *Moby Dick*. Cowperwood, caught in the panic raised by the Chicago fire, tries to "weather the storm" (F, p. 190), thinking that "this storm would surely blow over" (F, p. 169), but when the clamor increases, he seeks "any port in a storm" (F, p. 373). He convinces the city treasurer Stener that "it's a case of sink or swim" for both of them (F, p. 203), and to try to save himself, commits a crime involving the city's "sinking fund" (F, p. 232), for which he is sent to prison. There he welcomes the sympathy of his cell overseer as "any straw to a drowning man."[14]

Like *Sister Carrie*, Cowperwood betrays his fear of the stormy world of finance by trying to construct quiet chambers where he may escape into an illusion of success and peace. In this tendency he is aided by Aileen, whose seduction is not accompanied so much by a desire to share Cowperwood's struggles as by a desire to find with him a relief from the storm; her dream is "a yacht on the sea with him, a palace somewhere—just they two" (F, p. 144). This palace of escape from struggle is, as in *Sister Carrie*, often given an *Arabian Nights* flavor. Dreiser describes the first liaison of the two thus: "There was a cold, snowy street visible through the interstices of the hangings of the windows, and gaslamps flickering outside. He had come in early, and hearing Aileen, he came to where she was seated at the piano. She was wearing a rough, gray wool cloth dress, ornately banded with fringed Oriental embroidery in blue and burnt-orange. . . . On her fingers were four or five rings, far too many—an opal, an emerald, a ruby, a diamond—flashing visibly as she played" (F, p. 137). Nor is Aileen the only one of Cowperwood's women to whom he is drawn because of "all the Orient richness she represented" (T, p. 37). When he tires of Aileen, he finds Stephanie Platow who is "like something out of Asia" (T, p. 212), and when he discovers Stephanie nude and "curled up in the corner of a suggestive oriental divan" with a newspaper reporter, he thinks that "in an older day, if they had lived in Turkey, he would have had her strangled, sewn in a sack, and thrown into the Bosporus. As it was, he could only dismiss her" (T, pp. 237–239). Later he is drawn to Berenice Fleming, "as charming a figure as one would have wished to see—part Greek, part Oriental" (T, p. 457), who can translate him "as by the wave of a fairy wand, into another realm" (T, pp. 393, 397). To her he holds out the possibility of a beautiful house to overcome the social stigma of her procuress mother, "almost an Arabian situation," as she thinks of it, "heightened by the glitter of gold" (*T*, p. 497).

However stormy the sea outside may be, the inside of Cowperwood's palaces are keyed to a painting which he purchased for his Chicago mansion—"A particularly brilliant Gerôme, then in the heyday of his exotic popularity—a picture of nude odalisques of the harem, idling beside the highly colored stone manquetry of an oriental bath" (*T*, p. 68). The palatial chambers which Cowperwood builds for his wives and mistresses, however, are not so much Levantine as Mediterranean, and his make-believe role is not so much master of a harem as a Renaissance merchant prince.[15] Yet none of Cowperwood's mansions finally gives him shelter from the storms of life. The treasures in his Philadelphia house are sold, and the palaces which await him are the battlemented towers of Moyamensing Prison (*F*, p. 366), and later the Eastern District Penitentiary of Pennsylvania, "not at all unlike the palace of the Sforzas at Milan" (*F*, 427). At the end of *The Titan* he is forced out of his New York mansion to come back to Chicago to defend himself in the Chicago city hall, a "large, ponderous structure of black granite . . . suggesting somewhat the somnolent architecture of ancient Egypt" which contains not isolated luxury but "a sea of unfriendly faces" and "as hungry and bold a company of gray wolves as was ever gathered under one roof" (*T*, pp. 542, 543). Like Hurstwood and Carrie, Cowperwood has been the dupe of a false Aladdin; the stormy waves and the cries of animal life enter even into his chambers, and he has "no ultimate peace, no real understanding, but only hunger and thirst and wonder" (*T*, p. 552). He discovers that he is "quite as other men, subject to the same storms, the same danger of shipwreck. Only he was a better sailor than most" (*T*, p. 166).

IV

For all its apparent concern with the workings of American society and legal machinery, *An American Tragedy* is, with the possible exception of *The "Genius,"* more an "interior" novel than anything which Dreiser had written up to this time. It is documentary, but it documents the internal states of Clyde Griffiths, rather than the risings and fallings of the public fortune of a man like Cowperwood. The symbolic structure of *An American Tragedy* is also significantly different. The conflict which gave *Sister Carrie* and the Cowperwood novels their central unity—the conflict between the seemingly impersonal, inhuman workings of an indifferent universe and the yearning of the individual for a realization of beauty and security—was presented in two opposing sets of images, the universe as a sea or a jungle and the world of dreams as a magic harbor or chamber. Now in *An American Tragedy* the animal imagery becomes so infrequent and diffuse that most of the examples seem to be the result of habit rather than of conscious intent; the few really functional instances are the concentration of references to Clyde as a harried animal in the short time between Roberta's death and his seizure by the agents of the law. Furthermore, the imagery of the sea and the tempest has almost entirely disappeared, or rather has been transformed into the more restricted images of a lake or a pool. What remains constant in Dreiser's imagery is the motif of *The Arabian Nights*. Although one may suspect that the *Arabian Nights* imagery of the early books derived from an unconscious imitation of nineteenth-century pseudo-romances and popular plays, Dreiser in *An American Tragedy* developed it more fully than in any of the earlier novels and used it to provide the central fable of Clyde Griffiths' life. In place of the tension between the actuality of a turbulent sea and the illusion of a secure chamber which provided the central contrast of the earlier novels, Dreiser has in *An American Tragedy* substituted the theme of the ambiguity of reality, symbolized by the glittering lake which is transformed into a pool of death, and an Aladdin's cave which is transformed into a tomb.

The imagery of *The Arabian Nights* provides the symbolic structure for *An American Tragedy*. Late in Clyde's trial, his defense attorney points to this structure most directly when he speaks of Clyde's attraction to Sondra as "a case of the Arabian Nights, of the ensorcelled and the ensorcellor . . . a case of being bewitched . . . by beauty, love, wealth, by things that we sometimes think we want very, very much, and cannot ever have."[16] Although Clyde does not understand what the lawyer means, and the lawyer himself is merely indulging in rhetoric for the jury, he has provided the key to Dreiser's dominant image of Clyde. Throughout its 800 pages the novel is permeated with the quality of Scheherazade's tales, from the beginning description of Clyde as a twelve-year old boy with "a certain emotionalism and exotic sense of romance" and a "vivid and intelligent imagination" (I,10) to the end in the death house, where Clyde is given a gift of a copy of *The Arabian Nights* by a man condemned to death "for poisoning an old man of great wealth" (II, 362,369). Again the language with which Dreiser explores Clyde's personality is less the language of science than the language of romance; "chemisms" are spoken of much less frequently than "dreams," the key word of this novel. Clyde has "wishes," "phantasies," and "visions"; he sees and hears "apparitions," "genii," "effrits," "ghosts," "giants," "ouphes," "barghests," and "ogres"; and he and the other characters are "ensorcelled," "enchanted," "enslaved," "infatuated," "entranced," and "transported" by "witchery" and by dreams which are "mysterious" and "insubstantial," and visions which "materialize."[17].

More particularly, three stories of *The Arabian Nights* sequence are relevant to the life of Clyde Griffiths—"The History of Aladdin, or the Wonderful Lamp," "The History of the Barber's Fifth Brother," and "The History of the Fisherman." As in *Sister Carrie*, it is the first of these stories which is most frequently mentioned, but here the parallels are more explicit. Like Aladdin, Clyde is a poor boy who disregards the advice of his parents; and like Aladdin, he is conducted into a cavern by a long-lost uncle, who tries to keep him imprisoned until he discovers the magic ring and lamp which provide him wealth, social position, and a beautiful wife. Clyde's imagination is his own genie of the lamp, however. Coupled with his inexperience, it is capable of transforming vulgarity and gaudiness into exotic beauty. When he first visits a house of prostitution, "having pushed through the curtains of heavy velvet . . . Clyde found himself in a bright and rather gaudy general parlor or reception room, the walls of which were ornamented with gilt-framed pictures of nude or seminude girls and some very high pier mirrors. . . . It was really quite an amazing and Aladdin-like scene to him" (I,63, 65). The hotel in which he works, however gauche Dreiser and the reader may find it, is to Clyde a wonder of his world: "[through] a green-marbled doorway . . . he beheld a lobby . . . more arresting, quite, than anything he had seen before. It was all so lavish. Under his feet was a checkered black-and-white marble floor. Above him a coppered and stained and gilded ceiling. And supporting this, a veritable forest of black marble columns as highly polished as the floor—glassy smooth. . . . He gazed about in awe and amazement" (I, 29–30). Later Dreiser carefully poses Clyde at the doorway to the Griffiths factory and then the Griffiths house in an attitude of awe at an excitingly new world (I, 189–190, 219–220), and magically these doors respond to his "Open, Sesame!" It must be remembered that many of Clyde Griffiths' dreams are accomplished. His dreams of a job as bell-boy at the Green-Davidson are fullfilled, and he is ecstatic in his delight: "Kind Heaven! What a realization of paradise! What a consummation of luxury!" (I, 33, 37); each tip is "a mysterious and yet sacred vision" (I, 41). His dream of an outing with Hortense Briggs is made possible by the sudden appearance of a Packard which belonged to "an elderly and very wealthy man who at the time was traveling in Asia" (I, 123). Later in Chicago his uncle, imagined as "a king of Croesus, living in ease and luxury there in the east" (I, 14), suddenly appears at the Chicago Union League Club to offer him a new opportunity just after Clyde had "wished and wished that he could get into some work where he could rise and be somebody" (I, 175). Still later we find Clyde canoeing on Crum Lake, lonely and wishing that Roberta Alden were with him, when she appears on the shore; Clyde's face is "lit by the radiance of one who had suddenly, and beyond his belief, realized a dream," while to Roberta, Clyde is "a pleasant apparition suddenly evoked out of nothing and nowhere, a poetic effort taking form out of smoke or vibrant energy" (I, 265). And finally Clyde, as the result of an accidental meeting at night before the gates of a Wykeagy Avenue palace, is taken up by Sondra Finchley, "a princess" (I, 315), a "goddess in her shrine of gilt and tinsel" (I, 323), "a star, a paragon of luxury and social supremacy" (I, 374), whose glances "enslave" him (I, 315, 323, 341, 374). Some of Clyde's wishes and dreams are indeed "materialized."

The successful Aladdin, however, was only one of the poor youths in *The Arabian Nights* sequence; Alnashar, the Barber's Fifth Brother, is in some respects closer to Clyde Griffiths. Alnashar, it may be remembered, is a lazy, imaginative, and talkative youth who inherits 100 drachms of silver, and invests his inheritance in a stock of bottles and glass objects which he displays for sale on a tray. While waiting for customers he dreams of how he will sell his glasses, reinvest his profits in more glasses, and so on until he has 100,000 drachms, which enable him to dress like a prince, give gifts to the grand vizier, and demand his beautiful daughter as a bride. Then after his marriage he will pretend to lose interest in his bride, and when she and her mother come to plead for his favor, he will push them away violently. At this point Alnashar's dream becomes so real to him that he thrusts out his foot and knocks his tray of glasses to the street, where they lie in fragments. Although Dreiser mentions Alnashar at only one point in the novel (I, 317), he describes Clyde's Alnashar dreams many times: "To be able to wear such a suit with such ease and air! To be able to talk to a girl after the manner and with the sang-froid of some of these gallants! . . . And once he did attain it—was able to wear such clothes as these—well, then was he not well set upon the path that leads to all blisses? . . . The friendly smiles! The secret handclasps, maybe—an arm about the waist of someone or another—a kiss—a promise of marriage—and then, and then!"[18] Furthermore, Clyde is like Alnashar, who continued to be victimized throughout his life because of his impractical dreaming, in that he never really *learns*. The "dream" just quoted comes when Clyde is fifteen; another, equally Alnashar-like, comes when he is twenty-one. Between the two he has had his dream of securing Hortense Briggs shattered by a discovery of her vulgar self-centeredness, his dream of rising in the hotel business shattered by a procession of unrewarding jobs, his dream of rising rapidly in the Griffiths factory shattered by the drudgery which his relatives prescribe for him, and his dream of having Roberta as lover without any responsibility for her shattered by the discovery of her pregnancy. Critics who emphasize society's responsibility for Clyde's failure forget how really foolish Clyde is. Mason, the district attorney who solves Clyde's murder plot and takes him into custody in less than four days time, contemptuously calls Clyde "a dunce" (II, 150), and Dreiser frequently underlines Clyde's thoughtlessness with phrases like "no thought," "none of the compulsion of the practical," "no serious consideration," "no more plan than this," "he hadn't really thought about that," "he had not even stopped to look," and "he had never thought of them" (II, 5, 8, 17, 61, 129, 135). Clyde's lack of practical wisdom cannot be explained by his limited childhood training, however unrelated his parents' religious teachings seem to be to "the world." Like Alnashar, he "had a soul that was not destined to grow up. He lacked decidedly that mental clarity and inner directing application that in so many permits them to sort out from the facts and avenues of life the particular thing or things that make for their direct advancement" (I,

174). The seeming inevitability of Clyde's failure depends upon our accepting the fact that he never learns from his experience, that he remains the adolescent dreamer into his twenties.

The third story of *The Arabian Nights* which has relevance to the novel is the "History of the Fisherman" who on the third cast of his nets into the sea brings up a jar from which, when it is unsealed, a black smoke issues into the shape of a genie, or efrit. The efrit has power to reward the fisherman for releasing it, but unaccountably proceeds to threaten the fisherman with death; finally the fisherman tricks the efrit into returning to the jar for a moment, and stoppers the jar with Solomon's seal forever. Clyde is neither so suspicious nor so resourceful as the fisherman. He is faced with a need to rid himself of Roberta Alden, who blocks his acquisition of Sondra as "the central or crowning jewel to so much sudden and such Aladdin-like splendor" (II, 8). Then he reads a newspaper account of a double drowning in another state just before he drives to a lake with Sondra and her friends. The conjunction of these three events is enough to bring forth "as the genii at the accidental rubbing of Aladdin's lamp—as the efrit emerging as smoke from the mystic jar in the net of the fisherman—the very substance of some leering and diabolic wish or wisdom concealed in his own nature" (II, 48). Dreiser combines the language of *The Arabian Nights*, Freudian psychology, and Christian theology as he personifies Clyde's "darker or primordial and unregenerate nature" and "his darkest and weakest side" as a "Giant Efrit . . . the Efrit of his own darker self," speaking in the "sealed and silent hall" of his brain in language ambiguously like that of the inscriptions on the walls of his parents' mission, "Behold! I bring you a way. It is the way of the lake" (II, 49–56). Before this "genii of his darkest and weakest side" Clyde seems powerless to stopper the jar of his secret wishes or to drive them away with his will.

Because he suggests "the way of the lake" (II, 53), the ambiguity of this genie is all the more terrifying. The life of the turbulent sea which surrounded Carrie and Cowperwood was unambiguous; it was a dangerous actuality, however unpredictable. Clyde, however, tries not so much to find a safe harbor from stormy seas as to find a place on a lake which will not change its character beneath him. It will be noticed that Clyde's love affairs are frequently prosecuted on water. He comes nearest to intimacy with Hortense Briggs (whose dream is a beaver coat) on the ice of a river near Excelsior Springs. When he arrives in Lycurgus, he soon begins to feel that his position as a Griffiths raises him above dancing to "Dream Boat" with Rita Dickerman and Zella Shuman, and he learns to swim, dive, and manage a canoe so that he will have the accomplishments valued by the Griffiths and their friends. As he paddles his canoe alone on Crum Lake, he discovers Roberta Alden on the shore and takes her into his canoe to pick water lilies, but even while he is on Crum Lake with Roberta he thinks that "had fortune favored him in the first place by birth, he would now be in some canoe on Schroon or Racquette or

Champlain Lake with Sondra Finchley or some such girl" (I, 263). Sondra, unlike Roberta, is literally at home on the lake, in her family's new bungalow on Twelfth Lake, "right down at the water's edge" (I, 153), and she appears in a Lycurgus parade as an Indian maiden in a flower-covered canoe on the Mohawk (I, 241). To Clyde, Roberta soon comes to symbolize everything associated with his unhappy past—poverty, naiveté, sensuality warring with an uncertain primness, at best Crum Lake; Sondra, on the other hand, suggests wealth, sophistication, an easy confident manner, the social climate of Twelfth Lake. Dreiser catches this opposition in a single image: outside the Griffiths factory where Roberta stamps collars and where Clyde is assistant foreman is the river; "through the many open windows that reached from floor to ceiling could be seen the Mohawk swirling and rippling. . . . always [seeming] to hint of pleasures which might be found by idling along its shores" (I, 243).

How is Clyde to rid himself of Roberta and get Sondra? "Because of his own great interest in . . . any form of water life" (II, 23), he is attracted to the newspaper story of the accidental drowning of a couple on Pass Lake, Massachusetts. Some days later, after a trip to Big Bittern Lake with Sondra and her friends, Clyde meets his "genii," the embodiment of his overwhelming desire to do away with Roberta: "Would you escape from the demands of Roberta that but now and unto this hour have appeared unescapable to you? Behold! I bring you a way. It is the way of the lake—Pass Lake" (II, 49). The way of Pass Lake, enacted on Big Bittern Lake, will be, Clyde thinks, the way for him to pass forever from Crum Lake to Twelfth Lake.

As Clyde, the witless Aladdin, stumbles toward a seeming solution to his troubles, taking Roberta up the Mohawk to Utica, then on to Grass Lake, and finally to Big Bittern Lake, his life becomes more nightmare than actuality. He leaves such obvious clues behind him that a country lawyer can arrest him forty-eight hours from the time that Roberta's body is discovered. It is not simply that Clyde is stupid or inept (he has considerable success in his relationships with Sondra and her friends); rather he is moving *in* a dream and *toward* a dream of release and oblivion. When he takes Roberta into the boat on Big Bittern Lake, he recalls the details of their first outing on Crum Lake, but *this* lake and *this* Roberta are unreal: "an almost nebulous figure, she now seemed, stepping down into an insubstantial rowboat upon a purely ideational lake." The lake itself is magically shifting in shape. Behind an island the lake seemed to contain another lake within it, "an especially arranged pool or tarn to which one who was weary of life and cares—anxious to be away from the strife and contentions of the world, might most wisely and yet gloomily repair . . . where there was no end of anything—no plots—no plans—no practical problems to be solved—nothing. . . . the water itself looking like a huge black pearl cast by some mighty hand, in anger possibly, in sport or phantasy maybe" (II, 70, 74).

The Way of the Lake proves illusory for Clyde. The Big Bittern is a real lake, composed of real water which remains on his suit even when he carries it in his bag to Twelfth Lake. The lake does not accept Roberta into nothingness, but gives her up on a grappling hook along with Clyde's camera containing the snapshots that he had taken of her just before her drowning. The Way of the Lake does not make Sondra secure for Clyde: he never sees her again after his arrest, and the few hours he has with her before his arrest are filled with suffering as he watches her play at drowning in her boat on Twelfth Lake. Clyde's trial is not so much an unjust dispensing of "justice," as some of Dreiser's critics have suggested, as it is an indication of how inexorably the world moves on, how far it is removed from a fairy tale. Clyde's killing of Roberta was an actual killing, not a magic way to success. His world was a world in which his actions were related to others, not merely existing in isolation. "How people seemed to remember things," Clyde marvels during his trial, "more than ever he would have dreamed they would have" (II, 229).

V

If the epigraph for *Sister Carrie* might have been "She was . . . a lone figure on a tossing, thoughtless sea," that of *The Bulwark* might have been "He leadeth me beside the still waters." The world of *The Bulwark* is no longer that of the turbulent sea or the savage jungle, no longer that of the ambiguous lake, but one in which the lion and the lamb finally lie down together along a quiet stream. Lever Creek, clear, cool, and quiet, meanders through the novel, lacing together the various episodes which take place upon it, introducing the major motifs, and providing the central image for the transcendental wisdom which Solon Barnes finally attains. It is a source of inspiration for Solon's father, who, when he comes to Thornbrough, sets about restoring the banks of the stream from "neglect and decay" to make them "not sinful or wasteful ever—just gay and clean."[19] His improvements to the arbor, the benches, and the paths along the stream lead Rufus Barnes to resolve the conflict between his Quaker desire for simplicity and his love of comfort; convinced that his accumulation of property is evidence of a stewardship intended by God, he has the motto "He leadeth me beside the still waters" painted on his bedroom wall (p. 26). It is beside the creek that Solon confesses his love for Benecia, who becomes his wife, and the creek becomes a symbol to them of the blessed, protected existence which they want for their children.

Nevertheless, the episode in which the young Solon, his future wife Benecia, and his cousin Rhoda catch the minnows in the Thornbrough pool with dip nets foreshadows the trials which later come to the Barnes family. Rhoda, who years later will assist two of Solon's children to escape the restrictions their father has placed upon them, sees the fishing merely as good sport: "We'll have some fun," she says. "See if we can't outwit some of these minnows" (p. 69). Benecia, whose later concern and affection for her children shows itself only in sentimental gestures, says "I don't want to keep any of the little fishes out of the water too long. . . . If I do catch any, I'll put them right back. That'll teach them to be more watchful" (p. 70). Solon's reply, "Teaching minnows to be careful will certainly keep thee busy," foreshadows his later role as law-giver, when he comes to believe that life is "a series of law-governed details [and] . . . that those who were caught in the nets of evil paid dearly in this world or the next, or both" (pp. 70, 90).

As Solon and his children leave Lever Creek, they enter the world of *Sister Carrie, The Financier,* or *An American Tragedy* with the characteristic violent sea and lake imagery of those novels. It is on the beach of a lake that the boy Solon first meets violence in the person of Walter Hokutt, the town bully; and it is on the beach sands of Atlantic City that Solon's son Stewart is initiated into sex and later is involved in the seduction and death of a young girl, in a manner reminiscent of Clyde Griffiths' actions on the New York lakes. Solon's children share the dreams of success, longings for beauty, and strong sexual desires with Dreiser's earlier characters. His son Orville becomes a Gilbert Griffiths and his daughter Dorothea a Sondra Finchley, their Quaker upbringing adding only a certain blandness to their social-climbing. Isobel and Etta are college-educated Carries, filled with longings for beauty and excitement not to be found at Thornbrough. Stewart, as we have said, re-enacts Clyde Griffiths' entrapment by sexual desire and panic, and commits suicide while awaiting trial for his part in the death of a young girl. Solon himself is drawn into the Cowperwood world of finance, where he finds that the directors of his bank value him chiefly as a respectable front behind which they may manipulate their investments.[20]

Shocked by his own failure and the failures of his children, Solon leaves the bank in Philadelphia for the banks of Lever Creek. "Lift up your heads, you that have come through and beyond all outward washings, unto the Lamb of God, that your robes may be washed white in His Blood; that thereby you may overcome and then sit down in the Kingdom with weary Abraham, thoroughly tried Isaac, and wrestling Jacob," says a sermon given him by a friend (p. 296). If it is not literally true that Solon finds the Lamb of God near the Creek, he does regain through a mystical experience the love for "all people and things" which "raised him out of the black shadow of grief that had all but removed him from life itself, and now caused his sympathy and interest to reach out again—to [Etta] and Isobel, to the flowers and insects and the fish in Lever Creek" (p. 331).

Two incidents lead this "thoroughly tried Isaac" to humility and a new sense of the superiority of love over law. First, Solon sees "an exquisitely colored and designed green fly" eating the small bud of a plant; "why was this beautiful creature, whose design so delighted him, com-

pelled to feed upon another living creature, a beautiful flower? . . .
Which was intended to live—the fly, the bud, or both?" (pp. 316–317).
This scene is an obvious parallel to that in *The Financier* when the young
Cowperwood watches the lobster devour the squid and finds in that
elemental struggle a rationale for his own ruthless rise to power. But
Dreiser's animal world is no longer a savage jungle; it is a peaceable
kingdom. If the Quaker teachings of John Woolman, George Fox, and
Rufus Jones provided many of the ideas of *The Bulwark*,[21] the paintings of
the Quaker primitive, Edward Hicks, could have provided the imagery.
Instead of turning from Lever Creek to immerse himself again in the
financial world of Philadelphia, as Cowperwood would have done, Solon
Barnes goes on to examine the habits of fish, birds, butterflies, vines,
flowers, and grass. He experiences "a kind of religious awe and wonder"
recognizing that "surely there must be a Creative Divinity, and so a purpose, behind all of this variety and beauty and tragedy of life" (p. 317). In
this mood of wonder and resignation, Solon later steps near a puff-adder,
vicious and threatening in its appearance, but amenable to evidences of
Solon's good intentions toward it. As the snake quietly turns from its attitude of hostility and crosses over Solon's feet, Solon's sense of divine purpose becomes more explicit; not only is there a Creative Divinity with a
purpose, but this purpose is good: "Good intent is of itself a universal
language, and if our intention is good, all creatures in their particular
way understand, and so it was that this puff-adder understood me just as I
understood it. . . . And now I thank God for this revelation of His
universal presence and His good intent toward all things—all of His
created world. For otherwise how would it understand me, and I it, if we
were not both a part of Himself?" (p. 319).

This peaceable kingdom in which snakes discover good intentions
and flies eat flowers for the good of both is as far removed from the
Philadelphia financial world and the prison in which Solon's son commits
suicide in despair as the world of *The Arabian Nights* was from the everyday world of Carrie Meeber or Clyde Griffiths. But now the fairy land has
become the *real* world, and the world of struggle and torment only illusory. Even Etta, temporarily guilt-ridden by her disloyalty to her
father's teachings, is caught up in the experience of divine love, and she
regains her childhood wisdom—a "wisdom that is related to beauty only,
that concerns itself with cloud forms and the wild vines' tendrils, whose
substance is not substance, but dreams only, and those dreams are entangled with the hopes and the yearnings of all men" (p. 130). For the
Dreiser of *The Bulwark*, as for the boy Stewart Barnes, no longer was
there need for "fairy tales of Jack and the Beanstalk, Bluebeard, or Sinbad
the Sailor" to distract one from an actual world of struggle. "This mystic,
colorful world was fairy-land enough" (p. 142).

His primary groups of symbols—of water, animals, and fairyland—
have shifted in their suggestions through the course of his career and have

traced the central meaning of his novels. The water is first the turbulent sea of society, then the lake of private guilt, and finally the still stream of the Inner Light; the animals first inhabit a jungle but later a peaceable kingdom; and the hopes and desires of men turn out not to be false promises of a genie before Aladdin's Cave but the transcendental knowledge of the goodness of things which one discovers as he walks along Lever Creek. Dreiser's relentless questioning has taken him from the "external" naturalism of *Sister Carrie* and the Cowperwood books, through the "internal" naturalism of *An American Tragedy*, to the transcendental acceptance of *The Bulwark*.

Notes

1. *The Financier* (New York, 1927, rev. ed.), p. 135, F. O. Matthiessen, *Theodore Dreiser* (New York, 1951) and Alexander Kern, "Dreiser's Difficult Beauty," *Western Review*, 16 (Winter 1952), 129–136, find some merit in Dreiser's style. The common view is still that of Thomas K. Whipple, *Spokesmen: Modern Writers and American Life* (New York, 1928), pp. 71, 73: "His style is atrocious, his sentences are chaotic, his grammar and syntax faulty; he has no feeling for words, no sense of diction. . . . [His writing lacks] any sort of beauty—beauty of form, of imagery, of rhythm."

2. *Sister Carrie*, ed. Kenneth S. Lynn (New York, 1957), pp. 10, 11. Further references to *Sister Carrie* are made to this edition, and will be incorporated into the text. In his introduction to this edition Kenneth Lynn briefly discusses the sea imagery of *Sister Carrie*, as does Matthiessen, pp. 83–84.

3. When Hurstwood speaks of his own dissatisfaction with life, Carrie pities him: "To think . . . that he needed to make such an appeal when she herself was lonely and without anchor" (p. 119). When Drouet inquires about the frequency of Hurstwood's visits, Carrie lies to him because she is "all at sea mentally" (p. 125). Hurstwood himself is not immune to storms of feeling. When he watches Carrie play the role of "a cold, white, helpless object" in an amateur drama, he "blinked his eyes and caught the infection. The radiating waves of feeling and sincerity were already breaking against the farthest walls of the chamber. The magic of passion which will yet dissolve the world, was here at work" (p. 166).

4. Pp. 184–186. Hurstwood's relationship to his wife is also charted in terms of water. Because of his attraction to Carrie, the "river of indifference" (p. 128) which ran between Hurstwood and his wife is soon flooded by a storm, which approaches slowly; their arguments are "really precipitated by an atmosphere which was surcharged with dissension. That it would shower, with a sky so full of blackening thunderclouds, would scarely be thought worthy of comment" (p. 188). Searching for something to justify her jealousy, Mrs. Hurstwood awaits "the clear proof of one overt deed . . . the cold breath needed to convert the lowering clouds of suspicion into a rain of wrath" (p. 190). When she learns merely that Hurstwood has been seen riding with a strange woman, the incident is not conclusive enough. "Only the atmosphere of distrust and ill-feeling was strengthened, precipitating every now and then little sprinklings of irritable conversation, enlivened by flashes of wrath" (p. 191). But when the storm finally comes, with Mrs. Hurstwood's announcement that she has discovered enough about her husband to enable her to dictate terms to him her manner is so cool and cynical that "somehow it took the wind out of his sails. He could not attack her, he could not ask her for proofs. . . . He was like a vessel, powerful and dangerous, but rolling and floundering without sail" (p. 198).

5. Kenneth Lynn has observed the degree to which *Sister Carrie* is theatrical: "the theatrical world was to Dreiser a microcosm of the glamorous city, a quintessence of its artificial splendors" (p. xii). Though this is to some extent true, it misses the point. In *Sister Car-*

rie the shoe factory, the West Side flat, the street-car line, and the Bowery flophouse are closer to Dreiser's conception of the quintessence of the city; the theater is rather an escape from the city's ugly reality. It is the fairy tale world of illusion, an "elf land" toward which Carrie drifts to escape "the grim world without" (p. 341). The theater in which she first appears professionally is a "large, empty, shadowy playhouse, still redolent of the perfumes and blazonry of the night, and notable for its rich oriental appearance" (p. 345), and her first minor success comes as she plays "one of a group of oriental beauties who . . . were paraded by the vizier before the new potentate as the treasures of his harem" (p. 386) in a comic opera called "The Wives of Abdul." As her popularity increases, there are stage-door genii to offer her whatever she wants: "I could give you every luxury. There isn't anything you could ask for that you couldn't have . . . I love you and wish to gratify your every desire," and her $150 a week seems to be "a door to an Aladdin's cave" (pp. 410, 411).

6. Pp. 451–452. Hurstwood is "shut out from Chicago—from his easy, comfortable state" (p. 250) by having stolen money from Fitzgerald and Moy's; and no longer "subject to the illusions and burning desires of youth" (pp. 265–266), he is unable to conceive of himself as re-entering the gaudy chamber, which seems to him to be "a city with a wall about it. Men were posted at the gates. You could not get in. Those inside did not care to come out to see who you were. They were so merry inside there that all those outside were forgotten, and he was on the outside" (p. 297). His attempts to escape from the turbulent sea are mockeries. First he seeks refuge as a chairwarmer, "shielding himself from cold and the weariness of the streets in a hotel lobby" (p. 331); next he tries to escape into an illusion of activity, as in his rocking-chair he "buried himself in his papers. . . . What Lethean waters were these floods of telegraphed intelligence!" (p. 311); then there is the poker room where "visions of a big stake floated before him" before he loses half his money and walks out into the "chill, bare streets" (pp. 330, 332).

7. In addition to passages already cited, allusions to water, the sea, tides, storms, ships, and harbors may be found on pp. 9, 73, 74, 76, 110, 111, 145, 169, 188, 190, 193, 198, 206, 211, 213, 231, 252, 254, 255, 263, 273, 308, 314, 333, 356, 363, 380, 395, 402, 430, and 438. Additional allusions to chambers, caves, the theater, magic, and *The Arabian Nights* may be found on pp. 7, 9, 12, 14, 16, 17, 18, 22, 24, 26, 28, 30, 39, 41, 46, 52, 59, 65, 69, 72, 74, 76, 95, 102, 127, 140, 148, 162, 170, 200, 223, 225, 228, 255, 280, 281, 284, 287, 288, 289, 290, 294, 312, 314, 334, 397, 407, and 445. Carrie's preoccupation with clothes, which Matthiessen sees as representing her "craving for pleasure" (p. 70) and the "expression of 'pecuniary culture' " (p. 83), may also be seen as coverings from the weather, and thus allied to the "chamber" imagery. Allusions to clothing in the novel may be found on pp. 6, 7, 22, 23, 33, 39, 42, 48, 53, 58, 60, 61, 65, 72, 94, 251, 270, 278, 280, 285, 321, 343, and 394.

8. *The Financier* (New York, 1912; revised, 1927); *The Titan* (New York, 1914). Further references to *The Financier* and *The Titan* are made to these editions and will be incorporated into the text, with the titles indicated by *"F"* or *"T."* Although Dreiser revised *The Financier* extensively, the revisions of the imagery studied here were insignificant, and the greater accessibility of the revised edition argues for its use in this study.

Any extended consideration of *Jennie Gerhardt* (New York, 1911) must be omitted here. Written between *Sister Carrie* and *The Financier*, its major imagery is, as we might expect, divided equally between the sea and the animal world. For references to water, the sea, storms, and ships in that novel, see pp. 16, 17, 18, 90, 95, 99, 172, 177, 239, 274, 299, 364, 373, 398, 403, 417, and 419. For references to the animal world, see pp. 10, 35, 88, 100, 126, 130, 131, 133, 189, 190, 201, 203, 219, 223, 236, 238, 239, 277, 286, 295, 327, 370, 378, 404, 414, and 415.

9. See, for example, Harlan Hatcher, *Creating the Modern American Novel* (New York, 1935), p. 50; Kenneth S. Lynn, *The Dream of Success* (Boston, 1955), p. 52; and Charles C. Walcutt, *American Literary Naturalism, A Divided Stream* (Minneapolis, Minn., 1956), p. 204.

10. References to these animals, as well as to animal life in general, may be found in *F*,

pp. 2, 3, 5, 9, 17, 21, 34, 41, 42, 43, 69, 89, 101, 108, 123, 124, 125, 127, 128, 137, 140, 141, 150, 154, 164, 185, 189, 198, 199, 200, 202, 203, 205, 211, 214, 215, 220, 229, 244, 251, 253, 254, 255, 270, 298, 323, 327, 328, 332, 338, 350, 357, 359, 364, 376, 380, 393, 431, 436, 439, 441, 444, 464, 468, 471, 473, 485, 489, 493, 495, 501, and 502; and in *T*, pp. 7, 10, 19, 23, 24, 28, 30, 32, 45, 46, 47, 51, 60, 66, 67, 68, 70, 77, 83, 85, 101, 108, 109, 113, 114, 116, 120, 127, 128, 138, 139, 144, 145, 147, 148, 149, 150, 152, 155, 156, 157, 160, 162, 164, 167, 187, 188, 203, 206, 220, 221, 222, 230, 239, 248, 253, 262, 286, 303, 304, 316, 326, 331, 332, 338, 343, 351, 352, 355, 356, 357, 358, 361, 366, 374, 375, 386, 389, 393, 394, 396, 398, 406, 408, 410, 414, 419, 421, 432, 436, 437, 441, 458, 473, 479, 482, 489, 494, 501, 503, 508, 513, 514, 515, 516, 521, 532, 533, 534, 535, 539, 542, 544, and 550.

11. *F*, p. 202. Cf. "Might as well be tried for stealing a sheep as a lamb" (*F*, p. 339); "There is more than one way to kill a cat" (*T*, p. 303); "They're all as crooked as eels' teeth" (*T*, p. 47); and ". . . jumping around like a cat in a bag" (*T*, p. 331).

12. *T*, p. 10. In Philadelphia, "the city treasury and the city treasurer were like a honey-laden hive and a queen bee around which the drones—the politicians—swarmed in the hope of profit," and rival financiers have a regard for each other "as sincere as that of one tiger for another" (*F*, pp. 150, 185).

13. Cowperwood fancies himself to be quite a gay dog, and after several episodes of "puppy love" (*F*, p. 21), he meets Aileen Butler and thinks "some lucky young dog [will] marry her pretty soon" (*F*, p. 89). He pursues her much as he has followed his first business venture, like a "young hound on the scent of game" (*F*, p. 17); to Aileen, one of his most attractive features is his eyes, "as fine as those of a Newfoundland or a Collie and as innocent and winsome" (*T*, p. 7). These comparisons and others add an ironic force to the melodramatic clichés with which Aileen's father denounces him ("dirty dog") and which Aileen herself hurls at him again and again as their marriage crumbles: "You dog! you brute!" (*T*, pp. 145 ff.).

14. *F*, p. 438. Besides the storms of financial difficulty which Cowperwood constantly arouses and the "storm of words" which his schemes sometimes raise in the newspapers (*T*, pp. 255, 526), there are the tempests which his many love affairs engender. Aileen Butler's father is aroused to the pitch of a storm by Cowperwood's making her his mistress (*F*, p. 319); so is her brother Callum later (*F*, p. 477); meanwhile the first Mrs. Cowperwood's soul "rages" like a "tempest" (*F*, p. 406). Later, Cowperwood's involvement with Rita Sohlberg, although it fails to precipitate the "storm of public rage" which Cowperwood fears (*T*, p. 151), leads to "storms of disaster" (*T*, p. 160) in his union with Aileen, leading particularly to her "emotional storm" when she discovers that Cowperwood has had other mistresses than Mrs. Sohlberg (*T*, pp. 247, 248), as well as to "a storm of protest" in the home of Caroline Hand, one of the mistresses (*T*, p. 265).

15. The exterior of his office in Philadelphia is "early Florentine in its decorations" with a door panel featuring "a hand . . . holding aloft a flaming brand . . . formerly . . . a money-changer's sign used in old Venice"; and inside the gas lights are "modeled after the early Roman flame-brackets" (*F*, pp. 104, 105). He fills his house with bronzes of the Italian Renaissance and bits of Venetian glass (*F*, p. 453). For Aileen, then his mistress, he builds a secret meeting place which is "a veritable treasure-trove" (*F*, p. 161), and later a mansion in Chicago, the "Florence of the West" (*T*, p. 6), where the dining room is "rich with a Pompeian scheme of color" and "aglow with a wealth of glass" (*T*, p. 71), and the gallery contains Pinturicchio's portrait of Caesar Borgia, in whose career Cowperwood has recently begun to take an interest, befitting his reputation among his associates who think of him as "devil or prince, or both" (*T*, p. 164) and "a prince of politicians" (*T*, p. 220). Yet when Cowperwood, like Hurstwood, finds that it is easier to build his reputation in Chicago than in New York, where in spite of his wealth and power "he was not yet looked upon as a money prince," he decides that what he needs to fulfill his conception of himself is a new mansion built to imitate "the Italian palaces of medieval or Renaissance origin which he had seen abroad" and "a union, morganatic or otherwise, with some one who would be worthy to

share his throne" (*T*, pp. 438–439). When the house is completed, a newspaper account of it exaggerates only a little the surroundings of this self-made Borgia: "his court of orchids, his sunrise room, the baths of pink and blue alabaster, the finishings of marble and intaglio. Here Cowperwood was represented as seated on a swinging divan, his various books, art treasures, and comforts piled about him. The idea was vaguely suggested that in his sybaritic hours odalesques [sic] danced before him and unnamable indulgences and excesses were perpetrated" (*T*, pp. 541–542).

The "ideal . . . a wraith, a mist, a perfume in the wind, a dream of fair water" (*T*, p. 201) for which Cowperwood seaches is symbolized by the fountains which he installs in each of his houses, culminating in the "sunrise room" where "in a perpetual atmosphere of sunrise were . . . racks for exotic birds, a trellis of vines, stone benches, a central pool of glistening water, and an echo of music" (*T*, p. 440).

16. Theodore Dreiser, *An American Tragedy* (2 vols.; New York, 1925), II, 274. Further references to *An American Tragedy* are made to this edition, and will be incorporated into the text. Matthiessen, pp. 194 and 200, briefly treats the *Arabian Nights* theme in the novel. Dreiser's acquaintance with *The Arabian Nights* probably dates from his early childhood, but it was continued in the theaters and music halls of Chicago; see Robert H. Elias, *Theodore Dreiser: Apostle of Nature* (New York, 1949), p. 25. His interest in Eastern legend is to be seen not only in the frequent use of Oriental imagery in his major novels but also in his unfortunate excursions into such pseudo-Oriental tales as "Khat" and "The Prince Who Was a Thief" in *Chains* (New York, 1927).

17. I, 48, 175, 265, 331, 341, 376; II, 42, 48, 49, 56, 65, 118, 233, 274, 381. References to Clyde's dreams are found in I, 33, 84, 116, 136, 138, 175, 192, 228, 230, 309, 427, 428; II, 5, 16, 27, 31, 50, 133, 221, 229, 383, 385, 392, 405.

18. I, 26. A similar Alnashar dream is stimulated by Sondra Finchley: "Sondra, Twelfth Lake, society, wealth, her love and beauty. He grew not a little wild in thinking of it all. Once he and she were married, what could Sondra's relatives do? What, but acquiesce and take them into the glorious bosom of their resplendent home . . . he to no doubt eventually take some place in connection with the Finchley Electric Sweeper Company. And then would he not be . . . joint heir with Stuart to all the Finchley means" (II, 8).

19. Theodore Dreiser, *The Bulwark* (New York, 1946), p. 9. Further references will be incorporated into the text.

20. Dreiser worked on the novel which became *The Bulwark* at various times from 1912 until his death in 1945, and the middle portion of the completed novel was "largely a merging of three early, pre-*American Tragedy* typescripts" (Gerhard Friedrich, "A Major Influence on Theodore Dreiser's *The Bulwark, American Literature*, 29 May 1957, 189). It is therefore understandable that the incidents and imagery of the middle portion of the novel should recall those of the earlier books, and that the first and the last chapters should contain the bulk of the references to benign animals and to Lever Creek.

21. Friedrich, op. cit., and Gerhard Friedrich, "Theodore Dreiser's Debt to Woolman's *Journal," American Quarterly*, 7 (Winter 1955), 385–392.

Heathen Catacombs

David Weimer*

James had the gift, rare for a novelist, of poetic compression, so that even his briefer sentences can bare his sensibility as a whole. For all their differences, Crane's talent was also distinctly compressive and figurative. Dreiser's deepest impulses were to *explain*. Loose, expansive, discursive, his prose dips haphazardly into metaphor then suddenly out of it; his heavy mind lurches this way and that. He gives the impression of a writer bewildered by transitions, handling the larger ones with chapter divisions and others not at all. Short passages lifted from his fiction may or may not be representative of the whole: his explanations do not always square with his characters' behavior, his narrative lumber was often badly proportioned, ill-cut, poorly grained, mismatched and scored.

So Dreiser built to no great symbolic moments; but he has memorable small ones. They occur, unpretentiously, quite on the way to something grander, as we think of them at the time, as in the opening paragraphs of the first famous novel:

> When Caroline Meeber boarded the afternoon train for Chicago, her total outfit consisted of a small trunk, a cheap imitation alligator-skin satchel, a small lunch in a paper box, and a yellow leather snap purse, containing her ticket, a scrap of paper with her sister's address in Van Buren Street and four dollars in money. It was in August, 1889. She was eighteen years of age, bright, timid, and full of the illusions of ignorance and youth. Whatever touch of regret at parting characterized her thoughts, it was certainly not for advantages now being given up. A gush of tears at her mother's farewell kiss, a touch in her throat when the cars clacked by the flour mill where her father worked by the day, a pathetic sigh as the familiar green environs of the village passed in review, and the threads which bound her so lightly to girlhood and home were irretrievably broken.
>
> To be sure there was always the next station, where one might descend and return. There was the great city, bound more closely by these very trains which came up daily. Colum-

*Reprinted from *The City as Metaphor* (New York: Random House, 1966), pp. 65–77. Reprinted by permission of Random House, Inc.

bia City was not so very far away, even once she was in
Chicago. What, pray, is a few hours—a few hundred miles?
She looked at the little slip bearing her sister's address and
wondered. She gazed at the green landscape, now passing in
swift review, until her swifter thoughts replaced its impression
with vague conjectures of what Chicago might be.

Not all of Dreiser's world, by any means, is intimated in this passage
from *Sister Carrie*, but a generous part of it is. There is the youth's
journey from village—past nature—to the city, from known deprivations
to hoped-for privileges, the vague and simple emotions turned inward,
the rootlessness; there is the author's strangely mixed compassion and
detachment about all this. There is his documentary interest in time of
day, apparel and possessions, history and machinery. There is his absorption in movement: geographic, and of human individuals in transit
toward living.

It is a skillful beginning to the novel, and an introduction to the rest
of Dreiser's fiction as well. For we are brought close immediately to the
protagonist whose feelings about life will dominate the foreground of the
tale, and we are also made aware of the city which has generated or given
direction to the strongest of those feelings and on whose terms they are
fated to work themselves out. With variations, this is the pattern that
emerges early in all of the novels. (A partial exception is *The Bulwark*, a
stray pigeon on many counts.) The Columbus, Ohio, where Jennie
Gerhardt seeks her first job corresponds to Carrie's Chicago; it has 50,000
people in 1880, the novelist carefully informs us, and is the state capital,
with a sumptuous hotel and a resident United States senator that promote
in Jennie those longings for comfort and security better satisfied in
Cleveland and later Chicago. The Cowperwood trilogy opens with young
Frank, at ten years already sensible, vigorous, courageous, defiant, and
"forever pondering, pondering," looking straight toward the career in
money that his native Philadelphia seems irresistibly to offer. In *The
"Genius"* it is Eugene Witla and Chicago; in *An American Tragedy* the
dreamy Clyde Griffiths and a very metropolitan Kansas City. Private
longings and the public arena—Dreiser's scale is both intimate and vast.
He was the first powerful American novelist of the emotions, inferior to
Hawthorne and James in the capacity to analyze them but superior to
both in re-creating their texture. And before him only *Moby-Dick* and
James's international novels had been drawn on so prodigious a scale: for
the voyages between oceans and continents, now a commerce with cities.

A part of Dreiser's achievement rests in his having joined the two
spheres, in having shown how passion may be at once personal and social.
The yearnings of his major characters *belong* palpably to the city. So tiny
and shadowy is the settlement in *The Scarlet Letter* that one easily forgets
whether it is meant to be Boston or Salem, but the same doubt is almost
inconceivable in Dreiser's fiction. At the same time, very much as in the

Hawthorne novel, the course of passion in Dreiser's world is severely conditioned by the type of community in which it transpires. The various
adulteries, liaisons, flirtations, and clandestine desirings of his characters
are born or nourished in the peculiarly sensuous atmosphere of the city,
live feverishly in the anonymous cubicles the city provides and eventually
die from either a natural boredom or the city-bred logistical difficulties of
moving, quartering, and supplying all one's women. "The city has its cunning wiles," observes Dreiser of Carrie's pilgrimage to Chicago. The statement is redundant, amateurish, sententious—and completely true to his
feelings. "There are large forces which allure with all the soulfulness of
expression possible in the most cultured human. The gleam of a thousand
lights is often as effective as the persuasive light in a wooing and
fascinating eye. Half the undoing of the unsophisticated and natural mind
is accomplished by forces wholly superhuman. A blare of sound, a roar of
life, a vast array of human hives, appeal to the astonished senses in
equivocal terms." He is describing the emotional spectacle that throughout the quarter-century of his best work held him entranced.

The sense of painful wonder that the bare physical immensity of a
great city can arouse in the provincial soul Dreiser himself first experienced when he was twelve. The Chicago of 1884 excited and frightened him, and on a trip three years later he began to identify his ambitions with that expanding metropolis. New York too, as late as his early
twenties, struck him as "huge and powerful and terrible," as he afterward
remembered it, and the two characters that most nearly re-enact those
journeys, Carrie Meeber and Eugene Witla, marvel as he must have
marveled at the prairie gauntness of Chicago and the island splendor of
Manhattan. One is always lured in this way to seek the underlying
parallel in Dreiser's life, so autobiographical was he and so affectingly
tormented was that life. In his work this temptation is inescapable, I
think; and our inclination to read his tales as chronicles of an American
era or as illustrations of Nietzschean and social-Darwinist axioms is more
likely to grow than disappear. Such extrapolations are not necessarily unfortunate, and Dreiser himself would surely have welcomed them. But it
is well to be certain when we are talking about his novels as artifacts and
when we are not, and though many blunders have taught us this caution
with Melville and Whitman, we have not quite learned it with Dreiser.
Relying on that writer's autobiographical accounts, for instance, Matthiessen has said that Chicago "was to be etched in [Dreiser's] brain in an
endless series of pictures of tall new towers silhouetted against the lake, of
the black oily river as he hung along its bridges, of the immeasurable
energy that pulsated from the grain elevators and railroad yards and the
vast central building of the Board of Trade." These etchings do appear in
his nonfictional writings, and here and there in his novels, particularly in
The "Genius," where rather self-consciously he 'paints' (or etches) an
urban landscape. However, the visual memories of Chicago and other

American cities which Dreiser leans on most heavily for novelistic purposes are of ground floors rather than skylines, seldom of tall towers or grain elevators but commonly of low-lying residences.

There *is* architecture in Dreiser's novels, but it is domestic not public, and less important visually than thematically. This admirer of Alfred Stieglitz had a sharp eye for the urban pictorial, but the eye was not really "marvellous," as Dorothy Dudley claimed. He saw quickly, wrote rapidly, was not in the least concerned to reproduce meticulously in words the rich paintings set before us in James's late novels. His art may be that of a Hopper, as Alfred Kazin suggests, or a Sloan, whose grosser techniques and more darkly romantic realism seem to me more comparable to Dreiser's own; it is in any case an art of the bold sketch, with the artist going swiftly to what he wants. The architecture Dreiser chooses to present in this way is interestingly similar from novel to novel.

It is an architecture of façades, entrances, and interiors. The fact is, of course, telling. To have *access*—to the beckoning rooms of love and power—is overwhelmingly the passion gripping Dreiser's characters. They are outside, craving, and they want to be inside, enjoying. Theirs are the yearnings of children, prolonged into adulthood by a civilization that insists on the infantile joys of possession but allows only a charmed few to possess. At first, still largely guileless, artless, drawn by simple feelings within and apparently natural attractions of beauty without, they move as if in a spell toward the mansions of privilege. Clyde Griffiths, for example,

> found himself ambling on and on until suddenly he was out of
> the business district again and in touch with a wide and tree-
> shaded thoroughfare of residences, the houses of which, each
> and every one, appeared to possess more room space, lawn
> space, general ease and repose and dignity even than any with
> which he had ever been in contact. In short, as he sensed it
> from this brief inspection of its very central portion, it seemed
> a very exceptional, if small city street—rich, luxurious even. So
> many imposing wrought-iron fences, flower-bordered walks,
> grouped trees and bushes, expensive and handsome auto-
> mobiles either beneath porte-cochères within or speeding
> along the broad thoroughfare without.

This is the first of many walks Clyde takes from the obscure districts of Lycurgus, New York, to gaze at the bright exteriors of wealth. The scene has parallels in all but one of the other major novels. Jennie is "overawed" at the magnificent lobby of the Columbus hotel, Carrie is wholly enchanted by the lawns, entrance-ways, and glimpsed interiors of "palaces" along the North Shore Drive, Eugene by the "splendid houses" on Michigan and other avenues. Of the principal characters only Frank Cowperwood is not similarly awe-struck, but a cardinal point of his character is that he not be visibly overwhelmed by anything, and we learn all the same that he remembers his early visits to the homes of Butler the politician and others on fashionable Girard Avenue in Philadelphia and afterwards builds his own house with an unusually "arresting" façade.

One of Dreiser's relentless ironies is that these souls are always permitted some access to the social world whose façades they have admired but never win the full approval which they hoped that entrance would effect. Always, in what they most desire, they fail. Dreiser piles up plausible reasons for their failure: weak will or untoward circumstances, Clyde's inadequacies and then Roberta's tumble from the rowboat. And yet the aristocrats' unwillingness to accept an agreeable young Jennie or Clyde remains imperfectly explained. At an advanced point in the protagonist's social progress, realistic explanations become curiously irrelevant: he is simply destined to lose, in a fate only more totally imposed than that facing James's heroes and heroines, only less insistently explicit than that facing Faulkner's. The fact that Dreiser did not know very intimately the lives of the pedigreed rich helps us to understand the mystery but does not help us decide whether the mystery serves a literary end. In fact it does. The inscrutability of the world of privilege is a main element in what becomes from book to book a parable of the city.

Once there was a young man (in some versions a young woman) who found his home restrictive and left at the first chance for the center of the city. A creature of nature and custom, there he hoped to discover freedom from irksome restraint and also the approval of society. (Some say falsely that he sought only self-indulgence.) The great Mansion lured him; it seemed to promise both liberty and acceptance. He longed to enter.

There came a woman from inside the great Mansion who opened the door for him. But by this act she jeopardized her place in the Mansion. This was just, for the Mansion was Christian and like her new companion she was a Pagan. Wishing to be secure and yet to revolt, they turned elsewhere in the city to the Secret Room, where they could worship the gods of nature. But chance and the power of privilege betrayed them. The insider was compelled to choose between one god and many. She chose, unhappily. The outsider, given no choice, was driven from the Mansion.

The least allegorical of writers, nonetheless Dreiser returned to this story so often as to give it the force of allegory. For him it was the primordial tale of modern life, a tale which he could only repeat (with variations) since he could deduce no useful principles for conduct from it. The fundamental truth it appeared to demonstrate—who could be certain?— was that life in society was a trap. Of this truth the city was at once emblem and circumstance. "What a tangle life was," thinks Eugene, as in the pain of her child-bearing the sorrows of Angela's life and of his own merge in one great universal sorrow; and the sentiment echoes through all of the novels. Eugene's entanglements are many: his art, his business career, his relations with friends and women and himself have all become snarled. But one conflict has been common to them all—between conventionality and independence, the strangle hold of custom and the liberations of free action. This is the controlling theme of *The "Genius,"* whose thickly autobiographical stretches made for some of Dreiser's shrillest and also some of his most movingly impassioned writing, revealing how critical this theme was for him. Here the conflict is dramatized in parallel actions. Both the struggles between Eugene and his wife Angela and between Suzanne Dale and her mother are presented as inescapable clashes between fiercely independent and fiercely conventional personalities. Eugene is an artist, "pagan to the core"; Suzanne is possessed of "hard anarchic, unsocial thoughts." Angela and Mrs. Dale are managing types, who try implacably to discipline the two rebels as they have themselves been disciplined by their middle-class culture. Eventually Suzanne yields to her mother, in a denouement shaped more to Dreiser's past than to his characters', but the novelist's sympathies are overwhelmingly behind Eugene's struggle to be free.

The widowed Mrs. Dale, rich, of a famous New York family, owns many houses but prefers Daleview, the ancestral estate on Staten Island overlooking Manhattan and the harbor. Eugene is an occasional guest there until his passion erupts for Suzanne, whose mother then forbids him to enter the great house. The would-be lovers resolve to live privately in a studio, but the dream never materializes. Compelled to announce this plan, they are shocked to discover how vehemently Mrs. Dale and Angela react against it. The compromise with conventionality they looked to quickly vanishes; to enter society is to surrender one's freedom.

Because Eugene is "a painter," the secret room he conspires to share with Suzanne is to be a "studio"; but the word is also their attempt to romanticize a meeting-place for illicit love. The secret room in the other novels has less glamor, is usually a flat in an apartment-house or an apartment in a private dwelling. But whether as the comfortable place Drouet finds for Carrie on the West Side of Chicago, the ampler suite on the North Side where Lester Kane installs Jennie, or the old-fashioned bedroom Roberta rents at Clyde's insistence in Lycurgus, the room always lays claim to reputability. Of none is this truer than the Philadelphia chamber to which Frank Cowperwood is reduced to taking Aileen Butler, in a house of assignation. There the red-brick façade trimmed in white stone and the furnishings of the lovers' room ("showy but cleanly," parading the "commonplace idea of luxury which then prevailed") protest the respectability of the establishment, even as the Pinkertons (in the name of an implacable law) force the proprietress to reveal the whereabouts of the lovers. Even in their utmost conspiracy against the Mansion, the rebels still submit to the values it inspires.

Inside the room, moreover, the lovers are themselves divided in spirit. In that "Paradise" they love wildly, and they worry. For various reasons and in varying degrees they are shackled to the world of conventional opinion, at the same time that they pursue or drift into passion. Rejoicing in every "concealing, rewarding feverish night" with Roberta, while their clandestine affair is still young, Clyde thinks continually of his truly privileged relatives, the Griffiths, "and all they represented in his life and that of the city. Their great house closed and silent, except for gardeners and an occasional chauffeur or servant visible as he walked from time to time past the place, was the same as a shrine to him, nearly—the symbol of that height to which by some turn of fate he might still hope to attain." One day after her affair begins with Drouet, Carrie looks in the mirror (a sign, as in Hawthorne, that we are about to witness the truth). There "she saw a prettier Carrie than she had seen before; she looked into her mind, a mirror prepared of her own and the world's opinions, and saw a worse." The statement which follows defines Carrie's predicament and that of the other lovers: "Between these two images she wavered, hesitating which to believe."

The word "believe" seems to sound the one uncharacteristic note. For Dreiser's heroines and heroes are not really concerned with belief; but they think they are. They think that if only they can perceive the truth, can make the right decision, they will escape their predicaments. They are astonishing rationalists, true Americans, true Europeans. Whereas the objective fact about them is, Dreiser insists, that they "drift" or plunge as the great universal forces shove them from within or without. Their entrapment within the city is a spectacle for philosophic deliberation—but also for rejoicing. In Dreiser these moods are not easily separable: his fiction, even the meanest of it, is so impressive because he could link the particular swelling of emotion to general causes. But his fiction stirs us, as that of few other American writers can do, mainly because he celebrates natural human feeling. He has never been convinced of its inherent rightness, he simply *assumes* it. Dreiser is, in this respect, genuinely an innocent, as all of his heroes and heroines are innocents. He is aware of disastrous results, but not of evil. He is utterly secular, utterly profane, withal a transcendentalist.

Carrie's secret room in Chicago overlooks a park, Jennie's is near the lake. The touches are incidental, but not wholly so. Living close to nature is what the secret room offers, a nature interior but with its outward correspondences. Long passages near the beginning of her novel tell of Jennie Gerhardt's affinities with the natural world. "Where the sunlight was warm and the shadows flecked with its splendid radiance she delighted to wonder at the pattern of it, to walk where it was most golden, and follow with instinctive appreciation the holy corridors of the trees." Of all Dreiser's women she is the most saintlike, is in fact entirely a saint. Seeing her family in want, she accepts with few misgivings a surreptitious life with Lester that will eliminate that want. Some of the other lovers are a good deal more conscience-ridden, for example Roberta Alden, but they are all presented as innately good individuals. Even Frank Cowperwood's drive for power and Eugene Witla's for success are essentially ingenuous. They are creatures of Emerson's imagination, and of Whitman's.

But though they are not corrupted by society, as Emerson's were, they are painfully coerced by it. In Dreiser there is none of Emerson's sense that the individual can rise superior to society, not even in the manipulative career of Cowperwood, who is repeatedly struck down, thwarted, and only fleetingly through his money ventures manages to establish any clear relationship to a world outside himself; nor is there any sense as in Whitman that the individual can fuse his experience with that of any human group. Dreiser's individual is always at bottom adrift in the metropolis. He can only salvage some part of what he is born with, his emotive nature, and hope to give it spasmodic expression. His desire is not to be self-reliant but to be free; not to fulfill himself through adventure, in the manner of the Romantic hero, but to preserve some passional identity. So it is that sexual relations become diluted in Dreiser's fiction from pure ends into means as well, largely meaningless for the women and sometimes compulsive for the men. The love that begins in feeling ends in fear—of the "world's opinion." And that opinion, in the guise of conscience, easily invades the secret room. Conscience, in Dreiser's view, is absolutely social: Carrie's is constructed of "past environment, habit, convention." The Pinkertons need not tap at the door; the Mansion need only exist, and exert its overwhelming appeal.

In Dreiser's cities that is the function of the Mansion: to stand resplendently, to epitomize success, which is to say the approval of the existing social order. Whatever increase in freedom it seems to promise is largely illusory, as Clyde Griffiths discovers inside the Finchleys' home. The servility the Finchley world demands and its fundamental coldness are wonderfully evoked by the scene in the big kitchen one night when Clyde, seated at a servants' table by Sondra, stares wild-eyed at the rich display of pots and pans and silver service. His dalliance there with the daughter of the mansion is entirely chaste, "without lust, just the desire to constrain and fondle a perfect object." Meanwhile, the pagan Roberta lies in her room across the city; yet life with her offers no clear-cut alternative. Indeed the very character of the secret room foretells the outcome: *it too belongs to the city.* The pagans cannot make love under the elms or on the beach; to live according to nature they must occupy a room. And having surrendered so much of nature to custom, they find they must give up still more. Passion leads to Roberta's pregnancy, to Eugene's exhaustion, and in the web of social convention in the city these also become snares.

But one cannot live outside the city. Dreiser sees small-town or rural life for the most part as "narrow," and pushes it away toward the edge of his fiction. That average human beings should be lured to the city and trapped there—that is the dilemma. And while aspects of their travail draw from Dreiser a certain pleasure and thoughtfulness, the spectacle as a whole arouses chiefly his involved, compassionate regret. Dreiser bears comparison with Conrad and Hardy at many points, but above all in this; and in this he contrasts sharply with Lawrence, whose obsessive fear that passion would be killed in the modern world resembles Dreiser's in some respects but whose aloofness from his characters differs conspicuously from Dreiser's helpless identification with them. For all Dreiser's naïveté and because of it, he manages to convey the incredible poignance of lives in which feelings always overflow the vessels built to contain them, in which the deeper passions are always being channeled and dammed up. "O burning human appetite and desire on every hand!" In the city desire is increased, made furtive, and finally destroyed. And there is no way out.

The Romantic Dilemma

Richard Lehan*

Dreiser was caught between a world of dreams and a world of reality. He worked hard for social change and yet for most of his life he believed that man was the victim of an environment over which he had no control. As a romantic, he believed that it was possible for him to pursue an idealized self. As a Spencerian naturalist and later as a mechanist, he also believed that he functioned within fixed and prescribed limits. The contradictions in Dreiser's thinking would even be greater if Herbert Spencer's philosophy were not so highly romantic, if Spencer himself had not tried before him to reconcile the romantic and naturalistic mind.

Dreiser began reading Spencer in the summer of 1894 when he was a reporter on the Pittsburgh *Dispatch*. Spencer's *First Principles* (the introductory volume to *Synthetic Philosophy*) "quite blew me, intellectually, to bits," says Dreiser.[1] One can imagine the young Dreiser, totally unfamiliar with the complex problems of metaphysics and science, having trouble with Spencer's writing. *First Principles* is not an easy book to read, and the fact that Dreiser read it—and supposedly profited from the reading—proves how eagerly he must have been looking for answers to his religious questions. Certainly, Spencer would have been talking to him on an emotional as well as an intellectual level because Dreiser would find in Spencer's writings just what he wanted to find.

Spencer begins *First Principles* by questioning the logic of religious absolutists, those who cannot conceive of a self-existent universe and yet insist that a self-existent creator is at the source of the universe.[2] Spencer was not, however, directly attacking religion but was trying, in part, to reconcile religion with science. He insisted that an "Inscrutable Power" existed and that its presence was "manifested to us through all phenomena."[3] Like the romantics, he believed in a "Reality which is behind the veil of appearance,"[4] was concerned with how this "Reality" could be perceived and interpreted, and insisted that "our knowledge of the external world can be but phenomenal . . . the things of which we are conscious are appearances."[5]

*Reprinted from *Theodore Dreiser: His World and His Ideas* (Carbondale: Southern Illinois University Press, 1969), pp. 45–53. Copyright © 1969 by Southern Illinois University Press. Reprinted by permission of Southern Illinois University Press.

Physical matter thus holds the secrets of life—a romantic idea; but at this point Spencer begins to deviate from romantic thought. He maintains first that matter "is expressed in terms of the quality of chemical force it exerts."[6] Motion thus becomes force, and Spencer's real concern is describing the various forces which are in conflict for "any force manifested implies an equal antecedent force from which it is derived, and against which it is a reaction."[7]

Since an action engenders a reaction, force is constant, and matter is in constant motion. The sun's heat will raise vapor to a height at which it condenses and falls as rain, the rain being in direct relation to the gravitational force the sun's heat overcame in raising the atoms of water to a condensation point. Spencer uses this example to illustrate how two opposite forces (the heat of the sun and the temperature of the atmosphere) are here at work, interacting upon the other, and the effect of the two producing the chemical reaction we call rain.

If matter in motion is really chemical force at work, and if man is composed of matter, then man too must be controlled by chemical force. By this logic, Spencer destroys the religious definition of man and reduces him to a chemical organism. In fact, Spencer believes that intelligence in man is directly related to "the proportion of phosphorous present in the brain" which is at a minimum "in infancy, old age and idiocy, and the greatest during the prime of life."[8]

Dreiser's use of Spencer's ideas led him directly into the romantic dilemma. Dreiser maintained, on the one hand, that man is "incurably romantic" and that "it is only by acting in the name of . . . an ideal that . . . [the ideal] is brought to pass."[9] On the other hand, he also maintained, unaware that he was contradicting himself, that man could not realize his ideals because "at his best he is a product of heat and gases generated in amazing variety by so infinitesimal a thing as the sun" and that man is born "to desire that which he has not" and to press "pathetically against his wretched limitations, wishing always to know more and more, and as constantly being denied."[10]

Dreiser's inability to reconcile his romantic aspirations with his belief in a world of physical limits led in his fiction to the displaced hero—the man whose desire for essential self-fulfillment is in conflict with his environment. A destructive principle inheres in Dreiser's thinking: man is born to yearn and desire, and yet he lives in a world of limits. He is born to be one step behind himself, urged on by desire; and yet such struggle brings into operation a destructive counter-force. He believes he is independent, a creature of free will; and yet he is a mere tool of his appetites, of physical needs, of other men, and of the universe. Dreiser, in short, believed that man was a creature of illusion, who longed for an ideal commitment in a world where force and circumstance canceled out ideals.

Since man is composed of matter, he is very much a part of a mechanistic and chemical process. "With a gloomy eye," Dreiser wrote, "I began to watch how the chemical—and their children, the mechanical forces operated through man and outside him."[11] Man was a part of a bitter struggle, of which he had no real understanding. Life fed on life—the animals lived off each other and men lived off the animals—and Dreiser never abandoned his belief in this "law of life," even though he wavered on whether or not this happened by accident or by design, whether the force had or did not have an intelligence behind it.

Dreiser's early free-lance writing documents his belief that life is based upon combat. In a newspaper article on swordfishing (July 24, 1904), he talked of the fisherman to whom "the sea is a vast opposing force," wherein swordfish "so eagerly and relentlessly pursued by men, in turn are savagely and relentlessly pursuing other fish, and these are in turn pursuing others, until the smallest is reached, and the evidence of the strife becomes indiscernible."[12] He used the same metaphor in an essay for *Tom Watson's Magazine*, "A Lesson from the Aquarium" (January, 1906) and, of course, used it once again at the beginning of *The Financier*. If we are not aware that life feeds on life, Dreiser maintained, it is because the big meat producers do the slaughtering. In "Our Red Slayer," he described a man in tarpaulin, stabbing animals in the throat so they would bleed to death as they came along a conveyor belt. "We have been flattering ourselves," Dreiser concluded, "that our civilization has somehow got away from this old-time law of life living on death, but here . . . stands our salaried red man who murders our victims for us."[13]

Like Spencer, Dreiser came to believe in the law of conflicting forces. His world was a realm of forces at war, a realm of opposites. One thing is known by its opposite, and opposites set the limits of human conduct. Life becomes a tug-of-war, and all matter is in a process of action and reaction. Man finds himself caught in a mechanistic process where he is both pulling and being pulled from a fixed center of energy—fixed to the extent that the balance of power (once it has been established) is never destroyed. This is Spencer's theory of the "suspended equation." Dreiser directly acknowledged Spencer when he discussed this principle in *A Book About Myself*,[14] and he indirectly acknowledged Spencer in his early writings. In one of his *Ev'ry Month* essays, for example, he described a major New York social event, the Bradley Martin Ball, where "representatives of half the wealth of New York were on the floor" and where glamorous personalities arrived, amidst "the throng of gay carriages . . . the swish of silk, and the sound of music." At this point, however, Dreiser began to question the imbalance of wealth and wondered why so many were "without and miserable." He concluded with an idea straight from Spencer—that one extreme would and should (Dreiser here became exhortative) engender its opposite: "There is a general feeling," he warned, "that life should be equally balanced. Nearly everyone feels that such wide contrasts between extreme luxury and extreme poverty are a little bit odd."[15]

The language here reveals that Dreiser was talking for the "people."
He goes on, in this issue of *Ev'ry Month*, to suggest that the people,
represented by Clarence Lexow, would seriously limit the power, wealth,
and privileges of both Tammany Hall and the Trusts, that a counter-
influence was finally being asserted, and that Lexow's struggle would
bring the very rich (of which there were few) and the very poor (of which
there were many) into a realm of greater "balance."[16] Like many of his
contemporaries, Dreiser applied Spencer's law of conflicting forces to
social as well as natural processes. The great men of economic and
political power reached a certain point at which they brought into operation a series of counter-forces that arrested their advancement. Dreiser
believed that extreme wealth was a corollary to extreme poverty, that the
rich could not exist without the poor. As some men became wealthy, other
men by necessity became poor. Money, like energy, had fixed limits, and
the rich and the poor lived in an inverse ratio to each other. Forces within
nature and society were in furious combat. All matter was in constant motion, setting its own limits through a process of action and reaction.
"Great forces are at work," Dreiser said, "strong ones, and our little lives
are but a shadow of something that wills activity."[17] Even the box cars
that fascinated Dreiser as they went streaming into the night were a part
of this process, held together in fact by atoms—with a "central spicule of
positive energy about which revolve at great speed lesser spicules of
negative energy"—so that the cars are "as alive as life," "their journeys" a
proper symbol of man's "equally restless" nature.[18]

Man's restlessness reflected the flux of life itself. Man was never at
one with himself or with his environment. His desires were always one
step ahead of his achievements—desires that were limited only by the
reality of death. Like all matter, man had limits, was caught in the flux of
growth and decay, and lived in a world of change. Change, in fact,
proved that life was in motion, that opposites canceled each other out,
that the new replaced the old. Sensitive to beauty in the commonplace,
Dreiser saw a flock of pigeons in flight as a symbol of life in perpetual motion—hence perpetual change:

> I have seen them [the pigeons] at morning, when the sky
> was like silver. . . . I have seen them again at evening, wheel-
> ing and turning. . . . [I have seen them] in the sunset, against
> the . . . storm clouds, when the turn of a wing made them
> look like a handful of snowflakes . . . I have watched them
> soaring . . . running like children, laughing down the wind.[19]

The churn of the sea also became a symbol of life in flux, man caught in
the process of change. Dreiser would stare out from the New York docks,
watch ocean liners move into the Atlantic, and see in the scene both life's
beauty and "the tang of change and decay . . . the gradual passing of all
things—yourself—myself—all."[20]

Dreiser was obviously riding the high crest of romanticism. The impermanence of man, his insignificance in the face of time, his inability to arrest the moment—all of these themes run through romantic poetry, and Dreiser was just as overcome by nostalgia—by the passage of time—as a Keats or a Shelley. We can see this in an essay like "A Vanished Seaside Resort." We can see it again in the *Ev'ry Month* article in which Dreiser, echoing Shelley's "Ozymandias," pondered the mutability of man.

> You see a great temple stand, and it looks permanent. . . .
> But . . . when it crumbles you realize it is only frail stonework
> after all.[21]

A *Hoosier Holiday* is, of course, an exercise in nostalgia, Dreiser visiting the Indiana of his youth; and so, in part, is A *Traveller at Forty*, particularly the moving scene in which Dreiser visits the medieval town of Mayen, Germany, his father's birthplace. Dreiser also wrote a long essay, never published to my knowledge, in which he contrasted old and new New York—and regretted the change. "There was a time (1896 to 1910) when New York seemed to put its best foot forward. It had a smart air. The principal streets were trim and elegant. Today it has a sloppy and down-at-the-heels look."[22]

Since man is limited by time, success becomes a tenuous matter. Not only does the energy used in attaining it feed upon itself, leaving one vulnerable in a world where life destroys life, but even at the moment of greatest success the skull is still just beneath the skin. One seemingly rises to fall. The pattern of rise and fall, the journey from success to failure, obsessed Dreiser from his very earliest days. In one of his early essays, "Whence the Song" (December, 1900), Dreiser described a young song writer's climb to the top and then his descent, until at last "a black boat steaming northward along the East River to a barren island and a field of weeds carries the last of all that was so gay . . . of him who was the greatest in his world."[23]

A Potter's Field burial, like that of Hurstwood's, horrified Dreiser; and he saw in Hurstwood a man whose fate could have been his own father's, his brother Rome's, his brother-in-law Hopkins', or his own. Hurstwood was a projection of his secret and unexpressed fear of what might yet await him. No one was safe from a sudden reversal of fate. In another essay, Dreiser again charted the career of a young man—a millionaire piano manufacturer named Weber—who arose "from obscurity, through gilded and flittering resorts, into the asylum and the Potter's field." His concern was again with those "unnamed" buried in Potter's Field, which he described as "the driftwood from the wrecks upon the surging sea of yonder metropolitan life."[24] If the city was a place of wonder and opportunity, it was also a place of fear and failure.

Since Dreiser was obsessed with the theme of man's limits—of energy as fixed matter and of failure as something built into the pursuit of success—it is not surprising that he worked this theme into his first novel,

Sister Carrie. The story of Carrie is a necessary corollary to the story of George Hurstwood: the energy that Carrie used in driving to the top is in inverse relation to the momentum Hurstwood lost in his fall to the gutter. Dreiser carefully leaves Carrie's fate undisclosed: she had not yet reached the limits that will reverse the pendulum swing of her career. Carrie embodies the spirit of youthful aspiration, Hurstwood the spirit of middle-aged desperation: their two stories together reveal the pattern of all life.

Even the superman has limits. While he may try to rise above the ordinary man—may lust for inordinate wealth and power, may feel he is beyond good and evil—the masses will restrain him with their more ordinary lives and with their rigid moral values. Whether one is as seemingly self-sufficient as Frank Algernon Cowperwood or as seemingly helpless as George Hurstwood, he functions within the limits of these dynamics. All men live within circumscribed contexts, contexts which are the result of antithetical forces at work.

Just as the swing of two pendulums may be different—the arc of one higher than the other—the very swing of the pendulum away from its center produces in both an equal force in the opposite direction. Both Cowperwood and Hurstwood broke conventions in their pursuit after money and pleasure, and both became the victim of rigid conventionality. While their lives are vastly different, while the pendulum swing of their careers follows a different arc, their fates prove a common principle is at work when they both become the victims of Spencer's "equivalence of forces."

What went up had to come down, and Dreiser came to believe that some day in America there would be social and economic "equity" (an important word in his lexicon). And what was generally was also individually true. One had only so much energy, and at some point even the rich and powerful reached a limit in their upward drive and began the downward trip that ended in death. This is the reason that Dreiser told the complete story of Frank Algernon Cowperwood's life—from birth to death, from the moment he started to acquire his fortune to the time the fortune was dissipated after his death.

Dreiser's characters were the victims of the romantic dilemma: they yearned after the infinite while they were restrained by the physical; their genius was negated in the play of forces; their aspirations were in conflict with time; and their ideals were in conflict with society. Once Dreiser accepted Spencer's theory that man was mere matter, the motives of his characters became conditioned impulses and their dreams were negated on the lowest level of chemical play. Once the artist accepted the values of the tycoon, he became schizophrenic. Shelley and Babbitt, Thoreau and Yerkes, warred inside Dreiser, while cosmic and social forces warred outside.

Out of Dreiser's romantic dilemma came the displaced hero: the man who has a place in the world but cannot find it. He lives in a world where men prey on each other, where strength and subtlety are all important, and where law and justice are often used by selfish men to restrain those who oppose them. He unwittingly aspires to goals that are transient and beyond his grasp. He is never satisfied with his origins—his family or his present position—and struggles for wealth and recognition. In more sensitive moments, he intuits the beauty of life, but this only makes him more discontent with himself and his materialistic society. He is concerned with mutability, with birds in flight, water in motion, and crowded cities where men sweep by like rivers to the sea. He longs for stability but is caught in flux. He is a step behind himself, restless and yet with nowhere to go, duped by his own aspirations. He is, in a word, a victim: a victim of his temperament, a victim of time, a victim of a society that he cannot fully accept or totally reject, a victim of a world that is in constant struggle. Most of all, he is the victim of his romantic illusions: his belief in the possibility of self-fulfillment and purpose when life, in reality, is moving in a furious circle, the center holding all in balance, like a raging whirlpool going nowhere.

Notes

1. *A Book About Myself* (New York, 1922), p. 457.

2. Herbert Spencer, *First Principles* (London, 1893), p. 35.

3. *Ibid.*, p. 108.

4. *Ibid.*, p. 110.

5. *Ibid.*, p. 158.

6. *Ibid.*, p. 179.

7. *Ibid.*, p. 192c.

8. *Ibid.*, p. 215.

9. Theodore Dreiser, "The Realization of an Ideal," *The Color of A Great City* (New York, 1923), p. 108.

10. Theodore Dreiser, "Man and Romance," *Reedy's Mirror*, Aug. 28, 1919, p. 585. This article, which McDonald does not include in his bibliography, can be found among the Dreiser papers at the University of Pennsylvania.

11. *A Book About Myself*, p. 458.

12. Theodore Dreiser, "Hunting for Swordfish," *Sunday Magazine* for July 24, 1904, pp. 11–12, U. of P.

13. Theodore Dreiser, "Our Red Slayer," *The Color of A Great City*, p. 135.

14. See *A Book About Myself*, pp. 457–58.

15. *Ev'ry Month*, March 1, 1897, p. 2.

16. *Ibid.*, p. 3.

17. Theodore Dreiser, "The Beauty of Life," *The Color of A Great City*, p. 170.

18. Theodore Dreiser, "The Car Yard," *The Color of A Great City*, pp. 72–73.

19. Theodore Dreiser, "The Flight of Pigeons," *The Color of A Great City*, p. 74.

20. Theodore Dreiser, "The Waterfront," *The Color of A Great City*, p. 10.

21. *Ev'ry Month*, December 1, 1896, pp. 5–6.

22. Theodore Dreiser, "Greenwich Village," partly handwritten, partly typed manuscript. U. of P.

23. Theodore Dreiser, "Whence the Song," *Harper's Weekly*, December 8, 1900, pp. 1165–66A; reprinted in *The Color of A Great City*, p. 154.

24. *Ev'ry Month*, December 1, 1896, p. 4.

American Literary Naturalism:
The Example of Dreiser

Donald Pizer*

American literary naturalism has almost always been viewed with hostility. During its early years the movement was associated with Continental licentiousness and impiety and was regarded as a literature foreign to American values and interests. "We must stamp out this breed of Norrises," a reviewer of *McTeague* cried in 1899.[1] In our own time, though antagonism to naturalism is expressed more obliquely, it is as deeply rooted. A typical discussion of the movement is frequently along the following lines.[2] The critic will examine the sources of naturalism in late nineteenth-century scientism, in Zola, and in post-Civil War industrial expansion. He will note that to a generation of American writers coming of age in the 1890s the mechanistic and materialistic beliefs of contemporary science appeared to be confirmed by American social reality and to have been successfully applied to the writing of fiction by Zola. But he will also note that Stephen Crane, Frank Norris, and Theodore Dreiser were often muddled in their thinking and inept in their fiction, and he will attribute these failures to their unfortunate absorption of naturalistic attitudes and beliefs. Our typical critic will then discover a second major flowering of naturalism in the fiction of James T. Farrell, John Steinbeck, and John Dos Passos in the 1930s. He will remark that scientism has been replaced by Marxism and that the thinking of this generation of naturalists is not so much confused as doctrinaire, but his account of their work will still be governed by the assumption that naturalism is a regrettable strain in modern American literary history.

Indeed, the underlying metaphor in most accounts of American fiction is that naturalism is a kind of taint or discoloration, without which the writer would be more of an artist and through which the critic must penetrate if he is to discover the essential nature and worth of the writer. So those writers who most clearly appear to be naturalists, such as Dreiser and Farrell, are almost always praised for qualities which are distinct from their naturalism. We are thus told that Dreiser's greatness is not in

*Reprinted from *Studies in American Fiction*, 5 (Spring, 1977), 51–63. Reprinted by permission of *Studies in American Fiction*.

144

his naturalism[3] and that he is most of all an artist when least a philosopher.[4] And so the obvious and powerful thread of naturalism in such major figures as Hemingway, Faulkner, and (closer to our own time) Saul Bellow is almost always dismissed as an irrelevant and distracting characteristic of their work.

This continuing antagonism to naturalism has several root causes. One of the clearest is that many critics find naturalistic belief morally repugnant. But whereas earlier critics stated openly their view that naturalism was invalid because man was as much a creature of divine spirit as animal substance, the more recent critic is apt to express his hostility indirectly by claiming that naturalistic novelists frequently violate the deterministic creed which supposedly informs their work and are therefore inconsistent or incoherent naturalists. On one hand, this concern with philosophical consistency derives from the naturalist writer's interest in ideas and is therefore a justifiable critical interest. On the other, there seems little doubt that many critics delight in seeking out the philosophically inadequate in naturalistic fiction because man is frequently portrayed in this fiction as irredeemably weak and deluded and yet as not responsible for his condition. It is the rare work of fiction of any time in which threads of free will and determinism do not interweave in a complex pattern that can be called incoherent or inconsistent; on strictly logical grounds man either has free will or he does not. Yet it is principally the naturalistic novel which is damned for this quality, which suggests that it is the weighting of this inconsistency toward an amoral determinism—not its mere presence—that is at stake.[5]

Another source of the hostility of modern critics to the naturalistic novel lies in recent American political history. American naturalism of the 1890s was largely apolitical, but in the 1930s the movement was aligned with the left wing in American politics and often specifically with the Communist Party. In the revulsion against the Party which swept the literary community during the 1940s and 1950s, it was inevitable that naturalistic fiction of the 1930s would be found wanting because the naturalists of that decade, it was now seen, had so naively embraced some form of communist belief. The most influential critical discussions of American naturalism during the 1940s and 1950s—Philip Rahv's "Notes on the Decline of American Naturalism," Malcolm Cowley's "A Natural History of American Naturalism," and Lionel Trilling's "Reality in America"[6]—have as an underlying motive a desire to purge American literature and its historiography of an infatuation with an alien and destructive political ideal.

A final reason for the antagonism toward naturalistic fiction is that several generations of academic critics have been attracted by an increasingly refined view of the aesthetic complexity of fiction. They have believed that a novel must above all be organic—that is, the product of a romantic imagination—and they have found principally in the work of

Hawthorne, Melville, Faulkner, and to a lesser extent James, that enlargement of metaphor into symbol and that interplay of irony and ambivalence which bring fiction close to the complex indirection of a metaphysical lyric. Stephen Crane is the only naturalistic writer whose fiction satisfies these expectations, and his work is generally held to be uncharacteristic of the non-artistry of a movement more adequately represented by Dreiser.[7]

I do not wish to suggest by this brief survey of the critical biases which have led to the inadequate examination of American naturalism that there are not naturalistic novels which are muddled in conception and inept in execution. But just as we have long known that the mind-set of an early nineteenth-century critic would little prepare him to come to grips with the essential nature and form of a romantic poem, so we are coming to realize that a generation of American critics has approached American literary naturalism with beliefs about man and art which have frequently distorted rather than cast light upon the object before them.

Theodore Dreiser is the author whose work and career most fulfill the received notion of American naturalism; indeed, it is often difficult to determine the demarcation between literary history and critical biography in general discussions of American naturalism, so completely is Dreiser as thinker and writer identified with the movement in America. It would be instructive, therefore, to test the example of Dreiser—to note, initially and briefly, those characteristics of his career and work which lead us to describe him as a naturalist; and then, more fully, to examine some of the naturalistic elements in his fiction. But unlike so much of the criticism of naturalism which I have been describing, I do not wish to undertake this test with the assumption that Dreiser's fiction is confused in theme and form because he is not a consistent naturalist or that his work is best when he is least naturalistic. In short, I do not wish to consider his naturalism as an unfortunate excrescence. Rather, I want to see how his naturalistic predispositions work in his fiction and whether or not they work successfully.

Dreiser was born an outsider. His parents were of Catholic, German-speaking immigrant stock and throughout Dreiser's youth the large family was agonizingly poor. As a young man Dreiser sought the success and position which his parents had lacked and also shed the religious and moral beliefs which, he believed, had appeared to shackle them. While a young reporter in Pittsburgh in the early 1890s, he found his deepest responses to life confirmed by his reading of Herbert Spencer and Balzac. There were, he believed, no discernible supernatural agencies in life, and man was not the favored creature of divine guidance but an insignificant unit in a universe of natural forces. Although these forces, whether biological or social, were the source of racial progress, they often crushed the individual within their mechanistic processes. Like many of his generation, Dreiser found that the observed realities of American society supported this theory of existence. The mills and libraries of Pittsburgh were evidence of progress, but the lives of the immigrant foundry workers—to say nothing of the lives of Dreiser's own errant sisters and brothers—appeared dwarfed and ephemeral compared with the grinding and impersonal power of a vast economic system and a great city. Yet the city itself, as Balzac had amply demonstrated, was exciting and alluring, and not all were crushed who sought to gain its wonders. In *Sister Carrie* Dreiser was to write, "Among the forces which sweep and play throughout the universe, untutored man is but a wisp in the wind."[8] But though Hurstwood is swept away by these forces, and though Carrie's career is that of a storm-tossed ship, Carrie survives and indeed grows in understanding by the close of the novel. So accompanying Dreiser's endorsement of an amoral determinism there exists a disconcerting affirmation of the traditionally elevating in life—of Carrie, for example, as a figure of "emotional greatness," that is, of imaginative power. Forty-five years after *Sister Carrie* Dreiser joined the Communist Party while celebrating in his last two novels the intuitive mysticism at the heart of Quaker and Hindu belief. Here, in brief, at the two poles of his career and work is the infamous intellectual muddle of Dreiser and, by extension, of naturalism itself. And this muddle appears to be matched by a corresponding lack of control and firmness in fictional technique. Dreiser documents his social scene with a pseudo-scientific detachment yet overindulges in personal philosophical disquisitions; he attempts to write a "fine" style but produces journalistic cliché and awkwardness.

So in most important ways Dreiser fulfills the conventional definition of the American naturalist. All the major paradoxes are present: his identification with the "outsider," which was to lead to a contemptuous view of the main stream of middle class American life, yet his lifelong worship of "success"; his acceptance of a "scientific" mechanistic theory of natural law as a substitute for traditional views of individual insight and moral responsibility, yet his affirmation of many of these traditional views; and his deep response to a major European novelist, including the form of his fiction, yet his seeming neglect of style and form. I cannot hope to discuss these major characteristics of Dreiser as a naturalist as each appears in his eight novels. But I can pursue the vital naturalistic theme of mechanistic determinism in two of his principal novels, *Jennie Gerhardt* and *An American Tragedy*, and thereby reach toward at least a modest understanding of the example of Dreiser.[9]

Dreiser began *Jennie Gerhardt* in early 1901, soon after the publication of *Sister Carrie*. He wrote most of the novel during the next two years, though he did not complete it until late 1910. Like *Sister Carrie*, *Jennie Gerhardt* is about a girl from a poor family who has several sexual affairs with men of higher station but who emerges from her adventures not only unsullied but also elevated in character and insight. The novel differs from *Sister Carrie* primarily in Dreiser's characterization of Jennie and of Lester Kane, the principal man in Jennie's life. Kane, at least on the surface, is a more powerful, successful, and contemplative figure than Hurstwood, and Jennie differs from Carrie in that she is a warm and generous giver rather than a taker.

In the course of the novel, Jennie is seduced first by Senator Brander, by whom she has a child, Vesta, and then by Lester Kane. She and Kane are attracted to each other by a powerful natural "affinity" and they live together contentedly for several years. But because Lester is gradually forced to accept that a permanent union with Jennie would adversely affect his business career and the comfortable certainties of his social and family life, they do not marry. Eventually they part, Lester marries Letty Gerald, a woman of his own class, and Jennie suffers the death of both her father and Vesta.

One of the major scenes in *Jennie Gerhardt* is Lester's visit to Jennie after the death of Vesta. Deeply depressed by Vesta's death and by his realization that he erred in leaving Jennie, Lester tells her

> it isn't myself that's important in this transaction [that is, life itself] apparently; the individual doesn't count much in the situation. I don't know whether you see what I'm driving at, but all of us are more or less pawns. We're moved about like chessmen by circumstances over which we have no control.[10]

This famous pronouncement, which has supplied several generations of literary historians with a ubiquitous image for the philosophical center of American naturalism, requires careful analysis both in its immediate context and in relation to the novel as a whole if it is to be properly understood.

Whatever the general truth of Lester's words, they represent a personal truth. His pawn image expresses both his sense of ineffectuality in the face of the central dilemma of his life and a covert supernaturalism which has characterized his thought throughout the novel despite his overt freethinking. Earlier he had attributed his difficulties merely to bad luck. But by the time he and Jennie separate, he has elevated and generalized "fate" into a specific force which is at once social, supernatural, and (as far as he is concerned) malevolent:

> It was only when the storms set in and the winds of adversity blew and he found himself facing the armed forces of convention that he realized he might be mistaken as to the value of his personality, that his private desires and opinions were as nothing in the face of a public conviction; that he was wrong. The race spirit, or social avatar, the "Zeitgeist," as the Germans term it, manifested itself as something having a system in charge, and the organization of society began to show itself to him as something based on possibly a spiritual, or, at least, supernatural counterpart (pp. 373–74).

Lester's speculative statement that men are but pawns in the control of circumstances is thus in part an explanation and a defense of his own conduct. In particular, it is a disguised apology to Jennie for his failure to marry her when he could have done so. But it is also a powerful means of characterizing Lester. Throughout his life he had lived for the moment and had postponed making decisions about the direction of his life. But the decisionless flow of time contained an impetus of events which constituted an implicit and irreversible decision, and when Lester at last awoke to the fact that his life had been decided for him, he bitterly and angrily blamed fate.

Because Lester is a perceptive and on the whole an honest figure, his belief that men are pawns involves more than a rationalization of his own indecisiveness and ineffectuality. His belief also aptly characterizes social reality as that reality has been dramatized in the novel. The pressure of circumstances on Lester in his relationship with Jennie has indeed been intense, from their initial meeting within the convention of a seduction—a convention which appeared to preclude marriage—to the later opposition of Lester's personal, business, and socials worlds to the continuation of the relationship. In a passage cut from Chapter XL of the final holograph of the novel, Dreiser himself, as narrator, echoed Lester's attribution of superhuman powers to social force. "The conventions in their way," he wrote, "appear to be as inexorable in their workings as the laws of gravitation and expansion. There is a drift to society as a whole which pushes us on in a certain direction, careless of the individual, concerned only with the general result."[11]

In his final position as one deeply puzzled by the insignificance of the individual, Lester therefore reflects a persistent strain in Dreiser's thought. Before making his pawn speech to Jennie, Lester had "looked down into Dearborn Street, the world of traffic below holding his attention. The great mass of trucks and vehicles, the counter streams of hurrying pedestrians, seemed like a puzzle. So shadows march in a dream" (p. 400). The scene effectively images both Lester's and Dreiser's belief that life is a helter-skelter of activity without meaning either for its observers or for the "shadows" who give it motion. As a man aware of the direction of modern thought, Lester is able to give this view of life an appropriate philosophical framework. In the years that pass after Vesta's death, his response to life, Dreiser tells us, becomes "decidedly critical":

> He could not make out what it was all about. In distant ages a queer thing had come to pass. There had started on its way in the form of evolution a minute cellular organism which had apparently reproduced itself by division, had early learned to combine itself with others, to organize itself into bodies, strange forms of fish, animals, and birds, and had finally learned to organize itself into man. Man, on his part, composed as he was of self-organizing cells, was pushing himself

> forward into comfort and different aspects of existence by
> means of union and organization with other men. Why?
> Heaven only knew. . . . Why should he complain, why
> worry, why speculate?—the world was going steadily forward
> of its own volition, whether he would or no. Truly it was (pp.
> 404–05).

It must not be assumed, however, that Lester's pessimistic response
to the "puzzle" of man's role in a mechanistic world is Dreiser's principal
and only philosophical theme in *Jennie Gerhardt*. For Jennie, though not
Lester's equal in formal knowledge or in experience, is his equal in the
"bigness" of her responsiveness to the underlying reality of life, and she
discovers not only puzzlement and frustration in life but also an in-
eradicable beauty. Dreiser therefore follows his comments on Lester's
critical outlook with an account of Jennie's final evaluation of life. This
evaluation, because of its source and its strategic location, has significance
equal to Lester's beliefs. Jennie, Dreiser writes,

> had never grasped the nature and character of specialized
> knowledge. History, physics, chemistry, botany, geology, and
> sociology were not fixed departments in her brain as they were
> in Lester's and Letty's. Instead there was the feeling that the
> world moved in some strange, unstable way. Apparently no
> one knew clearly what it was all about. People were born and
> died. Some believed that the world had been made six thou-
> sand years before; some that it was millions of years old. Was it
> all blind chance or was there some guiding intelligence—a
> God? Almost in spite of herself she felt that there must be
> something—a higher power which produced all the beautiful
> things—the flowers, the stars, the trees, the grass. Nature was
> so beautiful! If at times life seemed cruel, yet this beauty still
> persisted. The thought comforted her; she fed upon it in her
> hours of secret loneliness (p. 405).

Jennie and Lester's complementary views of life represent Dreiser's
own permanent unresolved conception of the paradox of existence. To
both figures the world "was going steadily forward of its own volition,"
apparently guided by some unknowable power. Individuals counted for
little in this process, but individuals of different temperaments might respond to the mechanism of life in different ways. One kind of temperament might be bitter and despairing, another might affirm the beauty
which was inseparable from the inexplicable mystery of life. It has frequently been noted that Dreiser himself held both views at different stages
of his career—that he stressed a cruelly indifferent mechanistic universe
in *Hey Rub-a-Dub-Dub* (1920) and a mechanistic world of beauty in *The
Bulwark* (1946). It has not been as fully realized that he held the two positions simultaneously as well as consecutively and that he gave each position equal weight and dramatic expression in *Jennie Gerhardt* without

resolving their "discrepancy." For to Dreiser there was no true discrepancy; there was only the reality of distinctive temperaments which might find truth in each position or, as in his own case, of a temperament which might find an element of truth in both. Dreiser's infamous philosophical inconsistency is thus frequently a product of his belief that life is a "puzzle" to which one can respond in different ways, depending on one's makeup and experience.

The naturalistic "philosophy" of deterministic mechanism in Dreiser's novels is therefore usually secondary, within the fictional dynamics of each novel, to the role of the concept as a metaphor of life against which various temperaments can define themselves. Or, to put the matter another way, Lester's belief in one kind of mechanistic philosophy and Jennie's in another are less significant fictionally than the depiction of Jennie as a woman of feeling and of Lester as a man of speculative indecision. But it should also be clear that in attributing a secondary fictional role to the mechanistic center of *Jennie Gerhardt* I am not saying that the philosophy muddles the novel or that the novel is successful for reasons other than the philosophy. I am rather saying that the philosophy and the fiction are one and inseparable. As a late nineteenth-century novelist, Dreiser absorbed and used naturalistic ideas. But he did not do so, at his best, in a way which can be distinguished from his absorption of an understanding of character and of experience in general. It is this unity of understanding and of purpose which gives Dreiser's novels their power. At his most successful, Dreiser embodies in his novels the permanent in life not despite the ideas of his own time but because, like most major artists, he uses the ideas of his own time as living vehicles to express the permanent in man's character and in man's vision of his condition and fate.

Most students of American literature are aware that Dreiser derived the central plot and much of the detail of *An American Tragedy* from the Chester Gillette-Grace Brown murder case of 1906. Less commonly known is that although Dreiser's principal source—the reports of Gillette's trial in the New York *World*—presented him with a wealth of detail about Gillette's life in Cortland (the Lycurgus of the novel) leading up to the murder of Grace Brown, it offered only a few hints about Gillette's experiences before his arrival in that city. Thus, Book One of *An American Tragedy*, which deals with Clyde's early life in Kansas City, is in a sense "invented." Such major events of this portion of the novel as Clyde's sister's pregnancy, his job at the Green-Davidson Hotel, his longing for Hortense, and the automobile accident which concludes the book have no source in Gillette's life.

Because Dreiser in Book One is "inventing" a background for Clyde it is possible to view this section of the novel as the application to fiction of a simplistic deterministic ethic in which the author crudely manufactures hereditary and environmental conditions that will irrevocably propel the protagonist toward his fate. So, in Book One, we are offered Clyde's weak and fuzzy-minded father and coldly moralistic mother. We discover that Clyde is a sensitive youth who longs for the material and sensual pleasures of life but lacks the training, strength, and guile necessary to gain them. Ergo: weakness and desire on the one hand and irresistible attraction yet insurmountable barriers on the other will resolve themselves into an American tragedy.

Dreiser in this opening section of the novel is indeed seeking to introduce the deterministic theme that a young man's nature and early experience can solidify into an inflexible quality of mind which will lead to his destruction. Yet once said this observation is as useless to criticism as the equally true statement that *King Lear* is about the failure and triumph of love. For Dreiser in Book One of *An American Tragedy* is not a simple and simple-minded naturalist applying a philosophical theory to documentary material but rather a subtle fictional craftsman creating out of the imagined concrete details of a life an evocative image of the complex texture of that life.

Clyde's desire for "beauty and pleasure"[12] in Book One is in direct conflict with his parents' religious beliefs and activities, and thus Clyde's dominant impulse from early boyhood is to escape. At fifteen he makes his first major break from his parents' inhospitable mission existence and toward the life he desires when he gets a job as assistant clerk at a drugstore soda fountain. This position, with its accompanying "marvels" of girls, lively talk, and "snappy" dressing, offers a deeply satisfying alternative to the drab religiosity of Clyde's boyhood. He recognizes the appeal of this new world "in a revealing flash":

> You bet he would get out of that now. He would work and save
> his money and be somebody. Decidedly this simple and yet
> idyllic compound of the commonplace had all the luster and
> wonder of a spiritual transfiguration, the true mirage of the
> lost and thirsting and seeking victim of the desert (I, 26).

Dreiser's summary of Clyde's response to the lively worldliness of the soda fountain introduces a theme, and its imagery and tone, which pervades the entire novel. Clyde's need—his thirst—has the power to transform "spiritually" the tawdry and superficial world of the drugstore into the wondrous and exalted. So frequent and compelling is Dreiser's use of "dream" in connection with Clyde's longing that we sometimes fail to realize that his desires also have a basically religious context in which his "dream" is for a "paradise" of wealth and position ruled by a "goddess" of love. Clyde, at this moment of insight at the soda fountain, is truly converted. He has rejected the religion of his parents only to find a different kind of heaven to which he pledges his soul with all the fervor and completeness of his parents' belief. Yet like their "cloudy romance" of a heaven above, Clyde's vision of a "paradise" below is a "true mirage." He has thus not really escaped from his parents, and his initiation into life at the soda fountain and later at the Green-Davidson is no true initiation, for he has merely shifted the nebulous and misdirected longings of his family from the unworldly to the worldly. He still has the naiveté, blindness, and absolute faith of his parents' enthusiasm and belief. And because he is, like them, a true believer, he does not learn from experience and he does not change.

Clyde's job as a bellhop at the Green-Davidson is both an extension and an intensification of his conversion experience at the soda fountain. To Clyde, the hotel is "so glorious an institution" (I, 33), a response which at once reflects the religiosity of its sexual attractions and their embodiment in a powerful social form. The Green-Davidson has both an intrinsic and an extrinsic sexuality. So deep and powerful is Clyde's reaction to its beauty and pleasure—to its moral freedom, material splendor, and shower of tips—that he conceives of the hotel as a youth does his first love. The Green-Davidson to Clyde is softness, warmth, and richness; it has a luxuriousness which he associates with sensuality and position—that is, with all that is desirable in life: "The soft brown carpet under his feet; the soft, cream-tinted walls; the snow-white bowl-lights set in the ceiling—all seemed to him parts of a perfection and a social superiority which was almost unbelievable" (I, 42). "And there was music always—from somewhere" (I, 33). Clyde thus views the hotel both as "a realization of paradise" and as a miraculous gift from Aladdin's lamp, two images of fulfillment which, in their "spiritualizing" of his desires, appropriately constitute the center of his dream life.

But the hotel has a harsh and cruel sexuality in addition to its soft, warm, and "romantic" sensuality. Older women and homosexuals prey on the bellhops, who themselves frequent whores, and the hotel offers many instances of lascivious parties on the one hand and young girls deserted by their seducers on the other. Clyde, because of his repressed sexuality, cannot help responding to this aspect of sex with "fascination" despite his fears and anxieties. The sexual reality of the hotel is thus profoundly ambivalent. Clyde longs above all for the "romance" of sex and for warmth and a sense of union, but the overt sexuality which he in fact encounters is that of hardness, trickery, and deceit—of use and discarding. Both Clyde's unconscious need and his overt mode of fulfillment join in his response to Hortense. " 'Your eyes are just like soft, black velvet . . .,' " he tells her. " 'They're wonderful.' He was thinking of an alcove in the Green-Davidson hung with black velvet" (I, 112). Clyde unconsciously desires "softness" and later finds it in Roberta, but he is also powerfully drawn by the "hardness" of wealth and sexual power which he is to find in Sondra and which he first encounters at the Green-Davidson. Thus he endows Hortense with an image of warm softness which reflects his muddled awareness of his needs. For though Hortense is properly associated in his mind with the Green-Davidson because of their similar sexual "hardness," she is incorrectly associated with an image of softness and warmth.

Clyde's belief that the Green-Davidson is a "glorious . . . institution" also represents his acceptance of the hotel as a microcosm of social reality. So he quickly learns that to get ahead in the world—that is, to ingratiate himself with his superiors and to earn large tips—he must adopt various roles. So he accepts the hierarchy of power present in the elaborate system of sharing tips which functions in the hotel. So he realizes that he must deceive his parents about his earnings if he is to have free use of the large sums available to him as an eager novice in this institution. And because the world of the Green-Davidson—both within the hotel and as hotel life extends out into Clyde's relations with the other bellhops and with Hortense—also contains Clyde's introduction into sexual desire and sexual warfare, he assumes that the ethics of social advance and monetary gain are also those of love. Thus, when in Lycurgus he aspires to the grandeur of Sondra and her set, his actions are conditioned by an ethic derived from the Green-Davidson—that hypocrisy, dishonesty, role-playing, and sexual deceit and cruelty are the ways in which one gains what one desires and that these can and should be applied to his relationship with Roberta.

The major point to be made about Dreiser's rendering of the Green-Davidson Hotel as an important experience in Clyde's life is that we respond to his account not as an exercise in determinism but as a subtle dramatization of the ways in which a distinctive temperament—eager, sensitive, emotional, yet weak and directionless—interacts with a distinctive social setting which supplies that temperament with both its specific goals and its operative ethic. Again, as in *Jennie Gerhardt*, there is a naturalistic center to this fictional excellence. It is correct to say that Clyde's life is determined by his heredity and environment. But, once more, as in *Jennie Gerhardt*, the naturalism and the fictional strength are inseparable. The naturalism is not an obstacle to the excellence but the motive thrust and center of the bed-rock fictional portrayal of how people interact with their worlds and why they are what they are.

To sum up. One of the major conventions in the study of American naturalism is that naturalistic belief is both objectionable in its own right and incompatible with fictional quality. But the example of Dreiser reveals that the strength often found in a naturalistic novel rests in the writer's commitment to the distinctive form of his naturalistic beliefs and in his ability to transform these beliefs into acceptable character and event. We are moved by the story of Jennie and Lester and by the account of Clyde's career not because they are independent of Dreiser's deepest beliefs but rather because they are successful narratives of man's impotence in the face of circumstances by a writer whose creative imagination was all of a piece. Until we are willing to accept that the power of a naturalistic writer resides in his naturalism, we will not profit from the example of Dreiser.

Notes

1. Quoted by Franklin Walker, *Frank Norris: A Biography* (Garden City, N.Y.: Doubleday, Doran and Co., 1932), pp. 222-23.

2. The most characteristic discussions of American naturalism occur in histories of American fiction. See, for example, Harry Hartwick, *The Foreground of American Fiction* (New York: American Book Co., 1934), pp. 3-20; George Snell, *The Shapers of American Fiction, 1798-1947* (New York: E. P. Dutton and Co., 1947), pp. 223-48; Frederick J. Hoffman, *The Modern Novel in America* (Chicago: H. Regnery, 1951), pp. 28-51; and Edward Wagenknecht, *Cavalcade of the American Novel* (New York: Holt, 1952), pp. 204-29. But see also Oscar Cargill, *Intellectual America* (New York: Macmillan Co., 1941), pp. 82-175, and Lars Ahnebrink, *The Beginnings of Naturalism in American Fiction* (Cambridge: Harvard Univ. Press, 1950).

3. Charles C. Walcutt, *American Literary Naturalism: A Divided Stream* (Minneapolis: Univ. of Minnesota Press, 1956), p. 220.

4. Eliseo Vivas, "Dreiser, An Inconsistent Mechanist," *Ethics* (July, 1938); revised version, *The Stature of Theodore Dreiser*, ed. Alfred Kazin and Charles Shapiro (Bloomington: Indiana Univ. Press, 1955), p. 237.

5. Two extreme examples of this position are Randall Stewart, *American Literature and Christian Doctrine* (Baton Rouge: Louisiana State Univ. Press, 1958), pp. 114-20, and Floyd Stovall, *American Idealism* (Norman: Univ. of Oklahoma Press, 1943), pp. 134-36.

6. The essays were published originally in 1942, 1947, and 1950 respectively.

7. See, for example, Charles Thomas Samuels, "Mr. Trilling, Mr. Warren, and *An American Tragedy*," *YR*, 53 (1964), 629-40. Samuels finds *An American Tragedy* inept beyond belief.

8. *Sister Carrie* (New York: Doubleday, Page and Co., 1900), p. 83.

9. Portions of the discussion of *Jennie Gerhardt* and *An American Tragedy* which follow appear in different form in my *The Novels of Theodore Dreiser: A Critical Study* (Minneapolis: Univ. of Minnesota Press, 1976). I do not wish by my emphasis on the deterministic thread in naturalism to appear to be supporting a return to a simplistic definition of naturalism as "pessimistic determinism" or some such formula. I have devoted much effort over two decades in various critical studies of individual naturalists as well as in more general essays on the movement as a whole to the position that naturalism is a complex literary movement in which distinctive writers combine in their works distinctive strains of traditional humanistic values and contemporary deterministic belief. Rather, I seek in this essay to suggest that just as we were long guilty of not recognizing the element of covertly expressed traditional value in most naturalists, so we have also been guilty of an uncritical disparagement of the more readily identifiable deterministic strain in their work.

10. *Jennie Gerhardt* (New York: Harper and Brothers, 1911), p. 401. Citations from this edition appear hereafter in the text.

11. In the Theodore Dreiser Collection, University of Pennsylvania Library; quoted by permission of the University of Pennsylvania Library.

12. *An American Tragedy* (New York: Boni and Liveright, 1925), I,5. Citations from this edition appear hereafter in the text.

Sister Carrie

"Sister Carrie": A Strangely Strong Novel in a Queer Milieu

William Marion Reedy*

A novel that a man will read through at one sitting is, in these days of novels *ad nauseam*, a rarity, and yet the writer found one the other day,—a novel that has been neither extensively advertised by its publishers, Doubleday, Page & Co., nor enthusiastically reviewed, if, indeed, it has been reviewed at all, in any of the journals of criticism. The title of the novel is "Sister Carrie." The author is Theodore Dreiser.

Now, it isn't at all a nice novel. Neither is it nasty, which is supposed to be the antonym of nice. It is a story of the seamy side. It deals with the "fall" of a girl who goes to Chicago from a little Wisconsin town, and, strange to say, though the situation is treated with a calm frankness of tone, the fall is a fall upwards. The author writes with a startling directness. At times this directness seems to be the frankness of a vast unsophistication. Without any brutalities whatever, he is, nevertheless, intensely realistic in his painting of the methods which are employed, circumstance and temperament assisting, in the luring from sordid and dull and wearisome loneliness of innocence a girl by a flashy and flighty drummer. The peril of the girl who ventures into a great city to earn a living, without any training or moral preparation for the ordeal, is shown with a simplicity and strength that are the more impressive for being recorded in the strain of one who thinks the incident quite a frequent and a natural, though regretable, occurrence.

The scenes of the book are laid always among a sort of people that is numerous but seldom treated in a serious novel. And, for all its easy acceptance of the situation, this novel, "Sister Carrie," is a very serious production. Its veritism out-Howells Mr. Howells and out-Garlands Mr. Hamlin Garland. One would think that, with a factory girl for a heroine, with a fatuously empty-headed drummer for a leading figure and with a manager of a fashionable saloon for the dominating male character, such a novel would descend to depths unplummeted even by Mr. Albert Ross. But the book doesn't plunge into the obscurely salacious at all. It is, in

*Reprinted from St. Louis *Mirror*, 10 (January 3, 1901), 6–7, under the pseudonym of "Litte."

spite of veritism, very much restrained. It is photographically true and yet there is an art about it that lifts it often above mere reporting. And there grows upon the reader the impression that there lurks behind the mere story an intense, fierce resentment of the conditions glimpsed.

The girl's experiences in a shoe factory, her life in a small, dismal flat, and her easy surrender to a tawdry masculine charm and a coarse kindness, are revealed with a convincing truth to character and to conditions in a great city like Chicago. The vain, silly, kindly drummer introduces the girl to the saloon manager *Hurstwood*, who wins her by his superior personality and, finally, after quarrelling with his wife and taking $10,000 from the safe of his employers, forces her to accompany him to Montreal, where he "marries" her, without the formality of divorcing his wife. The manager returns the stolen money, is not prosecuted, and the pair go to New York, where he becomes a partner in another saloon. Wrong as all this is, the girl always has something sweet and fine in her character. She is hardly to be called by so harsh a word as vulgar. She is even good, though in a negative fashion. She is not glorified in the least, not a particle idealized and yet she holds one's sympathies with a strange security. She has a natural talent for the stage, unwittingly discovered at an Elks' entertainment, though, in New York, she settles down to a quiet domesticity, all ignorant of her supposed husband's peculation or the truth of his departure from Chicago.

Hurstwood, however, fails, and it is in the delineation of the man's gradual sinking or slinking into degradation that the author shows his real power. The slow slackening of will, the subtle growth of indecision and self-abandonment, the loosening of all manly fibre, the crumbling, rotting of character in a kind of narcotic procrastination touched with fitful gleams of paretic, puling pride, until he comes to beggary on the streets, and final rest in a fifteen-cent room with the gas out but turned on—all this is shown with a power which no endeavor to keep awake a critical attitude can resist. The terrible slowness of the ruin of a man, the descent marked by the clever, casual bringing to light of little, obscure symptoms, is hideously oppressive—all the more so that the man was only a saloon manager and a character, in the beginning, conceived upon so high a plane of attractiveness as to verge closely upon the absurd. The narrative of *Hurstwood's* progress down hill is, in what some would call, "journalese," but it is a tale with no abuse of words, and with no over-use of detail. Vulgar as the fellow *Hurstwood* was at first, vile as he was, even, there is that tragedy in his descent of the Avenues of failure which moves the heart. *Carrie*, forced to earn her living in the chorus, becomes, finally, a comic opera "queen," and her star rises in glory as *Hurstwood's* goes out in the dark.

The woman, *Carrie*, is a reality all through the book, as real, to be paradoxical, as she is, to a certain extent, shadowy. The drummer you have met often, and liked, with a touch of contempt. The scenes in which the drama works out are all well realized. The separation of the drummer and the girl, when he discovers *Hurstwood* has won her affection, acutely develops the strong hint of the pathetic in *banale* situations which is more frequent than is often imagined. Indeed this queer, *banale* atmosphere hanging over the story is of the essence of the fascination of the volume. The tragedy and romance is of the commonest kind of common people, yet the spell is there. There are times when the tale seems like to lapse into the veriest bathos of the cheapest sort of novel, but so sure as this is imminent the indeterminate somewhat in the writer suddenly bursts forth and informs the characters with a vivid vitality. The book is, as one might guess from what has gone before, very uneven, but the best of it is undeniably worth while and the worst of it seems, in some inexplicable fashion, to be a support to the best. At times the whole thing is impossible, and then again it is as absolute as life itself. The writer errs frequently in the selection of the material for his pictures, the incidents that he portrays, but the story, as a whole, has a grip that is not exercised upon any unwholesome taste. You read it through with interest and a stirring of the emotions, and when you sit down to write a criticism of it you find yourself trying, as it seems, to write and analyze the charm away. But you cannot. The charm, despite violence to taste and hovering intimations even of absurdity, remains superior to and defiant of analysis.

With the Novelists

Anonymous*

It is essentially a serious study that Theodore Dreiser presents in his novel, "Sister Carrie"—so serious, indeed, that the author cannot forbear more or less moralizing as his narrative unfolds. Were it not for this extraneous element of observation persistently injected, the story would make a greater impression, for there is that in it which of itself holds the attention despite certain crudities in the actual recountal of events. It is a sordid enough drama, to be sure, this narrative of the fortunes of a young woman who comes to Chicago to seek employment, and, disheartened by her first struggle with the world, and the repellent atmosphere of her sister's house, takes what apparently is an easy road to comfort and the satisfying of her yet almost dormant ambitions. But, from first to last, the delineation of Carrie Meeber is calculated to create an impression, and what is true in her case is even more marked in the portrayal of one of the men who play their parts in Carrie's life history. Indeed, although this is scarcely in the author's plan, the attention is focused even more directly on the figure of George Hurstwood than on Carrie herself, and there is nothing in the novel more convincing in quality than Mr. Dreiser's sketch of Hurstwood's last days, an outcast and a beggar in the streets of New York. In this particular description he does what we think will be conceded to be his best work. Hurstwood, the man who fails, partly, it may be said in charity, as the result of circumstances that are too much for him, but largely because of an inherent weakness, is a character drawn with that skill which comes only from understanding. He is typical in his heyday as manager of one of Chicago's showy saloons; he is typical on his downward path, and only too typical in his last stages, when Carrie, who had been trapped first into leaving Chicago with him, and later by an illegal marriage, feels that as an act of self-preservation she must leave him to work out his fate alone.

The effect that Hurstwood produces on the reader is due, in large measure, to the fact that the man's pitiful career is allowed, practically, to tell its own story. Carrie is more nebulous, because Mr. Dreiser envelops her to a considerable extent with his own imaginings, which have a tendency to blur what is clear cut in the record of her struggle with

*Reprinted from Newark *Evening News*, June 8, 1907, Second Section, p. 12.

the forces surrounding her, and of her ultimate success in her chosen pro-
fession—that of the stage. But these imaginings cannot obscure her salient
points, nor does the author have any intention of glossing over her
mistakes, careful as he is to explain how it is natural for her to make them.
It is the ugly truth that Carrie lacks moral fiber in accepting the offer that
her first admirer, Charles Drouet, makes her, and that she has no scruples
in deceiving Drouet, no matter how little she thinks that she owes him. To
the end she is strangely heedless of her past—calloused, perhaps, expresses
it better than any other word. Intellectually developing, as she does, her
moral nature seems to be quite at a standstill, and, although in her vicissi-
tudes she never loses a certain innate reserve and simplicity, her final
aspirations, as her first, are inseparably connected with her own well-
being. The fine instincts imparted by religion do not touch her life—this
explains much—and her relations with humanity are not, it is to be admitted, such as to lead her to an exalted conception of duty. It may be
that Mr. Dreiser has in mind the emphasizing of these very lacks. At any
rate, his heroine disappears, as she appears, with certain vague longings
for happiness, only more conscious that, with the resources at her command, she cannot look for anything approaching complete realization.
An analysis of limitations is what the author, to all intents, offers.

"Sister Carrie" is, as has been said, a sordid tale; but in its
disagreeable features Mr. Dreiser seeks to appeal to the thoughtful rather
than to those persons greedily desirous of the sensational in fiction. There
are passages which one more practised in writing would have omitted or
modified; still even in these, regrettable as their presence may be considered, it is only fair to recognize that it is not the author's object to provide what is merely unpleasant or suggestive.

Theodore Dreiser's "Sister Carrie"

Harris Merton Lyon*

That American readers have paid little or no attention to this work is by no means surprising; that British critics have welcomed it enthusiastically is to be taken as a matter of course. And in France, were Mr. Dreiser's book written in French and about characters which would interest the French, he would probably gain some of the praise and recognition which he justly deserves. He will not, it is safe to say, be applauded by America for some years to come, and then the praise will not be given on account of his "Sister Carrie" but on account of his later and more mature work, if there shall be any.

To me the volume has essential elements of greatness. It is the "biggest" thing I have read in the way of fiction—long fiction, synthetic fiction—since George Douglas' "House With the Green Shutters." The heroine of the book is not a nun, as her title would seem to indicate, but is a simple little Hoosier girl who goes up to Chicago in August, 1889, to seek her fortune. In 550 pages her pitiful moves on the chess board of life are revealed, and at the end of the game Mr. Dreiser leaves us with the question as to whether she has won for herself a victory or not. Ostensibly she has. Has she?

Two other characters in the book are wrapped up in her fortunes and influence her strongly—Drouet, the "drummer," and Hurstwood, the manager of a saloon. At a glance the reader will see this book is a document concerning the average middle class American; it is an attempt to do, with an Indiana woman, what Flaubert did with a woman of the provinces, though Carrie is by no means a Madame Bovary. It is an attempt to catch, with the spirit and scope of Balzac, the humdrum life of our bourgeoisie. The "drummer," so well has Mr. Dreiser depicted him, would, it is no exaggeration to say, live and be intelligible for all time, were he to be wiped as a class from the face of the earth tomorrow. Hurstwood—as for Hurstwood there is something uncanny about him, he is so true to life. In Mr. Dreiser's hands he is triumphantly analyzed. Hurstwood reminds you of yourself, of each one of your friends. He

*Reprinted from Houston *Post*, June 9, 1907, p. 26. Copyright 1907 the Houston *Post*. Reprinted by permission.

epitomizes your theory of life. He is the greatest thing in the book, from every point of view.

To tell you the plot of the story would be to destroy for you that inestimable pleasure which comes with perusing any slow revelation of relentless tragic forces, moving with Greek-like logic from cause to effect. Suffice it to say Carrie goes up in the world, Hurstwood goes down, and Drouet, the drummer, does the only thing which he is capable of doing—he stands still. But the whole result is absolutely masterful, ruthless, fascinating. It is as big, as vital, as American as Frank Norris' "Octopus"; only it lies in a far different field. It is more of the color-of-life found in Norris' "McTeague." It is a book that I have read twice and intend to read and reread. Nowadays in the United States you do not find busy people doing this sort of thing with very many books.

Mention has been made casually of Flaubert, Balzac, and Frank Norris in connection with Mr. Dreiser's work. It is true, I think, that these elements are found there. Flaubert is but hinted throughout, by means of the author's impersonal attitude. Certainly it would be ridiculous to speak of Mr. Dreiser in the same breath with the French master as regards technical finesse. Mr. Dreiser can not punctuate. He knows nothing of sentence and paragraph structure. He sees a scene, a situation, a crisis in huge, massed effects. Details, from their human side, are regarded by him with a painstaking nicety; but from the technical side of the craftsman, the word-artisan, he flouts them and lumbers over them, disdainful, with an uncouth grandeur. The book was first published seven years ago. For a man under 30 it is a most remarkable performance. Yet it is to his lasting discredit that, upon its present reissue, he lacked the energy, the concentration, the pride in his work which should have impelled him to use his more mature powers in correcting his dishevelled youthful technique. He should have edited this new edition of "Sister Carrie" with infinite pains.

"People in general attach too much importance to words," says Mr. Dreiser, somewhere in the first part of his novel. Evidently he doesn't. As a matter of fact, they are the only tools with which he has to communicate his information and his analyses; and it is to be regretted that he allowed himself to be slipshod in his methods. If he had the craftsmanship of Maupassant his "Sister Carrie" would be ten times more powerful.

The Balzac-like treatment, the Balzac-like attitude, is everywhere apparent. Mr. Dreiser speaks of department stores. He is writing for all time. "Should they ever permanently disappear," he adds a complete description of them, tedious but thorough. The art of suggestion is unknown to him. He begins to work out his character of Drouet, the "drummer." "Lest this order of individual should permanently pass," says Mr. Dreiser, "let me put down some of the most striking characteristics of his most successful manner and method." A page is given up to this cause, unmindful of the fact that it, of course, impedes the direct progress of the story. Many of Mr. Dreiser's American critics seizing upon this didactic crochet of his, have concerned themselves solely with this matter, utterly ignoring the great human force of the book. A recent namby-pamby reviewer in that namby-pambiest of molly-coddle literary magazines, the Bookman, was utterly myopic, and hence futile, in this respect. Perhaps this critic was unconsciously celebrating the criticism which the great American public will make upon Mr. Dreiser's work. It is slow; it is devious; and a public used to reading novels of the quick, snappy, rapid order will find "Sister Carrie" a difficult book to skim through. There are innumerable, weighty batches of Mr. Dreiser's philosophy thrown gratuitously about in his work. They clog the dramatic action, but in their way they are germane to his analysis of character, and they are decidedly worth while. If you make up your mind to read "Sister Carrie" make up your mind before you begin that you will conscientiously spend a week in the reading. Read him as you would Thackeray, not as you would read Dumas.

A word about the circumstances under which this book is composed will help to give you an advance estimate of its style and treatment. It was being written at the time when Frank Norris, filled with the abounding roughness and vigor of the West, was electrifying the atmosphere of our literary circles with his study of "McTeague," the huge San Francisco dentist, and with the first novel of his proposed "trilogy," "The Octopus." Norris was young; so young that his great work was loose-jointed. His synthesis was a synthesis of gristle, not of bone. His main ideas were detached from the body of his work, indiscriminate, incoherent. When the young men of the time began to catch the sympathy of Norris' reckless force, they, too, plunged into big things recklessly. Willy-nilly, helter-skelter their dreams took the shape of mal-formed prose. They were so strong that they stood without needing the strong steel understructure of restrained technique, the hidden girder which supports the masterpiece. It was at this time and under these conditions that Mr. Dreiser was working on his book.

"Sister Carrie" is, for today at least, a book for the few; not for the many. It never would have "run" as a serial in the Ladies' Home Journal, or in one of our 15-cent, popular magazines—for the home. It has been adjudged "immoral" by some of our very best citizens. Carrie, while fully meaning to do so, never quite managed to get a proper marriage certificate; and Drouet and Hurstwood, although happy-go-lucky, lackadaisical villains, are nevertheless felt to be villains by the public conscience. There is nothing in the book to offend any serious-thinking person; it is not an esoteric, a lubricious, a salacious book in any way whatsoever. It is simply the calm, impassioned, impersonal statement that such-and-such forces worked thus-and-so about a woman and a man produced such-and-such results. I mention this point to warn those who might read the book and choose to be offended at it, at me, at this journal, and at Mr. Dreiser afterward. It is no more immoral than Pinero's "Iris."

I also mention this because it brings opportunity for me to explain, in part, my interest in such books as "Sister Carrie." I see in "Sister Carrie" one more evidence of a broader American intellectual freedom. Possibly the day may come when George Moore's "Memoirs of My Dead Life" will not have to be expurgated, as for children, when it is being issued in the United States. No wonder England, no wonder France, no wonder Germany looks patronizingly down upon us—a nation of grown men and women for whom publishers must expurgate books before we are allowed to read them! "The land of the free," "freedom of the press"—the words are empty. We are free to swallow literary pudding out of a decidedly tin spoon. England, insular England, speaks contemptuously of our "rudimentary state of civilization." Politically, commercially and otherwise the sneer falls as water upon a duck's back; but, when our continental cousins mean intellectual civilization, their sneer sinks in. The time is coming some say—I care not whether it is within twenty-five years or within a century—when the United States will have to "stand for"—if it comes to the point of compulsion—an American Tolstoi, Turgenieff, Flaubert, Balzac, Nietzsche, Wilde, de Maupassant.

"Sister Carrie," tentative and insecure as it is, is a step in the right direction.

*   *   *   *   *   *   *

"Sister Carrie"

Joseph H. Coates*

Quite apart from its intrinsic merit as a work of literary art, "Sister Carrie" has, for the discriminating, in a marked degree the special interest which any writer's first novel possesses in proportion to the peculiarly individual power it may show as a promise for the future. In this, Mr. Dreiser's book is especially noteworthy, since rarely has a new novelist shown so singular a power of virile earnestness and serious purpose with unusual faculty of keenly analytic characterization and realistic painting of pictures. His people are real people; he compels you to know them as he knows them, to see the scenes amid which they move as he sees them. He shows absolute sincerity, he plays you no tricks; he is rigidly uncompromising, he scorns to tamper with the truth as he knows it, he refuses any subterfuges or weak dallying with what, to him at least, are the crucial facts of life. One may not always accept his philosophy fully and without reserve, but he himself believes in it. That is the general impression the book creates, and he possesses, therefore, a compelling individuality which is bound to make its mark.

The story is of Caroline Meeber, a girl of eighteen bred in a small country village where her father is a miller, who comes to Chicago to seek an independent livelihood by the work of her hands. She has never been away from home before; she knows nothing about the life of a great city, so strange and marvellous to her inexperienced girlhood. She has come, impelled by some restless but vague and as yet unconscious craving for happiness; and happiness in her crude and immature imaginings is confused with pleasure and the sensation of the stir of life, as it is with so many of her brothers and sisters the world over. This impressionable girl, unsuited for any successful struggle with hardship by temperament or training, is thrown into the whirlpool of city life during the years when character is beginning to form; and she is weighted by a soft attractiveness of face and gentleness of heart. In the opening chapter, on her way to Chicago she meets Drouet, a travelling salesman, who greatly influences her career. Later, she met Hurstwood, the manager of a fashionable drinking resort and in his way a man of respectable position. The condi-

*Reprinted from *North American Review*, 186 (October, 1907), 288–91. Reprinted by permission of the University of Northern Iowa.

tions under which she comes to live are not justified, nor excused, by any acceptable code. But they are not uncommon, and Mr. Dreiser handles them with such delicacy of treatment and in such a clean largeness of mental attitude, that they simply enforce an impressive moral lesson. The inevitable growth of her initial yielding softness into a hard cold selfishness at the last, but which yet fails to escape from the power of unsatisfied longing, is traced with much skill and with a logic which seems unanswerable. And the parallel working out of Hurstwood's character is surely a convincing piece of literary art.

"Sister Carrie" is a sombre tale. It does not leave you with a bad taste in the mouth, as one says, but with something very like a heartache; an effect even more pronounced here than in Mrs. Wharton's powerful novel, "The House of Mirth," to which it bears a notable similarity in the underlying theme, although widely different in most else. Mr. Dreiser belongs to the realistic school much more distinctly than Mrs. Wharton; he falls below her in grace and beauty of style and in her own characteristic literary art, but he gains in power and in vividness perhaps. The stories told are not the same, the methods of telling differ, but the *motif* in each is at the root of it essentially the same; the tragedy of human beings who, in our present social order, do not escape the crushing weight of a surrender to primal human impulses. The two books seem inevitably in the same class; they enforce a like moral. One is the complement of the other, with little or no superficial resemblance between them other than that each is of great and sombre power and deals with the same theme—the aberrations of social mankind, in America, in its search for pleasure and in its attempts at some basis for sex relations. In the two books the practical difference is only in the variables, the theme itself is constant. Mrs. Wharton works out her problem on one side, the complex laborious pleasure-seeking cult among that small and comparatively insignificant group, the idle rich; Mr. Dreiser is concerned with the greater and far more important class, the working-people from whose ranks it is that the upper strata of the future are to inherit character; for in this country, at least, the proletary of to-day begets the leader of to-morrow. It is the great lower and middle classes, if there are such things, that count.

Human nature is a tolerably constant quantity; men and women are pretty much alike in all times and places, and in all environments. Class distinctions, so far as the humanity of their elements is concerned, are more apparent than real; men are of the same nature everywhere. To find a great difference in essential quality between the very rich and the very poor, the very good and the very bad, the very cultured and intelligent and the very ignorant and stupid, we must, after all, take our measurements with a micrometric scale, so to speak; if we attempt to gauge these human differences by the finger of God, they are hard to find. No doubt, one bacillus differs from another in length, but you cannot mark it by a yard-stick. So that the "drummer" and the saloonkeeper who are arbiters of destiny for Sister Carrie are essentially of the same sort as the men who riot in "The House of Mirth," except that they appear to have retained more human quality of redemption; and the Lily Barts of the world of fashion are but Sister Carries after all. Indeed, the title of Mr. Dreiser's book is, no doubt, intended to suggest the kinship of the world.

And in these days, perhaps more markedly in America, the process of breaking down the class barriers, of interfusion of the social strata, is taking place with notable directness. Not only are the upper social ranks, or what passes for such, being constantly recruited by those who have lately risen from the lower stratum, but the economic change in industrial conditions is more and more bringing all humanity into closer touch; with the result that the high and mighty influence, as never before, the desires and the ambitions, the passions, too, of those who are low in social degree. As Mr. Dreiser puts it:

> "The great create an atmosphere which reacts badly upon the small. This atmosphere is easily and quickly felt. Walk among the magnificent residences, the splendid equipages, the gilded shops, restaurants, resorts of all kinds; scent the flowers, the silks, the wines; drink of the laughter springing from the soul of luxurious content, of the glances which gleam like light from defiant spears; feel the quality of the smiles which cut like glistening swords and of strides born of place, and you shall know of what is the atmosphere of the high and mighty. Little use to argue that of such is not the kingdom of greatness, but so long as the world is attracted by this and the human heart views this as the one desirable realm which it must attain, so long, to that heart, will this remain the realm of greatness. So long, also, will the atmosphere of this realm work its desperate results in the soul of man. It is like a chemical reagent. One day of it, like one drop of the other, will so affect and discolor the views, the aims, the desires of the mind, that it will thereafter remain forever dyed. A day of it to the untried mind is like opium to the untried body. A craving is set up which, if gratified, shall eternally result in dreams and death. Aye! dreams unfulfilled—gnawing, luring, idle phantoms which beckon and lead, beckon and lead, until death and dissolution dissolve their power and restore us blind to nature's heart."

So that, from the sociological point of view, the study presented in this book of existing conditions operating on human impulses which are inextinguishable, and often dominating, is of timely import. There are signs that the future of the race in this country may be more perilous than its past has been; it is possible one of those racial crises which are constantly recurring in the history of mankind, may be on the way. "Sister Carrie" is a book to be reckoned with, just as the social conditions—or defects—on which it rests must be reckoned with.

A Picture of Conditions

F. O. Matthiessen*

*   *   *   *   *   *   *

Dreiser is a primary example of the frequent American need to begin all over again from scratch. His case would seem to be different from that of Whitman, who found the gap so wide between what he had to say and any usual poetic form that he could not possibly bridge it. But in Whitman's day American poetry had hardly any tradition behind it, whereas fiction had been accruing a considerable background since Hawthorne had felt the thinness of his resources. Yet Dreiser was the representative of a far cruder America than Hawthorne's. He was only half-educated, and was scarcely a conscious artist at all when he set out to write *Sister Carrie*. In an authentic sense he was a primitive, not unlike the occasional American sign painter who has found that he possessed the dogged skills to create a portrait likeness, and then has bent all the force of a rugged character to realize this verity.

Opinions have been sharply divided as to Dreiser's skills in the most rudimentary element of his craft, the ability to tell a story. Some readers feel that he loses its movement in his crowded mass of details. But Ford Madox Ford held that "the difference between a supremely unreadable writer like Zola and a completely readable one like Dreiser is simply that if Zola had to write about a ride on a railway locomotive's tender or a night in a brothel, Zola had to get it all out of a book. Dreiser has only to call on his undimmed memories, and the episode will be there in all its freshness and vigor." Although the comparison seems to ignore the tremendous sweeping energy of (say) *Germinal*, and thus is unjust to Zola, Ford did hit at the center of what Dreiser has to offer. When he wrote *Sister Carrie*, he was hardly concerned with the intricacies of a plot as Hardy contrived one. So far as he was aware of a model at all, it was Balzac's direct way of presenting solid slabs of continuous experience. Looking back at the finished result, he said: "It is not intended as a piece of literary craftsmanship, but as a picture of conditions done as simply and effectively as the English language will permit." This dodges the

*Reprinted from *Theodore Dreiser* (New York: William Sloane, 1951), pp. 59–88. Copyright 1951 by William Sloane Associates, Inc. Reprinted by permission of William Morrow & Co., Inc.

question just as Whitman had done when he declared: "No one will get at my verses who insists upon viewing them as a literary performance." Their suspicion of the polite literature of their own times drove them both to this reckless extreme, and we may begin to understand Dreiser's feeling when we recall the reception of *Sister Carrie* by those who were looking for "literary" effects.

Why his "picture of conditions" then seemed revolutionary in America is perhaps the aspect of Dreiser that is hardest for us to grasp now. Yet, as Masters was to put it: "Forty years ago when you wrote *Sister Carrie*, there was one ideology by which to write the novel about a woman. It was to prove that as a matter of Christian sin, not even of cause and consequence . . . the woman was punished. You cleaned up the country and set the pace for the truth, and freed the young, and enlightened the old where they could be enlightened." Masters's rhetorical flourish sprang from his memory of how grimly oppressive the limitations of honest speech had been for a young man in 1900.

Carrie not only escaped punishment—Dreiser did not even regard her as sinful; and this was the crux of his defiance of late nineteenth-century conventionality. Only he hardly thought of it then as a defiance. He was simply writing what he knew. For doing no more—and no less—than this he would be hailed by Sherwood Anderson as the stalwart opener of doors for the next generation. Dorothy Dudley, who as a descendant of Fuller's inner Chicago and a graduate of Bryn Mawr, knew the convention from the inside, would strike as her leading theme that: "In the midst of a ruling tameness, or at least of a tameness dictated by those ruling here toward the last third of the last century, Dreiser was one of those born outside the convention, and living outside of it."

We have now moved so far from that convention that the contemporary effort to suppress *Sister Carrie* may strike us as only a curious freak—though we must not lose sight of the continuing effort today to suppress novels of more than Dreiser's naturalistic frankness. For we have by now so long defied the genteel tradition that we now tend to idealize it, to feel a nostalgic longing for it as an escape from our world which seems to us so much more brutal than Dreiser's. But if we are to appreciate, not the final value of Dresier to readers today, but the first great contribution that he brought to his contemporaries, we must remember that Santayana coined the phrase "the genteel tradition" to describe what he considered the most dangerous defect in American thought.

Observing our dominant New England culture, Santayana believed that its deep-rooted error was that it separated thought from experience. Among the legacies of a colonial culture is the habit of thinking of creative sources as somehow remote from itself, of escaping from the hardness and rawness of everyday surroundings into an idealized picture of civilized refinement, of believing that the essence of beauty must lie in what James Russell Lowell read about in Keats rather than in what Walt Whitman saw in the streets of Brooklyn. The inescapable result of this is to make art an adornment rather than an organic expression of life, to confuse it with politeness and delicacy. Even Howells, who set himself to record ordinary existence, could drift into saying: "Elsewhere we literary folk are apt to be such a common lot, with tendencies here and there to be a shabby lot . . . but at Boston we were of ascertained and noted origin, and a good part of us dropped from the skies. Instead of holding horses before the doors of theaters; or capping verses at the plow tail; or tramping over Europe with nothing but a flute in the pocket; or walking up to the metropolis with no luggage but the MS. of a tragedy; or sleeping in doorways or under the arches of bridges; or serving as apothecaries' prentices—we were good society from the beginning. I think this was none the worse for us, and it was vastly the better for good society."

With the last decades of the nineteenth century, as the new industrial cities filling up with new immigrants from central and southern Europe were less and less like London, the further mistake was made of thinking of literature as somehow dependent upon the better-born groups of richer standing. Even Edith Wharton could be oblivious to American actualities to the extent of saying: "How I pity all children who have not had a Doyley, a nurse who has always been there." Her autobiography is filled with so many similar notations that one realizes how much she had to overcome before she could take literature seriously.

Almost twenty years after *Sister Carrie* Logan Esarey would write in his *History of Indiana:* "From Crawfordsville also came Meredith Nicholson, one of the most widely known Indiana literary men at present. Like all literary men of Indiana he comes of good stock and enjoyed a first class education." One might dismiss this as merely "official" history, but Stuart Sherman was holding the same assumptions in 1915, in an essay in the *Nation* on "The Barbaric Naturalism of Theodore Dreiser." Objecting to the "animal behavior" of the novelist's characters, Sherman was not above attributing it to the fact that Dreiser sprang from the German rather than the Anglo-Saxon element of our "mixed population." Since Dreiser did not share in the moral ideas of our older heritage, he portrayed a "vacuum, from which the obligations of parenthood, marriage, chivalry and citizenship have been quite withdrawn. . . . Hence Mr. Dreiser's field seems curiously outside American society."

This was the kind of attack that continued against Dreiser after he had published five novels. At the outset of his career, the barriers erected by such standards might well have seemed impossible to break through. He knew what was expected from Indiana writers. Two of them were just then contributing to the immense vogue of historical romances. Charles Major's *When Knighthood Was in Flower* (1898), the romantic tale of the second marriage of "Mary of France" to Charles Brandon, was even more popular than Maurice Thompson's *Alice of Old Vincennes* (1900), whose picture of Indiana differed from Dreiser's memories not only because it dealt with frontier days. The most successful Indiana writers of Dreiser's own day would be Booth Tarkington, who had just issued *The Gentleman from Indiana* (1899), and Gene Stratton Porter. Mrs. Porter's sentimental portrayal—particularly in *Freckles* (1904) and *A Girl of the Limberlost* (1909)—of adolescent heroines in the Indiana swampland was to make her the American writer with the largest sales during the first quarter of the twentieth century, with a total of more than eight million copies.

For a writer with no sense of living tradition to protect him, such pressures of taste can be of imponderable weight. Tarkington adjusted himself easily to the current demands. The hero of his first work was the editor of a country newspaper nominally crusading against political corruption, but the milieu is handled in the tones of a light operetta. Dreiser never held any animus against Tarkington's vogue. In his later essay, "Indiana: Her Soil and Light" (1923), he linked Tarkington with Riley in their evocation "of a general geniality and sociability . . . which those who are most intimate with it are pleased to denominate 'homey' or 'folksy.' " These words have been especially prevalent in our Middle West, and another Middle Westerner, born in the same year and month as Dreiser, Vernon L. Parrington, would be more rigorous in judging the corruptions to which they are liable at the hands of authors whose smoothness is the twentieth-century face of gentility. The limitation of Tarkington's pleasant "neighborliness" is that it has little hard core of actuality. Parrington's description was accurate: "a purveyor of comfortable literature to middle-class America."

What prevented Dreiser from being seduced by the wistful charm that he knew to be the standard literary product of his native state was simply the accumulation of all the facts of his existence as we have sketched them from his birth. He could not have been a Tarkington if he had tried. He could never have acquired the lightness of touch that was at Tarkington's command from the time he was at Princeton. Dreiser was the immigrant's son from the wrong side of the tracks, who broke through the genteel tradition by no conscious intention, but by drawing on a store of experience outside the scope of the easily well-to-do—experience which formed the solid basis for all his subsequent thought.

When he began to develop Carrie Meeber's story, he remembered what had happened to one of his sisters, who had been supported in Chicago by an architect and had then felt herself much more deeply attracted by the manager of Hannah and Hogg's, a well-known eating and drinking establishment. Only later did she discover that he was married, but by then he was enough in love with her to persuade her to elope to Toronto, explaining that while drunk he had stolen fifteen thousand dollars from his employers. He was soon filled with remorse and sent back most of the money, and the owners agreed not to press the case against him. But the papers were filled with it, and the only reason the Dreisers were not involved in the scandal was that their daughter had been living under an assumed name. The couple had settled in New York where they supported themselves and two children in part by renting rooms to girls whose habits they did not scrutinize. It was to them that another sister of Dreiser's first turned when she was made pregnant by the son of a rich family who would do nothing about it. Later on, the ex-manager was to prove none too faithful to Dreiser's sister; and still later, when Dreiser was first in New York, they were having a hard time making both ends meet. Stuart Sherman might declare such material to lie "outside American society"; but, so far as Dreiser changed these details in his novel, he somewhat softened the actuality.

In her excited discovery of Chicago, Carrie is essentially Dreiser himself. Leaving her home in Wisconsin, where her father is a day laborer in a flour mill, in the summer of 1889, she approaches the city with the same "wonder and desire" that Dreiser had felt in approaching it a couple of summers earlier. For her too it is "a giant magnet." She experiences the same timidity in looking for work, the same dread of being rebuffed, and when she has landed her first job—cutting shoes—she walks to it through the "walled canyons" with the same overwhelmed sense of smallness. But the new department store windows speak to her even more importunately than they had to him, seeming to say: "You need me! You need me! You need me!" Only in this case the quotation is from Dreiser's autobiography, rather than from his novel.

But Dreiser is also Drouet, the "masher," the flashy dresser. Or at least in his early poverty he had aspired to such clothes as he describes with intimate thoroughness when Drouet first speaks to Carrie on the train and so impresses her by his pink-and-white-striped shirt, his cuff links set with agates, the Elks' insigne on his watch-chain, his highly polished tan shoes, and his gray fedora hat. Dreiser realized that he was presenting the new manifestation of a type, "a class which at that time was first being dubbed by the slang of the day 'drummers.' " One recalls the transfixed if horrified fascination with which James was to record, in a long passage in *The American Scene*, the ubiquity of the type in our new business civilization. But Dreiser felt at home with Drouet, though he probed at once to the bottom of the man's shallow vanity. It has been noted that in Drouet's rapid "technique" for engaging Carrie's attention Dreiser is also close to one of George Ade's *Fables in Slang*; but this would appear to be a common indebtedness to American ways.

In a more profound sense Dreiser is also Hurstwood. Or rather, Hurstwood, basking in the blaze of lights and dark polished woodwork of Fitzgerald and Moy's and affable with the rich and well-placed members of his clientele, is at home in the splendor that had exercised such a tug upon Dreiser, the outsider looking in. And when later in New York, Hurstwood, no longer in his luck, begins to sag step by step down into the bottomless pit of poverty, Dreiser renders every detail of what he himself most dreaded.

The most valuable thing that Balzac had taught him was to regard the ever-changing surfaces of the new American cities as having historical importance. Dreiser could scarcely share Balzac's confidence that he was "the secretary to society"; but, having found that St. Louis or Pittsburgh was in its basic human passions no different from the great world's capital, he could hold his material in serious perspective. From his opening pages he believed that he was adding to the American record, introducing Drouet in detail "lest this order of individual should permanently pass." Impressed as he was throughout his life by the "newness" of his world, he was concerned to note such things as that Hurstwood, at his moment of crisis, just after taking the money, calls Carrie from a drugstore which contained "one of the first private telephone booths ever erected." These details are presented more baldly than they would be in more sophisticated fiction. Dreiser tells us that "At that time the department store was in its earliest form of successful operation, and there were not many. The first three in the United States, established about 1884, were in Chicago." In the light of this method of documenting his milieu, we become even more aware why Dreiser no less than Carrie was awed by the great new buildings. With an equal sense of adding to architectural history, Louis Sullivan had made, in some of these stores, the finest contributions of his functionalism.

It has often been remarked that Dreiser describes objects as though no one else had ever described them. His realization that all of his surroundings were changing continuously and rapidly served not only to detach him from them but also to make him want to seize upon them before they disappeared. This again was a great asset for his work. He recalled that not even the name "North Shore Drive," where Carrie goes riding with Hurstwood, dated back a dozen years. When he located the room of Carrie's chorus-girl friend in New York on 19th Street near Fourth Avenue, he noted that it was in "a block now given up wholly to office buildings." The lapse of time here between "then" and "now" was scarcely six years, but the fact that Dreiser could regard the change as constituting history was one of the chief reasons why his narrative has so much weight. It was why Floyd Dell would feel that Dreiser had conveyed Chicago in its full density, whereas Norris, in *The Pit*, seemed to him to have sketched it in merely as a theatrical backdrop.

Dreiser had a particular fondness for reproducing the interiors in which his characters lived. The bleakness of Carrie's sister's flat, where she stays at first, could have been selected from many memories. The apartment overlooking Union Park in which Drouet establishes Carrie is located where Dreiser had taken a room when he was a beginning reporter; but he fills it with bric-à-brac and a Brussels carpet "with gorgeous impossible flowers" which are more suitable to Carrie.

The heroine he installs here is very different from any that James or Hawthorne would have portrayed, to cite Dreiser's chief American predecessors who built novels around the characters of women. James deliberately sought out the exceptional case, an Isabel Archer or a Milly Theale, whose intense consciousness was her main resource, and his main way of measuring values. For the vibrations of her inner life took her to heights of perception and appreciation not to be reached by the crude or the unaware. Dreiser tells us at the outset that Carrie "was possessed of a mind rudimentary in its powers of observation and analysis. . . . In intuitive graces she was still crude." And he soon adds: "It must not be thought that anyone could have mistaken her for a nervous, sensitive, high-strung nature." James would have thought that a nature so lacking in the inner no less than the outer endowments which made the exceptional American girl the heiress of all the ages was not worth treating at all.

Hawthorne would have been even more puzzled by some of Dreiser's assumptions about her. Hawthorne had taken the view that Hester Prynne possessed a deeper moral nature than her Puritan judges, but he could hardly have understood Dreiser's remark that Carrie "was saved because she was hopeful." Dreiser did not think very consistently in such terms, since he had immersed Carrie in a world apart from all theological sanctions, the actual existence that he knew. Yet the title of the novel appears as *The Flesh and the Spirit* in Dreiser's first agreement with Doubleday, and it is instructive to observe the kind of allegorical pattern he had in mind. When Carrie first goes out with Drouet for an evening, Dreiser remarks that she "had no excellent home principles fixed upon her." When she accepts the salesman's further attentions, Dreiser adds that she had "only an average little conscience."

But he does not develop the struggle between forces in these conventional terms. Carrie's craving for pleasure, as represented by money and chiefly by clothes—the "things" which the fastidiousness of James's Fleda Vetch would have rejected as beneath her—is described at first as being the chief "stay" of her otherwise timid nature. Yet she is too full of "wonder" ever to be greedy. Dreiser also emphasizes that she feels "the constant drag to something better." This is suggested initially in her gradual realization that she possesses an emotional depth quite beyond the scope of the genial but egotistic drummer. Hurstwood is drawn to her by something more tender and appealing than he has found in any other woman. But Dreiser manages to crystallize her essential quality only when she gets a casual chance to appear in amateur theatricals, and unexpectedly reveals something of "the sympathetic, impressionable nature," the "pathos" of the true actress.

The potentiality glimpsed here is what Dreiser had in mind when speaking of "the spirit," as he does in several of his chapter titles. These are oddly cast in the language of magazine verse, and most of them even fall into metrical lines of eleven or twelve syllables. They throw considerable light on Dreiser's intentions. "The Lure of the Spirit: The Flesh in Pursuit" serves as the title for the two successive chapters in which Hurstwood, having witnessed her performance in Augustin Daly's *Under the Gaslight*, begins to be seriously stirred by her, and begs her to come away with him. Not knowing that he is married, she agrees on condition that he marry her. When she discovers the true state of affairs, she is "a spirit in travail." Then—in a more complex sequence than the bare facts of Dreiser's sister's situation—Hurstwood, who does not divulge that he has stolen the money, persuades her to take the train on the pretext that Drouet has been injured and is in a hospital outside the city, and only then reveals that he and she are bound for Montreal. The chapter-title reads "A Pilgrim, An Outlaw: The Spirit Detained." Dreiser continues to think of Carrie as an ignorant but slowly wakening seeker after some deeper significance in life. The first chapter after their arrival in New York is "The Kingdom of Greatness: The Pilgrim Adream." But it is only after Hurstwood has drifted far into the maelstrom of misfortune that she realizes that she must strike out for herself, and thinks of trying her lot on the stage, in a chapter headed "The Spirit Awakens: New Search for the Gate."

"The flesh," as embodied in Hurstwood, is scarcely conceived as evil. In the account of Carrie's "pilgrimage," Dreiser is mainly concerned with her growth into possession of a gift, of whose existence she has been wholly unaware. She is passive rather than active, receptive rather than aggressive, and is spurred on mainly by what he calls her "helpful, urging melancholy." By the end of the book he is attributing "emotional greatness" to her of the unconscious sort that, without knowing it, can project on the stage an expression of universal longing, what Dreiser's forebears would have called *Sehnsucht*. In a brief epilogue akin to those that Balzac sometimes used, Dreiser returns to his own kind of moral judgment of her: "Not evil but that which is better, more often directs the steps of the erring. Not evil, but goodness more often allures the feeling mind unused to reason." But Carrie is not happy. Dreiser's last phrase to describe her spirit is "a harp in the wind." She has seen through her tinsel pleasures with Drouet. She has grown beyond the sphere of Hurstwood. And she finds herself essentially solitary. Dreiser takes leave of her, saying: "Know then, that for you is neither surfeit nor content. In your rocking-chair by your window dreaming, shall you long, alone. In your rocking-chair by your window, shall you dream such happiness as you may never feel."

The core of Dreiser's problem in endowing Carrie with the reality we find in the heroines of Hawthorne and James has already been suggested by the stilted language of the chapter titles. Carrie is real when her heart is fixed on a little tan jacket with large mother-of-pearl buttons, "which was all the rage that fall." She is real, for one thing, because that final phrase comes naturally both to her and to Dreiser. Through Carrie, also, Dreiser found a register for what Floyd Dell called "the poetry of

Chicago," noting that Dreiser looked not "to see the badness of the city, nor its goodness," but "its beauty and its ugliness," and that he saw "a beauty in its ugliness." But Carrie is a much less likely vehicle for the realization at which Dreiser himself was just arriving, a realization of some of the attributes of the artistic temperament. We have a hard time believing in her "emotional greatness" as she works her way up from chorus girl to star, largely because from the moment Dreiser introduces her as "a half-equipped little knight" he has tinged his conception with banality and sentimentality. Dreiser's realm of "the spirit," in rejecting conventional standards, is so loosely defined and moreover so cluttered with clichés that it is hard to respond any longer to his sense of liberation in it. His most serious inadequacy in presenting his heroine is not what Mrs. Doubleday thought—that Carrie is too unconventional—but that she is not unconventional enough. The only way we could sense what Dreiser calls her "feeling mind" would be to see her deeply stirred, and this she never is. Her affairs with Drouet and Hurstwood are so slurred over, in instinctive accordance with what was then demanded of fiction, that they are robbed of any warmth. She is never a woman in love.

The central vitality of the novel, however Dreiser may have conceived it, lies in Hurstwood. In handling him, Dreiser seems to have learned for himself what Taine had urged upon the French novelists: "Man cannot be separated from his milieu; he leaves his imprint upon his exterior life, his house, his furniture, his affairs. . . ." Hurstwood's solid, hearty manner, just like his clothes—"not loud, not inconspicuous"—gave to Fitzgerald and Moy's the air that it needed. Its life was his life. We feel this in a redoubled sense when we see him at home, in the marriage that has become a "tinder box," his wife cold, self-centered and ambitious, his son and daughter wanting from him only money, the whole relationship becoming drier and drier and waiting only to flare into an explosion. Dreiser's emphasis here is on the opposite side of Taine's proposition. A man hardly exists apart from the milieu that nourishes him. The Hurstwood who is so affable with John L. Sullivan is driven into morose silence in such a household.

In his relationship with Carrie we feel his physical presence throughout, as we do not feel hers, even though Dreiser skirts the details of his passion. He is a man of forty, slowly but deeply aroused again to what Dreiser calls "the tragedy of affection." Another of Dreiser's basic assumptions comes out in the scene of Hurstwood's crisis, exactly midway through the book, the scene in which, having quarreled bitterly with his wife who has begun to learn of his interest in Carrie, he steals the money. We can understand why Dreiser found this scene so hard to write when we note how he transformed the bare facts. Chance is the controlling force in Dreiser's world, and chance presides over this scene. Hurstwood has had no previous thought of stealing. He has been spending the evening in the bar, drinking a little more than usual with some of the clientele because of his upset state of mind. When he steps into his office at the closing-up hour, he finds that the daytime cashier has forgotten to lock the safe, a thing that has not happened before. Glancing into the safe before locking it himself, he is surprised to see far more money than he thought Fitzgerald and Moy usually left there. He picks up the parcels of bills and mechanically counts them. Only then, "floundering among a jumble of thoughts," does temptation strike him. Here is his means of escape with Carrie. But he puts the money back in its drawer. Then he takes it out again, and feels it "so smooth, so compact, so portable." He puts it into his hand satchel. Then in a moment of revulsion, he starts to replace it in the safe; but, while the bills are in his hands, he pushes the door in his excitement and the lock clicks shut. This is the same kind of crisis that will lie at the core of *An American Tragedy*. There is no doubt about Hurstwood's desire to steal. But the act is an accident.

This central image of insecurity—and the full picture of Hurstwood's wavering back and forth is masterly—symbolizes the whole society that Dreiser evokes. It is a society in which there are no real equals, and no equilibrium, but only people moving *up* and *down*. The thoroughness with which he pursues this fact provides him with the successive links in his structure. Carrie feels herself above the "common" machine girls, but is at first dazzled by Drouet. The salesman in turn admires the substantial manager, regards Fitzgerald and Moy's as "a way-up swell place," and is attracted there by "his desire to shine among his betters." As always with Dreiser, only the massed details themselves rather than any summary of them can convey the solidity of their effect. Here is Hurstwood's knowledge of where he stands: "He knew by name, and could greet personally with a 'Well, old fellow' hundreds of actors, merchants, politicians, and the general run of successful characters about town, and it was part of his success to do so. He had a finely graduated scale of informality and friendship, which improved from the 'How do you do' addressed to the fifteen-dollar-a-week clerks and office attachés, who, by long frequenting of the place, became aware of his position, to the 'Why, old man, how are you?' which he addressed to those noted or rich individuals who knew him and were inclined to be friendly. There was a class, however, too rich, too famous, or too successful, with whom he could not attempt any familiarity of address, and with these he was professionally tactful, assuming a grave and dignified attitude, paying them the deference which would win their good feeling without in the least compromising his own bearing and opinions. There were, in the last place, a few good followers, neither rich nor poor, famous, nor yet remarkably successful, with whom he was friendly on the score of good-fellowship. These were the kind of men with whom he would converse longest and most seriously. He loved to go out and have a good time once in a while—to go to the races, the theatres, the sporting entertainments at some of the clubs. He kept a horse and neat trap, had his wife and two children, who were well established in a neat house on the North Side near Lincoln Park, and was altogether a very acceptable individual of our great American upper class—the first grade below the luxuriously rich."

The last detail is what so rankles with his family, whose eyes are fixed exclusively upon the select social world into which they have hardly begun to penetrate. It is revelatory of Dreiser that he puts his successful manager somewhat higher in the scale than he objectively belongs. The range which Dreiser can encompass from his own knowledge is from the bottom up to Hurstwood, whose domain is the kind to which Paul had introduced him. Beyond this lies the distant realm which Dreiser had not yet—had even less than Mrs. Hurstwood—perceived at first hand. It is no wonder that he was able to endow each stage of aspiration with its glowing, if frequently mean, eagerness.

With the shift to New York, Dreiser's main dramatic contrast begins slowly to establish itself. Here Carrie is to rise, while Hurstwood is gradually to sink. The chapter after their arrival begins: "Whatever a man like Hurstwood could be in Chicago, it is very evident that he would be but an inconspicuous drop in an ocean like New York." Here again Dreiser reflects on the dwarfing effect surroundings can have upon the individual: "The great create an atmosphere which reacts badly upon the small." Hurstwood must start all over again under an assumed name, and the establishment with which he gets connected is very shabby in contrast with what he had left behind him. He goes along for three years with "no apparent slope downward," but Dreiser adds that when a man of Hurstwood's age is no longer advancing, the balance is inescapably "sagging to the grave side."

Hurstwood thinks of himself as "outside a walled city," the sounds of his old life being buried more and more remotely within. His real start down begins when the owner of the land on which his bar is located decides to sell it, and Hurstwood is out of a job. He follows want ads that lead nowhere, until he is asking himself "What's the use?" Dreiser records each stage of his relapse into apathy, none of them quite perceptible to Hurstwood until it has engulfed him. There is the first time that he lounges in the lobby of a Broadway hotel instead of pursuing any further fruitless leads—an act for which he has contempt, and which he then repeats. He begins to shave every other day, every third day, every week. By then he is hardly looking at the want ads any more. In a flash of his old cocksure independence he tries his hand at a poker game, but loses. It is at this point that Carrie, frightened by the realization of where they have drifted, makes her resolution to try to get a job. Although Hurstwood feels a faint stirring of shame at her suggestion, this is overcome by his heavy lassitude. He now takes charge of the household details, and when he runs up as much of an account as one grocer will stand and then shifts to another, Dreiser remarks: "The game of a desperate man had begun."

To prove to Carrie and himself that he can still do something, he tries to work as a scab motorman during a strike, but is pulled down from his car and shot at. As he retreats again to rocking and dozing by the radiator, he dwells more and more in the past, even to hearing scraps of old conversation: "You're a dandy, Hurstwood." It is shortly after this that Carrie leaves him. The changing circumstances have long since moved them far apart. Through the people living across the hall she has met a young engineer named Ames, who talks to her about books she has never heard of, and she senses in him someone superior to Hurstwood. She never has a very coherent idea of Hurstwood's troubles. Dreiser makes the point that Hurstwood never told her about stealing the money, which he had sent back from Montreal. As he becomes completely altered from the handsome magnetic man she first knew to the drab figure brooding over his newspaper in the corner, her feelings cool. Her "heart misgave her" at walking out. "She did not want to make anyone who had been good to her feel badly." But she does not see how she can support them both and have enough left for the clothes she needs for her new career.

Dreiser effectively offsets the line of her rise against that of Hurstwood's decline. When she first attracts the critics' attention, he reads of it "down in a third-rate Bleecker Street hotel." " 'Well, let her have it,' he said, 'I won't bother her.' " He still had that much grim pride. But there surged up before his eyes "a picture of the old, shiny, plush-covered world . . . with its lights, its ornaments, its carriages, and flowers. Ah, she was in the walled city now!" But Dreiser underscores this with irony. Carrie feels for the moment, to be sure, as though the door had opened "to an Aladdin's cave." She soon realizes that she has not really arrived anywhere. "If she wanted to do anything better or move higher she must have more—a great deal more."

Dreiser's use of such contrasting scenes in the final chapters is his most effective structural device. These chapters also contain one of the major accounts of the nature of poverty in American fiction. Melville had comprehended in *Redburn* the utter misery of the slums. But he had seen these in Liverpool; the cities of his still largely pre-industrial America had not yet yielded anything quite so menacing. But by Dreiser's time the distance had widened between the promise of Jefferson's America and the actualities of McKinley's. A perception of the change had been at the heart of Henry George's *Progress and Poverty*. It gave a peculiar urgency to his descriptions of conditions, as Bernard Shaw discerned: "Some of us regretted that he was an American, and therefore necessarily about fifty years out of date in his economics and sociology from the point of view of an older country; but only an American could have seen in a single lifetime the growth of the whole tragedy of civilization from the primitive forest clearing."

Being poor, as many Europeans have observed, can be particularly savage in a country where the *mores* of individualism consider it a disgrace, and where the official attitude is therefore tempted to pretend that poverty does not exist. The popular fiction of Dreiser's day had made it seem almost as remote as sex. In Carrie's eyes, "Everything about poverty was terrible," but its full quality enters the book only after Hurstwood is down to his last fifty cents. He gets a job in the basement of a hotel, falls sick with pneumonia, and is sent to Bellevue. From that point it is a short step to begging. One of the most effective dramatic passages is where Hurstwood, crossing Broadway one night, notices an ex-soldier who, as Dreiser remarks, "having suffered the whips and privations of our peculiar social system, had concluded that his duty to the God which he conceived lay in aiding his fellow-man." He stands on a corner soliciting money for beds, at twelve cents apiece, for a file of men who knowing that this is his nightly practice gather behind him out of the shadows. Here Dreiser can make a full contrast between the world of splendor and the world of misery, the world he had longed for and the world he dreaded, the world into which Carrie has entered and the world into which Hurstwood has sunk. Having loitered to watch a man in evening dress hand a bank note to the captain, Hurstwood edges up to the end of the line. Dreiser calls this chapter "Curious Shifts of the Poor," and one of the reasons why its details stand out with particular mastery is that he was drawing on an article he had written under the same title for *Demorest's* the year before. By introducing Hurstwood into his picture, he has given it a dynamic emotional center such as none of his articles could have.

Hurstwood's self-reliant pride is now spent. He hangs around the theater door determined that Carrie must help him. But the scene of their meeting is brief and bleak. Seeing that she is frightened at his shabby appearance, he resents her even as he asks for money. She hurriedly pulls out the contents of her purse, but it amounts to only nine dollars in all. The next step down will be when Hurstwood is begging and sometimes sleeping in the park, not even aware of the sign "blazing" her name in a new show. Here Dreiser drew again on his article for an account of the breadlines. He knew that they were a constant feature of the city even in times of prosperity, "when little is heard of the unemployed." But one reason why his picture has so much objective weight is his resistance to any tendency to sentimentalize it. His article had concluded that "the individuals composing this driftwood are no more miserable than others," that in fact some of them had been coarsened by their experience to suffer less than some of their sympathizers. The tap-root of Dreiser's feeling probed to a far deeper level than any facile pity. Dorothy Dudley perceived its source when Dreiser told her that he had broken off his manuscript because he "felt unworthy" to write about Hurstwood's decline. "I think," she said, "that I have not heard elsewhere such abject reverence in the face of misery as suddenly sounded in this man's voice. If genius is caring for human beings more than others know how to care, then Dreiser has genius."

By now Hurstwood, to whom "life had always seemed a precious thing," has "about concluded that the game was up." He remembers a lodging house that has small, close rooms with gas jets, but then reflects that he has not the necessary fifteen cents—not even enough money to kill himself. He begs from a gentleman coming out of a barber shop, but when he unexpectedly gets a quarter the idea of death fades out of his mind for the time being. But as the worst winter weather sets in, he has less and less to eat. One evening, so exhausted as to be hardly clear where he is going, he shambles into Broadway at 39th Street, and is face to face with a large poster of Carrie. Despite his previous resolve not to go near her again, he makes a confused lunge at the stage door. But the attendant pushes him away, and he slips and falls in the snow.

At that moment, as Hurstwood moves to his end through a succession of contrasts, Carrie is sitting in her apartment at the Waldorf, reading *Père Goriot,* which Ames had recommended to her. She is stirred by the old man's sufferings and feels sorry for the people outside in the storm. Her thoughts are interrupted by her actress friend Lola, who is standing at the window. " 'Look at that man over there,' laughed Lola, who had caught sight of someone falling down. 'How sheepish men look when they fall, don't they?' "

At that moment Drouet, who is also now located in New York, is shaking the snow from his ulster in the lobby of the Imperial. He is on his way up, in charge of a branch office. Impressed by seeing Carrie on the stage, he has brashly slurred over the fact that she left him, and has tried to renew the contact, only to learn quickly from her manner that he is out for good. On this evening he is gaily waiting for another of his endless parade of girls.

Shifting his focus once more, Dreiser turns for a page to Hurstwood's wife and daughter and the rich husband the girl has landed. They are on an eastbound train on their way to a vacation in Italy, and they now have the cold hard luster to which they had aspired. A few days later Hurstwood will go to his suicide, and not even Carrie will be aware of it.

By picking up and dropping again the threads of these other lives in his final pages, Dreiser enforces our sensation of isolation, of a world divested of lasting human contacts. This has been accumulating from the start of the book. Once Carrie is in the city, we hear no more of her family in the country. Once she has left her sister's with Drouet, she apparently never sees her again. In New York she reflects: "I have been in this house with nine other families for over a year and I don't know a soul." Hurstwood has no relation with Shaughnessy, his three-year associate in the bar, that lasts a moment beyond the sale of the property. When Carrie has her first success and her picture in the papers, she can think of "no one she knew well enough to send them to." The continual emphasis on such details makes us realize that Dreiser conceives of the city as a jungle in a broader sense than that in which Upton Sinclair was to conceive it. Not just the poorest in the stockyards are oppressed by its naked struggle, but people on all levels who, moving up or down, are rarely able to meet and embrace as equals.

Dreiser's few basic and recurrent symbolic images serve to underscore this view. The symbol he makes most of—as we have already seen—is that of clothes, which Veblen was singling out at the same time, in *The Theory of the Leisure Class*, as giving a peculiarly representative expression of "pecuniary culture." Clothes in Dreiser are the chief means of display, of lifting a character above where he was, and by that fact above someone else. They lure—but really they separate.

His use of other images is rudimentary; he hardly thinks of them as a resource; but for this very reason there is a particular significance in a cluster that helps to create the *movement* of life as he feels it. As Carrie steps out of the train in Chicago, she is—in the last phrase of the opening chapter—"a lone figure in a tossing thoughtless sea." Other water-images heighten the sense of division. When Carrie has left the factory girls behind her, it is "as if some great tide had rolled between them." More recurrent are the phrases which project Dreiser's feeling that people are swept by forces far beyond their control. "The little shop-girl was getting into deep water. She was letting her few supports float away from her." One of the most effectively condensed similes, foreshadowing Hurstwood's disastrous career, is that which epitomizes his break with his wife: "He was like a vessel, powerful and dangerous, but rolling and floundering without sail." From this point increasingly Dreiser sees his characters as "drifting." He uses this word very often, perhaps more often than he realized, though not often enough to make the reader too conscious of it. Carrie, caught between Drouet and Hurstwood, is described as "an anchorless, storm-beaten little craft which could do absolutely nothing but drift." Later she will be "drifting" out of Hurstwood's life, as he is "drifting farther and farther into a situation which could have but one ending." By the close not only the crowd outside the flop-house are "of the class which simply floats and drifts, every wave of people washing up one, as breakers do driftwood upon a stormy shore."

Dreiser's other chief image of movement is, curiously enough, one of slow calm within the ceaseless flux. The first night at her sister's flat Carrie "drew the one small rocking-chair up to the window, and sat looking out upon the night and streets in silent wonder." She soothes herself again and again "rocking to and fro," thinking, as in the scene with which Dreiser ends the book. Hurstwood takes similar refuge. The evening when Carrie is about to leave him, "all unconscious of his doom, he rocked and read his paper." Here Dreiser's repetition—there are more than a couple of dozen instances—probably becomes too obtrusive. But his instinctive fondness for this image is very revealing of the rhythm of experience he is projecting. The back-and-forth sway of the chair can do nothing to arrest the drift of events. Both movements are slow, but one is inexorable.

Incidentally, Dreiser's own fondness for a rocking chair, which many interviews with him noted, suggests a physical basis for the rhythm of his thoughts. The slowness with which things occur in his novels is one of the ways by which he gives them weight. He has very little of the psychologist's skill in portraying the inner life of his characters, but he is caught by an overwhelming sense of the flow of life, mysterious beyond any probing. He remarks of Hurstwood that his apathy was "almost inexplicable," and some readers are impatient at Dreiser's frequent lack of skill in detailed motivation. What he has expressed at the core of *Sister Carrie* has been well described by Charles Walcutt in the course of pointing out how basically Dreiser differs from Zola: it is "this quality of life—shifting, elusive, unaccountable—that holds our attention, rather than the spectacle of carefully analyzed forces operating under 'experimental' conditions. . . . Dreiser does not make even a pretense of controlling his conditions and discovering truths about the nature of human psychology and physiology." Where Zola's theory would "put most emphasis—on the extraction of laws about human nature—Dreiser is most uncertain and most sure that no certainty can be attained."

A novel resulting from such a reading of existence is, not surprisingly, more impressive in its main sweep than in all its details. The same thing is true of Dreiser's style. Emerson found Whitman's language a strange "mixture of the *Bhagvat-Geeta* and the *New York Herald*." Dreiser's mixture was even stranger since his journalistic usages were not counterbalanced by any pure body of poetry or scripture. The passages conveying the "glamor" of the city as Carrie felt it, in a chrome equivalent of *The Arabian Nights*, are in a sense accidental rather than intentional. He is not deliberately using Carrie as a register, as a later master of our city speech might have. He himself felt the city in the same way, but when he strove for effect he merely fell into the stilted usages of magazine fiction: "Thus was Carrie's name bandied about in the most frivolous and gay of places, and that also when the little toiler was bemoaning her narrow lot." If one began enumerating the fancy clichés that spatter his pages—"lightsome," "halcyon," "prancing pair of bays," "airy grace"— one might conclude that this writer could not possibly break through to freshness. But what bothered his first reviewers was the opposite tendency, the extent to which Dreiser introduced words from his own conversation: "flashy," "nobby," "truly swell saloon," "dress suit affair." Objections on these grounds led him to say (at the time of the book's reissue in 1907): "To sit up and criticize me for saying 'vest' instead of 'waistcoat'; to talk about my splitting the infinitive and using vulgar commonplaces here and there, when the tragedy of a man's life is being displayed, is silly. . . . It makes me feel that American criticism is the joke that English authorities maintain it to be."

But once more this partly dodges the question, and also fails to do justice to the firm body of what he achieved. Charges of clumsiness have been repeated against him so often that they have obscured the many passages where, like the journeyman painter, he has a mastery of the plain style. When his mind was most absorbed with what he had to say, the flourishes of the feature-writer fell away, as did also the cumbersome, only half-accurate abstract terms ("affectional," "actualities"). Then he could write long passages where nothing is striking except the total effect. He is at his rare best in conveying the first understated rift between Hurstwood and Carrie, with everything keyed down to the neutral phrases that passed between them over the supper table. Or in conveying the brutal blankness of Hurstwood's separation from his partner Shaughnessy, or the pitiful blankness of the scene where Hurstwood begs from Carrie. Or in the entire chapter dealing with the streetcar strike, or in that one on the "curious shifts" of the poor. It is impossible to suggest the power of these in brief quotations, or in anything short of the whole. The same would be true of the pages in which Hurstwood moves towards his end through a winter evening, which is portrayed in uniform tones of "somber" and "thickening" air, "dirty store fronts," and "dingy brown" snow. This is the close of the passage, after Hurstwood has paid his fifteen cents and gone to his small room:

"Now he began leisurely to take off his clothes, but stopped first with his coat, and tucked it along the crack under the door. His vest he arranged in the same place. His old wet, cracked hat he laid softly upon the table. Then he pulled off his shoes and lay down.

"It seemed as if he thought a while, for now he rose and turned the gas out, standing calmly in the blackness, hidden from view. After a few moments, in which he reviewed nothing, but merely hesitated, he turned the gas on again, but applied no match. Even then he stood there, hidden wholly in the kindness that is night, while the uprising fumes filled the room. When the odour reached his nostrils, he quit his attitude and fumbled for the bed.

" 'What's the use?' he said weakly, as he stretched himself to rest."

There are no words here for ornament, and the predominating monosyllables are right for the basic simplicity. The only three-syllabled word in the first paragraph is one that calls attention to Dreiser's tragic irony. His resolve taken, Hurstwood can be "leisurely," though his leisure will be only in the "rest" of death. Dreiser's feeling for the dignity of man, even at the last extreme, comes through in Hurstwood's calmness. But the key-word in bringing out Dreiser's attitude towards life is "kindness." Even at its worst, life contains something which he, with full compassion for his beaten hero, will not reject, but will embrace with tenderness.

Dreiser and the Plotting of Inarticulate Experience

Julian Markels*

If one thinks that such thoughts do not come to so common a type of mind—that such feelings require a higher mental development—I would urge for their consideration the fact that it is the higher mental development that does away with such thoughts. It is the higher mental development which induces philosophy and that fortitude which refuses to dwell upon such things—refuses to be made to suffer by their consideration. The common type of mind is exceedingly keen on all matters which relate to its physical welfare—exceedingly keen. It is the unintellectual miser who sweats blood at the loss of a hundred dollars. It is the Epictetus who smiles when the last vestige of physical welfare is removed.

Sister Carrie

By now the cataloguing of Dreiser's limitations has settled into a rather dry routine: his turgid and graceless style, which led F. R. Leavis to observe that Dreiser writes as if he hasn't a native language; his limited insight into the psychology of his characters; his wearisome attention to detail; and his editorial pretentiousness and inconsistency, in which he often seems bent on making metaphysical mountains out of mechanistic molehills. Such characteristics are not mere superfluous gimcrackery but part of Dreiser's substance, inseparable from his fictional method and from the conception of human experience that he attempts to shape in his fiction. Yet to pigeonhole Dreiser in this way is to obscure the fact that not all of his substance is composed of such defects. Equally the product of his method and conception, when he is at his best, is a powerful sense of the mystery underlying human experience, of the fathomless processes which hold our lives in suspension, of the deep sources of pain and desire with which our human condition confronts us—in short, of what Dreiser himself called the wonder of life. Even if he is not a Balzac or a Dickens or a Dostoevsky, the whole of Dreiser's substance is frequently rich and moving and powerful. It is time finally to acknowledge him as our own and go

*Reprinted from *Massachusetts Review*, 2 (Spring, 1961), 431–48. Copyright © 1961 by the *Massachusetts Review*. Reprinted by permission of the Massachusetts Review, Inc.

on from there—to explore his quality and unravel his meaning for us. If we cannot afford to ignore his limitations, neither can we afford to let him lie bound in that literary dungeon to which he has been consigned for some years by the neoliberal Zeuses of contemporary criticism.

The greatest obstacle in the way of such an enterprise is not that Dreiser writes as if he hasn't a native language, but that as critics we are unprepared to pass beyond that fact. We are disconcerted to read a statement like Saul Bellow's in his review of F. O. Matthiessen's book on Dreiser: "But it is very odd that no one has thought to ask just what the 'bad writing' of a powerful novelist signifies." Such a remark suggests that in some significant way we are estranged from the novel as a literary form, that to recover Dreiser we must recover the suppleness of certain critical faculties which have been until recently the victims of atrophy.

The first, if indirect step, in such a recovery is to confront the fact that Dreiser's artistic purposes made no strenuous demands upon his style, which after all may be true of a novelist though not of a poet. Dreiser could on occasion produce a kind of "good writing," so that his characteristic style is the result not only of ineptness but of a choice of relevant means for communicating what he had to. At scattered moments in his writing there is a compactness and fluency which usually passes unnoticed. There is, for example, this paragraph from *An American Tragedy:*

> The impact of this remark, a reflection of the exact truth, was not necessary to cause Clyde to gaze attentively, and even eagerly. For apart from her local position and means and taste in dress and manners, Sondra was of the exact order and spirit that most intrigued him—a somewhat refined (and because of means and position showered upon her) less savage, although scarcely less self-centered, Hortense Briggs. She was, in her small, intense way, a seeking Aphrodite, eager to prove to any who were sufficiently attractive the destroying power of her charm, while at the same time retaining her own personality and individuality free of any entangling alliance or com- promise. However, for varying reasons which she could not quite explain to herself, Clyde appealed to her. He might not be anything socially or financially, but he was interesting to her.

Eliminate the flatulent next-to-last sentence, change the paren- thetical into a subordinate clause, and you have in this passage a piece of smooth and deliberate prose such as might have been written by an im- itator of Henry James. Just as it stands the passage has a liveliness and precision which, if more prevalent, would make Dreiser's style less vulnerable to attack. But such writing is not frequent and hence not memorable in Dreiser; and indeed, he writes in this way only when, as in the present instance, he is taking time out to summarize previously recounted information. When his eye is on his main business his ear goes flat, and he characteristically writes the thick prose by which we remember him.

The source of his power and his meaning for us lies elsewhere, then, and I think it is in his method of arranging the episodes of his plots in order to dramatize with perfect coherence that absence of foreordained purpose in the universe, and its corollary, the hegemony of chance, of which he speaks so awkwardly in his "philosophical" writings. Not consistently but in long and powerful sequences, Dreiser's plot construction results in a fully credible image of human experience as an amoral process; it implies the possibility of human purpose and dignity arising out of a necessary immersion in this process; and hence Dreiser's method excludes the deterministic pathos of the conventional naturalistic novel, which conceives of human experience as the closing of a trap rather than the unfolding of a process. Frequently in Dreiser's novels the moment-to-moment action gives us no reason to desire or expect either good or bad fortune for the characters, no reason to feel hopeful, fearful, sad, or angry on their behalf. We are convinced instead that for them whatever is, is right; and we are moved by the mystery of their experience being so coherently purposeless and yet possibly resulting for them in an enlargement of being. When we see Carrie Meeber respond to her experience directly in fear and desire, without imposing upon it any moral categories or expectations, when we see her enlarge her worldly status and her human identity by her unquestioning submission to the "whatever is" of her experience, then we know why Dreiser attributes to Carrie the quality of "emotional greatness." When we see Hurstwood and Clyde Griffiths ruined by an equally emotional and unquestioning submission, then perhaps we know in a glimmer what Dreiser must have meant by the mystery and terror and wonder of life.

Such knowledge arises from a rhythm in the sequence of Dreiser's episodes rather than from anything that can be communicated by a graceful style. It is the rhythm of inarticulate human experience, undifferentiated and hence by definition without style. Matthiessen suggested rightly that Dreiser's sea imagery, his symbol of the rocking chair, and his own fondness for a rocking chair, all point to "a physical basis for the rhythm of his thoughts." But where the imagery and symbols are only its symptoms, the "physical basis" itself is established by Dreiser's method of construction, which is his true source of strength. It is also the source of his weakness, as I will indicate later, in that his method of construction disables Dreiser from portraying the emergence in human experience of moral consciousness and its corollary, literary style.

I

In the opening sequence of *Sister Carrie*, in which Carrie arrives in Chicago wholly inarticulate, Dreiser employs his method with powerful effect and absolute credibility. The design of the novel's first eight chapters makes perfectly logical and coherent Carrie's silent drifting toward her own good, and at the same time the irrelevance of any moral categories by which she might judge or be judged. On the trip from her country home to make her way in the city, Carrie meets Drouet, whose gaudiness of dress and ostentatious *savoir-faire* impress her simply because they are new in her experience. Then the drabness of her life in the city, with its round of hunting, holding and losing rough factory jobs which pay no more than her board in the dreary apartment of her listless sister and surly brother-in-law Hanson, makes the elegance of Drouet seem all the more attractive. When she has lost her job and is ready to go home in despair, she meets Drouet, who offers to provide the clothes and luxuries which she had come to the city to acquire. After much vacillation, she accepts his offer; and after he has taken her to dinner and to see *The Mikado,* a play that arouses in her "vain imaginings about place and power, about far-off lands and magnificent people," she becomes his mistress.

This material is not highly arresting. It seems an obvious occasion for the method of documentary determinism, in which Carrie is overwhelmed by the sheer weight of accumulated details exhibiting the drab restrictiveness of her environment and the bright expansiveness of Drouet's. But while Dreiser in fact presents an enormous amount of documentary detail, he does not simply pile it up to create an environmental "force" which explains Carrie's fall; and Matthiessen certainly was wrong when he suggested that Dreiser's characteristic method of construction is "Balzac's direct way of presenting solid slabs of continuous experience." The experience presented is indeed continuous, but its distinctive quality is that it is not presented in solid slabs that might make us aware of a shaping environment. Instead Dreiser breaks up and alternates in a precisely elaborated pattern the two main groups of details, so that the larger dialectic of the whole sequence is mirrored and repeated a hundred times in the minute episodes of the unfolding action. Though a Jamesian concern with the conscious life is alien to Dreiser, he works with a similar intensity of focus upon "manners" as the primary stuff of experience. And this makes Carrie's negotiation with her environment seem not so much a helpless response to overwhelming forces as a necessary immersion in a fundamental process.

In Chapter One, Carrie meets Drouet on the train, and is impressed with the vivacity, opulence, and assured contentment that he exhibits. At the end of the chapter Carrie, greeted at the Chicago station by her grim sister, immediately becomes aware of the sharp contrast between the "cold reality" represented by Minnie, and the "world of light and merriment" represented by Drouet. In Chapter Two, Dreiser documents Minnie's cold reality: her taciturn husband, who works in the stockyards and makes monthly payments on two parcels of real estate; and her threadbare third-floor apartment, with its general atmosphere of "a settled opposition to anything save a conservative round of toil." Carrie responds to this atmosphere by writing Drouet that she cannot receive him at her sister's. Thus the first two chapters establish the two poles of Carrie's world and of her range of awareness, the field of her experience at this early stage. And they initiate that process of shuttling back and forth from one pole to another which is to lead finally to an enlargement of identity accompanied by a rise in worldly status.

Chapter Three, which concerns Carrie's search for a job, is a microcosm of the entire method. In ten pages Dreiser reports nine separate encounters with prospective employers, not to mention time off for lunch. In her first, second, fourth, sixth and eighth attempts, Carrie is met with cold rebuffs which plunge her into hopelessness. In her third, fifth and seventh encounters she is given a friendly reception which raises her spirits, but no job; and in her ninth and last try she gets a job in a shoe factory at $4.50 a week. The whole design is typified in the episode where Carrie acts on the advice of a friendly employment manager that she look for work in a department store. She becomes almost exuberant as she walks through the store and sees the elegant lady shoppers and the lovely clothes she might buy if she gets the job. Then she meets the gruffest employment manager in her experience so far, who not only refuses her a job but virtually chases her out of the store. But such incidents are immediately erased from memory once she lands a job, and finally she comes home elated, remembering Drouet, certain that she will be happy in Chicago.

Chapter Four shows the step-by-step undermining of this elation. It begins with Carrie's fantasies of opulence as she sits in her rocking chair and spends her money in her mind many times over. Then the Hansons refuse to go to the theater with her to celebrate her success; and when she stands in the doorway to soak up the exciting life of the city as a substitute for going to the theater, her brother-in-law manifests cold disapproval. Her distress is complete when on her first day of work she is exposed to the stiff boredom of her job and the callowness of the young men who work with her.

Then Dreiser reverses direction again, leaving Carrie at the bottom and taking us to the "top," to witness a conversation between Drouet and Hurstwood in the "truly swell saloon" of Fitzgerald and Moy's. Here he expands and fills in with detail our image of Drouet's world, just when that world seems more inaccessible than ever to Carrie. In Chapter Six, Dreiser returns to Carrie, who is thoroughly disappointed in her job and in mounting friction with Hanson as she stands again in the doorway. She gets sick and loses her job, and on the fourth day of looking for work she runs into Drouet, who takes her to lunch in a fine restaurant, recognizes her distress, and gives her twenty dollars for clothes. In Chapter Seven, Carrie's worry about accepting the money is gradually purged—by her continued failure to find work, by further manifestations of Hanson's antagonism, and by Drouet's increasing generosity. The chapter ends with her moving into a place of her own, paid for by Drouet. And Chapter Eight, the last in the sequence, ends with her going to the theater at last, and with her seduction. Then Dreiser begins the pattern all over again, with a chapter about Hurstwood, the upper pole of the second major sequence.

Instead of piling up his material in solid slabs, then, Dreiser separates and stretches it out in minute gradations, and then shuttles Carrie back and forth. Hanson's cold disapproval of her aspirations is a single fact of the story; but Dreiser exhibits it on three distinct occasions, and each time after Carrie has had a success which gives rise to those aspirations. And her exposure to Hanson is usually followed by her exposure to Drouet. Her two main possibilities are presented to her mind serially and alternately instead of in simultaneous pairs, and the alternations are so swift that she has time to respond only in feeling but not in judgment to one set of circumstances before it is succeeded by its opposite. In view of her limited experience at this early stage, it is entirely credible that she should be aware at each moment only of what that moment brings. Nothing in her life has equipped her to stand apart from each moment and locate it in some larger system of expectations or judgments. Her consciousness of her identity does not precede, but arises out of, the ebb and flow of her experience. And this makes us feel that only by submitting to this ebb and flow, only by being loyal and responsive to each of her facts as it presents itself in turn, may Carrie attain her identity.

The sign of her emotional depth and of the wonder of life is that Carrie does attain her identity through such a seemingly aimless process. She arrives in Chicago a mere undifferentiated blob of feelings, just barely articulate. But her passage through the dialectic of desire and frustration does in fact enlarge her scope and refine her powers of discrimination. By responding only with her feelings she comes to perceive what James's heroines were spared any need to learn: that wealth is valuable not merely for itself, but as equipment for a free life in which one might engage the world in its full variety and complexity. To be sure, Drouet is no man to be chosen by a sophisticated woman. But his generosity and his buoyant appetite for living offer unmistakably richer possibilities than the Hansons' conservative round of toil or the young factory workers' crude fun. Drouet offers Carrie a way out of the spiritual death in which her environment does indeed threaten to trap her, an avenue leading toward the center of life. And when we see Carrie installed as Drouet's mistress, we are aware in her of a new presence, the weight of an actual person. She had learned to dress and move her body gracefully. She is acquiring the habit of speaking several sentences consecutively. She had begun to discriminate the tones of the world around her. As the process continues and her immersion is renewed, she learns to perceive Drouet's limitations and outgrows him too.[1] Her progress from Drouet to Hurstwood to Ames is marked by a continuing enlargement of identity and inner-direction. She is transformed from an amorphous into a differentiated human being.

The impression created by the plot that life is an amoral process is reinforced by Dreiser's descriptions of his characters. Even those more articulate than Carrie, like Drouet, are not permitted any long-range motives, which might imply a significant degree of moral awareness. Drouet gives Carrie twenty dollars out of an immediate generosity, not as part of a deliberate plan to seduce her. Like Carrie, he takes each moment as it comes:

> Now, in regard to his pursuit of women, he meant them no harm, because he did not conceive of the relation which he hoped to hold with them as being harmful. He loved to make advances to women, to have them succumb to his charms, not because he was a cold-blooded, dark, scheming villain, but because his inborn desire urged him to that as a chief delight. He was vain, he was boastful, he was as deluded by fine clothes as any silly-headed girl. A truly deep-dyed villain could have hornswaggled him as readily as he could have flattered a pretty shop girl. His fine success as a salesman lay in his geniality and the thoroughly reputable standing of his house. He bobbed about among men, a veritable bundle of enthusiasm—no power worthy the name of intellect, no thoughts worthy the adjective noble, no feeling long continued in one strain. . . . In short, he was as good as his intellect conceived.

He *bobbed about*, without needing or wanting to chart his course, but merely riding the waves of his "chief delight." Dreiser assigns Drouet not a dramatic persona capable of exerting influence, but rather a *gestalt*, a circumscribed field of activity which impinges upon the field of Carrie's passivity. He is simply *there* as one element in the total process which the plot unfolds. And the other characters are similarly adjusted and absorbed into the medium of the plot. They do not make the story, the story manifests them.

II

In 1916 Dreiser described to H. L. Mencken how he began writing *Sister Carrie*:

> Finally—September 1899 I took a piece of yellow paper and to please him [Arthur Henry] wrote down a title at random—*Sister Carrie*—and began. From September to Oct. 15th or thereabouts I wrote steadily to where Carrie met Hurstwood. Then I quit, disgusted. I thought it was rotten.

Whether or not his critics agree with Dreiser, this section of the novel has never commanded their attention. Their general impression seems to be that he outgrew the fumbling methods of composition that characterize his earliest work. It is all the more striking, then, to notice that Dreiser employs precisely the method I have described in what are perhaps the two most admired sequences in all his novels, the decline of Hurstwood in *Sister Carrie*, and, twenty-five years and five novels later, the events in *An American Tragedy* beginning with Clyde Griffiths' arrival in upstate New York and ending with the drowning of Roberta Alden.

The long grade of Hurstwood's decline is so familiar that I will not rehearse its details here. The little episode where he decides to turn on the gas but hasn't money for a flophouse room in which to do it, then begs a quarter, then decides to use the money for food and carry on awhile longer, is typical of the whole sequence and identical in design to the earlier episodes involving Carrie. The sequence in *An American Tragedy* warrants attention, however, because it shows the fundamental character of Dreiser's plastic power unchanged after the major span of his writing career, and because it may serve to clear up a traditional misunderstanding of the form and underlying conception of that novel. Everybody knows that Dreiser was using a murder case reported in the papers, the drowning of Grace Brown by Chester Gillette in Moose Lake, New York, in 1906. When Dreiser locates the drowning two-thirds through the 800-page novel, having told in minute detail the grim story of his hero's life beginning at age twelve, critics on the scent of naturalism assume that he has been spending his time building up a great weight of environmental forces that are to crush Clyde and explain the murder. But none of the mountainous information about Clyde's early life is even relevant to explain the murder. His early history interests us in the same way the first chapters of a biography do, as a segment in the total process of a man's life. The murder is fully explained by the events immediately leading up to it, beginning with Clyde's arrival in Lycurgus. It is the perfectly logical result of a process which is again exhibited in Dreiser's method of arranging his episodes. Only this time, as befits the amoral character of that process, the hero emerges at the ebb rather than the flow of fortune.

After a boyhood with "the flavor of sand," to use Alfred Kazin's phrase for Dreiser's own boyhood, Clyde Griffiths is brought to Lycurgus, New York, to work in the shrinking room of his uncle's collar factory. At first he forms social attachments with people of his own class; but once he has glimpsed the elegant and genteel world of his cousins and Sondra Finchley, he snobbishly fancies himself above his former friends and cuts himself off from them. But then his cousins and Sondra go off for their summer holidays, leaving Clyde isolated and lonely at the time when Roberta Alden arrives on the scene. Clyde and Roberta form an attachment, and as their romance develops he persuades her to move and take a room with a private entrance. Roberta no sooner compromises herself by

this action than Sondra returns to town and arranges to have Clyde invited out in high society. Then, at the moment when Clyde has finally
"arrived" socially, Roberta, who now looks faded compared to Sondra
but whom Clyde has been seeing and deceiving out of pity and guilt,
discovers that she is pregnant.

All the remaining details—the series of attempts to get an abortion,
Clyde's refusal to marry Roberta, his planning of the murder—are arranged in the same pattern. Like Carrie, Clyde is shuttled ceaselessly back
and forth. Unequipped to anticipate or judge his experience by previously
formulated standards, he responds logically to each circumstance as it
arises, taking his facts one by one. At no single point before the end of the
sequence are we well enough informed to pass judgment on what is happening. But at the end no judgment is possible. Everybody—Clyde,
Samuel Griffiths, Sondra, Roberta—has been moderately but not unduly
selfish. Like Drouet, each one has merely performed according to his
gestalt. If anybody had taken a firm stand at any single point, catastrophe
might have been averted. But nothing in the situation facing any single
character has indicated the necessity for such a stand. By his characteristic arrangement of episodes, Dreiser creates a firm pattern for the inscrutable, patternless drift of experience.

I do not mean to deny, however, that Clyde Griffiths and Hurstwood
before him are "victims." Indeed, it is perhaps more forlorn and helpless
to be a victim of the blind drift of cosmic chance than of the determinate
and hence remediable forces engendered by society. But it is also more
dignified, and truer to the condition of being human rather than a
laboratory animal. In Dreiser's sense we are all victims equally, so that
the fact when applied to Hurstwood or Clyde Griffiths is merely a *donnée*
of their existence, not a special occasion for pity or anger on their behalf.
In the article on "The Curious Shifts of the Poor" from which much of the
account of Hurstwood's decline is taken, Dreiser ends his description of
the Bowery *Lumpenproletariat* by saying, "the individuals composing
this driftwood are no more miserable than others." They and Hurstwood
are no more victims than Carrie, who drifts upward instead of
downward. And when Dreiser claims for Carrie the quality of "emotional
greatness," he implies that it is not mere chance that her victimization
should lead to success and Hurstwood's to death. He implies that a purposive and meaningful life may emerge from the meaningless drift of experience, and with it a personal "style" which might in turn demand embodiment by an appropriate literary style. And it is precisely at the point
where he tries to fill out this implication, to dramatize the emergence of
consciousness, purpose and style, that we may discover the limitations of
Dreiser's method and his genuine weakness as a novelist.

III

To fully perceive this weakness, first we must make what I believe is a Dreiserian distinction between being articulate and being conscious. A person may be articulate in learning to recognize his desires, to name them, and to pursue their objects actively instead of passively. Consciousness requires further the ability to judge those desires, to anticipate the consequences of pursuing them for some larger system of values, and hence to become responsible for one's active choices. To grow from articulateness into consciousness is to step from an amoral into a moral world of experience; and it is precisely in portraying that step that Dreiser's method proves inadequate. The method works successfully only when the characters are, so to speak, below the threshold of consciousness. It works successfully to bring Clyde Griffiths to the murder at the end of Book Two of *An American Tragedy*. Then Book Three is devoted mainly to Clyde's debate with himself (and Dreiser's debate with us) whether he should become conscious of the implications of his act and accept responsibility for it. In *Sister Carrie* the method works successfully to the point where Carrie prefers Hurstwood to Drouet. And it is most significant that once Dreiser brings Carrie to that point, he does not know what to do with her, and shifts the entire focus of the novel from her rise to Hurstwood's decline, where again the method works successfully to record a fall below the threshold of consciousness into an undifferentiated state of being comparable to Carrie's at the beginning. Carrie's rise during the second half of the novel is so clearly directed toward the emergence of consciousness that we have no reason to doubt Dreiser's intention here. This crucial result of her immersion in the drift of experience is pointed at and argued. But it never acquires sufficient dramatic weight to balance Hurstwood's decline. The ultimate weakness of *Sister Carrie* is the thinness and lack of warmth, the pasteboard quality of the heroine during the last half of the novel. For Dreiser was unwilling, perhaps unable, to find a method for depicting the manifestations of Carrie's enhanced powers in conscious and morally responsible actions.

Dreiser's tenacity in clinging to his characteristic method forces him to give increasingly inconsistent accounts of Carrie once she begins reaping the fruits of her career. The ripest fruit in her harvest is her relationship with Ames, who is introduced at Carrie's final stage of development as an unmistakable representative of the conscious life. She has only a few brief conversations with this shadowy young man, who "seemed wiser than Hurstwood, saner and brighter than Drouet," in his belief that self-aggrandizement is mere vanity, that one must read important books rather than sentimental novels, and that finally one must be selfless. In their last talk, after Carrie has become a successful comedienne, Ames urges her to give up comedy and try for serious parts, where her talents will be more valuable to others and will therefore endure:

> . . . You have this quality in your eyes and mouth and in your
> nature. You can lose it, you know. If you turn away from it
> and live to satisfy yourself alone, it will go fast enough. The

look will leave your eyes. Your mouth will change. Your power
to act will disappear. You may think they won't, but they will.
Nature takes care of that.

Here is Carrie's final attainment, the knowledge that if she lives only to
satisfy herself she will lose herself. Her ceaseless drifting toward only
what satisfies herself has led her to confront finally the demand of Nature
that she consciously shape her experience to run in the channels of
selflessness. Here more than anywhere in Dreiser is the justification for
Eliseo Vivas' remark that "there is more to his own concrete dramatic picture of men and society than he finds room for in his mechanistic
philosophy." But it is also true that at this moment Dreiser's dramatic picture is not very roomy either. In the sketchy characterization of Ames we
have another instance of Dreiser's intention made perfectly clear but not
rendered dramatically effective. And in his refusal to let Carrie take up
the challenge of Ames' suggestion, he is squelching her arbitrarily. We
have watched her ascend from the Hansons to Drouet and from Drouet to
Hurstwood. Now, when Hurstwood is left behind and Ames appears,
Dreiser becomes fussy and hesitant at the prospect of making Carrie as
conscious and responsible as Ames challenges her to be.

Indeed, as if the record of Carrie's relation with Ames were not
already sufficiently thin and halting, in other passages late in the novel
Dreiser undermines Ames' position and the resolution which Ames proposes to Carrie. Dreiser allows Carrie brief glimmerings of consciousness, but only to remember her early career in Chicago in terms that
attribute to it a rationale as thoroughly inconsistent with the facts as
Ames's challenge and the entire role he plays are consistent. When
Hurstwood stops looking for a job, Carrie remembers scornfully that in
her early struggle in Chicago she never stopped trying; she decides that
now, as in Chicago, she will try to get an acting job "as a last resort in
distress." The facts are that although she did struggle valiantly in
Chicago, she also eventually stopped trying, and was ready to pack up
and go home when Drouet rescued her; and that her Chicago venture as
an amateur actress was not a last resort in distress (though she had begun
to tire of Drouet), but something arranged entirely by Drouet, signed,
sealed and delivered on a platter without Carrie's lifting a finger. Dreiser
makes her remember these things as if she had planned and pursued her
goals systematically. And this engrafted rationale leads him into a damaging confusion in his final portrait of Carrie. Near the end of the novel,
long after her last interview with Ames, and after her resounding success
on the comic stage has brought her a salary of $150 a week, we are told:

> It does not take money long to make plain its impotence,
> providing the desires are in the realm of affection. With her
> one hundred and fifty in hand, Carrie could think of nothing
> particular to do. . . . Her clothes had for some time been
> wholly satisfactory. Another day or two and she would receive

another hundred and fifty. It began to appear as if this were
not so startlingly necessary to maintain her present state. If she
wanted to do anything better or move higher, she must have
more—a great deal more.

For most of her life her desires were in fact in the realm of money. But
now that her experience with Ames has transformed them into desires for
affection, now that money has shown its impotence, she decides she must
have more money.[2] The whole paragraph until the last sentence is a con-
firmation in her own experience of what Ames had told her. But instead of
letting her mind drift in characteristic fashion to memories of Ames, as
earlier it drifted to Drouet or Hurstwood in similar situations, now
Dreiser intervenes with a false explanation which makes Carrie inaccessible to the wisdom derived from her own immersion in the drift of experience. Dreiser increasingly stiffens to resist the deepest implications of
his own method as that method threatens to project Carrie across the
threshold of consciousness into the arms, so to speak, of Ames.

Thus at the beginning of his career in *Sister Carrie* and at its height in
An American Tragedy, Dreiser balks at portraying the life of consciousness and responsibility which arises logically out of his own conception of the inarticulate drift of experience. He arbitrarily qualifies
Carrie's emergence into consciousness, and later he can do no more than
make Clyde Griffiths' similar emergence the subject of an essentially
unresolved debate. And without a dramatically rendered life of moral
consciousness there is no demand for style. There is in fact an implicit
denial of style, so that finally it is accurate to say that Dreiser's style is the
necessary defect of his virtue. In its meandering syntax, its fuzzy diction,
its jerky rhythms and abrupt transitions, Dreiser's style is almost wholly
unarticulated. And in this respect it simply affirms the inarticulateness of
his characters. A coherently inflected style would attribute to the
characters a personal "style" appropriate only to a degree of consciousness
that Dreiser does not allow them; it would arrest the flow of experience
created by his method of plotting; it would embody the results of the process rather than the process under way. Dreiser's own style actually helps
to articulate his vision of life as an amoral process containing its own
coherent rhythm, bearing us along mysteriously and challenging us to
become conscious of ourselves.

The somehow unexpected power achieved despite his style by
Dreiser's method of plotting may serve to remind us of the enormous
resources of the novel as a genre. We often hear nowadays that the novel
is dead or dying, having exhausted its materials, with the possible exception of those relating to the condition of the self. Dreiser's power is unexpected because he is not directly concerned with the self, because in his
gallery of characters there is so little of that "self-presence" which Ortega
y Gasset told us is the sign of greatness in the novel and the one necessity
for its continuance as a literary genre. Dreiser's novels do not bear the sign

of greatness, but they show how various and new may be the novel's sources of life, for they derive their vitality precisely from Dreiser's ability to portray human experience before "self-presence" is achieved, to portray human beings in the process of becoming differentiated and conscious of themselves.

Dreiser's portrayal may remind us too that we still struggle to become conscious of ourselves and to locate the responsibilities that genuinely arise from our condition of life. It is traditional to compare Dreiser to James and find him parochial and thick-headed in his inability to portray the conscious life. But the social facts out of which James was able to imagine the conscious and moral life simply did not exist for Dreiser. And they do not exist for us. Dreiser's facts, which are our facts, are still largely inscrutable. And Dreiser's parochialism is simply part of a national phenomenon in our life and letters during this century, from the aloof clinical observation of the unconscious life in Stephen Crane's *Maggie* to the forced rejection of the conscious life in the novels of Ernest Hemingway. We smile nowadays to think how Dreiser's great contemporary Clarence Darrow made a monkey out of Bryan at the Scopes Trial. We too often forget the enormous waste of Darrow's granite courage and high intelligence engaged at the level of such monkeyshines. It is Dreiser's distinction that, despite his personal philosophy, as an artist he was often able to cut beneath the parochial oversimplifications of his time—from Social Darwinism and Zolaism to *nada* and Marxism and the honor of the South—to a core of substance that remains a central preoccupation of our best contemporary novelists. One might almost say that writers like Saul Bellow and Herbert Gold pick up where Dreiser left off, trying to discover by their art the point at which emerges from the amoral drift of experience a universal content for our proper consciousness of ourselves, the conditions under which we might honestly assume our responsibilities. Where Dreiser was able to imagine coherently the processes of experience but not the self-presence of his characters, the younger writers create characters superbly endowed with self-presence but still searching to attune themselves to the fundamental processes of human experience. Such writers may be said to represent the conscience of America. And that is why, for this reader, to look back at the American novel in the twentieth century is to find Dreiser, with his stubborn yet hopeful challenge to immerse ourselves in the dark processes of life, standing at the center of the field of vision.

Notes

1. Claude M. Simpson, who has studied the original manuscript of *Sister Carrie* from which Dreiser made cuts for the published version, tells me that Dreiser deleted a number of short passages describing Carrie in the process of outgrowing Drouet, and that these were arranged largely in the manner I have described. I am indebted to Professor Simpson for many

valuable suggestions concerning *Sister Carrie*, and for his article, *"Sister Carrie* Reconsidered," *Southwest Review*, 44 (Winter, 1959), 44–53.

2. There are objections to my reading here, on the grounds that "more" is ambiguous or even that it refers clearly to "affection" rather than "money." I can only rely on an ear which I hope is by now attuned to Dreiser's syntactical ambiguities, on other evidence for exactly the same kind of confusion in the later characterization of Carrie, and on the whole of the last sentence quoted. In that sentence, "better," "higher," and "more" all refer to "her present state." And Carrie's "present state" is founded on clothes and money, not affection.

The Finesse of Dreiser

Ellen Moers*

We are reading Dreiser again. Without benefit of editorial fanfare or critical hoopla, a revival is upon us, solidified by that blessed invention of the fifties, the quality paperbook book, with its attraction for the young, the poor, the serious, the curious, the follower of fashion—for, in short, the reader. There are seventeen Dreiser volumes now in paper, including seven different imprints of *Sister Carrie*. (For the record, which has its interest as a signpost to taste, there are also seven Ambassadors, fourteen Red Badges of Courage, ten Moby Dicks, fifteen Scarlet Letters, twelve Huckleberry Finns.)

Young people have good reason to be reading Dreiser, as they obviously are, beyond the fact of his quality. He forms a bridge between the self-consciously inarticulate poets and novelists of their generation (the devotees of what Robert Brustein has called the Cult of Unthink) and the humanitarians of the last century, for whom the inability to articulate was in itself tragic, even disgusting. It is as the novelist of the inarticulate hero that Dreiser comes again upon the literary scene.

"One thing that you are to be praised for is that you have always been low," Edgar Lee Masters wrote Dreiser; "you have always loved low company, as Hawthorne and Emerson did and Whitman and before them as Goethe did. This passion conduces to honesty." But how is Dreiser in fact *low*? What is the social milieu of his novels? It is not low, certainly, in the Marxist sense, which seems relevant only because Dreiser's final political stand was with the Communist Party. Dreiser never wrote a proletarian novel: his favorite characters are an actress, a saloonkeeper, a traveling salesman, an art-collecting financial manipulator, a street preacher, a painter, a mistress, a bellboy. The fringe figures, wasters and spoilers and enjoyers, were for Dreiser, as for his master Balzac, the irresistible subject.

Dreiser's characters are low in the sense of being stupid. Carrie and Jennie and Clyde would probably rank well below the norm in any verbal intelligence test. Neither sentimentality nor disgust mars Dreiser's han-

*Reprinted from *American Scholar*, 33 (Winter, 1963), 109–14. Copyright © 1963 by the United Chapters of Phi Beta Kappa. Reprinted by permission of the publisher and Martin Mayer.

dling of inarticulate people—although both these patronizing attitudes repeatedly disfigured the "naturalist" tradition to which he is supposed to belong. That Dreiser loved his helpless, unconscious people has often been said, but he did so with the very special love of a sibling, carrying with it acceptance, identification, shame, detachment and an honesty related to the contempt that is bred by familiarity. In the most literal sense, as his letters and autobiographical writings show clearly, Dreiser wrote as a brother. This is the central fact about his work, far more important than the clichés thrown at him in the 1930's and '40's: that he was a peasant, a linguistic imigrant, a naturalist, a People's realist, an American and so on.

One of Dreiser's sisters ran off with a married saloon-manager who stole money to keep her (Carrie); one bore a rich man's illegitimate child (Jennie Gerhardt); one brother hung around hotel lobbies looking for easy money, got into trouble and ran off to peddle candy on trains (Clyde). His beloved brother Paul, the song writer "Dresser," ran away from the seminary where he was training to be a priest, spent some time in jail and lived off the bounty of a "madam" on his easy-going way to success. Without much in the line of theory, using only family materials, Dreiser could easily work out a view of life somewhat at variance with the conventional homilies of his day. More important, from the contrast between day-by-day life as it was lived by his brothers and sisters, and life as it was played out in popular melodrama, he devised a literary style that gave form, and even heroism, to the inarticulate.

Dreiser's triumph in this enterprise is Clyde Griffiths in *An American Tragedy*, the last novel published in his lifetime and the sum of his experience as man and artist. But from his first novel, *Sister Carrie*, he addressed himself to the problem of expressing the inexpressibles and, what is more, carried it off with virtuosity and delicacy. These two books are Dreiser's masterpieces. The *Tragedy* is in every way more profound, more complex in structure, more rich in suggestions. That is where we are to look for the tragic sense, the compassion and the sociological subtlety that have won Dreiser the respect, if not the affection of his readers. But Dreiser would never have been able to manage the complex architectonics of *An American Tragedy* without his abundant natural, literary gifts as a novelist, which *Sister Carrie* most patently displays. Like *The Scarlet Letter*, which appeared exactly fifty years earlier, *Sister Carrie* is one of those first novels that show off the almost shameless virtuosity of the novice.

Dreiser wrote *Sister Carrie* somewhat by accident, at the insistence of a friend. He was already, in 1900 (like Hawthorne in 1850), a mature man and an experienced writer; he was the author of so many competent magazine articles (many of them showing a verbal smoothness lacking in *Sister Carrie*) that he had been listed by *Who's Who*. He had also written a few short stories, also at the urging of his friend, but what he really wanted to write was plays, not fiction. "Had I been let alone," he told Mencken, "I would have worked out in that form." *Sister Carrie* shows it.

It is, as no later Dreiser book would be, a novel of *scenes*, some of them so "gorgeous" that they remain in the mind like things in *Madame Bovary* or *Anna Karenina*.

There is, for example, the Hurstwood-Carrie love scene, acted out in a slow-moving horse-drawn carriage pacing along the flat, new, empty stretches of Washington Boulevard; the opening scene, Carrie's meeting with Drouet in the railroad car; Carrie's night of triumph on the stage, before an audience of "stout figures, large white bosoms, and shining pins" that includes her two blazing lovers; and the final stunningly illuminated scenes of Hurstwood in degeneration, one bum among many on a snowy night in the Bowery:

> In the drive of the wind and sleet they pushed in on one another. There were wrists, unprotected by coat or pocket, which were red with cold. There were ears, half covered by every conceivable semblance of a hat, which still looked stiff and bitten. In the snow they shifted, now one foot, now another, almost rocking in unison.

Rhythmic effects of every variety (the train, the streetcar, the carriage horse, the shuffling feet of the bums, the rocking chair) are scattered through the novel so profusely that its lyrical quality becomes at times almost too rich. There are effects of light and color that point to Dreiser's early and lasting passion for painting and architectural decoration, which has hardly been taken seriously by his critics. There are contrapuntal effects with speech—urban and rural; common, middling and "cultivated"; slang and theatrical bombast—that very few other novelists (James Joyce is one) have ever attempted. To say that the best scenes in *Sister Carrie* are cinematic rather than theatrical is another way of saying that Dreiser was a born, virtuoso novelist, for the movies learned more from the novelist than from the playwright. But it is often helpful, as Robert Penn Warren has shown in an essay on *An American Tragedy*, to write of Dreiser's effects in terms of the "sweep of the lens," the "shift of focus," the "movie in our heads."

If there is a crucial scene in *Sister Carrie*, on which the success of the book hangs, it is the early episode in the downtown restaurant, where Carrie is "seduced" by Drouet. This is hardly one of the memorable showpieces of the novel, yet it goes far to set the tone of the whole. For here Dreiser must take a stupid, commonplace girl, whose only charm is her youthful prettiness (and a certain something else that must here be established finally for the reader) and turn her into a heroine—without letting her think or feel or behave in the heroic style. She must take the first decisive step of her life—down a path that she, her family, her world know to be morally wrong—without seeming to understand what she is about and without incurring the reader's exasperation or provoking his blame. For Dreiser has set himself the task of making Carrie sufficiently null to skirt moral criticism, but vital enough to personify the creative force itself—to be, in effect, his Emma Bovary.

The writing in the seduction scene is careful to the point of finesse—a word I would like to bring forward in connection with Dreiser, if only because it challenges the old and worn-out complaints against his style. In one of the recent favorable statements about Dreiser (they are still relatively rare) Saul Bellow asked a useful question about the nature of "bad writing" by a powerful novelist, but moved away from the answer with the lamest recommendation: that "Dreiser's novels are best read quickly." The reverse is true. "Fine" writing (some of James's or Virginia Woolf's, for instance) often fails on slow and close examination, while the coarse, dense, uneven language of the more subtle novelists (like Dickens) yields surprising rewards—and explanations of the art of fiction—to the careful reader.

Dreiser has brought the farm girl, Carrie Meeber, to Chicago, introduced her to the drab home of her married sister, sent her about the city looking for poorly paid, tedious work, and then had her fall ill and lose her job at the outset of her first winter in the big city. Now he sets the stage for temptation. Carrie is spending her fourth weary day of job-hunting wandering the downtown streets of the city with a borrowed ten cents in her pocket for lunch, when Dreiser confronts her with that delectable specimen of brainless virility, Drouet, the traveling salesman Carrie had met on the train but had not seen again since her arrival in Chicago. Four pages later Carrie has taken money from Drouet, and the loss of her virtue is in plain view. But the scene ends as Dreiser has it begin: unstrained, calm, inevitable in a comfortable, flat sort of way, even cosy. Here is the beginning, several pages into Chapter VI:

> . . . Suddenly a hand pulled her arm and turned her about.
> "Well, well!" said a voice. In the first glance she beheld Drouet. He was not only rosy-cheeked, but radiant. He was the essence of sunshine and good-humour. "Why, how are you, Carrie?" he said. "You're a daisy. Where have you been?"
> Carrie smiled under his irresistible flood of geniality.
> "I've been out home," she said.
> "Well," he said, "I saw you across the street there. I thought it was you. I was just coming out to your place. How are you, anyhow?"
> "I'm all right," said Carrie, smiling.
> Drouet looked her over and saw something different.
> "Well," he said, "I want to talk to you. You're not going anywhere in particular, are you?"
> "Not just now," said Carrie.
> "Let's go up here and have something to eat. George! but I'm glad to see you again."
> She felt so relieved in his radiant presence, so much looked

after and cared for, that she assented gladly, though with the
slightest air of holding back.

"Well," he said, as he took her arm—and there was an exuberance of good-fellowship in the word which fairly warmed
the cockles of her heart.

The literary clichés in this last sentence are ugly, but they have a purpose: to throw into relief Drouet's final *"Well"*—which is positively
elegant. In this short passage Drouet speaks that homely Americanism five
times; more than "Say!" and "George!" his other expletives, it is his
trademark. Dreiser was a master of the use of senseless speech to establish
character—and those who believe that mastery does not enter here need
only examine the hundred different cries of inarticulate passion expressed
by Clyde Griffiths' "Gee!" or compare Drouet's speech with Carrie's. In
this passage, as throughout the novel, Carrie says almost nothing. Her
short, primer sentences carry the flat farm twang without Dreiser's insisting on it: "I've been out home," "I'm all right," and "Not just now."

It is relatively easy for Dreiser to show why Carrie succumbs to
Drouet, but much trickier to establish that this timid farm girl—naïve,
compliant, decently conventional and without a notion of the seductive
arts—can tie Drouet to the most permanent relationship of which he is
capable, move on to a more complex lover, prompt Hurstwood to a crime
of Balzacian dimensions and then move on again to solitary theatrical
triumphs. Carrie hardly talks or thinks, but the warmth of her presence
must be at the center of every scene in which she appears. To the men
around her she must, without word, respond; here as everywhere, she
smiles.

In this scene Dreiser first sets forth the idea that Carrie's fall is to be a
triumph, that her sexual adventures stimulate the unfolding of her
temperament, much as the sun's heat brings the plant to flower. The per-
vading atmosphere, the underlying sensual image of this scene is, in fact,
physical warmth. It emanates from Drouet, who (in the passage I have
quoted) is "rosy-cheeked," "the essence of sunshine" to whom Carrie is the
"daisy" of the farm. His *geniality* and *exuberance* are the sun that *warms
her heart*. Dreiser uses the word *radiant* twice at the opening of the scene
to characterize Drouet, and the shining, gleaming, warming quality of
the man is reinforced in the restaurant episode that immediately follows.
Drouet summons the "full-chested, round-faced" Negro waiter with a
hissing "Sst!" and his ordering of the meal, punctuated with the waiter's
repeated "Yassah," turns into a little duet full of sizzling *ss* sounds. (It
does not include the silent Carrie; but its last line is "Carrie smiled and
smiled.") Drouet's apotheosis as a warming, radiating presence comes,
again with intricate sound effects, as the waiter returns, bearing on his
"immense" tray the "hot savoury dishes."

Drouet fairly shone in the matter of serving. He appeared to
great advantage behind the white napery and silver platters of

the table and displaying his arms with a knife and fork. As he cut the meat his rings almost spoke. His new suit creaked as he stretched to reach the plates, break the bread, and pour the coffee. He helped Carrie to a rousing plateful and contributed the warmth of his spirit to her body until she was a new girl. He was a splendid fellow. . . .

Now Dreiser has been careful, in the opening chapters of the novel, to show that Carrie, although momentarily unfortunate, is *not* in the grip of a massively malign fate. She is *not* starving; she is far from destitution; she has two decent homes to go back to. What is at stake is not Carrie's survival but her growth. Dreiser has therefore established the sense of spreading cold that grips Carrie, a cold which is seasonal and physical but also emotional, and to which this scene, full of Drouet's "radiant presence," provides a warm alternative. The whole cold-warmth pattern has been cued to the reader with a sentence about the difficulty of *transplantation* "in the matter of flowers or maidens," which focuses our attention on Carrie as an organism, significantly a plant rather than an animal, whose response to temptation will be less conscious than instinctive.

About a page before Carrie meets Drouet, Dreiser announces the arrival of cold weather with a few carefully composed sentences (the penciled manuscript, ordinarily clean, shows erasures and excisions):

> There came a day when the first premonitory blast of winter swept over the city. It scudded the fleecy clouds in the heavens, trailed long, thin streamers of smoke from the tall stacks, and raced about the streets and corners in sharp and sudden puffs. Carrie now felt the problem of winter clothes.

Carrie falls ill. "It blew up cold after a rain one afternoon. . . . She came out of the warm shop at six and shivered as the wind struck her." A "chattering chill" follows; "she hung about the stove." She recovers, goes out again to look for work, but hates to return to her sister's home at night: "Hanson [her brother-in-law] was so cold." This sort of preparation throws into relief the sunny radiance of Drouet and the answering, smiling warmth of Carrie. It also clarifies, in the most prosaic way, her acceptance of Drouet's money, which Carrie takes to buy the warm clothing she needs for the winter. But the whole cold-warmth pattern, and the accompanying suggestions of sun, heat and soft, young greenness, are there to be drawn on when, at the close of the scene, Dreiser makes the transfer of money a climactic act.

When *Sister Carrie* was new it was regularly denounced, even by the firm that published it, as an immoral and indecent book. Inevitably, later critics, even those so well disposed as F. O. Matthiessen, have reproached Dreiser for his timidity in avoiding sexual contact between his characters. It is true that Dreiser never removes Carrie's clothes or shows her in the act of love. (When, much later, he came to handle sex openly, as in *The Stoic*, the effect is breathless and not quite sane—directing our attention more to Dreiser's temperament than to that of his characters.) What I have called the seduction scene in *Sister Carrie* culminates in nothing more physical than a pressing of hands. Yet Carrie's acceptance of Drouet's money points clearly and richly to her acceptance of Drouet as a lover, not merely because we know that this is the way the world (and the novel) goes, but because Dreiser's language drenches the transfer of money itself with sexual excitement.

Here is how he does it. The food is served. The man and the girl sit across the table from each other, talking banalities. A sexual current arises, for the first time, between them, and is phrased by Dreiser with deliberation: a matter-of-fact, businesslike sentence, then a colloquialism Carrie herself would use, then a literary sentence, suggestively metaphorical:

> She felt his admiration. It was powerfully backed by his liberality and good-humour. She felt that she liked him—that she could continue to like him ever so much. There was something even richer than that, running as a hidden strain, in her mind. . . .

It is important here that our attention be focused on Carrie, and her wordless, actually thoughtless reaction to Drouet's masculinity. (Dreiser cut from the beginning of the scene a sentence about Drouet's liking for Carrie's "mould of flesh" that might have spoiled the tone of the scene.) Drouet looks, admires, and then acts; in two sentences rich with suggestion, he begins to fondle—his cash.

> There were some loose bills in his vest pocket—greenbacks. They were soft and noiseless, and he got his fingers about them and crumpled them up in his hand.

The first physical contact then takes place, in words that seem to do nothing but state a gesture, but the key suggestion of warmth is there:

> She had her hand out on the table before her. They were quite alone in their corner, and he put his larger, warmer hand over it.

Drouet "pressed her hand gently . . . he held it fast . . . he slipped the greenbacks he had into her palm. . . ." Carrie takes the money, agrees to meet Drouet again, goes out onto the street. The last sentences of the chapter resolve the play of hands of the climax, and refer back to the gesture ("Suddenly a hand pulled her arm and turned her about") with which the scene opened. They also resolve the underlying imagery of the whole: the exchange of warmth, the soft greenness of the farm warmed by the heat of the sun.

> Carrie left him, feeling as though a great arm had slipped out before her to draw off trouble. The money she had accepted was two soft, green, handsome ten-dollar bills.[1]

What did Dreiser *avoid* doing with this scene? There is no sentiment, no moralizing, no foreshadowing of conclusions. Carrie's charm for Drouet has been established without destroying her simplicity of temperament; and Drouet's masculine heat has pervaded the scene without the element of lust. Drouet remains vulgar and coarse, but not disgusting. The natural forces of growth and change, the mysteriously casual interactions of creature with environment that always roused in Dreiser the emotions of wonder and awe, have been suggested by a metaphorical (but essentially novelistic) language which in turn gives a surprising eloquence to this tawdry encounter between trivial personalities. The people, Carrie and Drouet, are neither glorified nor idealized.

Two chapters and several days, perhaps weeks, later, Carrie becomes Drouet's mistress. Dreiser puts off the denouement, and indeed avoids presenting the event directly to the reader, not from mere prudery but from a conscious desire to destroy the significance of the act as action, to minimize the element of free will (in which he was a strenuous nonbeliever) and to make credible the lack of reflection in such a girl as Carrie. So we are given much detail about Carrie's shopping and pleasure in her new clothes; about Drouet's pleasure in her appearance and care for her material comfort; and about all the practical problems arising from Carrie's move out of her sister's home and into an apartment Drouet takes for her.

Dreiser's commentary insists, too heavily but never stupidly, on the importance of money, the force of instinct, the significance of habits—abstract topics that drain from Carrie's action the last vestige of moral or sentimental tone. He is particularly careful to keep Carrie's mind blank, her speech halting. A thought of home brings a gesture of despair and a query from Drouet: "What's the matter?" Carrie answers with a line that is at once accurate American slang and literal truth: "Oh, I don't know." Carrie recognizes in a crowd of poorly-dressed factory girls a face she had known at work, and for the first time senses some of the consequences of her move from decent poverty to comfortable disgrace. Her reaction is again a gesture, a start, and Drouet's comment pulls us up with its irony: " 'You must be thinking,' he said."

Dreiser cut from the manuscript a long paragraph making clear how aware he was of the literary significance of what he was doing. The paragraph comes near the beginning of Chapter VIII, after Carrie has gone to Drouet's apartment but before she takes him as her lover. The book as it stands retains nearly all of Dreiser's original reflections on the moral implications (or lack of them) of Carrie's actions; but this excluded paragraph probes—in language so clumsy as to justify the excision—the stylistic problems of inarticulate fiction.

> We are inclined sometimes to wring our hands much more profusely over the situation of another than the mental attitude of that other, towards his own condition, would seem to warrant.

People do not grieve so much sometimes over their own state as we imagine. They suffer, but they bear it manfully. They are distressed, but it is about other things as a rule than their actual state at the moment. We see, as we grieve for them, the whole detail of their blighted career, a vast confused imagery of mishaps, covering years, much as we read a double decade of tragedy in a ten hour [?] novel. The victim meanwhile for the single day or morrow is not actually anguished. He meets his unfolding fate by the minute and the hour as it comes.

So spoke the novelist who was, in every sense, the brother of Sister Carrie.

Notes

1. Dreiser thought at one point of using another transfer of money to prefigure Carrie's capitulation to Hurstwood, her second lover. For very good reasons he penciled the passage out of the manuscript, probably as soon as it was written. (The more subtle love affair between Carrie and Hurstwood would not have been glorified by such a transaction; and the climactic scene, Carrie's stage debut before both her lovers, would have lost some of its effectiveness, for Hurstwood was offering Carrie money to pay for the clothes she would wear on stage.) But Dreiser's choice of words for the discarded "money" scene is interesting. Hurstwood pulls out, not the loose, soft, noiseless, crumpled greenbacks of Drouet, but "a thin clean roll" of new hundred dollar bills. Taking off one bill, he "put it in her little green leather purse and closed it up."

Jennie Gerhardt

A Novel of The First Rank

H. L. Mencken*

If you miss reading *"Jennie Gerhardt,"* by Theodore Dreiser (*Harpers*), you will miss the best American novel, all things considered, that has reached the book counters in a dozen years. On second thought, change "a dozen" into "twenty five." On third thought, strike out everything after "counters." On fourth thought, strike out everything after "novel." Why back and fill? Why evade and qualify? Hot from it, I am firmly convinced that *"Jennie Gerhardt"* is the best American novel I have ever read, with the lonesome but Himalayan exception of "Huckleberry Finn," and so I may as well say it aloud and at once and have done with it. Am I forgetting "The Scarlet Letter," "The Rise of Silas Lapham" and (to drag an exile unwillingly home) "What Maisie Knew"? I am not. Am I forgetting "McTeague" and "The Pit"? I am not. Am I forgetting the stupendous masterpieces of James Fenimore Cooper, beloved of the pedagogues, or those of James Lane Allen, Mrs. Wharton and Dr. S. Weir Mitchell, beloved of the women's clubs and literary monthlies? No. Or "Uncle Tom's Cabin" or "Rob o' the Bowl" or "Gates Ajar" or "Ben Hur" or "David Harum" or "Lewis Rand" or "Richard Carvel"? No. Or "The Hungry Heart" or Mr. Dreiser's own "Sister Carrie"? No. I have all these good and bad books in mind. I have read them and survived them and in many cases enjoyed them.

And yet in the face of them, and in the face of all the high authority, constituted and self-constituted, behind them, it seems to me at this moment that *"Jennie Gerhardt"* stands apart from all of them, and a bit above them. It lacks the grace of this one, the humor of that one, the perfect form of some other one; but taking it as it stands, grim, gaunt, mirthless, shapeless, it remains, and by long odds, the most impressive work of art that we have yet to show in prose fiction—a tale not unrelated, in its stark simplicity, its profound sincerity, to "Germinal" and "Anna Karenina" and "Lord Jim"—a tale assertively American in its scene and its human material, and yet so European in its method, its point of view, its almost reverential seriousness, that one can scarcely imagine an American writing it. Its personages are few in number, and their progress is along a path that seldom widens, but the effect of that progress is

*Reprinted from *Smart Set*, 35 (November, 1911), 153–55.

ever one of large movements and large masses. One senses constantly the group behind the individual, the natural law behind the human act. The result is an indefinable impression of bigness, of epic dignity. The thing is not a mere story, not a novel in the ordinary American meaning of the word, but a criticism and an interpretation of life—and that interpretation loses nothing in validity by the fact that its burden is the doctrine that life is meaningless, a tragedy without a moral, a joke without a point. What else have Moore and Conrad and Hardy been telling us these many years? What else does all the new knowledge of a century teach us? One by one the old ready answers have been disposed of. Today the one intelligible answer to the riddle of aspiration and sacrifice is that there is no answer at all.

"The power to tell the same story in two forms," said George Moore not long ago, "is the sign of the true artist." You will think of this when you read "*Jennie Gerhardt*," for in its objective plan, and even in its scheme of subjective unfolding, it suggests "Sister Carrie" at every turn. Reduce it to a hundred words, and those same words would also describe that earlier study of a woman's soul, with scarcely the change of a syllable. Jennie Gerhardt, like Carrie Meeber, is a rose grown from turnip seed. Over each, at the start, hangs poverty, ignorance, the dumb helplessness of the Shudra—and yet in each there is that indescribable something, that element of essential gentleness, that innate, inward beauty which levels all caste barriers and makes Esther a fit queen for Ahasuerus. And the history of each, reduced to its elements, is the history of the other. Jennie, like Carrie, escapes from the physical miseries of the struggle for existence only to taste the worse miseries of the struggle for happiness. Not, of course, that we have in either case a moral, maudlin fable of virtue's fall; Mr. Dreiser, I need scarcely assure you, is too dignified an artist, too sane a man, for any such banality. Seduction, in point of fact, is not all tragedy for either Jennie or Carrie. The gain of each, until the actual event has been left behind and obliterated by experiences more salient and poignant, is rather greater than her loss, and that gain is to the soul as well as to the creature. With the rise from want to security, from fear to ease, comes an awakening of the finer perceptions, a widening of the sympathies, a gradual unfolding of the delicate flower called personality, an increased capacity for loving and living. But with all this, and as a part of it, there comes, too, an increased capacity for suffering—and so in the end, when love slips away and the empty years stretch before, it is the awakened and suspersentient woman that pays for the folly of the groping, bewildered girl. The tragedy of Carrie and Jennie, in brief, is not that they are degraded but that they are lifted up, not that they go to the gutter but that they escape the gutter.

But if the two stories are thus variations upon the same somber theme, if each starts from the same place and arrives at the same dark goal, if each shows a woman heartened by the same hopes and tortured by the same agonies, there is still a vast difference between them, and that difference is the measure of the author's progress in his art. "Sister Carrie" was a first sketch, a rough piling-up of observations and impressions, disordered and often incoherent. In the midst of the story of Carrie, Mr. Dreiser paused to tell the story of Hurstwood—an astonishingly vivid and tragic story, true enough, but still one that broke the back of the other. In *"Jennie Gerhardt"* he falls into no such overelaboration of episode. His narrative goes forward steadily from beginning to end. Episodes there are, of course, but they keep their proper place, their proper bulk. It is always Jennie that holds the attention; it is in Jennie's soul that every scene is ultimately played out. Her father and mother, Senator Brander the god of her first worship, her daughter Vesta and Lester Kane, the man who makes and mars her—all these are drawn with infinite painstaking, and in every one of them there is the blood of life. But it is Jennie that dominates the drama from curtain to curtain. Not an event is unrelated to her; not a climax fails to make clearer the struggles going on in her mind and heart.

I have spoken of reducing *"Jennie Gerhardt"* to a hundred words. The thing, I fancy, might be actually done. The machinery of the tale is not complex; it has no plot, as plots are understood in these days of "mystery" stories; no puzzles madden the reader. It is dull, unromantic poverty that sends Jennie into the world. Brander finds her there, lightly seduces her, and then discovers that, for some strange gentleness within her, he loves her. Lunacy—but he is willing to face it out. Death, however, steps in; Brander, stricken down without warning, leaves Jennie homeless and a mother. Now enters Lester Kane—not the villain of the books, but a normal, decent, cleanly American of the better class, well to do, level-headed, not too introspective, eager for the sweets of life. He and Jennie are drawn together; if love is not all of the spirit, then it is love that binds them. For half a dozen years the world lets them alone. A certain grave respectability settles over their relation; if they are not actually married, then it is only because marriage is a mere formality, to be put off until tomorrow. But bit by bit they are dragged into the light. Kane's father, dying with millions, gives him two years to put Jennie away. The penalty is poverty; the reward is wealth—and not only wealth itself, but all the pleasant and well remembered things that will come with it: the lost friends of other days, a sense of dignity and importance, an end of apologies and evasions, good society, the comradeship of decent women—particularly the comradeship of one decent woman. Kane hesitates, makes a brave defiance, thinks it over—and finally yields. Jennie does not flood him with tears. She has made progress in the world, has Jennie; the simple faith of the girl has given way to the pride and poise of the woman. Five years later Kane sends for her. He is dying. When it is over, Jennie goes back to her lonely home, and there, like Carrie Meeber before her, she faces the long years with dry eyes and an empty heart. "Days and days in endless reiteration, and then—"

A moral tale? Not at all. It has no more moral than a string quartet or the first book of Euclid. But a philosophy of life is in it, and that philosophy is the same profound pessimism which gives a dark color to the best that we have from Hardy, Moore, Zola and the great Russians—the pessimism of disillusion—not the jejune, Byronic thing, not the green sickness of youth, but that pessimism which comes with the discovery that the riddle of life, despite all the fine solutions offered by the learned doctors, is essentially insoluble. One can discern no intelligible sequence of cause and effect in the agonies of Jennie Gerhardt. She is, as human beings go, of the nobler, finer metal. There is within her a great capacity for service, a great capacity for love, a great capacity for happiness. And yet all that life has to offer her, in the end, is the mere license to live. The days stretch before her "in endless reiteration." She is a prisoner doomed to perpetual punishment for some fanciful, incomprehensible crime against the gods who make their mirthless sport of us all. And to me, at least, she is more tragic thus than Lear on his wild heath or Prometheus on his rock.

Nothing of the art of the literary lapidary is visible in this novel. Its form is the simple one of a panorama unrolled. Its style is unstudied to the verge of barrenness. There is no painful groping for the exquisite, inevitable word; Mr. Dreiser seems content to use the common, even the commonplace coin of speech. On the very first page one encounters "frank, open countenance," "diffident manner," "helpless poor," "untutored mind," "honest necessity" and half a dozen other such ancients. And yet in the long run it is this very *naïveté* which gives the story much of its impressiveness. The narrative, in places, has the effect of a series of unisons in music—an effect which, given a solemn theme, vastly exceeds that of the most ornate polyphony. One cannot imagine "*Jennie Gerhardt*" done in the gipsy phrases of Meredith, the fugual manner of James. One cannot imagine that stark, stenographic dialogue adorned with the brilliants of speech. The thing could have been done only in the way that it has been done. As it stands, it is a work of art from which I for one would not care to take anything away—not even its gross crudities, its incessant returns to C major. It is a novel that depicts the life we Americans are living with extreme accuracy and criticises that life with extraordinary insight. It is a novel, I am convinced, of the very first consideration.

*   *   *   *   *   *   *   *

Pathos and Dreiser

Warwick Wadlington*

I

One reason for the fascination Theodore Dreiser has held for critics is that it is possible to call him important or major without having to say that he is good. That is, because of the social and "philosophical" implications of his work, he seems to lend himself well to American Studies or to period studies, in both of which writers of inferior literary talents tend to be as significant as those of superior artistry, if not more so. Yet Dreiser's ramshackle house of fiction seems so obviously in defiance of the literary laws of gravity that for many commentators the primary question Dreiser poses is one of taste—the provocative and supremely difficult problem of aesthetics for those who agree with Henry James that "it comes back very quickly . . . to the liking."[1] Of the major American authors, Dreiser even more than Poe or Whitman or O'Neill forces upon our attention the vexing enigma of taste and prompts us to mistrust or to re-examine our instinctive (though, ideally, informed) responses to art. And the authentic but usually implicit question of aesthetic propriety, recurring in the Dreiser debate with the obdurate insistence of Dreiser's own prose, has a particular relevance to modern literature.

One way of properly distinguishing the kind of art Dreiser practices is to begin with the term almost universally applied to his distinctive tone—pathos. Along with satellites which cluster around it in Dreiser criticism, such as "compassion" and "pity," this word is used by admirers to call attention to the affective powers of Dreiser's work, and in a memorable instance by Lionel Trilling to excoriate the "doctrinaire indulgence" of Dreiser's "brooding pity" as a form of sentimentalizing the proletariat.[2] It is questionable, however, whether critics have always used the term correctly in regard to Dreiser or have seen that the pathetic is more than a matter of tone. Because of the very fact that it has been easy to agree that pathos is evident in Dreiser's work, the temptation has been to pass over the concept quickly without careful inspection. The tempta-

*Reprinted from *Southern Review*, 7 (Spring, 1971), 411–29. Reprinted by permission of Warwick Wadlington.

tion has been the stronger because of the pejorative, specifically maudlin, connotations of the word and because in writing criticism the natural tendency is to reach for adjectives like "tragic" which are forceful and honorific, if nothing else. As good rebellious scions of the Victorians—who at their best were masters of pathos—we feel queasy at anything we suspect of facile sentimentality. We are thus at some disadvantage in dealing with a continuing tradition of pathetic art. It is a familiar human habit to bend or transmute prestigious words and concepts rather than abandon them, so that by a sort of semantic momentum the term "tragic" will doubtless continue to be applied in our century to works and perceptions that are essentially pathetic. Even extra-literary usage militates against the purely descriptive employment of the adjectives—compare, for example, "a pathetic person" and "a pathetic attempt" with the "tragic" versions of these phrases.

Pathos is Dreiser's forte; it is the basic mode of his writing and the category of propriety by which his art may be fairly judged, understood, "tasted." If pathos, as I believe, tends to be obscured because it is at present taken for granted, my object is to make the concept more visible and in the process to contribute to an understanding of the tradition in which Dreiser writes. I will pay particular attention to *Jennie Gerhardt*, the novel which embodies Dreiser's pathos in its purest form. Although *Jennie Gerhardt* is in the second rank of Dreiser's achievement, behind *Sister Carrie* and *An American Tragedy*, and although the novel has had comparatively little close critical attention, it has been warmly praised, eliciting affectionate approval from many people, beginning with Dreiser himself. The pathos of this story of passive, suffering Jennie is in the one sense obvious; yet Dreiser uses the word "pathos" frequently to describe the situations, the fates, and the ultimate discoveries of many of his other characters as well. For all their differences, Carrie, Hurstwood, Witla, and Clyde Griffiths come to feel essentially the same thing that the superman Cowperwood does: "the pathos of the discovery that even giants are but pygmies, and that an ultimate balance must be struck."[3] Dreiser's habitual use of the term "pathos" is exact; his occasional substitution of the word "tragic" to describe the conditions of his characters is not. Since the confusion also seems to be common among his readers, it is helpful first to establish a working distinction, if not an absolute one, between these two terms in order to begin to see the place of the pathetic in Dreiser's fiction and, more generally, in modern writing. Absolute distinctions tend to break down when we descend from the stratosphere of ideal forms and attempt to apply them to specific, and thus wonderfully recalcitrant, works of literature; and so I will try to keep in mind that in practice "tragic" and "pathetic" are comparative terms like "little" and "big" and that one makes the most sense when it is brought into conjunction with the other.

II

The distinction that I wish to make between the tragic and the pathetic is similar in several respects to that which Northrop Frye develops between high mimetic and low mimetic tragedy and that which Robert B. Heilman establishes between tragedy and melodrama. Heilman says that in melodrama, "man is essentially 'whole,' " which means that the kind of inner conflict that is primarily significant in tragedy is muted and that the emphasis is instead upon man "pitted against some force outside of himself—a compact enemy, a hostile group, a social pressure, a natural event, an accident, or a coincidence."[4] Similarly, in the pathetic work man is integral: he may lack *completeness* as a human being, but he is not seriously divided against himself and does not find in himself a microcosmic struggle between good and evil, as he does in tragedy. In tragedy our attention is focused more upon a man who suffers disjunction within himself; in pathos, more upon a man who suffers disjunction with his world. It is a mistake to think of the pathetic character as solely or necessarily a weak, submissive figure—though of course pathos tends to feature women as protagonists, as for example in *The Duchess of Malfi*, *The Scarlet Letter*, *Madame Bovary*, *Miss Julie*, *Daisy Miller*, Joyce's "Clay," and *A Streetcar Named Desire*. The unsatiated, unappeasable conqueror is also a pathetic figure; for him, infinite yearning for complete but unattainable victory over the Other is an exquisite form of suffering, as it is in *Tamburlaine*, *The Jew of Malta*, *Hedda Gabler* (the woman as "conqueror"), *The Great Gatsby*, Camus' *Caligula*, Dreiser's own Cowperwood Trilogy, and as it is for Satan in *Paradise Lost*. In Aristotelian terms, the tragic character can be neither passive victim nor utter criminal. The pathetic character can be either, though he may be much else besides.

The key to the pathetic mode is above all suffering, the root meaning of pathos. In tragedy, suffering is both a cause and result of the extreme position the hero takes at the very boundaries of human experience, and in the end suffering and psychic divisiveness are transcended in some climactic epiphany. In pathos, suffering is primarily the cause and result of the unsuccessful attempt by the unified personality to reach an accommodation with his world either by submission or conquest, and suffering is endless, never to be transcended, ceasing only in death. The tragic hero has a destiny that he meets in a crisis of decision leading to an act of fatality. Typically, we are directly confronted with his death or exile in such a way that we are allowed—or forced—to detach ourselves from him in order to fix him in the total resolution and to see it whole. We thus experience self-transcendence, to use the terminology of Arthur Koestler (*Insight and Outlook*). In pathos, however, the protagonist is fated to a life of unresolved repetition or to a death which gives little or no sense of final resolution but comes only as the ultimate example of suffering or the longed-for release from it. Tragedy, although giving full weight to suffering, disorder, and flux, drives toward an affirmation of the permanent and the abiding beyond the phenomena of change and divisiveness. This is an affirmation of man's transcendent spirit too, a revelation of the awesome self-integrating resources of the hero. Tragedy is liberating, freeing us "with new acquist/Of true experience" of a reliable, comforting, though mysterious, Ground of Being both in the self and in the universe. Pathos is imprisoning, leading to a vision of a series of inescapable, concentric prisons—the self, society, nature—and the experience of evanescence and uncertainty in the universe. Yet it is important to see that pathos in general gains power insofar as it reminds us of transcendence and makes us aware of the missing connection with an ultimate permanence. In pathos we may be made as fully cognizant of the idea of a redeeming source by its effective absence as we are in tragedy by its mysterious presence. And this reminder of a failed possibility still yearned for makes the condition of imprisonment at once poignant and illuminating. The power of Dreiser's pathos is in large part ascribable to his ability to play off the confinement and alienation of his characters against their (and his) ineffable longing for permanence, for transcendence. His characteristic evocation of a longed-for, genuinely tragic world where pathos would be transcended is one indication of the way the two modes tend to move toward, complicate, and enrich each other.

For pure pathos and pure tragedy are theoretical extremes of the same spectrum, and it follows that a work may present a pathetic hero in a tragic world, and vice versa. The first of these cases is true in works which deal with conflicts between the gods or which directly involve the Absolute and a lesser being, as in Job, *Prometheus Bound*, and *Paradise Lost*. Job and Prometheus are both integral characters, innocent victims forcefully justifying themselves against an antagonist, yet they are granted a revelation of an order (either God or Fate) transcending suffering and impermanence; Satan's total commitment to evil and cosmic disorder necessarily denies him the tragic vision of the world achieved by Adam and Eve. Some of Euripides' plays may be seen as complex versions of the second, perhaps rarer, case: the hero tragically divided against himself who exists in a "pathetic" world where fundamental, ironic disorder is indicated.

Even though we are speaking of modes, not genres, and although the clearest examples of tragic structures are in drama, we may now profit from Aristotle's example and outline the beginning, middle, and end of tragedy and pathos. The tragic pattern begins with the hero in an outwardly peaceful world that is actually divided into spheres of good and evil, order and disorder. This world is an "unweeded garden"—often a plague-ridden kingdom (*Oedipus*) or one divided politically and morally (*Lear*)—in which the time is out of joint, imbalanced. The middle of the pattern is formed by the increasing division of the hero within himself, or his growing discovery that he and his world are correspondingly disjointed (*Hamlet*, of course, above all). *Agon* is internal as well as external, and the pattern is completed when the internal and external balances are righted through the interaction of the hero's subjective choice—or increased awareness—with an objective, impersonal fate. The liberating resolution of transcendent affirmation is often treated in terms of release from imprisonment or constraint, physical or metaphorical (*Samson Agonistes, Hamlet, Othello*).

By contrast, the pattern of pathos is looser, in keeping with the relative inconclusiveness of the mode. It is fundamentally one of dominance and submission, a continuing *agon* between an integrated individual and unified opponent. (The "opponent" may be a totally fragmented and multiplicitous world, but it faces the protagonist as a unit in that it is wholly opposed to him.) This pattern has no definite beginning—though often it begins, as does *Jennie Gerhardt*, with a presentation or a reminder of the protagonist's oneness with his unified world—and it is often open-ended or darkly speculative at the close (*The Scarlet Letter*, e.g.). The conclusion is dominated, moreover, by the imagery of confinement: the grave, the prison, and the cage, as in *The Duchess of Malfi, The Scarlet Letter*, "A Hunger Artist," "In the Penal Colony," *Jennie Gerhardt, An American Tragedy, The Stranger*, and *No Exit*. Since the protagonist is a "whole" character, and since in at least a superficial sense he is almost always defeated in his struggle with the world, what is finally at stake in pathos is the hero's ability to maintain his wholeness of character—not, as in tragedy, to re-achieve it. The self may be the first in a series of prisons, but it may also be able to "select its own society," in Emily Dickinson's words, and to retain its integral response to life even in the face of death and dissolution. Thus Job's "Though He slay me, yet will I trust in Him: but I will maintain mine own ways before Him" is echoed by "I am the Duchess of Malfi still" and by Lester Kane in *Jennie Gerhardt*: "The best we can do is to hold our personality intact." The attempt to avoid personal disintegration (which is the tragic condition) is the genuinely Quixotic aim of the pathetic hero, and his life's pattern of endless repetition makes of him a Sisyphus.

Indeed, Camus' *The Myth of Sisyphus* is a philosophy of pathos in much the same way Nietzsche's *The Birth of Tragedy* is a philosophy of tragedy. The utter divorce between the individual and his world that Camus calls the absurd is, in reality, a modern version of pathetic sensibility. Camus' philosophy is not only a rational exposition of the condition that has traditionally been depicted in the literature of pathos; it is an attmept to base a lifestyle upon this condition, as some nineteenth-century philosophies had been based upon an ostensibly tragic view of life. When Camus castigates the existentialists who attempt to transcend the chasm between man and his world by a "leap" of faith, his criticism is not only a metaphysical indictment but a literary judgment against tragedy in the modern age. Extending the logic of pathos, Camus in his essay counsels that men live in conscious defiance of their condition of alienation and make the most of lives of pointless repetition by seeking quantitative, not qualitative, experiences. In a tragic world, where men have a sense of fundamental, abiding value, quality of experience is most important. In the world Camus describes, the roles of conqueror, Don Juan, and actor are extreme examples of lives in which multiplication of ephemeral experience is important above all, for "The absurd man multiplies . . . what he cannot unify."[5] It is typical of the tragic hero that he comes to feel his own guilt and evil. Camus' hero, on the other hand, is a typical figure of pathos, for "He feels innocent. To tell the truth, that is all he feels—his irreparable innocence" (p. 39). Thus the absurd man attempts to retain his integrity: he is "attempting to be consistent" (p. 67). And when he is an artist, his mind, "ceasing to be renunciatory, flowers in images . . . [and] myths *with no other depth than that of human suffering and, like it, inexhaustible*" (p. 87; my italics).

Camus' intelligent and passionate exposition of the idea of the absurd is really a justification for the pathetic mode in our time, even if most pathos has somberly refused to go as far as Camus in making a virtue out of necessity and rejoicing in the paradoxical freedom of full consciousness of absurdity. Sartre's similar advocacy of a paradoxical freedom, absolutely self-generated, self-determined, and abjuring the necessity of external metaphysical foundation, takes the pathetic idea of the maintenance of the self one giant step further. For Sartre (as in *The Flies*) the life of freedom begins not only "beyond despair" but through and beyond pathos. Dreiser's Cowperwood and Witla are cut from the same cloth as Camus' conqueror-Don Juan figure; but Dreiser's views ruled out an existentialist solution to the pathetic impasse he came to repeatedly in his works. His increasing interest throughout his life in Transcendentalism is one evidence of his fascination with the idea of the self as the source of ultimate values. But just as, until the very end of his career, he could not accept the Transcendentalist idea of the individual's power to tap within himself the reliable permanence of the All, so too his Naturalistic view of the individual as driven by internal "chemisms" and pushed by largely deterministic external forces prevented him from coming to the existentialist version of "self reliance." Cut off from these solutions yet constantly compelled toward both of them, Dreiser has one recurrent idea: the stubborn preservation of the integrity of the personality, including its ability to yearn and thus to suffer.

From my brief discussion of pathos and tragedy it is apparent that a consideration of their subject matter and psychological form leads (and, I think, rightly) to the use of value-loaded words; but these prejudice opinion strongly in favor of tragedy as the "higher" form. Transcendence, freedom, permanence—these are in the province of tragedy, while their opposites most accurately delimit the constellation of the pathetic. It is easy to see why tragedy is frequently accorded the loftiest position in the aristocracy of literary types and why Heilman, for example, concludes that tragedy is healthier than what I call the pathetic. Simply to maintain one's standing as a human being, much less a liberal humanist, one wants to opt for the traditional "tragic values." But to apply ethical standards to a kind of writing requires the recognition of special dangers. Perhaps most important is the obvious fact that tragedy is the product of a particular sensibility and world-view on the part of both the author and his period of history. As Camus' essay should help us to see, where this sensibility and world-view do not obtain, the attempt to write tragedy will be unhealthy indeed—an abomination, a vacant verbal gesture. The odor of sickness is present in the modern confusion of both author and audience: for instance, Arthur Miller writes a defense of his "tragedy," *Death of a Salesman*, which is actually an excellent drama of pathos, and much of his public, believing him, is caught in a mesh of false expectations leading to rationalizations and to blindness about what is happening on the stage or in the text. Miller's error is a polemical one, readily pardonable in an author, but not a critic. Most commentators who try to deny the power and artistic merit of *Death of a Salesman* are in the anomalous position (characteristic of Dreiser criticism) of ignoring or denigrating the feelings aroused by direct response to the work because they cannot discover some prestigious sanction for them. Dreiser's titles present the issue squarely—*An American Tragedy, Tragic America*—yet perhaps because his work is so obviously not tragic the issue is either ignored or it is only half-heartedly taken up by such scholars as F. O. Matthiessen and Kenneth Lynn.

The inexhaustible human suffering of which Camus writes has established the focus of modern literature: a pathetic theme in which Job's God never comes to speak out of the whirlwind, so that man, pathetic and absurd, has continued to wait for Godot. Dreiser's characters wait too—rocking, or gazing, or planning, all of them are left finally waiting for the end of suffering.

III

Suffering and its Dreiserean synonym, yearning, have no beginning either in Dreiser's fiction; they are there, as pre-existing facts, immediately before us. *Jennie Gerhardt* begins with the heroine and her mother seeking employment at a hotel, where they have been driven by the inability of Papa Gerhardt to provide for them adequately. As the women scrub the stairs on their knees Jennie is both embarrassed before the men "passing constantly in and out" and attracted by this "kaleidoscopic world" (p. 6). In the background of this scene Dreiser depicts the impoverished Gerhardt home and the makeshifts of the poor-but-honest.

Then in the short second chapter there is a remarkable example of the sort of "fine writing" Dreiser liked to get off, especially in his early career. Brief as it is, the chapter is Dreiser's attempt to capture, as he says, "the spirit of Jennie." Dramatic action is scant: Jennie is outdoors with her younger brother and sister, expresses her yearning sense of nature's beauty, and upon being questioned by the children assures them that all nature's creatures have a home in the world. Seen as an introduction to Jennie's endless search for security in the novel, the chapter at once appears as Dreiser's effort at providing an enlarging framework for the heroine's "spirit" beyond the immediate social milieu of the story. The treatment of Jennie here as a child of nature is continued in the later descriptions of her "natural inheritance," where her beauty is seen in terms of timeless, evergreen nature (pp. 77–82) and her pregnancy is placed in harmonious context with the fertility of the great "all-mother" (pp. 93–100). Dreiser's attempts at lyricism, if they are noticed at all, are usually classified with his philosophizing as being among his more painful aberrations. Let us consider the passage at hand, however, not as an excrescence, but as an introduction to Jennie and to Dreiser's pathos.

The lyrical evocation of Jennie's spirit is startlingly Edenic following upon the suffocating materialism of both the hotel and the Gerhardt household, the one with its tinsel splendor and the other with its grubbing for food and coal. In its Edenic quality the scene defines Jennie's integral personality and her intimate sense of the natural world, described in prelapsarian terms as not only "perfect" but "conformable" to Jennie. There is an implication of timelessness too in Dreiser's perspective, which includes Jennie's "valued inheritance" of an Edenic world as well as a future when the earth "may . . . hope to hear . . . the song of goodness" that Jennie sings. Her awareness of the world is the medium for ours. The wood doves are "spirits of summer" whose call has a "spiritual quality" that drops "like silver bubbles" into her heart. The calm sky is described as a mystic sea, imaging the timeless, the enduring that both corresponds to and contrasts with the "sea of feeling" in Jennie which "stormed its banks." Staring at a "red island in a sea of silver," she feels that "Her soul was already up there, and its elysian paths knew the lightness of her feet" (pp. 15–18).

The overriding idea is that of nature as benevolent provider of a sanctuary for all living things. This theme, however, is put into the mouths of Jennie and the children, and their words give the idea of a domestic nature a slightly ironic cast. The children are rather incredulous in their questions about everything having a home, and Jennie responds "dreamily" and "deeply feeling the poetry of it" and "half believing her remark." Thus, although there is an identification of Jennie with the natural world, there is also an unmistakable insinuation that the self-sufficient permanence of nature is as distant from her as is the sky she yearns toward. Her "agony of poetic feeling" represents her sense of both affinity and distance, and this disparity finds substance in the imagistic tension between what she longs for and what she has.

For Jennie, Dreiser says, is a "daughter of poverty" and is "Caged in the world of the material . . ." (p. 15). The image of confinement looks forward, broadly speaking, to the whole novel, but particularly to the brilliantly executed last scene in which Jennie stands desolate behind the iron grating at the railroad station. Dreiser would have us see that Jennie is caged from the beginning of the novel, just as Clyde Griffiths in *An American Tragedy* is imprisoned by "tall walls" from first to last. In that work the wall images take on a variety of forms defining the exact nature of Clyde's physical and psychic entrapment. Analogously, the boundaries of Jennie's confinement increasingly come into focus throughout the book until we see that, as is typical of Dreiser, the social, material barrier the author overtly refers to in this second chapter stands for a more universal condition. All of Dreiser's protagonists share Jennie's initial instinctive sense of belonging to a particular world, except that for most it is symbolized by the city and not by Jennie's pastoral landscape. They somehow feel that their world—the city that looms magical, dreamlike, and compelling in the opening pages of Dreiser's novels—is rightfully theirs, as if by inheritance, and that they must achieve a more *perfect* harmony with this exciting "conformable" world, must come fully to possess and be possessed by an environment whose mores and processes they accept as the law of their behavior. Yet Dreiser's characters yearn infinitely, and therefore even if their world were not flawed, there is no Eden which can really be a refuge and a fulfillment for them—not until the bulwark Solon Barnes comes to terms with a snake.

The pathetic hero always tends to give the impression that he is somehow justified (Milton's Satan has been particularly troublesome to critics in this regard); integral and in that sense innocent, he is naturally associated with an Eden which he is trying to enter as his rightful place. Even in Cowperwood's world of cities and money, the Edenic motif enters into the judge's sentencing of the hero to prison: "You should have guarded the door of the treasury even as the cherubim protected the Garden of Eden . . ." (p. 425) Dreiser's primary bearers of the Edenic values—refreshing, eternal youthfulness combined curiously with a maternalistic security—are of course those fresh, whole young girls, like Jennie, whom his heroes are always pursuing. Clyde Griffiths' second thoughts on the attractions of the Union League Club sum up the positive ideal by a typical association of ideas: "It was such an Eveless paradise, that" (I, p. 204).

The opposing concepts of an Edenic world and a prison-cage drew Dreiser's imagination powerfully not only in *Jennie* but in *The Financier* and *An American Tragedy*, and it happens repeatedly that the latter image becomes gradually superimposed over the former as a dominant symbol of reality. Yet the Edenic idea never really disappears, for it is the key to the integral character and to the restless activity of the protagonist.

It may seem anomalous to speak of the activity of Dreiser's characters, since the immediate impression most of them give is one of almost somnolent passivity as they are pushed and pummelled by events and never seem able to make up their minds. I am arguing that the Dreiser character is not, as is so often implied, a psychologically passive creature, a *tabula rasa* shaped by the impingement of external phenomena. This description corresponds neither to the epistemology nor the psychology inherent in Dreiser's fiction. In his autobiographical writings Dreiser frequently refers to his own changeability and "uncertainty," and there is much of the author in his creations. But beneath a certain obvious exterior malleability, Dreiser's people must be posited as having a deep-structured active principle. At a level far below what Dreiser sometimes denigrates as "thinking"—logical, consecutive reasoning—this subterranean psychic activity performs one task above all: comparing a present external reality with some innate paradigm of ideality.

We sense this interior vitality as Dreiser's characters, after lengthy periods of quiesence, seem to flare suddenly to life. When an occasion appears to offer a correspondence to the internal paradigm, as it does, for example, in Carrie's early stage triumph as Laura, there is a surface, absorbed passivity even as the spark of recognition ignites; but this surface passivity merely allows the full play of the real, buried life that arises from the depths. "At the sound of her stage name Carrie started. . . . The feelings of the outcast descended upon her. She hung at the wing's edge, wrapt in her own mounting thoughts. She hardly heard anything more, save her own rumbling blood" (p. 201). As the stage role summons up the life of Carrie's innermost self, the strong, passionate quality of her voice and manner become "like a pathetic strain of music . . . ever a personal and intimate thing. Pathos has this quality, that it seems ever addressed to one alone" (p. 205). Carrie's passive-active dramatic ability, like the sobriquet Dreiser gives her of soldier of fortune, is the correlative of the vitality and the core of innate psychic activity that exists buried deep in all his characters, rising fitfully, "opportunistically," to the surface only when an external reality seems to promise fulfillment. But the promise is always illusory, and Carrie is typical in seeking endlessly through successive stages of apparent contentment that prove inadequate to the ideal pattern. Irving Howe has observed perceptively that "Dreiser's characters are romantics who behave as if the Absolute can be found, immaculately preserved, at the very summit of material power."[6] They feel this instinctive certainty because the paradigm for what they seek exists in all its dumb wholeness deep within them, so that the Absolute, the Eden, seems at once intimately theirs and yet oddly ungraspable.

The internal paradigm not only triggers the constant seeking, yearning quality of Jennie and all the others in Dreiser's gallery of men and women, but its inviolate wholeness structures their integral personalities. Dreiser is of course fascinated by the way external influences, events, accidents determine the direction seeking takes and the outward forms of immediate goals; but he is more moved by the individual's refusal to compromise the soul of integrality and by the ceaseless efforts to find its counterpart in the world. In the brief lyrical chapter we began by discussing, Dreiser summons up the "spirit of Jennie" by showing it projected "dreamily" against an objective world suffused with the coloring of her subjective ideal. Even at this point the world fails to match the Edenic spirit of the heroine, who desires to be integral with the universe as she is within herself. As Dreiser says later in the novel, she is "of that stable nature that rejoices to fix itself in a serviceable and harmonious relationship, and then stay so. For her, life was made up of those mystic chords of sympathy and memory which bind up the transient elements of nature into a harmonious and enduring scene" (p. 368). Jennie signally fails to find such a relationship, and she feels even as she is on the way to her first tryst in New York or while she is in a luxurious Egyptian hotel with her lover that these situations are inadequate to what she desires. What all of Dreiser's characters seek in the world is an answering reflection, an echo of themselves, or more exactly, of the innate personal ideal. Again *The Bulwark* is the exception that proves the rule; Solon Barnes does finally sense a comforting response from the natural world, a profound benignity that seems to answer his own.

To add a mythical reference to Camus' description of pathos, it is as if Narcissus looked into the water and saw no reflection. In Dreiser's work the horror of not finding such a reflection in the world is perhaps exceeded by the horror of finding one but not recognizing it—indeed, destroying it, as Clyde Griffiths does his female counterpart Roberta Alden in *An American Tragedy*: "And again he lowered his head and gazed into the fascinating and yet treacherous depths of that magnetic . . . pool . . . . A form . . . came nearer—clearer—and as it did so, he recognized Roberta struggling and waving her thin white arms out of the water and reaching toward him!" (II, p. 75)

The lack of reflection does not lead Dreiser's characters to self-alienation, to the sense that *they* are unreal. On the contrary, as the world repeatedly, painfully, fails to answer to the intense expectations springing from the internal ideal, objective reality pales before the undeniably felt reality of the self's paradigm. In the most solipsistic moods of Dreiser's fiction, the almost Chekhovian force of subjectivity radiating from the self's core makes it alone seem real and the world illusory, which is to say, infinitely alien. Immediately before Clyde gazes into the lake in the passage quoted above, Roberta seems to him to have "faded to a shadow or thought really, a form of illusion more vaporous than real." Authorial set pieces on life as illusion and dream are long and frequent in the novels, reinforcing the feeling of a character like Lester Kane, who articulates Jennie's culminating awareness: "The best we can do is to hold our personality intact," Kane says as he looks down from a window at the streams of vehicles and people moving like "shadows . . . in a dream" (pp. 400–401). Life "was mostly illusion . . . . That it might all be one he sometimes suspected. It was very much like a dream in its composition truly—sometimes like a very bad dream" (p. 413). In *The Financier*, Cowperwood is the "prince of a world of dreams" (p. 503) whose career of chicanery illustrates the natural law found in the illusionistic, deadly fish, the Mycteroperca. The paucity of Dreiser's stock of images often becomes a source of coherence and irony, and this is the case with the dream motif. The initially benign dreamlike quality of the world, the objectification of the viewer's subjective ideal, is transformed into a malign "bad dream" which, having denied its initial promise, seems to have no point of correspondence to the dreamer anymore. This grim dream vision is, nevertheless, coextensive with the imprisoning, dominating force of material reality. On the one hand, the much praised solidity of Dreiser's fictional environment underscores a fixed, blank imperviousness to human yearning; on the other hand, this very imperviousness causes the solid world to appear impalpable, transparent before the piercing light of desire. An alien, inescapable, impermeable reality and a baffled human consciousness committed to its own intactness to the point of solipsism—the paradoxically logical combination is pathos pushed to its fullest limits.

The idea that the world is both massively real and thinly unreal is also suggested by one of Dreiser's basic devices, the shift in perspective. Part of the sense of scale and relativity in Dreiser's work is produced by the overt editorializing on natural and cosmic laws, and part is achieved by the characteristic use of views-from-above: Carrie and Lester Kane looking down into the rushing night traffic, the distant point of view that ends Book Two and begins Book Three of *An American Tragedy*, Jennie Gerhardt seen in the timeless perspective of the natural processes of maternal nature. Most important are the changes in the reader's perspective necessitated by the circumstances of plot. Seen up close, in the right social context, Hurstwood, Senator Brander, Lester Kane, and Cowperwood all seem to be men whose ability and mental power have assured them a reliable stature in a stable, or at least predictable, milieu. But Dreiser repeatedly introduces new scales of measurement revealing superior hierarchies of force before which power and stability vanish like flimsy illusions. Hurstwood is powerful in Chicago, helpless in the larger scale of forces embodied in New York City; the apparently forceful and secure Brander suffers political defeat because of the intervention of a railroad corporation; the *enfant terrible* Kane is finally overcome in his desire for a life with Jennie by his father's opposition and by social pressure. But Dreiser is not primarily interested in making a comment about social hierarchies; he is interested in seeing in society an immediate representation of the cosmic scale of forces, as statements like this one demonstrate: "At the ultimate remove, God or the life force, if anything, is an equation, and at its nearest expression for man—the contract social—it is that also" (*The Titan*, pp. 550–551). In terms of this vast symbolic master scale of Dreiser's work, "giants are but pygmies," and Cowperwood and Clyde, Carrie and Hurstwood, Kane and Jennie, pathetic conqueror and pathetic victim, come together in a democracy of yearning and powerlessness. In this scale intellectual power or any other form of personal force seems ultimately negligible; and thus even before Hurstwood's decline his rational attempts to come to a decision about leaving his wife or robbing his firm's safe are treated ironically by Dreiser: "Meanwhile, he would have time to think. This process of *thinking* began by a reversion to Carrie . . . ." (p. 262); "Hurstwood could not bring himself to act definitely. He wanted to think about it—to ponder over it, to decide whether it were best" (p. 288). The "emotional greatness" (p. 410) specifically ascribed to Carrie Meeber is at base a capacity to desire. For Dreiser it is the sole attribute capable of matching the cosmic scale; it is both the most valuable possession of man and the source of his pathos.

Dreiser's shifts along the scale of power and desire contribute, moreover, to the rhythmic movement everyone notices in his novels. *Jennie Gerhardt* probably provides the best illustration of the form this movement gives to Dreiser's fiction. The rhythmic pattern is established by Jennie's successive attainment and loss of security as she goes from a romance with Senator Brander to various ménages with her family and with Lester Kane, from her family home to a symbolic benign natural context, from all of these to a final vision of utter aloneness. At first glance as one reads the novel the slow, regular rhythm seems to conform to the familiar pattern of the *Bildungsroman*, where individual development is the result of movement to and from, back and forth, between "city" and "country," social and natural; between places of permanence, order, and those of disorder, change. In the *Bildungsroman*, these antinomies are symbolic reflections of psychic reality, opposites which are reconciled in the synthesis of growth. In this way the protagonist is at least potentially a tragic character, except that usually he exists in a "comic" world where every action or situation is reversible—there is always a frontier to light out for, as in comedy there is always a rich uncle to bring lovers together again. However, the rhythmic movement of *Jennie* is in an important sense misleading, for there are no places of abiding value and permanent security in the novel. Each apparent haven, social or natural, turns out to be unreliable. *Jennie* demonstrates repeatedly that permanence is illusory and the evanescent is real. In all of Dreiser's novels except *The Bulwark*, the actual movement is one way, always *toward*: from a one-time condition of instinctive unity with the world to an irreversible condition of alienation. Yet if Dreiser inverts the pattern of the *Bildungsroman*, it is not true that he is simply writing a Naturalistic account of individual destruction. What is destroyed is not necessarily the individual, but rather the individual's sense of the world. There is no sudden tragic "fall" but instead the even paced, relentless drift of pathos.

Jennie is the typical Dreiser character in that she undergoes little if any real growth in the novel. She has a remarkable wholeness of being from the first, and this in fact is the attraction she holds for men like Brander and Kane. Following the tradition of the nineteenth-century novel, Dreiser refers to Jennie's new life and the broadening effect of her experiences. But it is clear that by "new life" Dreiser does not mean symbolic rebirth but only a new attempt to find a harmonious relationship with the world. Towards the end of the novel the ironic connotations of the phrase are spelled out in the emphasis on loss, with no compensating or transcending gain: "The new life was actually begun for her—a life without Lester, without Gerhardt, without anyone save Vesta" (p. 371). Jennie's achievement is that she is no less integral a character at the end of the novel than she was at the beginning; in this she is in the company of Carrie, Hurstwood, Witla, and Cowperwood.

IV

"A true sense of the pathetic" (*The Genius*, p. 237). Thus Dreiser assesses his own work through a critic's praise of Eugene Witla. We must, finally, grant Dreiser his *donnée*. We must grant his portrayal of large, common feelings that are often flat and lacking in sensibility without demanding that he deal with them in one of the currently intellectually respectable ways: satirizing them outright, making them the subject of black humor, or embodying them in grotesques in the manner of Sherwood Anderson, or William Faulkner, or Flannery O'Connor. Dreiser's best writing is a unique statement of the emotional intensity and affective capacity of man inarticulately possessing his selfhood and vainly striving to fit the world to its pattern. In giving us that untragic and undistorted statement Dreiser is more than a major figure, he is an accomplished writer in the pathetic tradition.

Notes

1. "The Art of Fiction," in *The House of Fiction: Essays on the Novel by Henry James*, ed. Leon Edel (London, 1957), p. 37.

2. *The Liberal Imagination* (Garden City, 1953), pp. 8–19. Trilling also says that *Jennie Gerhardt* provides the only exception to the rule that Dreiser's pity is either destructive of its object or is self-pity.

3. *The Titan* (New York: World Publishing Company, 1946), p. 551. Subsequent page references to the World editions of Dreiser will appear in the text.

4. Heilman, "Tragedy and Melodrama: Speculations on Generic Form," *Texas Quarterly* 3 (Summer, 1960), 47. See also Frye, *Anatomy of Criticism* (Princeton, 1957), pp. 36–40, 216–23. I find unsatisfactory Frye's distinction between high mimetic and low

mimetic tragedy (pathos) on the basis of the hero's power of action; several important pathetic heroes have powers "greater than our own"—Prometheus, Tamburlaine, Satan, and Dreiser's Cowperwood, for example. My major difference with Heilman's article, to which my debt is extensive, is my higher opinion of the non-tragic literature of suffering. Further acknowledgment of my indebtedness to the wealth of critical discussions of tragedy must be a general one, but readers will recognize echoes of Bradley and Kitto, among others.

5. *The Myth of Sisyphus and Other Essays*, trans. by Justin O'Brien (New York, 1955), p. 55. Subsequent page references to this edition will appear in the text. Cf. Strother B. Purdy, "*An American Tragedy* and *L'Étranger*," *Comparative Literature*, 19 (Summer, 1967), 252–268.

6. Howe, "Afterword," *An American Tragedy*. Signet edition (New York, 1964), p. 818.

The Cowperwood Trilogy

Dreiser's Novel

H. L. Mencken *

Theodore Dreiser's new novel, "The Financier," shows all of the faults and peculiarities of method that gave a rude, barbarous sort of distinction to his "Sister Carrie" and "Jennie Gerhardt," those arresting tales of yesteryear. The man does not write as the other novelists of his day and generation write, and, what is more, he does not seem to make any effort to do so, or to have any feeling that such an effort would be worth while. You may read him for page after page, held spellbound by his people and their doings, and yet not find a single pretty turn or phrase, or a single touch of smartness in dialogue, or a single visible endeavor to stiffen a dull scene into drama, or any other such application of artifice or art.

For all the common tricks of writing, in truth, he reveals a degree of disdain amounting almost to denial. He never "teases up" a situation to make it take your breath; he never hurries over something difficult and static in order to get to something easy and dynamic; he never leads you into ambuscades of plot or sets off stylistic fireworks; he never so much as takes the trouble to hunt for a new adjective when an old one will answer as well. In brief, his manner is uncompromisingly forthright, elemental, grim, gaunt, bare. He rolls over the hills and valleys of his narrative at the same patient, lumbering gait, surmounting obstacles by sheer weight and momentum, refusing all short cuts, however eminently trod, as beneath his contempt, and turning his back resolutely upon all the common lifts by the way.

But do I give the impression that the result is dullness, that all this persistent, undeviating effort leads to nothing but a confused and meaningless piling up of words? Then I have described it very badly, for the net effect is precisely the opposite. Out of chaos, by that unceasing pounding, order finally emerges. Out of the disdain of drama comes drama stirring and poignant. Out of that welter of words step human beings, round, ruddy, alive. In other words, Dreiser accomplishes at last, for all his muddling, what men with a hundred times his finesse too often fail to accomplish, and that is, an almost perfect illusion of reality. You may say that he writes with a hand of five thumbs, and that he has no more humor

*Reprinted from New York *Times Review of Books*, November 10, 1912, p. 654. Copyright © 1912 by the New York Times Company. Reprinted by permission.

than a hangman, and that he loves assiduity so much that he often forgets inspiration altogether, and you may follow up all of these sayings by ample provings, but in the end you will have to admit that Carrie Meeber is far more real than nine-tenths of the women you actually know, and that old Gerhardt's veritable existence is no more to be doubted than the existence of Père Goriot.

If "The Financier," on a first reading, leaves a less vivid impression than the two books preceding it, then that apparent falling off is probably due to two things, the first being that its principal character is a man and that in consequence he must needs lack some of the fascinating mystery and appeal of Carrie and Jennie; and the second being that the story stops just as it is beginning, (for all its 780 pages!) and so leaves the reader with a sense of incompleteness, of a picture washed in but not wholly painted. Final judgment, indeed, will be impossible until the more important second volume is put beside this first, for it is there that the real drama of Frank Cowperwood's life will be played out. But meanwhile there can be no doubt whatever of the author's firm grip upon the man, nor of his astute understanding of the enormously complex interplay of personalities and events against which the man is projected.

This Cowperwood is meant, I suppose, to be a sort of archetype of the American money king, and despite a good many little deviations he is probably typical enough. The main thing to remember about him is that he is anything but a mere chaser of the dollar, that avarice as a thing in itself is not in him. For the actual dollar, indeed, he has no liking at all, but only the toleration of an artist for his brushes and paint-pots. What he is really after is power, and the way power commonly visualizes itself in this mind is as a means to beauty. He likes all things that caress the eye—a fine rug, an inviting room, a noble picture, a good horse, a pretty woman, particularly a pretty woman. There is in him what might be called an aloof voluptuousness, a dignified hedonism. He is not so much sensual as sensitive. A perfect eyebrow seems to him to be something worth thinking about, soberly and profoundly. The world, in his sight, is endlessly curious and beautiful.

And with this over-development of the esthetic sense there goes, naturally enough, an under-development of the ethical sense. Cowperwood has little more feeling for right and wrong, save as a setting or a mask for beauty, than a healthy schoolboy. When a chance offers to make a large sum of money by an alliance with political buccaneers, he takes it without the slightest question of its essential virtue. And when, later on, the buccaneers themselves lay open for pillage, he pillages them with a light heart. And as with means, so with ends. When Aileen Butler, the daughter of his partner and mentor, old Edward Malia Butler, the great political contractor—when Aileen comes his way, radiant and tempting, he debauches her without a moment's thought of consequences, and carries on the affair under old Butler's very nose.

The man is not vicious: a better word for him would be innocent. He has no sense of wrong to Aileen, nor of wrong to Butler, nor even of wrong to the wife of his youth. The only idea that takes clear form in his mind is the idea that Aileen is extremely pleasing, and that it would be a ridiculous piece of folly to let her charms go to waste. Even when he is the conquered instead of the conqueror, not much feeling that an act of conquest can have a moral content appears in him. Old Butler, discovering his affair with Aileen, knocks over his financial house of cards and railroads him to prison, but he shows little rancor against Butler, and less against the obliging catchpolls of the law, but only a vague discontent that fate should bring him such hardships, and take him away from beauty so long.

This term in prison is a salient event in Cowperwood's life, but it cannot be said that it is a turning point. He comes out into the Philadelphia of the early seventies with all his old determination to beat the game. He has been defeated once, true enough, but that defeat has taught him a lot that easy victory might have left unsaid, and he has full confidence that he will win next time. And win he does. Black Friday sees him the most pitilessly ursine of bears, and the next day sees him with a million. He is now on his feet again and able to choose his cards carefully and at leisure. With the utmost calm he divorces his wife, tucks Aileen under his arm, and sets out for Chicago. There, where the players are settling down for the wildest game of money ever played in the world, he will prove that luck in the long run is with the wise. And there, in the second volume of this history, we shall see him at the proving.

An heroic character, and not without his touches of the admirable. Once admit his honest doubts of the workaday moralities of the world, and at once you range him with all the other memorable battlers against fate, from Prometheus to Etienne Lantier. The achievement of Dreiser is found in this very fact: that he has made the man not only comprehensible, but also a bit tragic. One is conscious of a serene dignity in his chicaneries, and even in his debaucheries, and so his struggle for happiness becomes truly moving. I am not alluding here to that cheap sympathy which is so easily evoked by mere rhetoric, but to that higher sympathy which grows out of a thorough understanding of motives and processes of mind. This understanding Dreiser insures. Say what you will against his solemn and onerous piling up of words, his slow plodding through jungles of detail, his insatiable lust for facts, you must always admit that he gets his effect in the end. There are no sudden flashes of revelation; the lights are turned on patiently and deliberately, one by one. But when the thing is done at last the figure of the financier leaps out amazingly, perfectly modeled, wholly accounted for.

So with the lesser personages, and particularly with Aileen and her father. Old Butler, indeed, is worthy to stand just below the ancient Gerhardt, by long odds the most real of Dreiser's creatures, not even excepting Carrie Meeber and Hurstwood. You remember Gerhardt, of course, with his bent back, his squirrel's economies, his mediaeval piety and his pathetic wonderment at the deviltries of the world? Well, Butler is a vastly different man, if only because he is richer, more intelligent, and more powerful, but still, in the end, he takes on much of that reality and all of that pathos, raging homerically but impotently against an enemy who eludes him and defies him and has broken his heart.

And so, too, with the background of the story. I can imagine nothing more complex than the interplay of finance and politics in war time and during the days following, when the money kings were just finding themselves and graft was just rising to the splendor of an exact science. And yet Dreiser works his way through that maze with sure steps, and leaves order and understanding where confusion reigned. Of tales of municipal corruption we have had aplenty; scarcely a serious American novelist of to-day, indeed, has failed to experiment with that endless and recondite drama. But what other has brought its prodigal details into better sequence and adjustment, or made them enter more vitally and convincingly into the characters and adventures of his people? Those people of Dreiser's, indeed, are never the beings in vacuo who populate our common romances. We never see them save in contact with a vivid and fluent environment, reacting to its constant stimuli, taking color from it, wholly a part of it.

So much for "The Financier." It is the prologue rather than the play. The real tragi-comedy of Cowperwood's struggle for power and beauty will be played out in Chicago, and of its brilliancy and mordacity we have abundant earnest. Dreiser knows Chicago as few other men know it; he has pierced to the very heart of that most bewildering of cities. And, what is more, he has got his secure grip upon Cowperwood.

Recent Reflections of a Novel-Reader

Reader

Anonymous*

The Financier is an imposing book, both in intention and execution. If it resembles a biography more than a work of art, that, doubtless, is an aspect of the matter with which the author deliberately reckoned before he began. The critic is entitled to ignore it in view of Mr. Dreiser's success in presenting an intimate picture of the development of a man of financial genius whose kind is only too common in America. Should the type become extinct (Heaven speed the day!) and the novel survive, our descendants will have in it the means of reconstructing for themselves the business life and immorality of a whole period.

The book details with endless particularity, but forcefully, the character and career of Frank Cowperwood, a Philadelphia boy: his rise in the financial world, his rocket-like descent to the status of a convict, and the means by which he, later, recoups his fallen fortunes. The picture includes his business associates, alleged friends, entire family connection, and the family of the girl whom he finally marries after a long *liaison*, wrecking a first marriage. The author has all these threads of his tapestry well in hand, and no less clear is his presentation of the ins and outs of Philadelphia politics, and the opportunities they afforded for unscrupulous money-making. So painstaking, so lavish of detail, so determined to cover the large canvas closely, is he, that he seems to propose to himself the feats of an American Balzac. If this is the case, he has made a good beginning and is alone in a field that is ready for harvest.

Perhaps the most extraordinary quality of this unusual book is the dryness of its atmosphere. We are reminded of those caverns where nothing ever decays, where all dead things lie mummified, retaining the outward aspect of life for centuries. This effect is, in part, intentional. I do not make out to my own satisfaction whether it is wholly so. Certainly Mr. Dreiser wishes us to feel the extreme aridity of nature in a man like Cowperwood, who sees life under the categories of strength and weakness, and in no other way; certainly also it is hardly possible to over-

*Reprinted from *Atlantic Monthly*, 111 (May, 1913), 689–91. Copyright © by the Atlantic Monthly Company, Boston, Mass. Reprinted by permission.

estimate the desiccating effect of absolute materialism in a man of his ability; doubtless, too, the environment and relations of such a man would inevitably tend to grow more and more arid. Still, one would like to ask the author if, as a matter of technique, this juicelessness of the money-maker might not have been brought out more poignantly by the introduction into the book of somebody with a soul—somebody, that is to say, who sees our existence under the categories of good and evil, right and wrong. This is the chief thing that gives atmosphere and perspective to life. Lust and greed, the pride of the flesh and the joy of life, are not shown in their proper values unless they are contrasted with something quite different. This something different, the spirit-side of life as opposed to the material side, is wholly omitted from *The Financier*. As the book stands, the part of foil is played by a hard-headed old contractor and politician, the father of the girl with whom Cowperwood becomes entangled. Butler is a soft-hearted parent, and is sufficiently shocked and vindictive on learning of the illicit relation in which his daughter exults. He is more nearly human than any other character of the tale, but even he fails really to touch the reader.

Since the death of Frank Norris, no American novelist has attempted anything on the scale of *The Financier*. Far apart in temperament and method, the two writers are alike in the resolution to do a big thing in a big way. For the novelist, I apprehend that the biggest way of all is one which is, as yet, closed to Mr. Dreiser by his philosophy. One must not be rash in formulating this philosophy, but it seems to be negative, to consist in the belief that life is an insoluble problem and that the existence of predatory types in nature and society justifies us in indicting that dark Will which places man in a universe where 'his feet are in the trap of circumstance, his eyes are on an illusion.'

Whatever the truth of such a philosophy, one thing is certain: the consensus of men's opinions through the centuries has demanded a different basis from this for the enduring things, the great things, in literature. And the long consensus of opinion is our only real criterion. But to quarrel with Mr. Dreiser upon this point is, after all, to praise him, since it makes clear the fact that his achievement must be looked at from the highest ground.

A man's philosophy is determined in part by his length of days. Knowing nothing as to the fact, I would place the author of *The Financier* near forty-three—too old for the optimism of youth, too young for the optimism of late middle life. If the horribly cold and insanely bitter realism of Strindberg melted at sixty, under the impact of life, into a believing mysticism, who can say what insight and tenderness, what softness of atmosphere and richness of feeling, a dozen years may not add to the already very notable performances of Mr. Dreiser?

*   *   *   *   *   *   *

Dreiser and His Titan

E. F. Edgett*

Voluble as Mr. Dreiser has been in "Sister Carrie," in "Jennie Gerhardt," in "The Financier," these novels have been the height of reticence compared with the license of incident and speech with which he has filled "The Titan." The second volume in "a trilogy of desire," it continues the record of Frank Algernon Cowperwood's exploits in love and finance. That hero, it will be remembered, found himself in prison towards the close of "The Financier" as the result more of a political conspiracy against him than of any wrong-doing, and it is his life following his emergence from about a year's confinement that Mr. Dreiser recounts in "The Titan." Fortune came to him again in response to the touch of the novelist's magician's wand, but since he was not looked upon fondly by the social and financial hierarchy of Philadelphia, he considered it wiser to seek other worlds. He chose Chicago and in the five hundred and more pages of "The Titan" we are told how he came, how he saw, and how he fought and conquered. With him also went the beautiful Aileen Burke, once his mistress and soon to be his wife after he had secured a divorce from the first wife whom he had deserted for her.

The gift of verbiage is certainly Mr. Dreiser's to command. He seems able to write of everything earthly with a hand that is unrestrained by any sense of the eternal fitness of things. He sees men and women, but he does not see them completely. He sees scarcely anything but the evil in them, and the pages of "The Titan" therefore become merely a record of the adventures in vice of Cowperwood and the creatures of both sexes with whom he surrounds himself. He lays equal emphasis upon the vices of politics and business and the vices of sex, and he makes Cowperwood an adept in both. His story is built up of alternate layers touching now upon Cowperwood's conquests in high finance and now upon his successes with women. It is in fact substantially two separate novels, and they could be easily separated and with but a few changes become independent stories.

The path of Cowperwood through the twenty years or so of his life upon which the story is founded is strewn with the relics of his personal dishonor. He can be true to no man and to no woman for even a moment. At times the novel becomes a list of his successes in business by means of

*Reprinted from *Boston Evening Transcript*, May 23, 1914, p. 8.

bribery; at other times it is a catalogue of his triumphs over women. He seems to be an all-conquering hero to the novelist who created him; to many of his readers he is nothing more than an unmitigated scoundrel. He attacks both the strong and the weak; the wives of men he despises and the daughters of his associates in business are alike his victims. Mr. Dreiser represents them as more tempting than tempted, but his attitude towards all mankind seems to be that there is no virtue in either man or woman. He seeks to show us not merely a fragment of the world in which evil is rampant; he endeavors to convince us that there is nothing but evil in the whole world and in all men and women. His Chicago is even worse than his Philadelphia; it is a hotbed of business crime and of social vice. His men have in them no good that Mr. Dreiser is able to discover.

A one-sided, serious view of life such as this betrays a lack of balance on the part of a novelist. However true it may be, it is not the whole truth. Such men as Cowperwood exist, but all men are not such men as he. The reader is certain, unless he happens to be a devotee of pornography for its own sake, to become utterly disgusted at the recital of Cowperwood's affairs with women, and he will search his vocabulary and easily find words wherewith to express his opinion both of the character and of the novelist. It is not of course the slightest use for us to seek or to find, or to use these words. They would defeat our own purpose. We leave them to the reader.

In spite of its tremendous shortcomings, "The Titan" nevertheless commands admiration and respect. Mr. Dreiser's knowledge of affairs in the world of business and society is remarkable. He is never at a loss for a scheme wherewith to explain Cowperwood's methods, or with his explanation of them. His pictures of the time and the place are vigorous and graphic.

*   *   *   *   *   *   *

With all his experience, with all his undoubted descriptive powers, with all his voluminous writing, Mr. Dreiser is unable to rid himself of the use of words and phrases that are an offense against good taste and the dignity of the English tongue. He persists in saying that a building is "located," in using the impersonal "one" as the antecedent of the personal "they," in placing something on "either" side when he means both sides, in "alluding" to an object or person that he specifically mentions, and in a thousand and one other tricks of speech that are the faults, doubtless, of the careless facility with which he writes. Whole sentences, too, may not infrequently be found that are sublime in their egregiousness, as "she stockinged her legs in brown silk," or "the colonel, who had a small, gray goatee and sportive dark eyes, winked the latter solemnly."

Understanding life so thoroughly, it is a pity that Mr. Dreiser cannot see all sides of it clearly. "The Titan" is a big book in size and intellectually, but it is by no means a great novel. It lacks the discretion, the restraint, the good taste, the normality essential even to an approach to perfection.

The Titan

H. L. Mencken*

After all, Dr. Munyon is quite right: there is yet hope. Sometimes, of course, it is hard to discern, almost impossible to embrace. Sweating through the best-sellers of the moment, shot from the presses in a gaudy cataract, one can scarcely escape a mood of intense depression, a bleak esthetic melancholia. What is to become of a nation which buys such imbecile books by the hundred thousand, and not only buys them, but reads them, and not only reads them, but enjoys them, gabbles about them, takes them seriously, even pays reverence to them as literature?

Publishers get rich printing that sort of "literature," and then use their money to bludgeon and browbeat all authors who try to do anything better. Imagine a young American bobbing up with a new "Germinal," or a new "Lord Jim," or a new "Brothers Karamazov"; what a job he would have getting it between covers! But let him rise shamelessly out of the old bog of mush, dripping honey and buttermilk, and at once there is silver in his palm and praise in his ear. The Barabbases fight for him, playing one another all kinds of sharp tricks; the newspapers record his amours, his motor accidents and his table talk; the literary monthlies print his portrait (in golf togs) opposite that of Gerhart Hauptmann; the women's clubs forget Bergson and the white slave trade to study his style. In the end, he retires to Palm Beach or Tuscany with a fortune, and so becomes a romantic legend, half genius and half god.

But, as I started out to say, there is yet a glimmer of hope. A small class of more civilized readers begins to show itself here and there; a few daring publishers risk a dollar or two on fiction of an appreciably better sort; the literary monthlies forget their muttons long enough to say a kind word for Joseph Conrad; now and then a genuine artist is seen in the offing. Fate, alas, conspires with stupidity to keep the number down. Frank Norris died just as he was getting into his stride; David Graham Phillips was murdered by a lunatic at the very moment of his deliverance; a dozen others, after diffident bows, have disappeared in ways just as mysterious. But there remains Theodore Dreiser, patient, forthright, earnest, plodding, unswerving, uncompromising—and so long as Dreiser keeps out of jail there will be hope.

*Reprinted from Smart Set, 43 (August, 1914), 153–57.

Four long novels are now behind him, and in every one of them one sees the same grim fidelity to an austere artistic theory, the same laborious service to a stern and rigorous faith. That faith may be put briefly into two articles: (a) that it is the business of a novelist to describe human beings as they actually are, unemotionally, objectively and relentlessly, and not as they might be, or would like to be, or ought to be; and (b) that his business is completed when he has so described them, and he is under no obligation to read copybook morals into their lives, or to estimate their virtue (or their lack of it) in terms of an ideal goodness. In brief, the art of Dreiser is almost wholly representative, detached, aloof, unethical: he makes no attempt whatever to provide that pious glow, that mellow sentimentality, that soothing escape from reality, which Americans are accustomed to seek and find in prose fiction. And despite all the enormous advantages of giving them what they are used to and cry for, he has stuck resolutely to his program. In the fourteen years since "Sister Carrie" he has not deviated once, nor compromised once. There are his books: you may take them or leave them. If you have any respect for an artist who has respect for himself, you may care to look into them; if not, you may go to the devil.

In all this, Dreiser runs on a track parallel to Conrad's; the two men suggest each other in a score of ways. Superficially, of course, they may seem to be far apart: the gorgeous colors of Conrad are never encountered in Dreiser. But that difference lies almost wholly in materials; in ideas and methods they are curiously alike. To each the salient fact of life is its utter meaninglessness, its sordid cruelty, its mystery. Each stands in amazement before the human tendency to weigh it, to motivate it, to see esoteric significances in it. Nothing could be more profoundly agnostic and unmoral than Conrad's "Lord Jim" or Dreiser's "Jennie Gerhardt." In neither book is there the slightest suggestion of a moral order of the world; neither novelist has any blame to hand out, nor any opinion to offer as to the justice or injustice of the destiny he describes. It is precisely here, indeed, that both take their departure from the art of fiction as we of English speech commonly know it. They are wholly emancipated from the moral obsession that afflicts our race; they see the human comedy as a series of inexplicable and unrepresentative phenomena, and not at all as a mere allegory and Sunday school lesson. If art be imagined as a sort of halfway station between science and morals, their faces are plainly turned toward the hard rocks of science, just as the faces of the more orthodox novelists are turned toward pansy beds of morals.

Conrad tells us somewhere that it was Flaubert who helped him to formulate his theory of the novel, with Turgenieff and the other Russians assisting. The influences that moulded Dreiser are not to be stated with such certainty. Here and there one happens upon what seem to be obvious tracks of Zola, but Dreiser, if I remember rightly, has said that he knows the Frenchman only at second hand. Did the inspiration come through

Frank Norris, Zola's one avowed disciple in America? Against the supposition stands the fact that "Sister Carrie" followed too soon after "McTeague" to be an imitation of it—and besides, "Sister Carrie" is a far greater novel, in more than one way, than "McTeague" itself. Perhaps some earlier and lesser work of Norris's was the model that the younger man followed, consciously or unconsciously. Norris was his discoverer, and in a sense, his patron saint, battling for him valiantly when the firm of Doubleday, Page & Co. achieved immortality by suppressing "Sister Carrie." (Some day the whole of this tale must be told. The part that Norris played proved that he was not only a sound critic, but also an extraordinarily courageous and unselfish friend.) But whatever the fact and the process, Dreiser has kept the faith far better than Norris, whose later work, particularly "The Octopus," shows a disconcerting mingling of honest realism and vaporous mysticism. In Dreiser there has been no such yielding. His last book, "The Titan," is cut from exactly the same cloth that made "Sister Carrie." Despite years of critical hammering and misunderstanding, and a number of attacks of a sort even harder to bear, he has made no sacrifice of his convictions and done no treason to his artistic conscience. He may be right or he may be wrong, but at all events he has gone straight ahead.

"The Titan" (*Lane*), like "Sister Carrie," enjoys the honor of having been suppressed after getting into type. This time the virtuous act was performed by Harper & Brothers, a firm which provided mirth for the mocking back in the nineties by refusing the early work of Rudyard Kipling. The passing years work strange farces. Today the American publisher of Kipling is the firm of Doubleday, Page & Co., which suppresed "Sister Carrie"—and "Sister Carrie," after years upon the town, is now on the vestal list of the Harpers, who bucked at "The Titan"! The grotesque comedy should have been completed by the publication of the latter work by Doubleday, Page & Co., but of this delectable fourth act we were unluckily deprived. Life, alas, is seldom quite artistic. Its phenomena do not fit snugly together, like squares in a checkerboard. But nevertheless the whole story of the adventures of his books would make a novel in Dreiser's best manner—a novel without the slightest hint of a moral. His own career as an artist has been full of the blind and unmeaning fortuitousness that he expounds.

But what of "The Titan" as a work of art? To me, at least, it comes closer to what I conceive to be Dreiser's ideal than any other story he has done. Here, at last, he has thrown overboard all the usual baggage of the novelist, making short and merciless shrift of "heart interest," "sympathy" and even romance. In "Sister Carrie" there was still a sop, however little intended, for the sentimentalists: if they didn't like the history of Carrie as a study of the blind forces which determine human destiny, they could wallow in it as a sad, sad love story. Carrie was pathetic, appealing, melting; she moved, like Marguerite Gautier, in an atmosphere of agreeable melancholy. And Jennie Gerhardt, of course, was merely another Carrie—a Carrie more carefully and objectively drawn, perhaps, but still one to be easily mistaken for a "sympathetic" heroine of the best-sellers. Readers jumped from "The Prisoner of Zenda" to "Jennie Gerhardt" without knowing that they were jumping ten thousand miles. The tear jugs were there to cry into; the machinery seemed to be the same. Even in "The Financier" there was still a hint of familiar things. The first Mrs. Cowperwood was sorely put upon; Cowperwood himself suffered injustice, and pined away in a dungeon.

But no one, I venture to say, will ever make the same mistake about "The Titan"—no one, not even the youngest and fairest, will ever take it for a sentimental romance. Not a single appeal to the emotions is in it; it is a purely intellectual account, as devoid of heroics as a death certificate, of a strong man's savage endeavors to live out his life as it pleases him, regardless of all the subtle and enormous forces that seek to break him to a rule. There is nothing in him of the conventional outlaw; he does not wear a red sash and bellow for liberty; from end to end he issues no melodramatic defiance of the existing order. The salient thing about him is precisely his avoidance of all such fine feathers and sonorous words. He is no hero at all, but merely an extraordinary gamester—sharp, merciless, tricky, insatiable. One stands amazed before his marvelous resourcefulness and daring, his absolute lack of conscience, but there is never the slightest effort to cast a romantic glamour over him, to raise sympathy for him, to make it appear that he is misunderstood, unfortunate, persecuted. Even in love he is devoid of the old glamour of the lover. Even in disaster he asks for no quarter, no generosity, no compassion. Up or down, he is sufficient unto himself.

The man is the same Cowperwood who came a cropper in "The Financier," but he has now reached middle age, and all the faltering weakness and irresolutions of his youth are behind him. He knows exactly what he wants, and in the Chicago of the early eighties he proceeds to grab it. The town is full of other fellows with much the same aspirations, but Cowperwood has the advantage over them that he has already fallen off his wall and survived, and so he lacks that sneaking fear of consequences which holds them in check. In brief, they are brigands with one eye on the *posse comitatus*, while he is a brigand with both eyes on the swag. The result, as may be imagined, is a combat truly homeric in its proportions—a combat in which associated orthodoxy in rapine is pitted against the most fantastic and astounding heterodoxy. The street railways of Chicago are the prize, and Cowperwood fights for control of them with all the ferocity of a hungry hyena and all the guile of a middle-aged serpent. His devices are staggering and unprecedented, even in that town of surprises. He makes a trial of every crime in the calendar of roguery, from blackmail to downright pillage. And though, in the end, he is defeated in his main purpose, for the enemy takes the cars, he is yet so far successful that he goes away with a lordly share of the profits, and leaves behind him a memory like that of a man-eating tiger in an Indian village.

A mere hero of melodrama? A brother to Monte Cristo and Captain Kidd? A play-acting superman, stalking his gorgeous heights? Far from it, indeed. The very charm of the man, as I have hinted before, lies in his utter lack of obvious charm. He is not sentimental. He is incapable of attitudinizing. He makes no bid for that homage which goes to the conscious outlaw, the devil-of-a-fellow. Even in his amours, which are carried on as boldly and as copiously as his chicaneries, there is no hint of the barbered Don Juan, the professional scourge of virtue. Cowperwood pursues women unmorally, almost innocently. He seduces the wives and daughters of friends and enemies alike; there is seldom any conscious purpose to dramatize and romanticize the adventure. Women are attractive to him simply because they represent difficulties to be surmounted, problems to be solved, personalities to be brought into subjection, and he in his turn is attractive to women simply because he transcends all they they know, or think they know, of men. There must be at least a dozen different maids and wives in his story, and in one way or another they all contribute to his final defeat, but there is nothing approaching a grand affair. At no time is a woman hunt the principal business before him. At no time does one charmer blind him to all others. Even at the close, when we see him genuinely smitten, an easy fatalism still conditions his eagerness, and he waits with unflagging patience for the victory that finally rewards him.

Such a man, described romantically, would be undistinguishable from the wicked earls and seven-foot guardsmen of Ouida and the Duchess. But described realistically, with all that wealth of minute and apparently inconsequential detail which Dreiser piles up so amazingly, he becomes a figure astonishingly vivid, lifelike and engrossing. He fits into no *a priori* theory of conduct or scheme of rewards and punishments; he proves nothing and teaches nothing; the motives which move him are never obvious and frequently unintelligible. But in the end he seems genuinely a man—a man of the sort that we see about us in the real world—not a transparent and simple fellow, reacting docilely according to a formula, but a bundle of complexities and contradictions, a creature oscillating between the light and the shadow, a unique and, at bottom, inexplicable personality. It is here that Dreiser gets farthest from the wallowed rut of fiction. The Cowperwood he puts before us is not the two-dimensional cut-out, the facile jumping jack, of the ordinary novel, but a being of three dimensions and innumerable planes—in brief, the impenetrable mystery that is man. The makers of best-sellers, if they could imagine him at all, would seek to account for him, explain him, turn him into a moral (*i.e.*, romantic) equation. Dreiser is content to describe him.

Naturally enough, the lady reviewers of the newspapers have been wholly flabbergasted by the book. Unable to think of a character in a novel save in terms of the characters in other novels, they have sought to beplaster Cowperwood with the old, old labels. He is the Wealthy Seducer, the Captain of Industry, the Natural Polygamist, the Corruptionist, the Franchise Grabber, the Bribe Giver, the Plutocrat, the Villain. Some of them, intelligent enough to see that not one of these labels actually fits, have interpreted the fact as a proof of Dreiser's incapacity. He is denounced for creating a Cowperwood who is not like other capitalists, not like other lawbreakers, not like other voluptuaries— that is to say, not like the capitalists, lawbreakers and voluptuaries of Harold MacGrath, E. Phillips Oppenheim and Richard Harding Davis. And one hears, too, the piping voice of outraged virtue: a man who chases women in his leisure and captures a dozen or so in twenty years is ungentlemanly, un-American, indecent—and therefore ought not to be put into a book. But I do not think that Dreiser is going to be stopped by such piffle, nor even by the more damaging attacks of smug and preposterous publishers. He has stuck to his guns through thick and thin, and he is going to stick to them to the end of the chapter. And soon or late, unless I err very grievously, he is going to reap the just reward of a sound and courageous artist, just as George Meredith reaped it before him, and Joseph Conrad is beginning to reap it even now.

*   *   *   *   *   *   *   *

The "Genius"

Desire as Hero

Randolph Bourne*

The insistent theme of Mr. Dreiser's work is desire, perennial, un-quenchable. The critic who would discuss him takes his life in his hands. He must either be denounced as an advocate of prostitution, or an ad-mirer of that second-rate pseudo-passion which Mr. Hearst and his able fictional lieutenants have made it their business to introduce to our American consciousness. A public which uses the word "sex" as in-discriminately as it does would be very hard to talk to on the subject of desire. As currently used, sex has a subtly derogatory sense. What it really means is, "We have no intention of making primary the values and im-plications which cluster around desire." A recent naïve critic expressed it exactly when he preferred Booth Tarkington to Tagore and Artzibashef because Tarkington makes business the master-motive of life, to which religion and sex are incidental. One simply takes them for granted in a turmoil the vortex of which is professional or business action. Of course no great Continental novelist ever believed this, Rolland or Dostoevsky or Tolstoi or Frenssen or Nexö, and it is in this contrast of values that we get our American uniqueness in the imaginative world. The major motive of these Continentals is almost always the inexorable desire of life, a desire which is no more physical than it is spiritual, a desire which consists often of walking in the mud with the face towards the stars. This push and yearning is what makes for religion and art in a kind of insatiable strain-ing towards realization and perfection. The East has too much of it and tries to put it to sleep. The West in the last century had almost too much, but struggled nobly to make something out of it. That struggle, embit-tered by a new knowledge of how meanly constituted the world was, pro-duced modern literature.

No matter how badly Mr. Dreiser might do his work, he would be significant as the American novelist who has most felt this subterranean current of life. Many novelists have seen this current as a mere abyss of sin from which the soul is to be dragged to the high ground of moral purpose and redemption, but this will not quite do. The great interpreters see life as a struggle between this desire and the organized machinery of ex-istence, but they are not eager, as we are, to cover up and belittle the

*Reprinted from *New Republic*, 5 (November 20, 1915), Fall Literary Review, pp. 5–6.

desire. There can be little creative imagination as long as we regard the motion picture trappings and action of life, the safe running in social harness, as "realer" than primeval or almost subconscious forces.

That Mr. Dreiser is our only novelist who tries to plumb far below this conventional superstructure is his great distinction. We have enough "red blood" in our fiction, but too much of it is patently compounded of carmine and water. And if we are to talk of bestiality, there is nothing more bestial than the romantic love of the conventional novel. What Mr. Dreiser has discovered is that "libido" which was nothing more than the scientific capturing of this nineteenth-century desire. You may come away from the Freudians and the Jungians chagrined at their technicalities and horrified at their phenomena, but you can scarcely deny that they have found and interpreted a central *leitmotiv* of our human living, which is immensely to illuminate our understanding of ourselves and the world about us. What Mr. Dreiser seems to me to do is to give us a crudely impressive fictional portrayal of this motive. His hero is really not Sister Carrie or the Titan or the Genius, but that desire within us that pounds in manifold guise against the iron walls of experience. Sister Carrie was a mass of undifferentiated desire, craving finery and warmth and light and sympathy quite as much as satisfied sex. The masculine Titan appeared in unpleasantly crystallized form of physical passion. In the Genius the libido takes the form of an insatiable desire which is sexual and yet incurably aesthetic. In his world, genuine spiritual monogamy would be an *idée fixe*, a kind of pathological petrifaction of desire. Here it is always overleaping the particular, seeking something elemental, almost metaphysical, that eludes the individual woman. The "Genius" himself calls it Beauty, and perhaps that is as good a word as any. Some magical manna he seems to seek in the women he is mad about. As they pass from his sight, that spirit merely becomes incarnated in another form. To those who would dismiss a character like Eugene Witla, the "Genius," as a beast, such an interpretation will seem over-idyllic. But he eludes moral capture. From Mr. Dreiser's first chapter we are out on a wider and more perilous sea.

Mr. Dreiser carries his hero over a restless field of adventure. From his boyhood in the Illinois town he takes him to Chicago and little jobs, until he discovers artistic talent and is drawn to the dazzling life of New York. (Mr. Dreiser never quite gets over this dazzle.) Studio life, exhibitions, social intrigue, come to a halt in nervous collapse and the effort to recover through hard physical labor. When the Genius's career revives, it is in the form of advertising art and the dizzy directorship of the United Magazines Corporations. Ultimately his good art reasserts itself, and he regains his place in the world. Through all of this runs the tragic stream of incontinence.

Mr. Dreiser writes of the erotic with an almost religious solemnity. There is something crudely massive about such a long epic of desire.

There is a touch of the same Greek tragic note which vibrates through "Spoon River Anthology." The Genius, swept away by girlish beauty, is himself bewildered by the vehemence of the Unknown Eros within him. That experience of such thrilling loveliness should end in such bitter and humiliating woe! Like Medea's "O wrath within me! Spare my children!" he feels himself haunted by this power not himself which makes for unrighteousness. The storms of angry chagrin which his unfaithfulness excites in his wife Angela bring him only the most undisguised astonishment. There is almost Greek irony too in the fact that the only good, responsible and dutiful act which he performs—his marriage to the devoted Angela—precipitates many of the horrors. When her child finally releases her in death from a purgatory of agonized jealousy, we are left with the unquenched Genius, worn but not repentant, restored to his painting and reconciled in a devotion to his unwelcome little daughter.

This does not pretend to be a solution. Through the chaotic welter of his artistic, business, and social career, the Genius wearily seeks a guiding thread which does not emerge. His researches in Herbert Spencer, cosmic philosophy, and Mrs. Eddy, are curiously typical manifestations of the libido. Mr. Dreiser seems to take them all very seriously, but he is honest in not making them points of satiation for weary desire. Very true also is the contrast between the Genius's hard and realistic art and his supersensuous life. He never becomes integrated, because with talent and passion and intelligence he yet finds himself in a world which is too diverse and too big for him. He is on a sea which is full of cross-currents where he cannot steer. The major current pulls him where he would not go. And the sea opens so far on every side that he does not know in what direction he wants to steer. One feels that this chaos is not only in the Genius's soul, but also in the author's soul, and in America's soul.

Mr. Dreiser compels and convinces almost entirely in spite of his method. He has no distinction of style. His conversation is negligible, and at time falls even below the level of cheapness. He is portentously wordy. He has no humor. And yet one reads him. In the 736 pages, one skips only the business and social details—which are too minute to be even good photography. One reads him because he never forgets that he is talking about life as it is lived, and because he takes it seriously. Even scenes of freezing realism like the birth of Angela's child do not offend as they might. He is always saved by a plodding sincerity. His people are rarely desirable or interesting. Yet they live and you cannot escape them.

And for all its dull and rather cheap texture, the book is set in a light of youthful idealism. Nobody but Mr. Dreiser could manage this fusion, but it is there. For the Genius the golden glow shines from everything. Always there is a sense of the miraculous beauty of girls, the soft clinging of charming atmospheres. Of sordid realists Mr. Dreiser is certainly the most idealistic. You cannot disillusion him. He still believes in, and still gives, a sense of the invincible virginality of the world.

I trust that the quotation marks in the title indicate Mr. Dreiser's realization that he has created only a second-rate personality, that he never, indeed, creates any but second-rate personalities. In the Genius he has made, however, a grandiose caricature of the masculine soul. And his real hero, anyway, is not his second-rate personality, but the desire of life. For this, much shall be forgiven him.

A Literary Behemoth

H. L. Mencken*

On page 703 of Theodore Dreiser's new novel, "The 'Genius' " (*Lane*), the gentleman described by the title, Eugene Tennyson Witla by name, is on his way to a Christian Scientist to apply for treatment for "his evil tendencies in regard to women." Remember the place: page 703. The reader, by this time, has hacked and gummed his way through 702 large pages of fine print: 97 long chapters: more than 300,000 words. The stagehands stand ready to yank down the curtain; messieurs of the orchestra, their minds fixed eagerly upon malt liquor, are up to their hips in the finale; the weary nurses are swabbing up the operating room; the learned chirurgeons are wiping their knives upon their pantaloons; the rev. clergy are swinging into the benediction; the inexorable embalmer waits in the ante-chamber with his unescapable syringe, his Mona Lisa smile. . . . And then, at this painfully hurried and impatient point, with the *coda* already under weigh and even the most somnolent reaching nervously for his goloshes, Dreiser halts the whole show to explain the origin, nature and inner meaning of Christian Science, and to make us privy to a lot of chatty stuff about Mrs. Althea Johns, the lady-like healer, and to supply us with detailed plans and specifications of the joint, lair or apartment-house in which this fair sorceress lives, works her miracles, trims her boobs, and has her being!

Believe me, I do not spoof. Turn to page 703 and see for yourself. There, while the fate of Witla waits and the bowels of patience are turned to water, we are instructed and tortured with the following particulars about the house:

1. That it was "of conventional design."
2. That there was "a spacious areaway" between its two wings.
3. That these wings were "of cream-colored pressed brick."
4. That the entrance between them "was protected by a handsome wrought-iron door."
5. That to either side of this door was "an electric lamp support of handsome design."
6. That in each of these lamp supports there were "lovely cream-colored globes, shedding a soft lustre."

*Reprinted from *Smart Set*, 47 (December 1915), 150–54.

7. That "inside was the usual lobby."

8. That in the lobby was the usual elevator.

9. That in the elevator was the usual "uniformed negro elevator man."

10. That this negro elevator man (name not given) was "indifferent and impertinent."

11. That a telephone switchboard was also in the lobby.

12. That the building was seven stories in height.

Such is novel-writing as Dreiser understands it—a laborious and relentless meticulousness, an endless piling up of small details, an almost furious tracking down of ions, electrons and molecules. One is amazed and flabbergasted by the mole-like industry of the man, and no less by his lavish disregard for the ease and convenience of his readers. A Dreiser novel, at least of the later canon, cannot be read as other novels are read, *e.g.*, on a winter evening or a summer afternoon, between meal and meal, travelling from New York to Boston. It demands the attention for at least a week, and uses up the strength for at least a month. If, tackling "The 'Genius,' " one were to become engrossed in the fabulous manner described by the newspaper reviewers and so find oneself unable to put it down and go to bed before the end, one would get no sleep for three days and three nights. A man who can prove that he has read such a novel without medical assistance should be admitted to the *Landwehr* at once, without thesis or examination, and perhaps even given the order *pour la mérite*. A woman of equal attainments is tough enough to take in washing or to sing Brünnhilde. . . .

And yet, and yet—well, here comes the inevitable "and yet." For all his long-windedness, for all his persistent refusal to get about his business, for all his mouthing of things so small that they seem to be nothings, this Dreiser is undoubtedly a literary artist of very respectable rank, and nothing proves it more certainly than this, the last, the longest and one is tempted to add the damnedest of his novels. The thing is staggering, alarming, maddening—and yet one sticks to it. It is rambling, formless, chaotic—and yet there emerges out of it, in the end, a picture of almost blinding brilliancy, a panorama that will remain in the mind so long as memory lasts. Is it ncessary to proceed against the reader in so barbarous a manner? Is there no way of impressing him short of wearing him out? Is there no route to his consciousness save laparotomy? God knows. But this, at all events, is plain: that no other route is open to Dreiser. He must do his work in his own manner, and his oafish clumsiness and crudeness are just as much a part of it as his amazing steadiness of vision, his easy management of gigantic operations, his superb sense of character. One is familiar with stylist-novelists, fellows who tickle with apt phrases, workers in psychological miniature, carvers of cameos. Here is one who works with a steam-shovel, his material being a county. Here is a wholesaler in general merchandise. Here, if such a fellow as Henry James be likened to a duellist, is the Hindenburg of the novel.

And what have we, precisely, in the story of Eugene Tennyson Witla? A tale enormous and indescribable—the chronicle, not only of Witla's own life, but also of the lives of a dozen other persons, some of them of only the slightest influence upon him. And what sort of man is this Witla. In brief, an artist, but though he actually paints pictures and even makes a success of it, not the artist of conventional legend, not a moony fellow in a velvet coat. What the story of Witla shows us, in truth, is very much the same thing that the story of Frank Cowperwood, in "The Financier" and "The Titan," showed us, to wit, the reaction of the artistic temperament against the unfavorable environment of this grand and glorious republic. If a Wagner or a Beethoven were born in the United States to-morrow it is highly improbable that he would express himself in the way that those men did; if a Raphael or a Cézanne, it is even more unlikely. The cause thereof is not that we disesteem music and painting, but that we esteem certain other arts infinitely more; particularly the art of creating vast industrial organisms, of bringing the scattered efforts of thousands of workers into order and coherence, of conjuring up huge forces out of spent and puny attractions and repulsions. Witla, as I have said, tries conventional art; he even goes to Paris and sets up as a genius of Montmartre. But his creative instinct and intelligence are soon challenged by larger opportunities; he is too thoroughly an American to waste himself upon pictures to hang upon walls. Instead he tackles jobs that better fit his race and time, and so, after a while, we see him at the head of a mammoth publishing house, with irons in half a dozen other fires—a boss American with all the capacity for splendor that goes with the species.

The chief apparent business of the story, indeed, is to show Witla's rise to this state of splendor, and its corrupting effect upon his soul. To this extent Dreiser plays the moralist: he, too, is an American, and cannot escape it altogether. Witla mounts the ladder of riches rung by rung, and at each rise he yields more and more to the lavishness surrounding him. He acquires fast horses, objects of art, the physical comforts of a sultan. His wife, out of Wisconsin, is hung with fragile and costly draperies; his home is a thing for the decorator to boast about; his very office has something of the luxurious gaudiness of a bordello. Bit by bit he is conquered by this pervasive richness, this atmosphere of gorgeous ease. His appetite increases as dish follows dish upon the groaning table that fate has set for him; he acquires, by subtle stages, the tastes, the prejudices, the point of view of a man of wealth; his creative faculty, disdaining its old objects, concentrates itself upon the moulding and forcing of opportunities for greater and greater acquisitions. And so his highest success becomes his deepest degradation, and we see the marks of his disintegration multiply as he approaches it. He falls, indeed, almost as fast as he rises. It is a collapse worthy of melodrama. (Again the moral note!)

I say that this rise and fall make the chief business of the story, but that, of course, is only externally. Its inner drama presents a conflict between the two Witlas—the artist who is trying to create something, however meretricious, however undeserving his effort, and the sentimentalist whose longing is to be loved, coddled, kept at ease. This conflict, of course, is at the bottom of the misery of all men who may be truly said to be conscious creatures—that is, of all men above the grade of car conductor, barber, waiter or Sunday-school superintendent. On the one hand there is the desire to exert power, to do something that has not been done before, to bend reluctant material to one's will, and on the other hand there is the desire for comfort, for well-being, for an easy life. This latter desire, nine times out of ten, perhaps actually always, is visualized by women. Women are the conservatives and conservators, the enemies of hazard and innovation, the compromisers and temporizers. That very capacity for mothering which is their supreme gift is the greatest of all foes to masculine enterprise. Most men, alas, yield to it. In the common phrase, they marry and settle down—*i.e.*, they give up all notion of making the world over. This resignationism usually passes for happiness, but to the genuine artist it is quite impossible. He must go on sacrificing ease to aspiration and aspiration to ease, thus vacillating abominably and forever between his two irreconcilable desires. No such man is ever happy, not even in the moment of his highest achievement. Life, to him, must always be a muddled and a tragic business. The best he can hope for is a makeshift and false sort of contentment.

This is what Eugene Tennyson Witla comes to in the end. Women have been the curse of his life, from the days of his nonage onward. Forced into their arms constantly by an irresistible impulse, an unquenchable yearning for their facile caresses, he has been turned aside as constantly from his higher goals and led into smoother and broader paths. Good, bad and indifferent, they have all done him harm. His own wife, clinging to him pathetically through good and evil report, always ready to take him back after one of his innumerable runnings amuck, is perhaps his greatest enemy among them. She is always ten yards behind him, hanging on to his coat-tails, trying to drag him back. She is fearful when he needs daring, stupid when he need stimulation, virtuously wifely when the thing he craves is wild adventure. But the rest all fail him, too. Seeking for joy he finds only bitterness. It is the gradual slowing down of the machine, mental and physical, that finally brings him release. Slipping into the middle forties he begins to turn, almost imperceptibly at first, from the follies of his early manhood. When we part from him at last he seems to have found what he has been so long seeking in his little daughter. The lover has merged into the father.

It is upon this tale, so simple in its main outlines, that Dreiser spills more than 300,000 long and short words, most of them commonplace, many of them improperly used. His writing, which in "The Titan" gave promise of rising to distinction and even to something resembling beauty, is here a mere dogged piling up of nouns, adjectives, verbs, adverbs, pronouns and particles, and as devoid of aesthetic quality as an article in the

Nation. I often wonder if he gets anything properly describable as pleasure out of his writing—that is, out of the actual act of composition. To the man who deals in phrases, who gropes for the perfect word, who puts the way of saying it above the thing actually said there is in writing the constant joy of sudden discovery, of happy accident. But what joy can there be in rolling up sentences that have no more life or beauty in them, intrinsically, than so many election bulletins? Where is the thrill in the manufacture of such a paragraph as that I have referred to above, in which the apartment-house infested by Mrs. Althea Johns is described as particularly as if it were being offered for sale? Or in the laborious breeding of such guff as this, from Book I, Chapter IV:

> The city of Chicago—who shall portray it! This vast ruck of life that had sprung suddenly into existence upon the dank marshes of a lake shore.

But why protest and repine? Dreiser writes in this banal fashion, I dessay, because God hath made him so, and a man is too old, at my time of life, to begin criticizing the Creator. But all the same it may do no harm to point out, quite academically, that a greater regard for fairness of phrase and epithet would be as a flow of Pilsner to the weary reader in his journey across the vast deserts, steppes and pampas of the Dreiserian fable. Myself no voluptuary of letters, searching fantodishly for the rare tit-bit, the succulent morsel, I have yet enough sensitiveness to style to suffer damnably when all style is absent. And so with form. The well-made novel is as irritating as the well-made play—but let it at least have a beginning, a middle and an end! Such a confection as "The 'Genius' " is as shapeless as a Philadelphia pie-woman. It billows and rolls and bulges out like a cloud of smoke, and its internal organization is as vague. There are episodes that, with a few chapters added, would make very respectable novels. There are chapters that need but a touch or two to be excellent short stories. The thing rambles, staggers, fumbles, trips, wobbles, straggles, strays, heaves, pitches, reels, totters, wavers. More than once it seems to be foundering, in both the equine and the maritime senses. The author forgets it, goes out to get a drink, comes back to find it smothering. One has heard of the tree so tall that it took two men to see to the top of it. Here is a novel so huge that a whole shift of critics is needed to read it. Did I myself do it all alone? By no means. I read only the first and last paragraphs of each chapter. The rest I farmed out to my wife and children, to my cousin Fred, and to my pastor and my beer man.

Nathless, as I have before remarked, the composition hath merit. The people in it have the fogginess and impenetrability of reality; they stand before us in three dimensions; their sufferings at the hands of fate are genuinely poignant. Of the situations it is sufficient to say that they do not seem like "situations" at all: they unroll aimlessly, artlessly, inevitably, like actual happenings. A weakness lies in the background: New

York is vastly less interesting than Chicago. At all events, it is vastly less interesting to Drieser, and so he cannot make it as interesting to the reader. And no wonder. Chicago is the epitome of the United States, of the New World, of youth. It shows all the passion for beauty, the high striving, the infinite curiosity, the unashamed hoggishness, the purple romance, the gorgeous lack of humor of twenty-one. Save for San Francisco, it is the only American city that has inspired a first-rate novel in twenty-five years. Dreiser's best books, "Sister Carrie," "Jennie Gerhardt" and "The Titan," deal with it. His worst, "The Financier," is a gallant but hopeless effort to dramatize Philadelphia—a superb subject for a satirist, but not for a novelist. In "The 'Genius' " he makes the costly blunder of bringing Witla from Chicago to New York. It would have been a better story, I venture, if that emigration had been left out of it. . . .

An American Tragedy

Theodore Dreiser:
An American Tragedy

T. K. Whipple*

Dreiser is one of those writers who are said to have historical importance, one of those trail-breakers, that is, who make a deep impress on their own time and who are known to later generations by reputation, but by reputation only. Dreiser's force and originality—greatness is not too strong a word—must become only more obvious with the passage of years; but surely that greatness will be taken more and more on faith. The labor of reading him, with the sense it brings of a grinding despair, as of being pursued in a nightmare over endless wastes of soft sand, is an experience, however profitable, that is too painful to be sought out by normal humanity.

To take the full measure of Dreiser's achievement, one must remember that Sister Carrie appeared in 1900 and Jennie Gerhardt in 1911, and that among the most popular and typical novels of those years were When Knighthood Was in Flower, Graustark, and Rebecca of Sunnybrook Farm. No wonder that from the first Dreiser was treated either to invective or to apologetics, and that his apologists dwelt on his intentions and on his personal qualities almost to the exclusion of his work. At least, at a time when fiction was a kind of confectionery, he was not facile, conventional, pretty and optimistic: at least, he meant well. And the critics who approved of his purpose—to tell the whole truth about American life as he saw it, even though he saw it as unpleasant—could not afford, in the bitter war being waged with the censors and the moralists, to question his literary success. Furthermore, his granite-like steadfastness and integrity, his insistence on seeing for himself, were so striking and so admirable that it was natural to praise the man and forget the novelist.

All Dreiser's virtues are as evident as ever in An American Tragedy; if they no longer shine quite so brilliantly and all-sufficingly, it is doubtless because the contrasting background has disappeared, owing in part to the lesson which Dreiser has himself taught. Fifteen years ago, An American Tragedy would have been a portent; now it is another of Dreiser's novels, much like its predecessors. More successful than The Financier, The

*Reprinted from *New Republic*, 46 (March 17, 1926), 113–15.

Titan, and The "Genius", less successful but also a more difficult under-
taking than Sister Carrie or Jennie Gerhardt, it marks a return rather than
an advance, a return from high finance and high sosciety, from elaborate
études de moeurs and minute accounts of social machinery, to the sort of
topic which Dreiser is best fitted to handle: the sordid and pathetic story
of a midwestern boy of the lower middle class whose weakness lands him
in disaster. It shows development only in that Dreiser tries to reach higher
emotional levels and greater intensity than he has attempted heretofore.
Otherwise, it is another manifestation of his familiar merits and defects:
in other words, it is a novel no other living American could have written—and also, probably, one which no other would have written.

An American Tragedy could have been written only by a man of
unusual power and magnitude. Even on the harshest critic Dreiser's
novels must leave an impression that the author has a kind of greatness.
The cause of this impression and the source of Dreiser's greatness I take to
be his emotional endowment—not so much an intensity as a tremendous,
steady, unfailing flood of feeling. He is distinguished from ordinary men
by extraordinary strength and volume of passion. Chiefly it shows itself in
his tragic sense, in his profound consciousness of the tragedy inherent in
all existence, in the very scheme of things—tragedy inescapable, essential,
universal, perceived by many, but by very few so overwhelmingly felt.
His brooding pity penetrates all life as he sees it, touching every human
being, from the most glittering superman to the forlornest prostitute, as in
An American Tragedy it touches everyone from the bellboys of the
Green-Davidson Hotel in Kansas City to the rich and beautiful Sondra
Finchley, social leader of Lycurgus, New York. Especially acute is his
perception of man's endless capacity for suffering, a trait which lends
dignity to even the weakest and most contemptible of Dreiser's creatures,
even to the elder Griffiths, the street-preaching derelict who is the hero's
father in An American Tragedy, just as Clyde's mother, for all her gro-
tesqueness, in her grief for her son illustrates Dreiser's saying that
"sometimes even the mediocre and the inefficient attain to a classic
stature when dignified by pain."

Dreiser's emotional capacity shows itself not only in his tragic sense
but also in his zest, his unflagging relish for actuality and his feeling of its
mystery. His is a romantic love of reality, charged with wonder and awe.
His love of life, good or bad, beautiful or ugly, is omnivorous; because it is
all strange, to him it is all exciting. To a curiosity so voracious and an interest so insatiable as his, nothing whatever seems dull or tiresome. Hence
comes his amazing faculty of observation and his relentless heaping up of
detail; hence also, therefore, the epic sweep often and rightly attributed
to his novels, which have the range and vastness pertaining to any minute
record of an enormous area of human life. This gusto, however, not content with imparting scope to his work, leads him into trouble, for because
of it he can resist no temptation to wander off into by-paths and tedious
digressions. Because he can bring himself to leave out nothing, he piles up

mountains of pointless minutiae, irrelevant and insignificant, and produces an intolerable tedium. He can never learn to omit, for his latest
novel is as overweighted as his earlier; on page 78 of the second volume
Clyde commits the murder which really ends his story; he is captured on
page 145; his trial drags along to his conviction on page 330; and his execution takes place on page 405. Not even The Financier so abundantly illustrates Dreiser's ability to make ten pages do the work of one. His emotion, when it shows itself as all-inclusive love of reality, is a source of
weakness as well as of strength.

Yet even these vast talus-heaps of detail are stirred by the tides of passion which surge under them. Somehow, in spite of everything, Dreiser
manages to communicate something of his feeling, which burns, though
dimly and feebly, even through the slag and dross of his writing. If many
readers regard his emotionality as merely sentimental, it is partly because
the childish crudity of his expression leads an appearance of falsity. When
the "Genius" exclaims "What a sweet welter life is—how rich, how
tender, how grim, how like a colorful symphony" and the author adds
"Great art dreams welled up into his soul as he viewed the sparkling deeps
of space," it is difficult, but also I think necessary, to believe that words so
inadequate and so false could be called forth by true emotion. An
American Tragedy contains some two hundred pages like the following:

> But, God, what was that?
> Oh, that terrible sound!
> Like a whimpering, screeching spirit in this dark!
> There!
> What was it?
> He dropped his bag and in a cold sweat sunk down,
> crouching behind a tall, thick tree, rigid and motionless with
> fear.
> That sound!
> But only a screech-owl! He had heard it several weeks before
> at the Cranston lodge. But here! In this wood! This dark! He
> must be getting on and out of here. There was no doubt of that.
> He must not be thinking such horrible, fearful thoughts, or he
> would not be able to keep up his strength or courage at all.
> But that look in the eyes of Roberta! That last appealing
> look! God! He could not keep from seeing it! Her mournful,
> terrible screams! Could he not cease from hearing them—until
> he got out of here anyhow?

Finally the author's agitation grows insufferable in the chapters
devoted to Clyde's experience in the death house, which rival a Hearst
paper's account of a popular murderer's last agonies. Dreiser's understanding of Clyde, his pity and sympathy, his remarkable imaginative
power, are rendered all but vain by the terms in which they are expressed,
terms which disgust fully as much as they move the reader.

Most of Dreiser's warmest champions, such as Mencken, grant that he cannot write, grant that he has no narrative sense and no sense of words or of style, that he is prolix and irrelevant, that his sentences are worse than chaotic, that he violates English and even American idiom; these foibles, however, they regard as but petty irritations which must be overlooked. But how can such writing be negligible? Dreiser could not write as he does, mixing slang with poetic archaisms, reveling in the cheap, trite and florid, if there were not in himself something correspondingly muddled, banal and tawdry. Furthermore, since a writer works through words alone and words are his only means of communication, a failure in writing is necessarily a failure in communication—and of Dreiser's failure the best that can be said is that it is incomplete. Somehow he contrives to give a sense of reality and veracity, as of a tremendous story which actually happened told by an inept, loquacious stutterer, himself deeply stirred, who sometimes unintentionally misrepresents the facts. In An American Tragedy he has particularly difficult problems in carrying the reader's belief—that so feeble a creature as Clyde would prove a social success and captivate Sondra Finchley, or would plan and carry out a murder. I cannot doubt Clyde's story in the main, but I cannot believe that it happened precisely as Dreiser has recounted it.

Dreiser's characterization suffers, and must inevitably suffer, from his incapacity to handle words. As in The Financier and The "Genius" he asserts that his heroes are brilliant and irresistible, yet shows them as vulgar dullards because he is unable to write good conversation, so in An American Tragedy he misses success because he cannot so use language as to communicate intense feeling. Not that the reader is unaffected—but the disparity between the author's perturbation and the inadequacy of his expression is almost grotesque. If Clyde and Roberta and the rest were not half concealed by a deluge of inept verbiage, An American Tragedy might well be one of the world's great novels.

Perhaps Dreiser's incompetence in the management of his medium is partly accounted for by the striking resemblance of his writing to the world which he depicts, a world chaotic and tawdry, without plan, purpose, or sense, lacking even the rudimentary organization of a wolf pack, a world offering no valid reasons for living, no reward which would appeal to a rational or civilized being, no prize save an economic success which can buy only physical luxury, inane display and vulgar snobbery. It is a brutal world, a free-for-all of personal aggrandizement, no more humane than the aboriginal jungle of sabre-toothed tiger and woolly elephant, a world seeking meretricious and gaudy in the absence of genuine satisfactions. Not only futile and wasteful, it is also tragic and passionate, for its inhabitants are endowed with desires and possibilities for which it affords no possible means of fulfillment. The strongest and coarsest are dissatisfied victors; the weak mill helplessly about, kicked and trodden upon. Dreiser's books are the stammering utterance of this pathetic and flashy disorder trying to speak.

Similarly, one might say that Dreiser's philosophy is this world trying to think. Being able to conceive nothing else, he assumes that human life everywhere has always been and must always be like the life he has himself known at first hand. His thought is simply a formulation of the beliefs which he has discerned in the practice of those about him. The official and avowed creed of his world—the taboo morality and silly ostrich-like optimism with which it oils the wheels of progress—he never tires of attacking; but the creed implicit in its actions he has exalted into a universal philosophy. He regards human existence as inevitably a bestial anarchy never under any circumsances capable of yielding better gratifications than the joy of fighting, sensual pleasure, and the parade of money. For all his onslaughts on the pious camouflage with which his compatriots conceal their motives and doings even from themselves, he has essentially accepted American life as he found it in the midwest of his younger years. He has felt and experienced his world too fully to be able to detach himself from it and try it by any other standards than its own. He has identified himself with it, and the union has brought forth the misbegotten Leviathans of his novels. Through this union he has taken into himself and so into his art the anarchy and the cheap barbarity of his surroundings.

Yet what a tremendous emotional pressure has gone into this identification, what power of realization! Of that power, the basis of life as well as of literature, surely Dreiser has more than any other living American. Furthermore, in the making of this vital contact with American life, Dreiser was the first, the pioneer. Herein lies the debt which all other writers owe to him—herein lies his greatness and his significance. No doubt it was necessary that someone should be sacrificed by being merged and sunk, and that he was chosen was Dreiser's fortune and misfortune. His real achievement is to be found in the work of others, work which he has helped make possible. And his contribution is not to literature alone; he has done more, directly and indirectly, than any other individual to rouse Americans to a consciousness of what American life is like and if an American civilization ever emerges, Dreiser's share in its making will not be small. That is what it is to have historical importance. Perhaps it is more than being a good novelist.

An American Tragedy

Robert Shafer*

I

Mr. Theodore Dreiser's critical friends have always been ready to admit his deficiencies as a literary artist, and these deficiencies are really extraordinary. Nevertheless, by universal consent Mr. Dreiser stands at the head of the realistic movement in American fiction, not merely because he is its pioneer, and has endured obloquy and even persecution for the Cause, but primarily on account of his seriousness and singleness of purpose, his depth of keen feeling, and his earnest reflectiveness. His work also anticipates in important respects the efforts of the post-realists and super-realists, so-called, and altogether has a present salience which insistently demands consideration.

The work, however, cannot be assessed—cannot indeed be understood—apart from the man; and fortunately Mr. Dreiser has written much about himself.[1] He was born in 1871 in Terre Haute, Indiana, of German Catholic parents who struggled vainly against poverty. In the schools of another Indiana town he received the elements of an education, but apparently learned little of value to him beyond reading and writing. In boyhood and youth, in school or out, he became acquainted with a number of the better-known writers, chiefly of fiction, of the nineteenth century, but without gaining from them more than momentary entertainment. He has said that as a boy he "had no slightest opportunity to get a correct or even partially correct estimate of what might be called the mental A B abs of life."

If the truth is to be told, one reason for this lay clearly within himself. For he was, as his records show him, a stupid boy and young man, lapped in vague reverie and hazy dreams of enjoyment, and roused slowly to puzzled observation and thought. "No common man am I," he used to tell himself when he was scarcely out of his 'teens, with no evident reason save that with adolescence came an intense craving for freedom from the shackles of common life—freedom to indulge fully his temperamental longing for sensuous and materialised delight. This self-

*Reprinted from *Humanism and America*, ed. Norman Foerster (New York: Farrar and Rinehart, 1930), pp. 149–69.

conceit helped to prevent him from learning what could have been learned during his boyhood, and, as he grew older, aroused in him bitter resentment against the limitations of his early environment.

Those limitations, at the same time, were extreme. The Dreiser household was one combining almost unrelieved ignorance with perfect tastelessness, presided over by a father whose consuming interest was a Catholicism degraded into mere ceremonies and prohibitions. Mr. Dreiser explicitly denotes the quality of the purifying influence dominant in the home and community of his youth: "One should read only good books . . . from which any reference to sex had been eliminated, and what followed . . . was that all intelligent interpretation of character and human nature was immediately discounted. A picture of a nude or partially nude woman was sinful. . . . The dance in our home and our town was taboo. The theatre was an institution which led to crime, the saloon a centre of low, even bestial vices. . . . It was considered good business, if you please, to be connected with some religious organisation. . . . We were taught persistently to shun most human experiences as either dangerous or degrading or destructive. The less you knew about life the better; the more you knew about the fictional heaven and hell ditto. . . . In my day there were apparently no really bad men who were not known as such to all the world, . . . and few if any good men who were not sufficiently rewarded by the glorious fruits of their good deeds here and now! . . . Positively, and I stake my solemn word on this, until I was between seventeen and eighteen I had scarcely begun to suspect any other human being of harbouring the erratic and sinful thoughts which occasionally flashed through my own mind."

By the time Mr. Dreiser had fairly formed the suspicion that, despite appearances, other people might not be much better than himself, his family had begun to break up, following the death of his mother, and he himself had been thrust into the world—or rather into Chicago, where the Dreisers by now lived—to earn his way. He did manage to spend one year at Indiana University, to the great improvement of his health, but with no positive intellectual benefit, so that he refused to waste a second year, which he might have had there. He confesses this, it should be said, in no boastful spirit. He was in fact made to realise at Bloomington that there were elements of knowledge which it would be useful to him to acquire—but he found the effort hopeless. His mind could not be constrained, and, besides, the deficiencies of his earlier schooling stood in his way. Hence he returned to Chicago, to become a collector for an easy-payment furniture shop.

It was at this time that his feelings—scarcely yet his imagination or his reason—were awakened by the spectacle of "America on the make." He found that spectacle intensely vital. At the same time, too, he was doing the first reading that really came home to him:—he was reading a daily column of Eugene Field's in a Chicago newspaper. It gave him the notion of doing something like that himself, and sent him hunting for a post on a news-sheet. This he finally obtained, and at the reporter's desk achieved his real education, one not beyond his grasp. His first instructor promptly informed him that "life was a God-damned stinking, treacherous game, and that nine hundred and ninety-nine men out of every thousand were bastards." The truth of this generalisation Mr. Dreiser proceeded to establish for himself, by observation of those of life's realities which constitute news, and by intercourse with fellow-journalists. He discovered that practically all men, high or low, were lying hypocrites, outwardly professing a fine morality, but privately violating this without hesitation whenever it would serve their turn in the pursuit of gain or in the satisfaction of lust.

This was the reality, at any rate, which the young reporter saw, and which, as he says, broadened considerably his viewpoint, finally liberating him "from moralistic and religionistic qualms." So liberated was he, indeed, that he came to judge men "thoroughly sound intellectually" in proportion as he found them "quite free from the narrow, cramping conventions of their day." So liberated was he that he came to see the "religionist" for what he was: "a swallower of romance or a masquerader looking to profit and preferment." He came also to see behind "the blatherings of thin-minded, thin-blooded, thin-experienced religionists" only "a brainless theory." Nor was this the limit of his discoveries. He came further to see that life was not simply a ruthless struggle for material advantages, because, howsoever ruthless and intelligent one's struggle, still, one might be defrauded by sheer accident. Chance seemed, at times, the final ruler of all things—many of the reporter's assignments combining "to prove that life is haphazard and casual and cruel; to some lavish, to others niggardly."

Mr. Dreiser, it is fair to say, was the more ready to learn these lessons of experience because, as he plainly tells his readers, he himself was lustful and passionately eager for the material satisfactions of life. He longed to join in the antics of the rich, who alone, as he judged, were bathed in happiness. He felt, as he gazed enviously upon the gilded sons and daughters of earth, that, from no fault of his, life was tragically cheating him. And this sense of grievance, feeding upon itself, passed easily through a sentimental phase into bitterness, as his reminiscences show: "Whenever I returned to any place in which I had once lived and found things changed, as they always were, I was fairly transfixed by the oppressive sense of the evanescence of everything; a mood so hurtful and dark and yet with so rich if sullen a lustre that I was left wordless with pain. I was all but crucified at realising how unimportant I was, how nothing stayed but all changed. . . . Life was so brief, . . . and so soon, whatever its miserable amount or character, it would be gone. . . . But I, poor waif, with no definite or arresting skill of any kind, not even that of commerce, must go fumbling about looking in upon life from the outside, as it were. Beautiful women, or so I argued, were drawn to any but me. . . . I should never have a fraction of the means to do as I wished or to share in the life that I most craved. I was an Ishmael."

Not always, of course, was Mr. Dreiser sunk in a bitterness induced by self-pity and sentimental regret. Often in moments of successful work or of flattering companionship he was quickly lifted up into a mood of expansive self-satisfaction, equally unbalanced. Then he would say to himself: "I must be an exceptional man. . . . Life itself was not so bad; it was just higgledy-piggledy, catch-as-catch-can, that was all. If one were clever, like myself, it was all right." It was indeed magnificent, so long as the slave of temperament could dream of his heroic future as something assured. But dreams, like life, were unstable, and the fever for self-advancement, becoming intolerable from its intensity, would transmute itself—not every time into frank self-pity—but sometimes into tearful "sympathy for the woes of others, life in all its helpless degradation and poverty, the unsatisfied dreams of people." And from the downtrodden for whom he wept he also drew a lesson. The hideous inequalities both of fortune and of capacity which he saw, proved to him that democracy, like morality, was a sham, a hollow convention, irrelevant, indeed opposed, to the facts of life and practice.

Mr. Dreiser's journalistic career took him from Chicago to St. Louis, and thence, with several stops on the way, to Pittsburgh, during a period of rather more than three years. In these years, he says, speaking of his "blood-moods or so-called spiritual aspirations," he was "what might be called a poetic melancholiac, crossed with a vivid materialistic lust of life." His body, he adds, "was blazing with sex, as well as with a desire for material and social supremacy." It is not surprising, consequently, that he found himself able to entertain carnal desires for several women at the same time—though this at first surprised him, and troubled him also, until his day of liberation from "moralistic qualms." It is not surprising either that he presently was captivated by a charming country girl, several years older than himself, who had no single idea and only one desire in common with him. He had welcomed his liberation from "moralistic and religionistic qualms" the more complacently because of the simplification of thought and conduct to which it pointed. From this time the conduct of life was to be straightforward as well as simple, in accordance with the brutish yet vital law of following your dominant impulse regardlessly, ruthlessly, slavishly. But now this liberation itself was mainly instrumental in plunging him into a new, long-continued, and grievous difficulty. For his simple country maiden, though she was drawn to him as he was drawn to her, was nevertheless rigidly conventional, immovably "moralistic," one of the predestined pillars of an ordered society and a stable family. She steadfastly refused to yield him her body without marriage, and he, alas, was not only unable to support her but deeply unwilling to marry her even if he could.

Clearly this pair did not understand all that divided them in spirit, but, still, Mr. Dreiser knew from the first some portion of the truth. For he knew what love really was: it was a mere "blood-mood"; it was a vivid lust crossed with poetic fires; it was irresistible, of course, but it was like everything else, transient, shifting, evanescent. He already suspected, as he later concluded, that monogamy—marriage indeed of any kind—was a debasing institution which not only killed the love that brought men to it, but also deformed and dwarfed their personalities. It might not harm stupid and lethargic men, but the man of individuality, at least, the highest type of citizen, required utter freedom to follow his vital impulses—required the joys of the sexual act "without any of the hindrances or binding chains of convention." He knew, in fine, that "the tug of his immense physical desire for his beloved" might easily have been satisfied, despite his poverty, without compromising the future, and without doing a hurt to society, had there only been "any such thing as sanity in life," outside of himself. He even knew, after the first raptures of idyllic feeling had passed, that any other beautiful woman would have served his need as well; but, nevertheless, he clung to this one, because in fact no beautiful woman whom he found accessible did keep alive in him the same fever of desire. Yet his beloved remained immovable, and so drew him on, through several years of miserably divided feeling, into a marriage finally accomplished after his carnal fires had cooled, owing to the passage of time and the casual ministrations of certain other fair creatures, more pliant, but unsatisfying.

I dwell upon this painful episode, following Mr. Dreiser's own example, because it tells so much. It was the crucial event of his early life, and it left an ineffaceable scar. The fact is, indeed, that without definite knowledge of this miserable union, it would not be easy to understand how Mr. Dreiser became so obstinately fixed in those notions of life which journalism and its associations gave him and which he was eager to accept. Without definite knowledge of this marriage, further, it would be impossible fully to understand his novels; for none of them could have been written quite as it stands save in the light of this afflictive experience of his, and several, it is extremely likely, could not otherwise have been written at all.[2]

Some knowledge of another side of Mr. Dreiser's life, however, during his years of work for the news-sheets, is also necessary for those who would understand his novels. He has told us that in St. Louis the great literary idol of his associates was Zola, and after Zola, Balzac. These novelists, and especially the former, were constantly held up to him as models by one of his assignment-editors, who made it abundantly clear what Zola stood for. Mr. Dreiser read none of the Frenchman's books at this time, but he did read an unpublished novel by two St. Louis newspaper men which made a deep and lasting impression upon him and which, as he later discovered, was wholly inspired by Zola and Balzac.

This was "the opening wedge for him into the realm of realism," and, too, "it fixed his mind definitely on this matter of writing," firing him with a desire to create someting of the sort himself. He thought the novel "intensely beautiful," "with its frank pictures of raw, greedy, sensual human nature, and its open pictures of self-indulgence and vice." In these indirect ways, evidently, Zola exerted upon the young reporter an influence real and significant. It was, indeed, probably much more important than the direct influence exerted by Balzac not long thereafter; though the accident which brought Mr. Dreiser to a fevered and ecstatic reading of many of Balzac's novels, while he was in Pittsburgh, marked what was for him "a literary revolution."

The crowning stage of Mr. Dreiser's education, however, was now to come, while he was still in Pittsburgh, with his discovery of certain of the writings of Huxley, Tyndall, and Herbert Spencer. Huxley, Mr. Dreiser credits with finally dispelling the "lingering filaments" of Christianity still trailing about him; and Huxley's work of dispersion was completed by Spencer's *First Principles*. This book wholly "threw him down in his conceptions or non-conceptions of life" by its "questioning or dissolving into other and less understandable things" all that he had deemed substantial. "Up to this time," he says, "there had been in me a blazing and unchecked desire to get on and the feeling that in doing so we did get somewhere; now in its place was the definite conviction that spiritually one got nowhere, that there was no hereafter, that one lived and had his being because one had to, and that it was of no importance. Of one's ideals, struggles, deprivations, sorrows and joys, it could only be said that they were chemic compulsions. . . . Man was a mechanism, undevised and uncreated, and a badly and carelessly driven one at that."

The seeming ill logic of some of these remarks—the sudden concern over spiritual things felt by one who had hitherto devoted himself wholeheartedly to the world by sensuous appearances—is not unimportant. Clearly Spencer's book left an abiding mark on Mr. Dreiser because it represented in a general way the abstract conclusion towards which his own observations had been pointing. Without knowing it, and without any attempt to set his intellectual house in order, he had himself been drifting towards a mechanistic naturalism. Spencer made him aware of this, and if, as he thought, that awareness left him crushed and hopeless, it at least seemed to clear his mind of rubbish, and to give his view-point self-consistency and finality. Nevertheless, he did not come forth a Spencerian; and, indeed, his debt to the *Synthetic Philosophy* may easily be exaggerated—the more easily because it really is important.

Mr. Dreiser emphasises the fact that his reading of the *First Principles* was followed by an emotional revulsion—a revulsion which the Synthetic Philosopher can scarcely alone have caused. And in truth just at the time when he stumbled upon Spencer his feelings were strained to the breaking point. He had just returned from a last desperate, yet unsuccessful, effort to seduce his country maiden, which left him crushed, not only by that defeat itself, but by the consciousness that the gratification he was bound to secure was now driving him towards a marriage for which he had no capacity, no desire, and no prospect of sufficient means. Moreover, immediately after his Western visit he had gone, for the first time, to New York, where he had received an extraordinarily vivid impression of all the glories and delights of that worldly success, with its attendant wealth, which he so intensely craved. The sight had fired him to renew his efforts after so grand a reward, but, at the same time, had made him gloomily feel his distance from it, lodging in his mind a stubborn doubt if it could, after all, ever be attained by him. The combined weight of these experiences had intensified his already bitter sense of the world's indifference to his desires and aims, of the world's unconscious cruelty, and of its brutal injustice. He had eagerly embraced the world at his earliest opportunity, had reviled those who opposed themselves to it—and what was the world doing for him, what was it not blindly and carelessly doing against him? He was brought to the point of sheer despair, and was ready to turn upon the world—yet not ready to turn his back upon it. For he had not the slightest conception of any other than sensuous and worldly values, of any other than material gratifications which might bring to him fulness of life. Years ago he had defiantly closed *that* door, without in the least knowing what he was doing, and it was never to be opened to him. He was miserably exasperated by defeat, but the world's appeal was still insistent and compelling, and would be heard and obeyed for many a year, whether or not it became suspect for a siren's call.

In these circumstances the *First Principles* came really as a god-send. The book had the impressive appearance of being the voice of science itself uttering at last the Truth. Yet its weight and authority left undisturbed Mr. Dreiser's worldliness and some of his dear prejudices. It left, indeed, everything as it was with him; but it did appear to rob everything of value, and so, as he thought, left him crushed and hopeless. Actually, however, it offered him a species of consolation for the crushed and hopeless state into which he had already been plunged by his efforts after a "realistic" way of life. A species of consolation;—because, though the dehumanised conception of the world and life presented by naturalism was "cold comfort," still, it did enable one who felt badly used to turn upon the universe and *say*, if not feel, that life was a meaningless and unimportant phenomenon anyhow.

The *Synthetic Philosophy*, Mr. Dreiser tells the world, "eternally verified" his "gravest fears as to the unsolvable disorder and brutality of life." Precisely; as these turns of phrase show, it left his feelings what they had been, likewise his desires and aims, and his sentimental humanitarianism and more. What Spencer gave him was something to fall back upon and *say* in hopeless or disillusioned moments, but something which, leaving him otherwise where he was, even helped to preserve him inviolate from self-criticism or self-discipline. Following the guidance of temperament and mood, he took from Spencer what he wanted, and nothing else; and it so happened that this included little or nothing specifically characteristic of Spencer as against various other naturalistic thinkers. The tone, indeed, of Mr. Dreiser's naturalism, as well as its emphasis upon accident and chaotic disorder, is not only more sophisticated than that of Spencer's, but abruptly contradictory of the Synthetic gentleman's grandiose fancy of one eternal, universal law infallibly working to bring about perfection in all things earthly.

His dark emotional naturalism—and, it may be added, several of the contradictions it has involved him in—bring Mr. Dreiser, as some of his readers have perceived, close to Thomas Hardy, in proportion as he is far from Spencer. He does not mention Hardy in the record of his development which I have been following, but he is said to have confessed to "an enchanted discovery" of that novelist in 1896, and his delight is what was to be expected. As far as one can see, however, his indebtedness to Hardy, though real, is not important.

II

This, in summary form, is the story of Mr. Dreiser's preparation for a novelist's career. His first novel was published in 1900, and his sixth in 1925. Though from an early time he has had warm friends amongst the critics, still, even the most devoted of these have harshly condemned some of his books; and, in general, critical opinion, when not predominantly hostile, has been sharply divided. Nevertheless, in the face of whatever difficulties, Mr. Dreiser has slowly won a leading position in the world of fiction, for reasons which I began by mentioning. And his sixth novel, *An American Tragedy*, was, upon its appearance, widely proclaimed a masterpiece.

Certainly, moreover, *An American Tragedy* is by all odds the best of Mr. Dreiser's novels, though perhaps not the most *interesting*. In it his language is still faulty, as in his earlier books; the quality of his style is mediocre, when not worse; his narrative is badly proportioned;—but, nevertheless, the novel also has excellences which its author had not previously achieved, and which are seldom to be found save in works of a serious and mature artistry. It has a sombre inevitableness, a self-contained adequacy, a restraint, dignity, and detachment which bespeak not merely the experienced craftsman, but also the workman's sure grasp of this theme united with a deeply emotional confidence in its truth and importance. A far higher intelligence is exhibited in its execution than in Mr. Dreiser's play, *The Hand of the Potter* (1918), whose theme is similar in several respects. If one should name a single change indicative of the intelligent masterliness of *An American Tragedy*, perhaps the most significant is the fact that in this book, for the first time, Mr. Dreiser has permitted his characters and events to speak entirely for themselves.

But though *An American Tragedy* marks a really notable advance in technique, and a heightened plausibility thus attained, partly through restraint, still, it exhibits Mr. Dreiser's thought and the essential quality of his realism entirely unchanged. How Mr. Dreiser reached a mechanistic naturalism has above been shown, and how he became conscious of the fact. The appropriate result was that all his novels became tales of human irresponsibility, constructed to illustrate life's contradiction of the hollow conventions of society, and life's obedience to blind laws which make the individual's experience a chaos with an end unrelated to desert. This is the theme of *An American Tragedy*, as of the earlier novels. It is a tale of human irresponsibility, supported by youthful prejudices never relinquished, built up on false antitheses, and capped by a merely circumstantial realism calculated to give the narrative a deceptive air of importance.

Youthful prejudice, for example, transparently dictates the important part played by religion in this novel. Religion is represented as an illusion capable of deceiving only those blind to life's realities—the hopelessly incompetent and unintelligent, those whose advocacy would itself discredit any doctrine. Religion's illusory nature is said to be self-evident, indeed, since it has much to say of Providence, yet manifestly bestows on the convert no worldly rewards, in satisfaction of the real needs and desires with which he is endowed, not by his own design or wish. Convention, too, is represented as a force which sways only the stupid and lethargic, which makes no demands entitling it to respect, and which the intelligent disregard deliberately, the temperamental wilfully. Intelligence itself is pictured as merely an instrument useful for devising methods of self-advancement;—in other words, as the servant of inborn temperament. And temperament is the one irresistible, compelling force in life, to which all else is ultimately obedient. Hence no one is really responsible for anything;—save, perhaps, the novelist who sees this important truth, at length, and by careful selection of appropriate matter is able to picture it for us.

Not even Mr. Dreiser's expert care and long practice, however, are sufficient to enable him to evade a difficulty inherent in the nature of his theme. For the predicament of Roberta Alden is infinitely sad, and her creator narrates her history and murder with an exemplary truthfulness which emphasises that sadness to the full. Nevertheless, the reader's sympathy is not invoked. The girl, on the contrary, is presented as the inevitable resultant of inheritance, environment, and sex, and she lives as an embodied energy rather than as a person. Extraordinary pains are taken, with all the multitudinous details of her story, to balance causes against effects, and she emerges a plausible creature. There is nothing incredible in her being just conventional enough and unwary enough and love-sick enough to suit the story's purpose; but, too, there is nothing in her nature or her history to render either important. Indeed, her grievous distress, leading up to her murder, takes on, under Mr. Dreiser's hand, the same significance as the squirming of an angleworm, impaled by some mischievous boy—no less, but certainly no more.

"Chemic compulsion" draws Roberta Alden as it draws other substances. "Chemic compulsion" epitomises the book. It "just happens"—and this is all—that "chemic compulsion" entangles Roberta with the squid—Clyde Griffiths, the defeated squid. For readers of Mr. Dreiser's "epic" tale, *The Financier*, who recall the apologue of the lobster and the squid cannot fail to recognise Clyde Griffiths as the embodiment of the latter—and his cousin Gilbert as the patient, triumphant lobster. The squid, it need scarcely be said, commands no more sympathy than Roberta;—indeed, most readers inevitably must sympathise with the spirit of the "irate woodsman's" brutal question during the trial. This undefiled son of the forest asked: "Why don't they kill the God-damned bastard and be done with him?" But, just for this reason, it has to be remembered that Mr. Dreiser exhausts every possible means so to account for Clyde as to preserve him from all blame. The squid is the complete plaything of "chemic compulsion," the paragon of irresponsibility, the perfect exemplar of the truth as the truth has been revealed to his creator.

This being so, it is little less than a miracle that Mr. Dreiser has contrived—through the infinite detail of a merely circumstantial realism—to save Clyde Griffiths' humanity sufficiently to maintain the reader's "suspension of disbelief" until the end of the book. Undoubtedly he has done so, though he has not succeeded in making all readers feel that patience has been adequately rewarded. They have been impressed, as is fitting before so monumental a composition; they have been troubled; they have not been recompensed. Eight hundred and forty pages devoted to the unconscionable prolongation of a mere sensational newspaper story! Remarks to this effect I have heard more than once; and they roughly indicate the real difficulty—the inevitably self-destroying effect of such an effort as Mr. Dreiser's, in proportion as it is successful.

This difficulty, however, does not actually lie in the plot of *An American Tragedy*, as the remark just cited implies. The bare plot of the *Agamemnon* of AEschylus might equally well form the basis of a mere sensational newspaper story, and Clytaemnestra in that play and in the *Choephori* makes for herself, not without seeming justice, the plea that is made for Clyde Griffiths. Not she, but Destiny, she says, through her its helpless instrument slew Agamemnon; and she also pleads that she did not make herself, yet can only act out her inborn nature. But it is not for his plots, nor because he was well acquainted with Mr. Dreiser's view of life, that AEschylus lives on still amongst us. His dramas have a perennial and deep value for mankind because, rejecting the plausible notion of "chemic compulsion," he struggled with profound conviction to convey a very different meaning through their form, characters, and action. Without evading any of its difficulty, he asserted his faith that Moral Law uncompromisingly governs the life of man, making for an order which is divine, in the face of a chaos intrinsically evil, and that men are fully, if tragically, responsible for the consequences of their acts, whatever their motives or compulsions, so that ignorance and self-conceit are equally as criminal as violence.

This is not to say all, of course, but it may suffice to show how AEschylus and, more clear-sightedly, Sophocles cut straight through to the centre of the human problem and propounded a solution which, if not the only one, nor by itself a complete one, is still, strictly speaking, irrefutable, being founded directly upon facts of experience which have not changed with the passing generations;—an unassailable solution, moreover, which gives weight and meaning to every individual and to all of his acts. And hence it is that the bloody and sensational fables of AEschylus and Sophocles, triumphantly formed in full harmony with their meaning, have an interest and value for men which time does not exhaust.

Mr. Dreiser's difficulty is not that he has different facts of experience to interpret;—he has precisely the same facts concerning an essentially unchanged human nature. His difficulty is that his mechanistic naturalism compels him so to select and manipulate facts of experience as to deny, through his narrative, that human life has any meaning or value. The attempt is suicidal, and the more consistently it is carried out the more completely is Mr. Dreiser forced to divest his creatures and their actions of any distinctively human quality and meaning. The more successful he is the more insignificant his work becomes. *An American Tragedy*, as I have said, is more skilfully, faithfully, and consistently executed on the naturalistic level than any of its author's earlier novels, and precisely for this reason it contains no single element of tragedy in any legitimate sense of the word, and it impresses thoughtful readers as a mere sensational newspaper story long drawn out. In other words, in proportion as Mr. Dreiser contrives to accomplish his self-imposed task he has nothing to tell us except that there is nothing to tell about life until it can be reduced even below the apparent level of animal existence, to the point where it becomes a meaningless chaos of blind energies.

Whether or not any real sense of the self-destroying character of this effort, to create a literature as valueless and insignificant as possible, will ever strike Mr. Dreiser's consciousness, I should not venture to guess. But only an obstinate self-conceit, or an invincible stupidity, one imagines, could have kept him from seeing the absurdities into which he was forced, in the course of half-a-dozen sentences, when he recently attempted to draw up a brief statement of his present belief. He wrote: "I can make no comment on my work or my life that holds either interest or import for me. Nor can I imagine any explanation or interpretation of any life, my own included, that would be either true—or important, if true. Life is to me too much a welter and play of inscrutable forces to permit, in my case at least, any significant comment. One may paint for one's own entertainment, and that of others—perhaps. As I see him the utterly infinitesimal individual weaves among the mysteries a floss-like and wholly meaningless course—if course it be. In short I catch no meaning from all I have seen, and pass quite as I came, confused and dismayed."[3]

To this point has Mr. Dreiser's naturalism driven him. If the general sense of this awkward yet mannered statement comprised the truth about him and his work, he would, of course, never have been asked to make it. He would, in all probability, have been confined long ago to an asylum; and he would certainly never have written any of his books. Those books, moreover, have manifestly not been written just for his own entertainment. They have been written because he felt he had something to say—because of his certainty that he had come to know the truth, as men in general knew it not. And with singular faithfulness of purpose and of industry, involving what for him must have been almost superhuman effort, because of his defects of mind and training, he has devoted himself to the struggle to express the truth as he conceived it—that is, to reduce it to consistency and give it coherent form. He has also neglected nothing, within his limits, to make it impressive. He has thus lived a rationally purposive life, reducing at least to symptoms of order the welter of his impressions and impulses, controlling at least fitfully his rebellious temperament, and mastering (or "sublimating") at least partially his almost pathological obsession by sex. For the sake of self-expression—or, as I shall presently suggest, of self-justification—he has thus achieved an appreciably disciplined life, and so has in his own person, against his own literary aim, furnished a convincing refutation of his philosophy. He has effectively proved that *An American Tragedy* gives form to a view of life as gratuitous as it is unmeaning.

Fortunately it is now realised by an increasing number of people that naturalistic philosophies are merely speculative ventures, which derive no valid support from "modern science." And it has, besides, been shown above how little "science" had to do with the formation of Mr. Dreiser's naturalistic prejudice. Mr. Dreiser, on his own showing, was first awakened to a sense of life as a problem to be solved by his discovery of the radical contrast between the ethical standards of his father and his church (as he understood its teaching), and his own spontaneous impulses and desires. His haphazard, undirected education gave him an unexcelled opportunity to learn that there were many others like himself, that they seemed to be the most vigorous members of their communities, and that they never hesitated to transgress every ethical standard, when they could get away with it, in their struggle for self-advancement and self-gratification. He treasured every impression which seemed to be on his side against ethical standards by which he stood condemned. His self-esteem had been gravely shocked by the discordance he had discovered, and he now found the means to restore it and, indeed, to strengthen it, by appeal from home and church to the larger world. Not he was in the wrong of it, but the "senseless," "impossible" theories which would have convicted him of shameful tendencies. "In shame there is no comfort, but to be beyond all bounds of shame," says one of Sidney's Arcadians, and this Mr. Dreiser might thenceforth have taken for his motto.

Governed by this apolaustic prejudice, he has since continued his transparent course of seeing only what he has desired to see, or rather of admitting the reality of only what has suited him, while setting down all else as either hypocrisy or delusion. And while it is true that no one escapes the necessity of bringing only a selective attention to bear upon the outer world, it by no means follows that we are all alike cut off from "reality." On the contrary, it does mean that the basis of our selective attention, the interests and purposes served by it, are of fundamental importance. And the disastrous effect of Mr. Dreiser's apolaustic prejudice is that it encouraged him in slavery to mere temperament, in helpless surrender to the chaotic flow of "natural" impulses, while it brought to his attention from the outer world only what fed itself, the antics of complicated beasts with strange illusions. The trouble with what he thus saw is not that it was non-existent, some gross trick of the fevered imagination;—it was there to be seen—it is there, in grievous plenty. No, the trouble is that none of it has positive significance. The naturalism which it fathers lights up the animal in man, but tells man nothing of that which positively distinguishes him from the beast—more, it vindictively denies that anything save hypocrisy and delusion does so distinguish him. And while it seeks to dissolve our humanity, it ends, as it ends in Mr. Dreiser, in a bottomless morass of misrepresentation and despair. This is the American tragedy of our confused age which constitutes the real import of Mr. Dreiser's masterpiece.

Notes

1. In that which follows I draw chiefly upon *A Book About Myself* (1922), but also make use of *A Hoosier Holiday* (1916), *Twelve Men* (1919), and *Hey Rub-a-Dub-Dub* (1920). *A Traveler at Forty* (1913) is also a revealing book.

2. I refer particularly to *Jennie Gerhardt* and *The "Genius."* Limitations of space unfortunately prevent me from considering here any save Mr. Dreiser's latest novel, *An American Tragedy*.

3. From the *Bookman*, 68 (Sept., 1928), 25.

Homage to Theodore Dreiser on the Centenary of His Birth

Robert Penn Warren*

* * * * * * *

An American Tragedy had a long history. As early as 1892 or 1893 Dreiser began collecting clippings on murder cases, always cases in which a girl was killed by her lover, and always because of ambition. As late as 1919 Dreiser had several chapters of a novel based on the case of a Baptist minister who seduced a girl and then, out of ambition, poisoned her when she became pregnant. Finally, out of this slow, mulling process, Dreiser found the focus for his murder story, and the particular story elected was one that had been collected years earlier, in 1906: the murder of the pregnant Grace ("Billie") Brown by young Chester Gillette, the son of a fanatically devout couple who had run a mission.

Born in the West, Chester had wound up, after two years at Oberlin College and much wandering, in Cortland, in upper New York, where he got a job in a shirt factory owned by an uncle, and promptly seduced one of the girls employed there. Meanwhile, he had penetrated the world of "society" in Cortland. At this juncture, Billie announced her pregnancy, and as her seducer withdrew more and more into his elegant life, she wrote him the letters that were to bring jurors to tears. Chester persuaded her to go on a trip with him, presumably to be married. At Big Moose Lake, he took her out in a rowboat. After he had hit her on the head with a tennis racket, she fell into the water and drowned. He left a straw hat (an extra provided for the occasion) to float on the water and announce his death, and fled the scene. He was captured, and in March, 1908, was executed.

The objective story of Chester is very close to that of Clyde, and Dreiser, rather than trying to disguise similarities, often insisted on them. He kept, for example, the initials of Chester Gillette for Clyde Griffiths, and the "B" of the nickname of Grace Brown for Bert, the nickname of Roberta Alden. For Clyde he kept the pseudonym of Carl Graham, which

*Reprinted from the *Southern Review*, 7 (Spring, 1971), pp. 383–410. Reprinted by permission of Robert Penn Warren. An earlier, and briefer, version of Warren's comments on *An American Tragedy* appeared in the *Yale Review*, 52 (Oct., 1962), 1–15.

Chester had used on the death trip with Billie. Big Moose Lake, where Billie died, becomes Big Bittern Lake. The tennis racket of Chester (an improbable object for a jaunt in a rowboat) is transformed into a camera, but both items are accoutrements of a vacation. The poor but respectable family of Roberta is like the Brown family. With only a little editing, the letters from Billie, which unstrung the jurors in the Herkimer County courthouse, become the letters of Roberta which unstring the jurors in the Cataraqui County courthouse.

Furthermore, in 1923 Dreiser made a tour of the region where Chester had acted out his sleazy story. He saw the pushing little cities, the rutted roads and isolated farms, the very lake where, years back, Billie Brown had died, the dark woods into which Chester had fled, the Herkimer County courthouse, where Chester had been convicted. Dreiser heard the cry of the weir-weir bird that Chester must have heard and that Clyde was to hear. Dreiser's imagination fed on fact: this was where *it* had happened, and this was where *it* would now happen. Fact is doom, the ultimate, irreversible doom, and he was writing a story of doom.

But Dreiser clung to the locale for another reason, too. The factual scene becomes the laboratory in which the experiment of Clyde Griffiths' life can be performed in its purity. Lycurgus is a little node on a fringe filament of the great industrial society; the remoteness, the very smallness of scale, the triviality of the stakes being played for against the terrible cost of failure (or success), the contrast of the whole human project set against the lurking darkness of the primal woods and waters—all these factors give the action a kind of paradigmatic precision of outline and archetypal clarity of meaning. There is nothing to distract us from the logic of doom and the irony of the doom. The factual scene becomes, in Dreiser's imagination, the action: in its factuality it becomes, as the city had become in *Sister Carrie*, the image of doom, fulfilled and complete in the moment when Clyde, after the deed, disappears into the shadow of trees. The nightmare self needed the mystic mirror of the world of fact in order to have its story clear. Rather, Dreiser needed to understand the nature of the nightmare self by brooding on a factual story which seemed to be a mirror, in order to elicit from his personal darkness of torturing potentiality the story lurking there.

The nightmare self had long needed to find its story, for we know how far back goes the file of clippings. But so much had to be understood before Dreiser could make the final effort of self-understanding that would be *An American Tragedy*. There had to be the antithesis between the world of Carrie and that of Jennie. There had to be the long exploration of the autobiographies. There had to be the self-glorification in *The Genius* and the Trilogy. There had to be, perhaps, Dr. Brill and his gospel of the meaning of the past in the living self. But Dreiser finally came into the time when he could recognize what the story of Chester Gillette really meant.

In an extremely interesting biographical-critical study called *The Two Dreisers*, Ellen Moers quotes Freud to the effect that a writer's subject is determined when "a strong experience in the present" awakens "a memory of an earlier experience . . . from which there now proceeds a wish which finds its fulfillment in the creative work." Applying this formula, Moers suggests that the "earlier experience" for Dreiser would have been his desire to get rid of his first wife Jug, and that the "strong experience in the present" would have been his falling in love with Helen Patges Richardson. But the first bloom of passion with Helen had scarcely passed before she, like Jug years back, began to pester him to marry her. Though Dreiser had long since got rid of Jug along with her nagging presence and her insatiable and burdensome sexuality, he had been lucky enough, or clever enough, to do so, not by a divorce but by a legal separation, thus converting the old liability into a new asset: a protection against future matrimony. *Plus ça change.* . . . If Helen was to get her way in the end, that end was a long time coming—only, in fact, a little more than a year before Dreiser's death, when Jug's death had removed, willy-nilly, the happy legal impediment and age had reduced Dreiser's powers of resistance.

Meanwhile, just back from California, at work on *An American Tragedy*, and in good health, Dreiser had moved out on Helen, now seeing her only as it suited his pleasure, in a sort of stop-gap or backstop way. He did, however, take the devoted but demanding lady on the tour of upper New York. In his passion for factuality, he even took Helen for a row on Big Moose Lake. During the little outing, she reflected: "Maybe Teddy will become completely hypnotized by this idea and even repeat it, here and now." Dreiser was not, in fact, trying to put himself imaginatively in the place of Chester or Clyde. He was not, in the end, trying to tell their story. He was trying to tell his own.

It was his own story that he had begun long ago in his first version of the murder story called *The Rake*. But between *The Rake* and the final version in *An American Tragedy*, he told it in *Dawn*—there the murder story without the murder. This is the story of his own growing up, the deprived one, the yearner, the quester. At the very end of *Dawn*, when the young Dreiser has entered into the temptations of the world, has committed fornication and has dared to enter the glitter of a real restaurant, we find, as a summary of his life thus far, the following self-portrait:

> I have to smile. Poor, cocky, hungry, without the faintest · notion of the deeps of luxury, expenditure, control, taste, here I was, assuming that I was reasonably near if not well within the gates! And at the same time, nervous as to the impending ills of a rake!

It is a strange phrase: "the impending ills of a rake." In the first place, the word *rake* does not occur (unless I have missed it) elsewhere in the autobiographies. We know that Dreiser did know the cautionary tales of harlot and rake and idle apprentice illustrated in Hogarth's work (even if, in the autobiography, he transfers Hogarth from his eighteenth century back to the reign of Charles II), and it is possible that he made some connection between Hogarth's grim warnings and his own account of the doom of a rake; and almost certainly the mature author of *Dawn*, looking back with pity and condescension on the poor, cocky, hungry boy, identified him, by the word *rake*, with the hero of the murder story he had long ago begun—and of all the murder stories he had collected and was to collect.

But what were the "impending ills of a rake"? In *Dawn*, this passage introduced the tale of the embezzlement of $25.00 to buy the fashionable overcoat necessary for a rake, and the loss of a good job. But the loss of a job or even a jail sentence is, we know, only the beginning of the ills of a rake: at the end we see the gallows or the chair. All the stories of the rake are murder stories, and the victim is always the trusting maid who loves not wisely but too well; and the common theme is the murder of love for gain and ambition. And that is the theme of the personal story of the young Dreiser up through *A Book About Myself*, which follows *Dawn* and which ends with the marriage to Jug—"after the first flare of love had thinned down to the pale flame of duty."

The tale had begun, however, even before Dreiser ever laid eyes on Jug. First, there is the boy "flaming with sex," ferociously masturbating, tortured by fear of "imaginary sex weakness." Next, there is the episode of the nameless little "reckless and adventure-looking Italian girl of not more than sixteen or seventeen," who in "an idle or adventuring mood," comes into the real estate office where the boy is alone for the afternoon, and lures and badgers him into the back room. Then comes the time when, heartened by the fact that the little Italian girl had seized him "convulsively and even affectionately" before lying back in a "smiling calm," he embarks on his own sexual adventures and establishes the pattern of his subsequent life—over which, we may surmise, the archetypal figure of the girl who, as though summoned by a dream, comes out of nowhere to give herself, and after the spasm, affectionate embrace, and smiling calm, disappears into nowhere, nameless and undemanding.

In this third phase, at the same time that the boy Dreiser, presumably freed from the fears of impotence, is seeking sex, he has the "giddy dreams" of the world of wealth, elegance, social position, and ostentation, visions of himself "in golden chambers," giving himself "over to what luxuries and delights." He longed to "succeed financially by marriage with some beautiful and wealthy girl," but he never met the dream girl who was both "rich" and "sensual."

What he met was little Nellie MacPherson, behind the cashier's desk in the laundry where he worked. She was pretty, gay, good-natured, quick at repartee, and sweet, but she was "embedded in a conservative and wholly religious family—Scotch Presbyterian"—as he was to find Jug embedded in her Missouri Methodism. In any case, Nellie was not the girl Dreiser would have chosen from the "veritable garden of femininity" that the laundry room was. She was merely what he, in his uncertainty, had to make do with. The best he could do was to act out the charade, and go regularly to her house where he basked in the respect and admiration of her family, where he secretly preferred the younger sister, where he spent endless hours cuddling Nellie and talking of their married bliss to come and systematically trying to seduce her. Though she was not "lustful" like the nameless little Italian girl, she was "passionate enough within her conventional tether," and now and then he almost "over-ran her good judgment." He had no intention of marrying her. His vainglorious ambitions lay elsewhere, even in the realm of intellectual achievement, and in *Dawn*, like Cowperwood looking back with pity on the "passionate illusion" of Aileen's girlhood love for him, Dreiser could write:

> I think I must have been her first serious affair. The pity of it was that she had no understanding of the type of youth she was dealing with, any more than I had of myself, and soon believed in the gushing phrases I lavished upon her.

It was all a charade. But even at the time when Dreiser was lavishing the "gushing phrases" on Nellie, he was trying them out on Alice, and we have the beginning of the pattern of the double (or multiple) romance which was to continue for Dreiser's life, and which is the central fact of the story of Clyde.

With Alice, who begins *A Book About Myself*, Dreiser repeated all the protracted deceptions and self-deceptions of planning for marriage, the reveling in imaginary bliss to come, the various gambits of seduction he had become acquainted with. He had been resentful of Nellie because, in spite of the "white tenseness" of her face and her "almost savage embraces," she would not surrender to him, but with Alice there was, in the end, another kind of resentment. Once Alice, "in her own home threw some pillows on the floor," and lay down and begged him to "love" her. Later Dreiser could write of the event: "I fancy she thought that if she yielded to me physically and found herself with child my sympathy would cause me to marry her." But she had mistaken her man, as Roberta was to mistake hers. In fact, there was no way for a Nellie or an Alice to win, neither by fending off this lover nor by surrending to him.

When at last Dreiser left Alice, whom he had cunningly not deflowered (cunningly, if his avowed motive is to be accepted), he went to St. Louis to a better newspaper job, and the letter she wrote him there had all the pathos of those of Billie Brown, or Roberta Alden. Dreiser, suffering loneliness, remorse, and self-pity, wrote her that he loved her and that her letter had torn his heart. But in looking back on that moment, he says, in *A Book About Myself*, of his letter: "But I could not write it as effectually as I might have, for I was haunted by the idea that I should never keep my word. Something kept telling me that it was not wise, that I didn't really want to."

The "something" was always there, pronouncing his doom. He yeared for love, but only, as he put it, "after I had the prosperity and fame that somehow I falsely fancied commanded love." If he was "blazing with sex," he was also blazing with the "desire for material and social supremacy—to have wealth, to be in society." That "something" was the voice of the anguishingly uncertain ego that had to have "prosperity and fame" before it could feel itself even to exist—or if existing, to be worthy of love. And the voice was so cold and commanding that it seemed the very voice of destiny. It was the voice that Clyde finally heard, as we shall see, the voice of the Efrit, the genie of *An American Tragedy*. The voice, for Dreiser as for Clyde, seemed detached from the self, and thus to exculpate the self:

> I saw myself a stormy petrel hanging over the yellowish-black waves of life and never really resting anywhere. I could not; my mind would not let me. I saw too much, felt too much, knew too much. What was I, what anyone, but a small bit of seaweed on an endless sea, flotsam, being moved hither and thither—by what subterranean tides?

By what subterranean tides? That is the question underlying *An American Tragedy*.

By the same token that Dreiser can exculpate the self as a victim of the subterranean tides, he can pity the self; and in the next stage, he can pity and bless Alice ("She wanted to unite with me for this little span of existence, to go with me hand and hand into the ultimate nothingness")—or Nellie, or Roberta, who had not understood the grip of the subterranean tides on Theodore Dreiser or on Clyde Griffiths.

There is, however, a third and most important stage in the natural history of pity. In *A Book About Myself*, at the end of the paragraph from which we have quoted the sentence on "prosperity and fame," Dreiser says: ". . . at the same time I was horribly depressed by the thought that I should never have them [prosperity, fame, love], never; and that thought, for the most part has been fulfilled." But after this self-pity, in the next paragraph, in the very next sentence we find:

> In addition to this, I was filled with an intense sympathy for the woes of others, life in all its helpless degradation and poverty, the unsatisfied dreams of people, their sweaty labors, the things they were compelled to endure—nameless impositions, curses, brutalities,—the things they would never have, their hungers, half-formed dreams of pleasure, their gibbering insanities and beaten resignations at the end.

This paragraph continues with a Whitmanesque catalogue of human sufferings and Dreiser's confession of the literal tears which we must believe he shed. But then the next two paragraphs return to the young man's preoccupation with his own defects and limitations, his obsessive fear of failure, his yearning looks into the house of "some kindly family" or through the "windows of some successful business firm" and his "aches and pains that went with all this, the amazing depression, all but suicidal."

The whole passage has its own deep intrinsic interest, but it has another interest as the background for the analysis of Clyde's stages of pity when he finds his sister in the lonely room, pregnant and abandoned. What I have been trying to demonstrate is that in *Dawn* and in the first twenty-two chapters of *A Book About Myself*, not only the basic personality and life pattern of Dreiser himself has been presented and analyzed, but that the basic characters, situations, and issues of *An American Tragedy* have been projected. All is ready. Life is there, ready for the understanding that will make art possible and the art that will make understanding possible. And at the end of this period Dreiser had even begun to write poems and had become friends with a newspaperman who had written a "Zolaesque" novel.

But there was to be an essential, intermediate stage in the process. Up to this moment, the elements that were to reappear in Dreiser's great masterpiece, and indeed, in his fiction in general, had been floating, not brought to focus in experience. The entrance of Sara White—poor Jug, who could not understand the subterranean tides—was to do this. In *The Two Dreisers*, Moers is right to insist on Jug's importance in the background of *An American Tragedy*. Her presence dominates the second half of *A Book About Myself*, and her story brings to focus all that had been diffused in Dreiser's experience. And the key episode occurs when a newspaperman, seeing the photograph of the twenty-two-year-old Dreiser's fiancée, declares that if he marries such a "conventional and narrow woman," and one older to boot, he'll be gone. He gives further advice: "Run with the girls if you want, but don't marry." Looking back on this moment, Dreiser wrote:

> She would never give herself to me without marriage, and here I was, lonely and financially unable to take her, and spiritually unable to justify my marriage to her even if I were. The tangle of life, its unfairness and indifference to the moods and longings of any individual, swept over me once more, weighing me down far beyond the power of expression.

Life's "unfairness and indifference to the moods and longings of any individual": the generalization of pity in the phrase "of any individual" is a mask for the self-pity. The whole phrase should be revised to read: Life's unfairness and indifference to the moods and longings of Theodore Dreiser—or Clyde Griffiths. Then we should find the premise: The moods and longings of Theodore Dreiser (or Clyde Griffiths) are the measure of justice. And from this premise flows the inexorable conclusion: Those who would contravene these sacred moods and longings shall have justice visited upon them.

Poor Jug. Poor Roberta.

An American Tragedy is the work in which Dreiser could look backward from the distance of middle age and evaluate his own experience of success and failure. We feel the burden of the personal pathos, the echo of the personal struggle to purge unworthy aspirations, to discover his own sincerity. We also feel, in this book, the burden of a historical moment, the moment of the Great Boom which climaxed the period from Grant to Coolidge, the half century in which the new America of industry and finance capitalism was hardening into shape and its secret forces were emerging to dominate all life. In other words, *An American Tragedy* can be taken as a document, both personal and historical, and it is often admired, and defended, in these terms.

As a document, it is indeed powerful, but such documentary power is derivative: The power of *An American Tragedy* is not derivative. The weight of Dreiser's experience and of the historical moment are here, but they are here as materials; in the strange metabolism of creation, they are absorbed and transmuted into fictional idea, fictional analogy, fictional illusion. The book is "created," and therefore generates its own power, multiplying the power implicit in the materials.

The thing in *An American Tragedy* most obviously created is Clyde Griffiths himself. The fact that Dreiser, in his characteristic way, chose a model for Clyde does not make Clyde less of a creation. Rather, it emphasizes that he is a creation; and the contrast between the dreary factuality of an old newspaper account and the anguishing inwardness of the personal story may well have served as a mirror for the contrast that always touched Dreiser's feelings and fired his imagination—the contrast between the grinding impersonality of the machine of the world and the pathos of the personal experience. In fact, the novel begins and ends with an image of this contrast: the family of street preachers, in the beginning with the boy Clyde and in the end with the illegitimate son of Clyde's sister Esta, stand lost between the "tall walls of the commercial heart of an American city;; and lift up their hymn "against the vast skepticism and apathy of life." The image of the boy Clyde looking up at the "tall walls" of the world is the key image of the novel. And of Dreiser's life.

The creation of the character of Clyde is begun by a scrupulous accretion of detail, small indications, and trivial events. We are early caught in the dawning logic of these details. We see the sidewise glances of yearning. We see how, when he discovers his sister Esta in the secret room, pregnant and abandoned, his first reaction is selfish; how only when she refers to "poor Mamma" does his own sympathy stir; how this sympathy is converted suddenly into a sense of world-pathos, and then, in the end, turns back into self-pity. We see him staring at the rich house of his uncle, and again when for the first time he lays eyes on Sondra, with "a curiously stinging sense of what it was to want and not to have." We see his real sadness at Roberta's jealousy, which he, also one of the deprived, can feel himself into, but we know that his pity for her is, at root, self-pity. We see him open the *Times-Union* to see the headline: *Accidental Double Tragedy at Pass Lake*. We see all this, and so much more, and remember his mother's letter to him after his flight from Kansas City: ". . . for well I know how the devil tempts and pursues all of us mortals, and particularly just such a child as you." And what a stroke it is to fuse the reader's foreboding interest with the anxiety of the mother!

For Dreiser's method of presenting the character is far deeper and more subtle than that of mere accretion. The method is an enlargement and a clarifying, slow and merciless, of a dimly envisaged possibility. We gradually see the inward truth of the mother's clairvoyant phrase, "such a child as you"; and the story of Clyde is the documentation of this.

A thousand strands run backward and forward in this documentation, converting what is a process in time into a logic outside of time. When back in Kansas City, we see Clyde's sexual fear and masochism in relation to the cold, cunning Hortense, we are laying the basis for our understanding of what will come later, the repetition with Sondra of the old relationship and the avenging of it on the defenseless Roberta. When in the room of women where he is foreman, Clyde looks wistfully out the window on the summer river, we are being prepared for the moment when he first encounters Roberta at the pleasure lake, and for the grimmer moment to come on Big Bittern Lake. When, on the night after the first meeting with Sondra, Clyde does not go to Roberta, we know that this is a shadowy rehearsal for the last betrayal and murder.

It is not only that we find, in an analytic sense, the logic of character displayed; in such instances we find this logic transliterated into a thousand intermingling images, and in this transliteration the logic itself becoming the poetry of destiny. We see the process moving toward climax when, on the train, on the death ride with Roberta, Clyde flees from his own inner turmoil into the objective observations which, in their irrelevancy, are the mark of destiny: *Those nine black and white cows on that green hillside*, or *Those three automobiles out there running almost as fast as the train*. And we find the climax of the process in the "weird, contemptuous, mocking, lonely" call of the weir-weir bird which offers a commentary on the execution, as it had on the birth, of the murderous impulse.

This transliteration of logic into a poetry of destiny is what accounts for our peculiar involvement in the story of Clyde. What man, short of saint or sage, does not understand, in some secret way however different from Clyde's way, the story of Clyde and does not find it something deeper than a mere comment on the values of American culture? Furthermore, the mere fact that our suspense is not about the *what* but about the *how* and the *when* emphasizes our involvement. No, to be more specific, our *entrapment*. We are living out a destiny, painfully waiting for a doom. We live into Clyde's doom, and in the process, live in our own secret sense of doom which is the backdrop of our favorite dramas of the will.

How deep is our involvement—or entrapment—is indicated by the sudden sense of lassitude, even relief, once the murder is committed; all is now fulfilled, and in that fact the drawstring is cut. With the act thus consummated, we may even detach ourselves, at least for the moment, from the youth now "making his way through a dark, uninhabited woods, a dry straw hat upon his head, a bag in his hand. . . ."

As a commentary on Dreiser's art, we can note how, after this sentence that closes Book II, Dreiser jerks his camera from that lonely figure and begins Book III by withdrawing into magisterial distance for a panoramic sweep of the lens: "Cataraqui County extending from the northernmost line of the village known as Three Mile Bay on the south to the Canadian border, on the north a distance of fifty miles. Its greater portion covered by uninhabited forests and. . . ." The whole effect is that of detachment; and with this we are restored, after a long painful while, to the role of observer, interested and critical, but not now involved.

But we shall not be long permitted to keep this comfortable role. Soon the camera will come close to the cell where Clyde waits, the focus will be sharpened. And in this constant alternation of focus, and shift from involvement to detachment, we find one of the deep art-principles of the work, one of the principles of its compelling rhythm. It is compelling because the shift of focus is never arbitrary; it grows out of the expressive needs of the narrative as Dreiser has conceived it, and out of the prior fact that the narrative is conceived as a drama between the individual and the universe.

Randolph Bourne once said that Dreiser had the "artist's vision without the sureness of the artist's technique." I have used the phrase "Dreiser's art" in full awareness that most critics, even critics as dangerous to disagree with as Lionel Trilling, will find it absurd; and in full awareness that even those who admire Dreiser will, with few exceptions, concede a point on "art," or apologetically explain that Dreiser's ineptitudes somehow have the value of stylistic decorum and can be taken as a manifestation of his groping honesty, and will then push on to stake their case on his "power" and "compassion."

But ultimately how do we know the "power" or the "compassion"— know them differently, that is, from the power or compassion we may read into a news story—except by Dreiser's control? Except, in other words, by his grasp of the human materials and his rhythmic organization of them, the vibrance which is the life of fictional illusion, that mutual interpenetration in meaning of part and whole which gives us the sense of preternatural fulfillment? Except, in short, by art?

There is a tendency to freeze the question of Dreiser as an artist at the question of prose style. As for prose style, Dreiser is a split writer. There is the "literary" writer whose style is often abominable. But there is another writer, too, a writer who can write a scene with fidelity if not always with felicity. But sometimes there is the felicity, a felicity of dramatic baldness: the letters of Mrs. Griffiths or Roberta; the scene of Roberta back home, in her mother's house, looking out at the ruined fields; the scene when Clyde first sees Sondra, with that "curiously stinging sense of what it is to want and not to have."

Words are what we have on the page of a novel, and words are not only a threshold, a set of signs, but a fundamental aspect of meaning, absorbed into everything else. Words, however, are not the only language of fiction. There is the language of the unfolding scenes, what Dreiser, in the course of composing the novel, called the "procession and selection of events," the language of the imagery of enactment, with all its primitive massiveness—the movie in our heads, with all the entailed questions of psychological veracity and subtlety, of symbolic densities and rhythmic complexities. I am trying here to indicate something of the weight of this language, or better, languages, as an aspect of Dreiser's art.

With this intention we can return to the question of the rhythm between detachment and involvement which manifests itself in shifts of pace and scale. But we may find the basis for another rhythm in the fact that the personal story of Clyde is set in a whole series of shifting perspectives. By perspective I do not mean a point of view in the ordinary technical sense. I mean what may be called an angle of interest. For instance, the picture of the organization of the collar factory in Lycurgus gives a perspective on life, and on the fate of Clyde; this is another contrast between a mechanism and man, a symbolic rendering of the ground idea of the novel.

But there are many perspectives. There is the perspective of the religious belief of the family, which returns in the end to frame the whole story; that of the world of the bellhop's bench in the hotel; that of sex and "chemism"; that of the stamping room in the factory with its mixture of sex, social differences, power, and money; that of the economic order of Lycurgus which stands as a mirror for the world outside; that of the jealousies and intrigues of the young social set of the town, jealousies and intrigues which, ironically enough, make it possible for Clyde to enter that charmed circle; that of justice and law in relation to the political structure of Cataraqui County; that of the death house.

Sometimes a perspective comes as an idea boldly stated, sometimes as implicit in a situation or person. In fact, all the persons of the novel, even the most incidental, are carriers of ideas and represent significant perspectives in which the story may be viewed. In the enormous cast there are no walk-ons; each actor has a role in the structure of the unfolding dialectic. And it is the pervasive sense of this participation, however un-formulated, that gives the novel its density, the weight of destiny.

If, as a matter of fact, the dialectic were insisted upon as mere dialectic we should not find this weight; and thi ⋮ the great difference in method from the Trilogy. We find the force here as the dialectic unfolds in personality, in the presentation of personality not as a carrier of idea but as a thing of inner vibrance. The mother, for instance, is a small masterpiece of characterization. She is the carrier of "religion," but with her own inner contradictions, she exists in her full and suffering reality, a reality which, at the end when she comes to join Clyde, affirms itself by her effect on everyone around. Roberta is fully rendered, not only in her place in the social and economic order and in her role as victim, but with the complexity of her humanity. When her friend Grace catches her in a lie about Clyde, she stiffens with "resentment" and this conversion of her self-anger into the relief of anger at her friend is a telling index, given in a flash, of the depth and anguish of her scarcely formulated inner struggle. She does not quite tell the truth to her mother about why she moves out of her first room. In the midst of her as yet submerged moral struggle she deceives even herself as to why she selects a room downstairs and with an outside door in the new house. She is a sufferer, but she is not beyond the flash of jealous anger when Clyde, with unconscious brutality, remarks that Sondra dresses well: "If I had as much money as that, I could too." And the scene in which Clyde tries to persuade her to let him come to her room is of extraordinary depth, coming to climax when he turns sullenly away, and she, overwhelmed by her fear and pain at her own rebelliousness, feels the "first, flashing, blinding, bleeding stab of love."

Even minor characters have more than their relation to the dialectic. The prosecuting attorney and the defending lawyers have their own depth, and their roles are defined by their personal histories. A character like Hortense may be merely sketched in, but she takes on a new significance when we see her, like Rita, as an earlier image of Sondra, who is—and let us dwell on the adjectives—"as smart and vain and sweet a girl as Clyde had ever laid eyes on." And if at first Sondra herself seems scarcely more than another example of the particular type of *femme fatale* destined to work Clyde's ruin, let us remember how Clyde, in his cell, receives the letter beginning; "Clyde—This is so that you will not think someone once dear to you has utterly forgotten you. . . . ." The letter, typewritten, is unsigned, but with it, in all the mixture of human feeling and falsity, Sondra, retroactively as it were, leaps to life.

As every person enters the story with a role in the dialectic, so every person enters with a human need which seeks fulfillment in the story. The delineation of this need—for instance, the portrait of the socially ambitious clerk in Lycurgus or the history of the prosecuting attorney Mason—serves to distract our interest from Clyde's personal story, to provide another kind of distancing of the main line of narrative. At the same time, in the extraordinary coherence of the novel, we finally see that such apparent digressions are really mirrors held up to Clyde's story, in fact to Clyde himself: in this world of mirrors complicity is the common doom. So here we have another version, in distraction of interest and realization of complicity, of the rhythm of approach and withdrawal.

There is, indeed, another sense in which the delineation of each new need compensates, in the end, for the distraction it has provoked. Each new need introduced into the novel serves as a "booster" to the thrust of narrative, each providing a new energy that, though at first a distraction, is absorbed into the central drive; and in the rhythm of these thrusts, we find another principle of the organization of the whole. Or to change our image, in the braiding together of these needs with the need of Clyde, we find a rhythm of pause and acceleration, the pulse of creative life. To put the matter in another way, the delineation of each new perspective, each new person, each new need acts as a new analysis of the dynamism of the story, for instance, the psychological makeup of the prosecutor, his frustrations and yearnings, are a part of the explanation of the course of justice. The delineation of each new perspective, each new person, each new need, reveals a new factor of motive; there is a progressive "unmasking" of the secret springs of the action, related in the end to the "unmasking" of life as a mechanism cursed with consciousness; and something of our own resistance to unmasking enters into the whole response to the story. This resistance, set against our natural commitment to the narrative, creates another sort of frustrating tension, and another sort of rhythm of withdrawal and approach. Furthermore, over against the unmasking of the mechanism of life is set the feel of life itself being lived in the urgency of its illusions; and the play between the elements of this contrast gives us another principle of rhythm, another principle by which the form unfolds.

We have spoken of the moment of withdrawal at the beginning of Book III, after we have left Clyde walking away from the scene of Roberta's death, into the forest. Our commitment to the movement of narrative leading to the death of Roberta has been so complete that now, with its accomplishment, the crime seems, for the moment at least, to split off from the subsequent story of consequences; and Dreiser, by the moment of withdrawal into distance, emphasizes the split. The split, coming about two-thirds of the way through the novel, has been felt, by some readers, as a grave flaw in the structure. The split is indeed real—a real break in emotional continuity. But we must ask ourselves whether or not this split serves, as the similar "split" in Conrad's *Lord Jim* or Shakespeare's *Julius Caesar*, to emphasize a deeper thematic continuity.

The story is one of crime and punishment. In the first two Books we see the forces that converge toward the death of Roberta, and in Book III we see the forces that are triggered into action by her death; that is, we see the relation of the individual personality, and individual fate, to such forces as a continuing theme. What, in other words, is the nature of responsibility in this world of shadowy complicities, where all things seem to conspire in evil? The shadowiness of the outer world is matched by the shadowiness of the inner world; at the very last moment in the boat Clyde does not "will" to strike Roberta—even her death is an accident. Then after the "accident," this shadowiness of the inner world emerges again with that of the outer. For instance, Jephson, one of the lawyers defending Clyde, creates a version of the accident; and then Clyde is persuaded, without much resistance, to testify to a "lie" in order to establish, as Jephson put it, the "truth."

This scene of the "persuasion" of Clyde is balanced by a later scene in which, after Clyde's conviction, the young preacher McMillan strips Clyde of all his alibis and equivocations, and prepares him for repentance and salvation. But just before the execution, even as Clyde assures his mother that God has heard his prayers, he is asking himself: "Had he?" And Clyde goes to his death not knowing what he really knows or feels, or what he has done. The theme of ambiguity, as of complicity, in varying manifestations, runs throughout. Clyde lives in the ambiguous mists of a dream and the most important thing shrouded from his sight is his own identity.

At the end, on death row, there is a little episode that returns us to the notion of dream and identity in the novel. One of the condemned waiting death is a man named Nicholson, a lawyer who has poisoned a client to gain control of his estate. Nicholson is clearly a man of breeding and education, and in spite of his criminality, has courage, humor, kindliness, and dignity. In short, he has a self that can survive his own criminality and its consequences. His role in the story is a thematic one. He is set in contrast to Clyde—who has no "self"—and undertakes to instruct him in the rudimentary dignity of having an identity. When he is to be executed, he sends two books to Clyde, *Robinson Crusoe* and the *Arabian Nights*.

Here we find repeated the little device with which Dreiser indicates his meaning when he gives us the last glimpse of Carrie, sitting in her rocking chair with a copy of *Père Goriot* on her lap, the study of another "little soldier of fortune." As the novel of Balzac, whose fiction long ago had made Dreiser aware of his own role as the "ambitious beginner," so the gifts of Nicholson summarize the theme of *An American Tragedy*. The two books provide the poles of Clyde's story.

The significance of *Robinson Crusoe* is clear. It gives the image of a man who is totally self-reliant, who, alone and out of nothing, can create a life for himself, a world. Even in shipwreck—in disaster—he asserts and fulfills the self (as, we may say, Nicholson does).

As for the *Arabian Nights*, Dreiser does not have to trust the reader for a last-minute interpretation. At the trial, while Jephson, one of the

defending lawyers, is leading Clyde in his testimony, we find the following passage:

> "I see! I see!" went on Jephson, oratorically and loudly, hav-
> ing the jury and audience in mind. "A case of the *Arabian
> Nights*, of the enscorcelled and the enscorcellor."
> "I don't think I know what you mean," said Clyde.
> "A case of being bewitched, my poor boy—by beauty, love,
> wealth, by things that we sometimes think we want very, very
> much, and cannot ever have—that is what I mean, and that is
> what much of the love in the world amounts to."

In this passage Jephson summarizes the whole story of Clyde, but the
terms of the summary have long since been established in the novel. At the
very beginning of his worldly career, in his "imaginary flights," the hotel
where he was a bellhop seemed a magic world, "Aladdinish, really": "It
meant that you did what you pleased." And this Aladdinish world, where
dream is law, appears again at the very crucial moment of the novel when
he contemplates the death of Roberta:

> Indeed the center or mentating section of his brain at this
> time might well have been compared to a sealed and silent hall
> in which alone and undisturbed, and that in spite of himself,
> he now sat thinking on the mystic or evil and terrifying desires
> or advice of some darker or primordial and unregenerate
> nature of his own, and without the power to drive the same
> forth or himself to decamp, and yet also without the courage to
> act upon anything.
> For now the genii of his darkest and weakest side was speak-
> ing. And it said: "And would you escape from the demands of
> Roberta that but now and unto this hour have appeared
> unescapable to you? Behold! I bring you a way. It is the way of
> the lake—Pass Lake. This item that you have read—do you
> think it was placed in your hands for nothing?"

Notice that the genie's argument involves the notion that all is "done
for" Clyde: the newspaper with the story of the death on Pass Lake, has
not been "placed" in his hands "for nothing." For this is the world where
dream is law, where every wish is fulfilled effortlessly and innocently.
The first Aladdinish dream, back in the Green-Davidson in Kansas City,
had merely been to be like the guests of the hotel: "That you possessed all
of these luxuries. That you went how, where and when you pleased."
Now the dream is different and dire. But the "Efrit" is ready still to show
how it may be gratified, effortlessly and innocently.

The fact that Dreiser divides the novel into only three Books falsifies
the intrinsic structure and blurs the fundamental theme. There are really
four basic movements of the narrative, and there should be four Books:
the story up to the flight from Kansas City, that of the preparation; the

story of the temptation leading to the death of Roberta; the story of the conviction, that of the ambiguities of justice; and the story of the search, as death draws near, for salvation and certainty as contrasted with ambiguity. In other words, the present Book III should be divided; and then in the latter half, related to other themes, especially to that of Aladdin, but more deeply grounded, the theme of identity would be specific and dominant.

Throughout the whole novel this theme has, in fact, been emerging. If, in the world of complicities and ambiguities, it is hard to understand responsibility, then how, ultimately, can one understand the self? If one's dream is to "have things done for you," if one is passive, how can there be a self? In fact, in this world of shadows Clyde has always sought to flee from the self. In all his self-absorption and selfishness, he has sought to repudiate the deepest meaning of self. He had longed to enter the "tall walls" of the world and find there a dream-self, a self-to-be-created, a role to play in the rich and thrilling world—a *role*, we may say, to take the place of a *self*. The very end of Book I, which has described Clyde's first attempt to enter the world, shows him fleeing from the wreck of the borrowed car: ". . . he hoped to hide—to lose himself and so escape. . . ." He wishes to escape responsibility and punishment; he does "lose himself," and early in Book II we learn that he has lost his name, to reassume it only when he can use it to advantage with his rich uncle from Lycurgus.

All the rest of the grim, sleazy story can be regarded as an attempt to repudiate the old self. And the repudiation of self is associated with Clyde's readiness to repudiate others: he is ashamed of his family; he drops new friends—Dillard and Rita, for example—as soon as he makes contact with his rich relations; he ends by murdering Roberta. Or it may be put that Clyde, having no sense of the reality of self, has no sense of the reality of others; and as we have seen earlier, even his pity for others is always a covert self-pity or a pity for the self that could not be, truly, a self.

At the end, in a last desperate hope, Clyde is forced by McMillan to recognize the truth that he has fled from responsibility and self. But even now, as Clyde tries to recognize this fact and thus discover and accept a self, he cannot be sure of who or what he is. His "tragedy" is that of namelessness, and this is one aspect of its being an American tragedy, the story of the individual without identity, whose responsible self has been absorbed by the great machine of modern industrial secularized society, and reduced to a cog, a cipher, an abstraction. Many people, including Serge Eisenstein who in his film made Clyde the mere victim of society, have emphasized the social determinism in *An American Tragedy*, and James Farrell succinctly summarizes this view:

> To him [Dreiser] evil is social: all his novels are concerned
> with social history, the social process of evil. Ambition, yearn-

ing, aspiration—these all revolve around this problem, and it in turn revolves around the role of money. He has related social causation . . . to the individual pattern of destiny.

Dreiser did indeed relate social causation to the individual pattern of destiny, but deeper than this story of the individual set against the great machine of the secularized society is the story of the individual set against the great machine of the universe—the story we find in the image of Cowperwood, in prison, staring up at the stars (in a scene that reminds us of Thomas Hardy), or in that of Clyde, after the death of Roberta, moving into the darkness of the woods.

No, these images are not adequate to focus the issue as it appears in, and informs, *An American Tragedy*. For man is not merely set against the machine of the universe, he is part of it; he *himself* is a machine. This was the doctrine that in the years leading up to the novel, Dreiser had been absorbing from Jacques Loeb, the great physiological researcher of the Rockefeller Institute, one of the pioneers in establishing the explanation of life by physico-chemical laws subject to exploration by the methods of the laboratory. Under the tutelage of Loeb, Dreiser had come to feel that the stars that are indifferent to man, or would cross him, are not in the sky but in his bloodstream and nerve cells and genes; and that man himself is the dark wood in which he wanders. Consciousness itself is merely a product of the physico-chemical process. And this brings us back to Dreiser's theme of illusion.

Success, power, place, wealth, religion, art, love—over and over, in one way or another, in fiction or autobiography, Dreiser had defined each of these things as an "illusion." Now, in *An American Tragedy*, he specifically comes upon his final subject, the illusion of the self; for, whatever its origins, consciousness, with all the pathos of aspiration and desire, exists. The "mulch of chemistry" in man that gives him all his other illusions, gives him this, the primary illusion; and the drama of self-definition remains crucial. The last anguish is the yearning for identity, for the illusion that is the fundamental "truth," and Clyde Griffiths, now past all the other empty yearnings that had merely been masks for this deepest yearning, longs for this certainty as he walks down the corridor toward the door that would close upon "all the earthly life he had ever known."

As soon as *An American Tragedy* was off the press, people began to ask what kind of tragedy, if any, it was. Clyde Griffiths scarcely seemed to be a tragic hero. He had not fallen from a great place. He was not of great scale. Rather than being a man of action, he was acted upon. By what criteria might he be called tragic? Even readers who felt the power of the novel were troubled by this title.

The puzzlement was compounded by the notion that, if Dreiser had used this title for his Trilogy (of which only two volumes had then appeared), nobody would have been surprised. Cowperwood, that is, appeared to be every inch the stuff of tragedy. If not of kingly blood, he was, like Tamburlaine, the stuff of which kings are made. His scale was beyond dispute, his power over men, women, and events preternatural. As for his ability to act, he was will incarnate in action. As far as the readers of 1925 were concerned, it seemed that one merely had to wait for the third volume to find the classic conclusion of a tragedy, complete with pity and terror; and even now, with *The Stoic* before us and the dwindling out of the hero with Bright's disease as the conclusion, we may still remember that Marlowe's character merely died a natural death too, without losing his franchise as a tragic hero.

The comparison of Cowperwood and Clyde is essential for an understanding of what Dreiser is about in *An American Tragedy*; and it is reasonably clear that Dreiser himself was thinking and feeling in these terms. The hard, hypnotic, blazing blue gaze of Cowperwood, before which men quailed and women shivered delightfully, is the central fact of his image, insisted upon again and again. Clyde's eyes, too, are central for his image and are insisted upon. In the very beginning, even as we are told that Clyde was "as vain and proud as he was poor," and was "one of those interesting individuals who looked upon himself as a thing apart" (as the young Dreiser had sung the refrain to himself, "No common man am I"), we see him studying his assets in a mirror: "a straight, well-cut nose, high white forehead, wavy, glossy black hair, eyes that were black and rather melancholy at times." It is those "deep and rather appealing eyes" that, when a girl cashier in a drugstore notices him, put him in the way of his first good job, in the Green-Davidson Hotel. And when the other bellhops take him to his first brothel, the prostitute, trying to overcome his timidity, says, "I like your eyes. You're not like those other fellows. You're more refined, kinda."

Many others, including, of course, Sondra, are to feel the peculiar attraction of his eyes, but they are most obviously important in the stages of the affair with Roberta. There is the moment when she first becomes aware of the "darkness and melancholy and lure of his eyes" and, at the moment of the first kiss, of the "dark, hungry eyes held very close to hers." Then, in the magnificent scene when, after she has refused to let him come to her room and he leaves her standing in the dark street, she, in the "first, flashing, blinding, bleeding stab of love," thinks: "His beautiful face, his beautiful hands. His eyes." At last, on Big Bittern Lake, trying to steel himself to the deed: "And his dark, liquid, nervous eyes, looking anywhere but at her." And in the instant when she becomes aware of his strange expression and makes her fateful movement toward him in the boat: "And in the meantime his eyes—the pupils of the same growing momentarily larger and more lurid. . . ."

The hard, blaze-blue glance of Cowperwood is the index of unrelenting, self-assertive male force. The dark melancholy gaze of Clyde is not an index of force: rather, of weakness, a device of blackmail by which, somehow, his weakness feeds on the kindly or guilty weakness of others so that pity is in the end converted into complicity. In *Dawn* Dreiser says that he gave way "to the whining notion that if something were done for me—much—I would amount to a great deal—a whimper which had taken its rise out of my self-exagerated deprivations. . . . And which of us is not anxious, or at least willing, to have things done for him?"

Cowperwood's glance is the mark of naked self-assertion, Clyde's gaze is a confession of the non-self—blank desire, a primal need to "have things done for him." The self of Clyde does not exist except in terms of desire—at root the desire to create a self worthy of the fulfillment of desire, to conceal the sniveling worthless self. When Clyde sees girls "accompanied by some man in evening suit, dress shirt, high hat, bow tie, white kid gloves and patent leather shoes," he thinks: "To be able to wear such a suit with such ease and air!" And if he did attain such raiment, would he not be "well set upon the path that leads to all the blisses?" And so Dreiser develops, not by a woman but by a man, Clyde or himself, the philosophy of clothes that he had begun in *Sister Carrie*: now at a deeper level, an existential level, a level at which we understand the inwardness of the sad little tale of his embezzlement of $25.00 for the flashy overcoat and of his passion for fame, both as manifestations of the need to create a worthy self, or to conceal the unworthy self.

To sum up, Cowperwood, with his brutal self-sufficiency, could make his way with women, but Clyde was like Dreiser, who could say of himself: "I was too cowardly to make my way with women readily; rather they made their way with me." So we see, for example, that Hortense, Rita, and Sondra "make their way" with Clyde; they have reasons for using him, Hortense for money, Sondra, to spite the Griffiths of Lycurgus. Clyde, with his dark, melancholy eyes, merely happens to be handy. Roberta, too, in her own fashion, makes her way with him, as Dreiser quite explicitly puts it, for she has been seized by the "very virus of ambition and unrest that afflicted him."

Her own purposes, however shadowy and unadmitted to herself, are at work, but these purposes are transformed into love, while the purposes of Clyde, in his shadowy inner world of self-concern and self-deception, are not. Since Roberta is in love, and he is not, he can dominate her. But there is another factor involved here. Sondra is in love with Clyde too, and he does not dominate her; rather, with her he remains the passive yearner, the one who must "have things done for him," and it is appropriate that she talks baby talk to him. Underlying the difference between his dominance of Roberta and his subservience to Sondra is the difference in social scale. To Sondra, Clyde feels socially inferior, this feeling of social inferiority fusing with his other feelings of weakness, but he had sensed that Roberta accepts him as a social superior who stoops to her, who can "do something" for her, and this feeling makes possible, fuses with, the sexual dominance here achieved for the first time.

So we find, in the instant when Roberta, alarmed by the expression on her lover's face, moves toward him in the boat, this fundamentally significant sentence: "And Clyde, as instantly sensing the profoundness of his own failure, his own cowardice and inadequateness for such an occasion, as instantly yielding to a tide of submerged hate, not only for himself, but for Roberta—her power—or that of life to restrain him in this way." Roberta, the one woman whom he, as a male, has been able to dominate, now seeks to dominate him: she would thwart his desire. And in this instant of her return to the old role all women had had with him, he sensed the "profoundness" of his own failure—that is, his life-failure, his sexual failure—and the "submerged hate" bursts forth, and poor Roberta pays for all the pent-up and undecipherable hatred and self-hatred Clyde had found in those relationships.

The hate that bursts forth from its secret hiding place, does not, it must be emphasized, eventuate in a simple act of will. Dreiser is explicit: "And yet fearing to act in any way. . . ." If the hand holding the camera flies out, the gesture is one of revulsion and self-protection, of flight, and of flight that somehow comes with an overtone of sexual flight. If Roberta falls into the water and drowns, he is "innocent." And here we are concerned with something different from a mere illustration of unconscious motive, for the episode has a deeper and more ironical implication in which the psychological dimension merges into the metaphysical. Clyde, the blackmailer with the dark, melancholy eyes, Clyde who wanted things done for him, Clyde the Aladdin with the magic lamp—in this, the great crisis of his life, his deepest wish comes true. The genie has served him faithfully, to the end: "For despite your fear, your cowardice, this—this—has been done for you."

His wish is his doom.

To return to our question, if Clyde is merely the passive yearner who "wants things done for him," in what sense is his story a tragedy? The first stage toward an answer may be in the adjective "American," which is best explained by a remark, in *A Hoosier Holiday*, about the atmosphere of American cities that, Dreiser says, he has always missed abroad; the "crude, sweet illusion about the importance of things material"—the importance, as he puts it elsewhere in a passage already quoted, of "getting on." Clyde's dream is that "crude, sweet illusion," tragic in that for this mere illusion all values of life, and life itself, will be thrown away.

But behind this illusion is the illusion that in terms of "getting on" a self may be created, or an unworthy self concealed and redeemed. So here, again, as in the Trilogy, illusion is the key. With Cowperwood the tragic effect lies in the fact that the hero of great scale and force spends himself on illusions—the illusions of will, love, and art. But the hero who seems so self-sufficient, whose "blazing trial . . . did for the hour illuminate the terrors and wonders of individuality," is in the end only, as Dreiser puts it in the epilogue to *The Financier*, the "prince of a world of dreams whose reality was disillusion." So Dreiser, in Clyde Griffiths, turns his attention to another "prince of dreams." What does it matter if Clyde cannot achieve the "soul-dignity," the sense of identity, that Cowperwood could feel even when, in prison, he stared up at the indifferent constellations, for even that sense of "soul-dignity," though it is the illusion that is the only "truth," is but an illusion.

In the story of Clyde, Dreiser is trying to write the root tragedy. It is a tragedy concerned, as tragedy must be, with the nature of destiny, but, as the root tragedy, it seeks the lowest common denominator of tragic effect, an effect grounded in the essential human situation. It is a type of tragedy based on the notion that, on whatever scale, man's lot is always the same. He is the mechanism envisioned by Jacques Loeb, but he is a mechanism with consciousness. His tragedy lies in the doubleness of his nature. He is doomed, as a mechanism, to enact a certain role. As a consciousness, he is doomed to seek self-definition in the "terrors and wonders of individuality," the last illusion and the source of final pain.

Some few human beings seem to avoid the doom. For instance, Clyde's mother praying, on the night of his execution, for the soul of her son. In her prayer she affirmed: "I know in whom I have believed."

Does she?

An American Tragedy

Irving Howe*

Do I exaggerate in saying that Theodore Dreiser has dropped out of the awareness of cultivated Americans? If so, it is but a slight exaggeration. Few young writers now model themselves on his career, and not many readers think of him as one of those literary figures whose word can transform the quality of their experience. Dreiser has suffered the fate that often besets writers caught up in cultural dispute: their work comes to seem inseparable from what has been said about it, their passion gets frozen into history.

Mention Dreiser to a bright student of literature, mention him to a literate older person, and only seldom will the response be a swift turning of memory to novels that have brought pleasure and illumination. Far more likely is a series of fixed associations—to a cragged, brooding, bear-like figure who dragged himself out of 19th Century poverty and provincialism, and in *Sister Carrie* composed a pioneering novel of sexual candor; or to a vague notion that the author of *The Financier* and *The Titan* turned out quantities of illtuned and turgid social documentation; or to a prepared judgment against a writer taken to be sluggish in thought and language, sluggishly accumulating data of destruction and failure, but deaf to the refinements of consciousness, dull to the play of sensibility, and drab, utterly and hopelessly drab in the quality of his mind.

The decline of Dreiser's reputation has not been an isolated event. It has occurred in the context, and surely as a consequence, of the counter-revolution in American culture during the past few decades. For readers educated in these years, Dreiser often became a symbol of everything a superior intelligence was supposed to avoid. For the New Critics, to whom the very possibility of a social novel seemed disagreeable; for literary students trained in the fine but narrow school of the Jamesian sensibility; for liberals easing into a modest gentility and inclined to replace a belief in social commitment with a search for personal distinction; for intellectuals delighted with the values of ambiguity, irony, complexity and impatient with the pieties of radicalism—for all such persons Dreiser

*Reprinted from *New Republic*, 151 (July 26, 1964), 19–21, and 151 (August 22, 1964), 25–28. Reprinted by permission of Irving Howe.

became an object of disdain. He stood for an earlier age of scientism, materialism, agnosticism: all of which were now seen as hostile to the claims of moral freedom and responsibility. He represented the boorishness of the populist mentality, as it declined into anti-Semitism or veered toward a peculiarly thoughtless brand of Communism. He could not think: he could only fumble with the names of ideas. He could not write: he could only pile words on top of each other. He cared not for art as such, but only for the novel as a vehicle of social and "philosophical" ideas. He was uneducated, insensitive—the novelist as mastodon.

So the indictment went, frequently right in its details, and when coming from so temperate a critic as Lionel Trilling often persuasive in result. If a few literary men, like the novelist James T. Farrell and the critic Alfred Kazin, continued to praise Dreiser as a writer of massive and poignant effects, if they insisted that attention be paid to the novels he wrote rather than his foolish public declamations, they were not much heeded in the last few decades.

But now, when Dreiser's prejudices have begun to be forgotten and all that remains—all that need remain—are his three or four major novels, it is time for reconsideration. The early praise these books received may have been undiscriminating: we are not obliged to repeat it. Dreiser's role in assaulting the taboos of gentility can no longer excite us as once it did his admirers. And as for his faults, no great critical insight is required to identify them, since they glare out of every chapter, especially his solemnities as a cosmic voice and his habit of crushing the English language in a leaden embrace. Yet these faults are interwoven with large creative powers, and it can be argued that for the powers to be released there had first to be the triggering presence of the faults. Let me cite an example.

As a philosopher, Dreiser can often be tiresome; yet his very lust for metaphysics, his stubborn insistence upon learning "what it's all about," helped to deepen the emotional resources from which he drew as a novelist. For he came to feel that our existence demands from us an endless contemplativeness, even if—perhaps because—we cannot think through our problems or solve our mysteries. In the frustrations he encountered when trying to extract some conceptual order from the confusion and trouble of existence, he grew more closely involved, more *at one*, with the characters he created, also confused and troubled.

In the first task of the novelist, which is to create an imaginary social landscape both credible and significant, Dreiser ranks among the American giants, the very few American giants we have had. Reading *An American Tragedy* once again, after a lapse of more than twenty years, I have found myself greatly moved and shaken by its repeated onslaughts of narrative, its profound immersion in human suffering, its dredging up of those shapeless desires which lie, as if in fever, just below the plane of consciousness. How much more vibrant this book is than the usual accounts of it in recent criticism might lead one to suppose! It is a masterpiece, nothing less.

Dreiser published *An American Tragedy* in 1925. By then he was 54 years old, an established writer with his own fixed and hard-won ways, who had written three first-rate novels: *Sister Carrie, Jennie Gerhardt* and *The Financier*. These books are crowded with exact observation—observation worked closely into the grain of narrative—about the customs and class structure of American society in the phase of early finance capitalism. No other novelist has absorbed into his work as much knowledge as Dreiser had about American institutions: the mechanisms of business, the stifling rhythms of the factory, the inner hierarchy of a large hotel, the chicaneries of city politics, the status arrangements of rulers and ruled. For the most part Dreiser's characters are defined through their relationships to these institutions. They writhe and suffer to win a foothold in the slippery social world or to break out of the limits of established social norms. They exhaust themselves to gain success, they destroy themselves in acts of impulsive deviancy. But whatever their individual lot, they all act out the drama of determinism—which, in Dreiser's handling, is not at all the sort of listless fatality that hostile critics would make it seem but is rather a fierce struggle by human beings to discover the limits of what is possible to them and thereby perhaps to enlarge those limits by an inch or two. That mostly they fail is Dreiser's tribute to reality.

This controlling pattern in Dreiser's novels has been well described by Bernard Rosenberg, a sociologist with a literary eye:

> "Emile Durkheim had suggested in Dreiser's day that when men speak of a force external to themselves which they are powerless to control, their subject is not God but social organization. This is also Dreiser's theme, and to it he brings a sense of religious awe and wonder. 'So well defined,' he writes, 'is the sphere of social activity, that he who departs from it is doomed.' . . . Durkheim identified social facts, i.e., the existence of norms, precisely as Dreiser did: by asking what would happen if they were violated. . . . Norms develop outside the individual consciousness and exist prior to it; we internalize them and are fully aware of their grip only when our behavior is deviant. Durkheim illustrated this proposition in a dozen different ways, and so did Dreiser."

In Dreiser's early novels most of the central characters are harried by a desire for personal affirmation, a desire they can neither articulate nor suppress. They suffer from a need that their lives assume the dignity of dramatic form, and they suffer terribly, not so much because they cannot satisfy this need, but because they do not really understand it. Money, worldly success, sensual gratification are the only ends they know or can name, but none of these slakes their restlessness. They grapple desperately for money, they lacerate themselves climbing to success, yet they remain sullen and bewildered, always hopeful for some unexpected sign by which to release their bitter craving for a state of grace or, at least, illumination. Dreiser's characters are romantics who behave as if the Absolute can be found, immaculately preserved, at the very summit of material power. Great energies can flow from this ingrained American delusion, both for the discharge of ambition and the aggressiveness of ego. And Dreiser too, because he had in his own experience shared these values and struggled, with varying effectiveness, to burn them out of his system—Dreiser too lived out the longings and turmoil of his characters.

Yet there is usually present in his early novels a governing intelligence more copious and flexible than that of the characters. This governing intelligence is seldom revealed through direct statement, either by characters or author. Taking upon himself the perils and sharing in the miseries of his characters, he leaves the privilege of admonition to others. Yet there is never really a question as to what his novels "mean," nor any serious possibility that the characters will usurp control. Through the logic of the narrative, we are enabled to grasp with an almost visceral intensity how shallow are the standards by which the characters live.

In these early novels society figures largely as a jungle; and with good reason—the capitalism of the early 20th Century closely resembled a jungle. The characters may begin with a hard struggle for survival, but far more quickly than most of Dreiser's critics allow, they leave it behind them. Having emerged from the blunt innocence of their beginings, they are now cursed with a fractional awareness. They can find neither peace nor fulfillment. In their half-articulate way Dreiser's characters are beset by the same yearnings that trouble the characters of Fitzgerald and many other American novelists: a need for some principle of value by which to overcome the meanness, the littleness of their lives. To know, however, that the goals to which one has pledged one's years are trivial, yet not to know in what their triviality consists—this is a form of suffering which overcomes Dreiser's characters again and again. In all its dumb misery, it is the price, or reward, of their slow crawl to awareness. One sometimes feels that in the novels of Dreiser there is being reenacted the whole progression of the race toward the idea of the human.

The prose in these early novels is often as wretched as unsympathetic critics have said. Dreiser had little feeling for the sentence as a rhythmic unit (though he had strong intuitive grasp of the underlying rhythm of narrative as a system of controlled variation and incremental development). He had a poor ear for the inflections of common speech, or even for the colloquial play of language. And worst of all, he had a weakness, all too common among the semi-educated, for "elegant" diction and antique rhetoric. Yet, despite the many patches of grey and the occasional patches of purple prose, Dreiser manages to accumulate large masses of narrative tension; he pulls one, muttering and bruised, into the arena of his imagination; and finally there is no recourse but surrender to its plenitude, its coarse and encompassing reality.

Not even Dreiser's philosophical excursions—bringing together nativist American prejudice with the very latest ideas of 1900—can break the thrust of these narratives. Dreiser's thought has by now been analyzed, mauled and ridiculed: his distortion of social life through metaphors of brute nature, his reduction of human motive to the malignant pressure of "chemisms," his toying with notions about "the superman" in the Cowperwood novels. But it hardly matters. One brushes all this aside, resigned to the malice of a fate that could yoke together such intellectual debris with so much creative power. One brushes aside, and reads on.

Though surely Dreiser's major achievement, *An American Tragedy*, is not the work of a master who, at the approach of old age, decides upon a revolutionary break from the premises and patterns of his earlier writing. For that order of boldness Dreiser lacked a sufficient self-awareness and sophistication as an artist; he was cut off from too much of the tradition of Western, even American, culture to do anything but continue with his version of naturalism. He was the kind of writer who must keep circling about the point of his beginnings, forever stirred by memories of his early struggles and preoccupations. All such a writer can hope for—a very great deal—is to mine his talent to its very depth; and that Dreiser did in *An American Tragedy*. Still, there are some changes from the earlier novels, and most of them to the good.

The prose, while quite as clotted and ungainly as in the past, is now more consistent in tone and less adorned with "literary" paste gems. Solecisms, pretentiousness and gaucherie remain, but the prose has at least the negative virtue of calling less attention to itself than in some of the earlier books. And there are long sections packed with the kind of specification that in Dreiser makes for a happy self-forgetfulness, thereby justifying Philip Rahv's remark that one finds here "a prosiness so primary in texture that if taken in bulk it affects us as a kind of poetry of the commonplace and ill-favored."

For the first and last time Dreiser is wholly in the grip of his vision of things, so that he feels little need for the buttress of comment or the decoration of philosophizing. Dreiser is hardly the writer whose name would immediately occur to one in connection with T. S. Eliot's famous epigram that Henry James had a mind so fine it could not be violated by ideas; yet if there is one Dreiser novel concerning which something like Eliot's remark might apply, it is *An American Tragedy*. What Eliot said has sometimes been taken, quite absurdly, as if it were a recommendation for writers to keep themselves innocent of ideas; actually he was trying to suggest the way a novelist can be affected by ideas yet must not allow his work to become a mere illustration for them. And of all Dreiser's novels *An American Tragedy* is the one that seems least cluttered with unassimilated formulas and preconceptions.

Where the earlier novels dealt with somewhat limited aspects of American life, *An American Tragedy*, enormous in scope and ambition, requires to be judged not merely as an extended study of the American lower-middle-class during the first years of the 20th Century but also as a kind of parable of our national experience. Strip the story to its bare outline, and see how much of American desire it involves: An obscure youth, amiable but weak, is lifted by chance from poverty to the possibility of winning pleasure and wealth. To gain these ends he must abandon the pieties of his fundamentalist upbringing and sacrifice the tender young woman who has given him a taste of pure affection. All of society conspires to persuade him that his goals are admirable, perhaps even sacred; he notices that others, no better endowed than himself, enjoy the privileges of money as if it were in the very nature of things that they should; but the entanglements of his past now form a barrier to realizing his desires, and to break through this barrier he must resort to criminal means. As it happens, he does not commit the murder he had planned, but he might as well have, for he is trapped in the machinery of social punishment and destroyed. "So well defined is the sphere of social activity that he who departs from it is doomed."

Now this story depends upon one of the most deeply-grounded fables in our culture. Clyde Griffiths, the figure in Dreiser's novel who acts it out, is not in any traditional sense either heroic or tragic. He has almost no assertive will, he lacks any large compelling idea, he reveals no special gift for the endurance of pain. In his puny self he is little more than a clouded reflection of the puny world about him. His significance lies in the fact that he represents not our potential greatness but our collective smallness, the common denominator of our foolish tastes and tawdry ambitions. He is that part of ourselves in which we take no pride, but know to be a settled resident. And we cannot dismiss him as a special case or an extreme instance, for his weakness is the essential shoddiness of mortality. By a twist of circumstance he could be a junior executive, a country-club favorite; he almost does manage to remake himself to the cut of his fantasy; and he finds in his rich and arrogant cousin Gilbert an exasperating double, the young man he too might be. Clyde embodies the nothingness at the heart of our scheme of things, the nothingness of our social aspirations. If Flaubert could say, *Emma Bovary, c'est moi*, Dreiser could echo, *Clyde Griffiths, he is us*.

We have then in Clyde a powerful representation of our unacknowledged values, powerful especially since Dreiser keeps a majestic balance between sympathy and criticism. He sees Clyde as a characteristic reflex of "the vast skepticism and apathy of life," as a characteristic instance of the futility of misplaced desire in a society that offers little ennobling sense of human potentiality. Yet he nevertheless manages to make the consequences of Clyde's mediocrity, if not the mediocrity itself, seem tragic. For in this youth there is concentrated the tragedy of human waste: energies, talents, affections all unused—and at least in our time the idea of human waste comprises an essential meaning of tragedy. It is an idea to which Dreiser kept returning both in his fiction and his essays:

> "When one was dead one was dead for all time. Hence the reason for the heartbreak over failure here and now; the awful tragedy of a love lost, a youth never properly enjoyed. Think of living and yet not living in so thrashing a world as this, the best of one's hours passing unused or not properly used. Think of seeing this tinkling phantasmagoria of pain and pleasure, beauty and all its sweets, go by, and yet being compelled to be a bystander, a mere onlooker, enhungered and never satisfied."

The first half of *An American Tragedy* is given to the difficult yet, for Dreiser's purpose, essential task of persuading us that Clyde Griffiths, through his very lack of distinction, represents a major possibility in American experience. Toward this end Dreiser must accumulate a large sum of substantiating detail. He must show Clyde growing up in a family both materially and spiritually impoverished. He must show Clyde reaching out for the small pleasures, the trifles of desire, and learning from his environment how splendid are these induced wants. He must show Clyde, step by step, making his initiation into the world of sanctioned America, first through shabby and then luxury hotels, where he picks up the signals of status. He must show Clyde as the very image and prisoner of our culture, hungering with its hungers, empty with its emptiness.

Yet all the while Dreiser is also preparing to lift Clyde's story from this mere typicality, for he wishes to go beyond the mania for the average which is a bane of naturalism. Everything in this story is ordinary, not least of all the hope of prosperity through marriage—everything but the fact that Clyde begins to act out, or is treated as if he had acted out, the commonplace fantasy of violently disposing of a used-up lover. This is the sole important departure from ordinary verisimilitude in the entire novel, and Dreiser must surely have known that it was. In the particular case upon which he drew for *An American Tragedy*, the young man did kill his pregnant girl; but Dreiser must nevertheless have realized that in the vast majority of such crises the young man dreams of killing and ends by marrying. Dreiser understood, however, that in fiction the effort to represent common experience requires, at one or two crucial points, an effect of heightening, an intense exaggeration. Clyde's situation may be representative, but his conduct must be extreme. And is that not one way of establishing the dramatic: to drive a representative situation to its limits of possibility?

In *An American Tragedy* Dreiser solved the problem which vexes all naturalistic novelists: how to relate harmoniously a large panorama of realism with a sharply-contoured form. Dreiser is endlessly faithful to common experience. No one, not even the critics who have most harshly attacked the novel, would care to deny the credibility of Clyde and Roberta Alden, the girl he betrays; most of the attacks on Dreiser contain a mute testimony to his achievement, for in order to complain about his view of life they begin by taking for granted the "reality" of his imagined world. Yet for all its packed detail, the novel is economically structured—though one must understand that the criterion of economy for this kind of novel is radically different from that for a James or Conrad novel. In saying all this I do not mean anything so improbable as the claim that whatever is in the book belongs because it is there; certain sections, especially those which prepare for Clyde's trial, could be cut to advantage; but the over-all architecture has a rough and impressive craftsmanship.

The action of the novel moves like a series of waves, each surging forward to a peak of tension and then receding into quietness, and each, after the first one, reenacting in a more complex and perilous fashion the material of its predecessor. Clyde in Kansas City, Clyde in Chicago, Clyde alone with Roberta in Lycurgus, Clyde on the edge of the wealthy set in Lycurgus—these divisions form the novel until the point where Roberta is drowned, and each of them acts as a reflector on the other, so that there is a mounting series of anticipations and variations upon the central theme. Clyde's early flirtation with a Kansas City shopgirl anticipates, in its chill manipulativeness, the later and more important relationship with Sondra Finchley, the rich girl who seems to him the very emblem of his fantasy. Clyde's childhood of city poverty is paralleled by the fine section presenting the poverty of Roberta's farm family. The seduction and desertion of Clyde's unmarried sister anticipates Clyde's seduction and desertion of Roberta. Clyde receives his preliminary education in the hotels where he works as bell-boy, and each of these serves as a microcosm of the social world he will later break into. Clyde's first tenderness with Roberta occurs as they float on a rowboat; the near-murder, equally passive, also on a rowboat. The grasping Clyde is reflected through a series of minor hotel figures and then through the antipathetic but complementary figures of his cousin Gilbert and Sondra; while the part of him that retains some spontaneous feeling is doubled by Roberta, thereby strengthening one's impression that Clyde and Roberta are halves of an uncompleted self, briefly coming together in a poignant unity but lacking the emotional education that would enable them to keep the happiness they have touched. There are more such balancings and modulations, which in their sum endow the novel with a rhythm of necessity.

Reinforcing this narrative rhythm is Dreiser's frequent shifting of the distance he keeps from his characters. At some points he establishes an almost intolerable closeness to Clyde, so that we feel locked into the circle of the boy's moods, while at other points he pulls back to convey the sense that Clyde is but another helpless creature among thousands of helpless creatures struggling to get through their time. In the chapters dealing with Clyde upon his arrival at Lycurgus, Dreiser virtually *becomes* his character, narrowing to a hairline the distance between Clyde and himself, in order to make utterly vivid Clyde's pleasure at finding a girl as yielding as Roberta. By contrast, there are sections in which Dreiser looks upon his story from a great height, especially in the chapters after Roberta's death, where his intent is to suggest how impersonal is the working of legal doom and how insignificant Clyde's fate in the larger motions of society. Through these shifts in perspective Dreiser can show Clyde in his double aspect, both as solitary figure and symbolic agent.

In the first half of the novel Dreiser prepares us to believe that Clyde *could* commit the crime: which is to say, he prepares us to believe that a part of ourselves could commit the crime. At each point in the boy's development there occurs a meeting between his ill-formed self and the surrounding society. The impoverishment of his family life and the instinctual deprivation of his youth leave him a prey to the values of the streets and the hotels; yet it is a fine stroke on Dreiser's part that only through these tawdry values does Clyde really become aware of his impoverishment and deprivation. Yearning gives way to cheap desire and false gratification, and these in turn create new and still more incoherent yearnings. It is a vicious circle and the result is not, in any precise sense, a self at all, but rather the beginning of that poisonous fabrication which in America we call a "personality." The hotels are his college, and there he learns to be "insanely eager for all the pleasures which he saw swirling around him." The sterile moralism of his parents cannot provide him with the strength to resist his environment or a principle by which to overcome it. The first tips he receives at the Green-Davidson hotel seem to him "fantastic, Aladdinish really." When he tries to be romantic with his first girl, the images that spring to his mind are of the ornate furnishings in the hotel. Later, as he contemplates killing Roberta, the very idea for the central act in his life comes from casual reading of a newspaper. It would be hard to find in American literature another instance where the passivity, rootlessness and self-alienation of urban man is so authoritatively presented. For in one sense Clyde does not exist, but is merely a creature of his milieu. And just as in Dreiser's work the problem of human freedom becomes critically acute through a representation of its decline, so the problem of awareness is brought to the forefront through a portrait of its negation.

Even sexuality, which often moves through Dreiser's world like a thick fog, is here diminished and suppressed through the power of social will. Clyde discovers sex as a drugstore clerk, "never weary of observing the beauty, the daring, the self-sufficiency and the sweetness" of the girls who come to his counter. "The wonder of them!" All of these fantasies he then focusses on the commonplace figure of Sondra Finchley, Heloise as a spoiled American girl. Apart from an interval with Roberta, in which he yields to her maternal solicitude, Clyde's sexuality never breaks out as an irresistible force; it is always at the service of his fears, his petty snobbism, his calculations.

Now all of this is strongly imagined, yet what seems still more notable is Dreiser's related intuition that even in a crippled psyche there remain, eager and available, the capacities we associate with a life of awareness. False values stunt and deform these capacities, but in some pitiful way also express and release them. Clyde and Roberta are from the beginning locked in mutual delusion, yet the chapters in which they discover one another are also extremely tender as an unfolding of youthful experience. That this can happen at all suggests how indestructible the life-force is; that Dreiser can portray it in his novels is the reward of his compassion. He is rarely sentimental, he reckons human waste to the bitter end; but at the same time he hovers over these lonely figures, granting them every ounce of true feeling he possibly can, insisting that they too—clerk and shopgirl, quite like intellectual and princess—can know "a kind of ecstasy all out of proportion to the fragile, gimcrack scene" of the Starlight Amusement Park.

Dreiser surrenders himself to the emotional life of his figures, not by passing over their delusions or failures but by casting all his energy into evoking the fullness of their experience. And how large, finally, is the sense of the human that smolders in this book! How unwavering the feeling for "the sensitive and seeking individual in his pitiful struggle with nature—with his enormous urges and his pathetic equipment!" Dreiser's passion for detail is a passion for his subject; his passion for his subject, a passion for the suffering of men. As we are touched by Clyde's early affection for Roberta, so later we participate vicariously in his desperation to be rid of her. We share this desire with some shame, but unless we count ourselves among the hopelessly pure, we share it.

Other naturalists, when they show a character being destroyed by overwhelming forces, frequently leave us with a sense of littleness and helplessness, as if the world were collapsed. Of Dreiser that is not, in my own experience, true. For he is always on the watch for a glimmer of transcendence, always concerned with the possibility of magnitude. Clyde is pitiable, his life and fate are pitiable; yet at the end we feel a somber exaltation, for we know that An American Tragedy does not seek to persuade us that human existence need be without value or beauty.

No, for Dreiser life is something very different. What makes him so absorbing a novelist, despite grave faults, is that he remains endlessly open to experience. This is something one cannot say easily about most modern writers, including those more subtle and gifted than Dreiser. The trend of modern literature has often been toward a recoil from experience, a nausea before its flow, a denial of its worth. Dreiser, to be sure, is unable to make the finer discriminations among varieties of experience; and there is no reason to expect these from him. But he is marvelous in his devotion to whatever portion of life a man can have; marvelous in his conviction that something sacred resides even in the transience of our days; marvelous in his feeling that the grimmest of lives retain the possibility of "a mystic something of beauty that perennially transfigures the world." Transfigures—that is the key word, and not the catch-phrases of mechanistic determinism he furnished his detractors.

Santayana, in his lecture on Spinoza, speaks of "one of the most important and radical of religious perceptions":

> "It has perceived that though it is living, it is powerless to live; that though it may die, it is powerless to die; and that altogether, at every instant and in every particular, it is in the hands of some alien and inscrutable power.
>
> "Of this felt power I profess to know nothing further. To me, as yet, it is merely the counterpart of my impotence. I should not venture, for instance, to call this power almighty, since I have no means of knowing how much it can do: but I should not hesitate, if I may coin a word, to call it *omnificent*: it is to me, by definition, the doer of everything that is done. I am not asserting the physical validity of this sense of agency or cause: I am merely feeling the force, the friendliness, the hostility, the unfathomableness of the world."

Dreiser, I think, would have accepted these words, for the power of which Santayana speaks is the power that flows, in all its feverish vibration, through *An American Tragedy*.

Mr. Trilling, Mr. Warren, and
An American Tragedy

Charles Thomas Samuels*

For a moment in *The Liberal Imagination* Lionel Trilling adopts the inspirational mode:

> . . . with us it is always a little too late for mind, yet never too late for honest stupidity; always a little too late for understanding, never too late for righteous, bewildered wrath; always too late for thought, never too late for naive moralizing. We seem to like to condemn our finest but not our worst qualities by pitting them against the exigency of time.

Aux barricades! In behalf of intellect and art, Trilling issued a challenge to admirers of Theodore Dreiser.

We know the famous case which Trilling made against him. Dreiser is not to be cherished for being true to life at the cost of art since he is "literary" in the worst sense; he is not to be forgiven for his intellectual vulgarity since his "anti-semitism was not merely a social prejudice but an idea, a way of dealing with difficulties": his was a failure of mind as well as art.

One would have thought the ghost exorcised. Trilling's case was sound—a writer's beliefs are neither separable from his art nor more valid than his means of expression. The very critics whom Trilling had to fight prove his point. Alfred Kazin valued Dreiser's fiction since "it hurts because it is all too much like reality to be 'art.' " Eliseo Vivas condoned Dreiser's prose because "the prose is the man."

Before Trilling, Dreiser criticism had begun to sound like a character reference or the introduction to an after-dinner speaker. Dreiser serving up great gobs of bleeding reality salted with his tears and garnished with prosy sincerity to a hall full of people who were already salivating. What difference does it make whether Dreiser is speaker or writer, waiter or cook if what you want is life in the raw?

The fight over Dreiser has always involved presumed relationships between "reality" and "art." Critics friendly to him define "reality" as a complex of anti-proletarian forces which Dreiser, fine human being that

*Reprinted from *Yale Review*, 53 (Summer, 1964), 629–40.

he was, hated, as good men ought. He was for *us* and against *them*: that conspiracy of wealth and power which oppresses and deprives us and then outrageously demands that we describe oppression and deprivation in fancy prose. Dreiser's friends always defend him as if he were Walter Reuther and you were a Rotarian. If you deride his mechanistic philosophy, you embrace the morality of the ruling class; if you detest his illiterate style, you admire the bloodless chic of *The New Yorker*; if you deplore his mindless devotion to detail, you probably hate life itself.

That line of defense is its own refutation.

In 1950, after Kazin's eulogies and Trilling's attack, the American Men of Letters series published posthumously the appreciation which was to do Dreiser justice. In it, F. O. Matthiessen shows how very temperate a responsible critic must be in Dreiser's behalf. Beginning with the usual references to Dreiser's person and his contemporary pertinence, Matthiessen proceeds to say everything that can be said about *An American Tragedy* as a work of art. He points to the structural parallels, the faithful depiction of milieu in the Green-Davidson Hotel, the tenderness and compassion which Dreiser has for his characters. Yet his chapter is full of poignant doubts and shame-faced disclaimers:

> For some readers interest breaks down under the sheer weight of details; for others the exhaustiveness of Dreiser's treatment is what builds up to an effect of final authority.

> A crucial element in our final estimate of this novel is how far [Dreiser] can enable us to participate in his compassion.

> Some of these details may seem stock in themselves, but . . .

> . . . what Clyde finds in his "baby-talking girl!" is what Dreiser never manages to convey to us concretely.

In conclusion, Matthiessen recalls Krutch's insistence that *An American Tragedy* was "the great American novel of our generation," but he continues with a more modest claim that comes nearer the truth:

> Clyde's whole experience was too undifferentiated, too unilluminated to compel the attention of some readers already habituated to the masterpieces of the modern psychological novel. But for young men growing up in the 'twenties and 'thirties here was a basic account of the world to which they were exposed.

Matthiessen's conclusion seemed the authentic farewell to that veteran warrior against Victorian morality and Social Darwinism. The late nineteenth century had asked what social classes owed one another, William Graham Sumner had answered "nothing," the Captains of Industry had agreed, and up went the breadlines, the apple-sellers, the strikes—the whole world over which Dreiser shed so many tears and such a quantity of typescript. It was a bloody and a good fight; but the old soldier was gone, and his book would live as a mute witness to the awful past.

Trilling riddled the body, but Matthiessen, turning it into a period piece, neatly interred it. But, in its Autumn 1962 number, *The Yale Review* staged an exhumation, by, of all people, Robert Penn Warren. As Mr. Trilling might have said, here is a "cultural episode."

After the battles and the insults, after Trilling's brilliant attack and Matthiessen's more damning defense, the former Southern Agrarian, New Critical fabulist of innate depravity pays homage to the Populist, illiterate poet of exculpation. Mr. Warren finds in *An American Tragedy* all Dreiser's well-known selling points. And because Mr. Warren *can* write, they now appear more palatable than anyone had thought them.

The relic is restored with a few cosmetic touches of the critic's art. An image here: "the image of the boy Clyde looking up at the 'tall walls' of the world is the key image of the novel." A touch of point of view there: at the close of Book II, "Dreiser jerks back his camera from [the] lonely figure and begins Book III by withdrawing into magisterial distance for a panoramic sweep of the lens. . . ." If the writing is bad, let's forget words. Behold "the language of the unfolding scenes, the language of the imagery of enactment, with all its primitive massiveness—the movie in our heads, with all the entailed questions of psychological veracity and subtlety, of symbolic densities and rhythmic complexities." Add a little "search for identity." And the "basic account" of a dead world lives again in its symbolically dense and rhythmically complex reenactment of the ritual search for identity.

But Mr. Warren has rewritten the book. Not the movie which George Stevens found in its pages: a film that *is* ritualistic (the love scenes), that does make Sondra desirable (Elizabeth Taylor) and Clyde a character (Montgomery Clift with his tubercular chest and hungry eyes). Not the troubling insight into a society which defiled sex by dirtying its face and laying it out for money. The words which are the book. The words which tell the story, which set the scene, which force you to believe in Dreiser's people and what they mean.

What are Dreiser's words like? First, as F. R. Leavis has said, they are like the work of a man who lacked a native language. Not only because of Trilling's "paste gems"—the "scene more distingué than this," the man "*soi-distant* and not particularly eager to stay at home." Dreiser's words travesty not only themselves but the hero they are meant to create. Clyde is introduced as a "tall and as yet slight figure, surmounted by an interesting head." Explaining the pained response to his family's sidewalk church which must convince us of Clyde's fine-grained soul and which must excuse his later repudiation of religion, Dreiser asserts: "all that could be truly said of [Clyde] now was that there was no definite appeal in all this for him."

Dreiser cannot make us see his characters (his only detailed descriptions are of clothes); he cannot create their responses; nor, despite his vaunted compassion, can he take us into his characters' hearts so that we may join him in his empathy. After a long and stormy scene in which Clyde feels the stirrings of healthy young libido, we get this:

> And suddenly now, as he felt this yielding of her warm body so close to him, and the pressure of her lips in response to his own, he realized that he had let himself in for a relationship which might not be so very easy to modify or escape. Also that it would be a very difficult thing for him to resist, since he now liked her and obviously she liked him.

The words fail to make us feel the heat of sex, the heat of life, which cannot be denied and which Lycurgus is evil for denying in order that business may be more efficient. When Dreiser talks of sex and man's destiny, "What man, short of saint or sage," Warren asks, could fail to respond "in some secret way however different from Clyde's way. . . ." Yet Dreiser speaks of sex as a "chemism," as the "sex lure or appeal," and Dreiser illustrates destiny merely by creating a character full of "mental and material weakness before pleasure," by presenting that character with pleasure and an impediment, and by drearily establishing the preconceived certainty that the character, since he lacks "mental and material" strength, will remove the impediment by whatever means. Sex becomes a behavioristic tic and destiny a charade.

The book's admired structural parallels reveal a want of invention. If Hortense is like Rita and Sondra, couldn't Dreiser have done without one of them? Must we have every bit of evidence, every "objection sustained," every hackneyed bit of journalese in the trial scene?

The novel is held together by its big scenes, but these invariably fall flat. This, for example, is Dreiser's description of the first meeting between Clyde and Roberta at Crum Lake:

> Almost before he had decided, he was quite beside her, some twenty feet from the shore, and was looking up at her, his face lit by the radiance of one who had suddenly, and beyond his belief, realized a dream. And as though he were a pleasant apparition suddenly evoked out of nothing and nowhere, a poetic effort taking form out of smoke or vibrant energy, she in turn stood staring down at him, her lips unable to resist the wavy line of beauty that a happy mood always brought to them.

All is seen through smoke and poetry (perhaps that accounts for "the wavy line"; Leslie Fiedler reminds us that Dreiser comes from "the kind of people who copulate in the dark and live out their lives without ever seeing their sexual partners nude . . ."). Then the apparition speaks:

> "My, Miss Alden! It is you, isn't it? . . . I was wondering whether it was. I couldn't be sure from out there."
>
> "Why, yes it is. . . ."

Thud.

But doesn't this dialogue faithfully reflect Dreiser's inarticulate characters? Some such argument has been the classic defense of Dreiser's unspeakable dialogue. Notice, however, how Dreiser expresses Roberta's thoughts:

> . . . in spite of her obvious pleasure at seeing him again, only thinly repressed for the first moment or two, she was on the instant beginning to be troubled by her thoughts in regard to him—the difficulties that contact with him seemed to prognosticate.

When Dreiser is faced with the task of describing Roberta's first, pathetic overtures to Clyde, this is what he comes up with:

> She wavered between loyalty to Clyde as a superintendent, loyalty to her old conventions as opposed to her new and dominating desire and her repressed wish to have Clyde speak to her—then went over with the bundle and laid it on his desk. But her hands, as she did so, trembled. Her face was white—her throat taut. [She speaks] "There's been a distake" (she meant to say 'mistake'). . . . In a weak, frightened, and yet love-driven way, she was courting him. . . .

Equally slight is Dreiser's equipment for creating the emotional expression of his characters. When they are happy they are always in Paradise, or the scene before them in Aladdinish; when they are impressed they say "Gee!"; when they are entranced they say "Thrilling!" when sad, they say "God!" The exclamation point is to Dreiser what the drum is to Eugene O'Neill.

In *An American Tragedy*, Dreiser is no more able to create scenes and characters than he is to write a sentence that is both moving and grammatical. Some of what I have said has been acknowledged. More crucial and less well-known is the book's confusion and dishonesty.

An American Tragedy is a thesis novel. Its thesis, moreover, is meant to be tragic, to appall and harrow. There but for the grace of God, we are meant to say. If you had been Clyde Griffiths. If you have been susceptible and poor. If you had wanted Roberta and had been denied her in the interest of more and better collars. If she wanted you but denied you in the interest of a mean little morality. If you loved her and she became pregnant and you had, by this time, fallen in love with another, more desirable woman who could give you all that your world valued. If narrow religious training had made you ignorant, and poverty had made you helpless, and hypocrisy denied you the only expedient that could have solved your dilemma. If you lacked convictions and strength, and had lately read a newspaper account of a tragedy suffered by a man in your situation. . . . Then, you should have come to murder. It was all circumstance and chemism. You could not help it. Weep for you.

Yet Dreiser seems to have doubted whether his readers would weep

for stupid, weak Clyde when Roberta was eqaully pathetic and appeal-
ingly feminine. Dreiser was not certain that our love would flow to the
unlovely. His was a compassion without courage. It could not hold Clyde
up before us and say: "He is abject and guilty, but he is human. That is
enough." Instead, at the very moment when Clyde is performing the
murder, Dreiser undertakes his rehabilitation.

In the scene to which the whole novel has been moving, Dreiser's
mechanism becomes psychomachia:

> . . . there had now suddenly appeared, as the genii at the ac-
> cidental rubbing of Aladdin's lamp—as the efrit emerging as
> smoke from the mystic jar in the net of the fisherman—the very
> substance of some leering and diabolic wish or wisdom con-
> cealed in his own nature, and that now abhorrent and yet com-
> pelling, leering and yet intriguing, friendly and yet cruel, of-
> fered him a choice between an evil which threatened to destroy
> him (and against his deepest opposition) and a second evil
> which, however it might disgust or sear and terrify, still pro-
> vided for freedom and success and love.

Suddenly, amoral, unreflective Clyde undergoes an inner moral
struggle. If he acts without moral qualm, we might regard him as a tool of
circumstance and so deny him our sympathy. We are not likely to approve
of a monster without shame, who moves toward crime like a sleepwalker.
So, at the last crucial moment, Dreiser gives Clyde a hitherto undemonstrated moral sense which recoils at a hitherto undemonstrated principle
of internal evil.

But there is another problem. If Clyde consciously chooses what he
knows to be wrong, he is more than the hand that held the weapon
through which the whole weight of the world came down on poor Roberta. If Clyde wills the crime, we may understand it, because of his past,
but we cannot excuse him for it. More important, we may deny him our
love.

Dreiser is caught between a mechanism that denies responsibility
and thereby a fully human response and a humanistic ethic which can only convince us of Clyde's profound guilt. He solves his problem
metaphorically, by making the indwelling evil inaccessible to Clyde's
will. The rational will is sealed off from the rest of its owner's psyche so
that Clyde can be both morally repelled and actually helpless to reverse
the course upon which he had been determined:

> Indeed the center or mentating section of [Clyde's] brain at
> this time might well have been compared to a sealed and silent
> hall in which alone and undisturbed, and that in spite of
> himself, he now sat thinking on the mystic or evil and terrify-
> ing desires or advice of some darker or primordial and
> unregenerate nature of his own, and without the power to

drive the same forth or himself to decamp, and yet also without the courage to act upon anything.

Circumstance drove Clyde to Big Bittern; when he arrives, the devil takes over. Society brought him to the lake; invincible depravity makes him a murderer. He had no more control over one than the other. What matter if this be faulty thinking; it is masterly emoting.

In the celebrated scenes which lead up to the crime, Dreiser finds still other sources of responsibility. The genii conquers Clyde and begins insinuating its orders:

> Go to the lake which you visited with Sondra! . . . Go to the south end of it and from there walk south, afterwards.

When the hapless couple arrive at the lake the genii is assisted by the landscape: the very trees suggest death—there is even a Poesque weirbird. The crime itself is covered by a veil of unreality: Roberta, "an almost nebulous figure . . . now . . . [steps] down into an insubstantial rowboat upon a purely ideational lake." Finally, when Clyde hits her with his camera, he does not intend to kill her, and she tumbles out of the boat by accident.

Lest the exculpation be incomplete, after the murder, Dreiser begins suggesting that other people are worse than Clyde. The prosecuting attorney uses the case for political gain while claiming righteous indignation. One of Clyde's lawyers had a Roberta in his youth, but, being rich, escaped the need to kill her. The coroner falsifies evidence, and people gape at Clyde out of some obscene prurience. Then, when Clyde is finally convicted, Dreiser submits us to a detailed account of his torments in the death house. And if all this were not enough—Clyde's essential innocence, his comparative virtue, his extreme suffering—Dreiser makes Clyde finally accept an essentially Christian view of his guilt from the Reverend McMillan: this despite the novel's theme and the repeatedly anti-clerical and anti-religious comments made both by Clyde and by his author.

Yet the novel's final confusion is the result of Dreiser's inability to recognize the form most appropriate to his insights. There is nothing wrong, as Mr. Trilling recognizes, with Dreiser's view of life as a struggle between inner drives and outer environment. But in a dramatization of such a viewpoint the antagonists must be individual men and the world which thwarts them. Yet Dreiser fails utterly to particularize the social and economic worlds of *An American Tragedy*. Clyde peering at the "tall walls" of the city is more than a key image; it is almost all we ever get of his confrontation with socio-economic reality. Outside of the Green-Davidson (which Dreiser, almost hysterically, asserts but does not dramatize as Sodom and Gomorrah) and the row of houses of Wykeagy Avenue, there is no outer world in Dreiser's book. The cream of the jest is that Dreiser fails to give us reality, fails to pile on the right details. Only in the melodramatic trial, which captures his imagination in much the same way that trials fascinated Mark Twain, do we get anything like the minute verisimilitude for which Dreiser has been admired. If you think of Flaubert, or Zola, or that underrated American naturalist Dos Passos, you will see how deficient Dreiser is exactly where you would expect him to be strong.

Dreiser's genius is for feeling, feeling uncontrolled by, unaided by thought. It is characteristic of his peculiar confusion that when he wished to tell a tale of American youth destroyed by the inequalities of a corrupt, money-mad class system he should have declined to do anything more than sketch the system so that he could devote all his effort to recreating a banal and wordless triangle between a weakly good-looking, utterly uninteresting man, and two women—one of whom is merely pathetic and the other of whom is capable not of conveying "the pain of wanting not having" but only pain.

Dreiser lacked more than art; he lacked a sense of what he lacked.

If I am right about the book, if it is worse than one gathers from Mr. Trilling's attack, why should a critic like Robert Penn Warren (who is also a better novelist than Dreiser) attempt at this late date to eulogize the giant from Terre Haute? Warren demonstrates a sense of his anomalous position. In his earlier essay, Trilling had articulated a conception of literary art which Warren himself had helped to create. In 1946, Trilling reminded his readers, with a fine note of exasperation, that in literature "from the earth of the novelist's prose spring his characters, his ideas, and even his story. . . ." Yet Warren now complains of the "tendency to freeze the question of Dreiser as an artist at the question of prose style."

We have a pertinent parallel for this strange debate. Some years ago, Trilling was involved in a position as uncharacteristic as Warren's eulogy of Dreiser's book. In 1948, he was asked to write the introduction to a new edition of *Huckleberry Finn*. (Warren's essay is likewise the introduction to a paperback reprint.) Though Twain's masterpiece has never been thought faulty on anything like the scale I have found relevant to Dreiser's book, the ending of *Huck Finn* is often roundly attacked. Trilling's introduction undertakes to defend the last fifth of the novel on formal grounds: Huck's abdication to Tom Sawyer aptly permits Huck "to return to his anonymity, to give up the role of hero. . . ." Coincidentally, T. S. Eliot published, two years later, an introduction to another edition of Twain's book, making an even more elaborate defense of the novel on formal grounds.

Three years after that, Leo Marx published a significant article in *The American Scholar* entitled "Mr. Eliot, Mr. Trilling, and *Huckleberry Finn*." After showing in convincing detail why the ending is objectionable, Mr. Marx makes some charges against the Eliot-Trilling effort at revaluation which are even more important than his critical remarks about the novel. Since he had demonstrated that the ending is a cruel travesty of the book's humane, unillusioned attack on hypocrisy and discrimination, Marx neatly proves that Trilling and Eliot had stressed form and ignored morality. He then shrewdly speculates that so egregious a blunder in critics so eminent could only result from an indifference to the book's moral point. Marx suggests that Trilling and Eliot could stomach the gratuitous brutality which Tom displays toward Jim in the "Evasion" and which Huck uncharacteristically approves because of their exclusive interest in personal development and related uninterest in morals operating in the social or political realms. They rejoice at the anonymity which will protect Huck's selfhood while they ignore its cost: Huck's immoral assent to the debasement of Jim. Huck's story is neatly rounded off, but the novel is about larger issues.

Mr. Marx's justly famous essay implies the intimate connection between form and content. The irony of the debate is that such a point had to be made against Mr. Trilling when Mr. Trilling had years earlier made the same point against the partisan admirers of Theodore Dreiser. How could Trilling acknowledge the connection between form and content when attacking Dreiser and ignore it when defending Twain?

This is to ask the same question about Robert Penn Warren. How could Warren admire Dreiser despite his formal incompetence when Warren's entire critical career has assumed the identity of theme and mode of expression? The answer to this question must be cautionary.

Trilling's essay on *Huck Finn* and Warren's essay on *An American Tragedy* share a common flaw which accounts for their surprising advocacy of shoddy materials. Both of them conceive the novel in terms of consistency of form and feeling; neither of them questions the consistency of form and idea. Thus Trilling can admire the formal excellence of language and structure in *Huck Finn*, noting that they cooperate to create a mood of nostalgia for the honest, untainted youth both of Huck and of America. In the same way, Warren can admire the formal excellence of plotting and pacing that produce a feeling of *"entrapment"* (his term and italics) in the heavy fate of Clyde Griffiths. Both critics ignore the assertions and insights which these moods and emotion are meant to sustain. The notorious unself-consciousness of Twain and Dreiser abet a criticial disposition to regard the novel as a personal reverie which cannot and should not be tested by any public canons of truth or logic. When Warren displaces Dreiser's mechanism from the center, finding "the real drama" in "the individual story," when Trilling ignores the social crime, finding the real meaning in Huck's individual development, they are subscribing to more than a radical shrinkage of the novels which they so admire: they are diminishing the novelist's role. Neither critic is interested in those large social or moral propositions subsumed within the structure of *Huckleberry Finn* or *An American Tragedy*. And by ignoring these propositions, each critic can impose, with fatal ease, a private intellectual bias on the reverie which he appreciates. So Trilling reads *Huck Finn* as nostalgia, while Warren reads *An American Tragedy* as a search for the self. No admirer of either critic needs to be told the marked affinity of each for the interpretation he advances.

Everyone sees himself in what he reads. But that is not the only error that needs guarding against. Too easy identification of critic and book could never have overcome the acknowledged convictions of Trilling and Warren, could not have produced contradictions as blatant as those which Marx pointed out in one and which I am attempting to show in the other. Both critics made their identifications and ignored their novels' fault because neither was thinking of what the writer meant to "say." Trilling implicitly, Warren explicitly voices indifference to theme. But what Marx asserts about *Huck Finn* and what I have asserted about *An American Tragedy* is that both novels suffer from faults which are conceptual or thematic. Moreover, the contradictory ending of *Huck Finn* and the pervasive confusion of *An American Tragedy* are, at the same time, formal flaws. The conclusion of *Huck Finn* is dull and unpleasant, and the whole of *An American Tragedy* is ponderous and vague. In short, the intellectual failing is first perceived as an artistic lapse. Conversely, to deny the artistic lapse is to ignore the intellectual failing. This Trilling and Warren both do, I suspect, because neither of them, when they wrote these essays at least, felt bound to regard the serious novel as essentially cognitive. If it is not that, what is it? If it is not making a statement about life, how can we call it "serious"? Why do we study it? Why do we teach it in the University? The neglect of the novelist's mind must not be authorized now. Those French theoreticians (Mme. Sarraute & Cie.) are even now outside the house of fiction waiting to sweep out people as well as ideas and leave only the furniture.

At the end of his essay, Marx called for "a criticism alert to lapses of moral vision." He could not have failed to be aware that Lionel Trilling is a critic of the deepest moral concern. If I call for a criticism alert to the cognitive content of fiction, I am also aware that Robert Penn Warren is our only distinguished novelist of ideas. Yet if Trilling can advocate a lapse in morality and Warren can advocate a lapse in mind, how much more must the rest of us be vigilant.

We have heard rather too much lately of the irrelevance of a writer's ideas. If we mean by that that a writer's ideas need not be agreeable, what honorable critic would disapprove? But it does not follow that a writer need not have ideas or that he may be more irresponsible in treating them than in treating characters or fashioning prose. Art may begin in reverie and solitude, but it performs in the rational daylight of the public world. The critic departs from that world to his cost. The artist departs from it to our deep impoverishment.

An American Tragedy: Theme and Structure

Sheldon Norman Grebstein*

With every passing year it becomes further apparent that there is a greatness in Dreiser which overleaps his defects and his limitations, his bunglings, contradictions, and intrusions. The greatness reached its apogee in *An American Tragedy* which, four decades after its publication in 1925, impresses us more and more as one of the enduring novels of our century. Such distinguished men of letters as Robert Penn Warren pay it homage, and it continues to provoke the most careful and respectful critical commentary, even from those who find Dreiser vulgar or irreverent. Because *An American Tragedy* is so large a novel and so far from a simple one, it might prove instructive to turn our scrutiny once again to this work which has already declared itself more than a curiosity, more than a document of the jazz age (although in part it is that, too), and attempt to explore some of its complexities of theme and structure.

Thematically, *An American Tragedy* is a resonant work which, like all enduring literary creations, reverberates on multiple levels of meaning, at one and the same time bearing individual, social, and universal implication. We need look no farther than the novel's title for an outline of its themes, each word in the title signifying a thematic dimension: "An"—a single but not singular tale; "American"—a tale somehow representative not only of a particular nation but also, as the word increasingly connotes, a social structure, an experience, a life-style; "Tragedy"—a tale which concerns the end of man and its import.

On the individual level, or the simple one-to-one application of the content of a literary work to some aspect of real life within the reader's actual (or potential) experience, Dreiser employed, as is widely known, the records of an actual crime as the basis for his novel. This was the case of Chester Gillette, nephew and employee of a wealthy shirt manufacturer of Cortland (Lycurgus), New York, in which Gillette was convicted for the murder of his pregnant sweetheart, Grace Brown, and executed March 29, 1908, after appeals had delayed the death penalty for almost two years. Although Dreiser's use of this material is of considerable in-

*Reprinted from *The Twenties* . . . , ed. Richard Langford (Deland, Fla.: Everett/Edwards, 1966), pp. 62–66. Reprinted by permission of Everett/Edwards, Inc.

terest, an exhaustive account of the matter is not pertinent here. Suffice it to say that Dreiser relied heavily upon documentary materials, altering fact in two significant areas, however, to better serve the purposes of fiction:

1. The details of the real crime are changed so that the crime in *An American Tragedy* has a stronger element of the accidental. To name only one important difference, in the Gillette case five doctors agreed that drowning was *not* the primary cause of Grace Brown's death; the murder weapon was allegedly a tennis racket carried into the boat by Gillette and later found with all its strings broken.

2. More important, Clyde Griffiths only partly resembles Chester Gillette. He is less athletic and physically effectual (Gillette's photographs show him a bull-necked, deep-chested young man—also, Gillette admitted during the trial that he had initiated sexual relations with Grace Brown by force); less poised and self-contained (if contemporary newspaper accounts can be believed, Gillette did not lose his nerve under stress of indictment and trial); less well-equipped intellectually (Gillette had attended Oberlin for two years and seems to have been quick-witted, or at least glib). Finally, in contrast to Clyde's passion for Sondra, it is doubtful that Gillette was enamoured of any one girl in the wealthier class to which, like Clyde, he had gained access.

Much of what is different from the novel's Clyde Griffiths and life's Chester Gillette was supplied by Dreiser himself, from the raw materials of his own youth. The moving from place to place; the shame at the poverty and ineffectuality of the parents, especially the father; the sister who was made pregnant and then deserted; the young Dreiser's burning sexual hungers frustrated yet intensified by parental thou-shalt-nots and his own fears of inadequacy; the lust for beauty which expressed itself in a fascination with fine things, money, prestige, and which became inextricably interwoven with Dreiser's sexual appetites; the pervasive guilt for all desires and deeds not consonant with the iron doctrines of the devoutly Catholic father—all this was Dreiser and was to become Clyde Griffiths. This transubstantiation does much to explain the peculiar poignancy of Clyde's characterization.

The total effect of Dreiser's alterations of Chester Gillette, conjoined with the projection of his own experience, is cumulatively much stronger than the individual changes themselves would seem to suggest. They result in a character who is far weaker than one might expect a murderer to be, yet who is more sympathetically and credibly motivated because he kills, or plans to kill, not only for money but for beauty and love. As Dreiser himself remarked in a letter protesting the diluted and cheapened film version which had been made of his novel, Clyde's affair with Roberta is not wholly sordid: "As they [the film's producers] picture it, there is nothing idyllic about it, and there should be—there must be. Until Sondra comes into his life, Clyde is content, more or less happy in his love life with Roberta." We recall, too, that as Clyde languishes in the death house for nearly two years the one element of his past he does not repudiate, the one element in the whole complex of factors leading to his fate which he continues to affirm and which sustains him almost to the end, is the vision of Sondra's beauty and the thrilling memory of her kisses. For better or worse he loves her more than he has loved anyone and to the limit of his capacity to love, and if his discrimination can be questioned, the fact of his feelings cannot. It is a fact which recommends Clyde to the reader's heart, if not to his approving judgment.

Just as the individual or personal thematic level of *An American Tragedy* is hardly simplistic, so its social content has at least two dimensions.

First, the novel is the fictional but not fictitious treatment of an all too common situation in American life, that in which some desperate young man kills his poor (and usually pregnant) sweetheart in order to marry his way up the social scale. It might be called the tragedy of the aspiring young man, the pregnant working girl, and the debutante. Although Dreiser chose the Gillette-Brown murder case as the basis for his story, he had dozens of similar episodes at his disposal. As a boy Dreiser had immersed himself in potboiling fiction, one of whose staples was the poor-boy-gets-rich-girl theme, and he had early concluded, both from his reading and experience that money, not achievement, was the chief American ideal. Moreover, as a young reporter in various cities Dreiser encountered at first hand similar cases, some of them involving murder. And when, Helen Dreiser tells us, many years later he was formulating plans for the book first titled "Mirage" and then "An American Tragedy," he studied fifteen such incidents before finally deciding on the Gillette case. Not only did the Gillette case conform to his thoughts, it had been so well publicized that it was still being discussed into the 1920's and its records were readily accessible.

To Dreiser, then, the story of Chester Gillette and others like him became symbolic of certain dominant forces in American life, and in the characters and events of *An American Tragedy* he dramatized trends that had been true for generations: the worship of the goal of success, together with the refusal to condone the methods and consequences it engendered; the excitation and prurient display of sexuality in all forms of entertainment, billboards, magazines, popular literature, yet the stern legal repression of all but the narrowest forms of sexual expression (in marriage for the purpose of procreation only); the pretense of democratic egalitarianism, yet the existence of rigid class stratification; the absurd idealization of women; the stifling influence of intrinsically false but powerfully institutionalized religious creeds—these were elements which for Dreiser had tarnished the once-luminous American Dream. And all this shapes the social purpose of *An American Tragedy*. In addition to its depiction of these broad issues, (and much of Dreiser's triumph in *An*

American Tragedy is that he depicts rather than editorializes), the novel indicts the legal system which could condemn and slaughter a youth whose real sin was weakness and real crime that of illicit sexual pleasure. The trial itself is vividly dramatized, with Dreiser demonstrating persuasively how Clyde becomes as much a victim of rigged evidence, political ambition, and public opinion as of "Justice;" *e.g.*, at one point in the proceedings a spectator speaks out in the voice of the people when he interjects: "Why don't they kill the God-damned bastard and be done with him?" Throughout, Dreiser is remarkably objective, but at moments toward the conclusion of his narrative, unable to restrain himself, he drops the guise of novelist and speaks with missionary fervor directly to the reader about the brutality of prisons, the death house, and by implication, the concept of justice which could tolerate such practices. Some critics would find this a flaw in the novel; nevertheless, there is probably no more trenchant argument against capital punishment in American literature.

Despite the weight of its social burden, *An American Tragedy* is much more than a tract, much more than a problem novel. Rather, it is a chronicle of American life. In the handling of his material Dreiser once again simply but effectively transformed history into art by means of a skillful manipulation of time. His main strategem was to move the time of the action forward about ten years, or just enough to make the book's composition and publication parallel the events it narrates. That is, unlike its documentary source the story begins sometime during the 'teens and ends in the '20's, rather than in the period before 1910, when the Zeitgeist belonged to the 19th century, not the 20th. Thus, as F. O. Matthiessen has noted, the novel occurs in and conveys a generalized atmosphere of the era following the end of the first World War, the historic moment parent to much of what we are now living. Although *An American Tragedy* is perhaps the most sober book of the decade, its cast nevertheless includes a number of authentic sheiks and flappers, of both high and low class, who dash around in automobiles, carry hip flasks, dance to jazz music, and neck—or worse. Even that elite group of young people of Lycurgus who comprise the Olympian company to which Clyde aspires display a freedom from parental restraint and a mobility unknown before the war. Certainly Hortense Briggs, one of the novel's minor triumphs of characterization and a girl best described in the parlance of the time as a tease and a gold-digger, could not have existed before 1920 as an accepted member of society.

In this respect it could even be said that *An American Tragedy* tells another part of the story Fitzgerald recorded in *The Great Gatsby*. The analogy need not be carried too far, but Clyde Griffiths and Jay Gatsby have kinship, as do Sondra Finchley and Daisy Buchanan. Clyde and Gatsby pursue the same dream, the dream of an orgiastic future embodied in a beautiful girl with a voice like the sound of money; both pursue it passionately but illicitly, and with similarly disastrous results. There the comparison of the two books should probably end, but clearly it is more than a coincidence that two novels so superficially different yet thematically so alike should be published in the same year and should come to the same mordaunt conclusions about American life.

It has already been remarked how *An American Tragedy* functions on the individual and social levels; it remains to be seen how the book fulfills the third and most profound thematic dimension—the universal—or, in brief, how it functions as tragedy. Here Dreiser has fused an individual but representative instance and a social milieu into the larger saga of what happens to any man whose desires exceed both his capacity to satisfy them and his ability to avoid retribution, since satisfaction can only come at the expense of others. On this level Dreiser is no longer a meliorist concerned with changing certain attitudes toward poverty or sex or crime. Rather, he is a tragedian, a tragic ironist, who confronts the problem of human destiny and demonstrates what can happen in a cosmos indifferent to human suffering but inhabited by humans who persist in finding meaning in their suffering. In *An American Tragedy* he gives us a synthesis of the two basic tragic situations of western literature, the tragedy of frustrated love and the tragedy of thwarted ambition, as played by a proletarian hero and as written by a compassionate agnostic.

The source of Clyde's anguish (and, we may conjecture, Dreiser's as well) is that he belongs neither to the old theistic world, with its assurance of certain certainties, however harsh, nor in the new existential one, in which man (like Mersault, also a condemned criminal, in Camus's *The Stranger*) can stoically accept and even find a sense of happiness in the benign indifference of the universe. Man's law has declared Clyde guilty but few of the men who judge him have been so fiercely afflicted by the same desires. Belknap, Clyde's lawyer, is one of the few who can be honestly sympathetic because he, too, had once gotten a girl into trouble. Like one of Dreiser's earlier characters, the hero of the play *The Hand of the Potter*, Clyde could well cry out as his only defense, "I didn't make myself, did I?" Consequently, Clyde can feel none of the guilt whose admission his fellows wish to exact from him, and although just before his execution he signs a Christian testimonial-warning to errant youth, he does so only to repay his mother and the Reverend McMillan for the love and spiritual labor they have lavished upon him. It is grimly ironic that Clyde goes to his death still unconvinced in his heart of his guilt, while the Reverend McMillan, closest to him at the end, leaves the death house both convinced of Clyde's guilt and shaken in his belief in the efficacy of his own Christian mission.

Although in his refusal to confirm Clyde's guilt, or to confirm the fact of human guilt at all, Dreiser has risked the approval of much of his audience—for most of us believe that without guilt tragedy can have no moral value and consequently result in no catharsis—his tough-mindedness and his refusal to compromise his position invoke our admiration. If he has rejected the Christian or moralistic solution to man's dilemma, the promise of redemption and salvation through suffering, he refuses equally to take comfort from the science-inspired creeds of Naturalism or Determinism, which imply that all problems, including evil, are soluble once we learn enough about them. Instead, Dreiser persists in employing as his tragic formula that which has never been quite compatible to western man: the tragedy of humans overwhelmed by an omnipotent external fate. Accordingly, he does not permit Clyde even that dignity which is the agnostic, humanistic substitute for redemption. In his very weakness Clyde Griffiths becomes a metaphor of human frailty, and in his refusal to accept guilt he signifies the futility of human thought and endeavor in the context of life's essential meaninglessness. The result could easily have been stark nihilism, yet somehow, perhaps because of the indefinable quality of what has been called Dreiser's brooding pity, Clyde's story is meaningful and poignant.

Purists in tragedy might argue that Clyde's fate is not tragic because his weakness does not permit sufficient struggle. Dreiser provides the basis for a reply. The death house is populated with others wiser and stronger than Clyde, e.g., Nicholson, the lawyer, who has had all the advantages Clyde lacked; these are men of different races, religions, backgrounds—a Negro, an Oriental, Italians, a Jew, Irish—and all share the same fate. Obviously the death house is another of Dreiser's metaphors of the human condition. It is the place, the metaphor implies, where all men, wise or stupid, weak or strong, meet because all are condemned to a common fate not because they have sinned but because they are men. To their credit, most of them—including Clyde—leave life more nobly than they have lived it.

To assert, then, as a number of critics have recently, that Dreiser's treatment of tragedy is inferior because of some supposed flaw in his tragic vision, his employment of inadequate heroes, his denial of free will, is neither to comprehend Dreiser's position fully nor to judge it fairly on its own terms, but really to disagree with it. Granting Dreiser his premises and placing him in the appropriate tradition of tragedy, one can only say that one prefers some other tradition, not that Dreiser fails. It is also likely that Dreiser's hostile critics have confused his world-view with his workmanship, attributing to one a defect of the other, for if Dreiser falls short he does so as a stylist rather than a tragedian (I speak here, of course, specifically about An American Tragedy). That is, we have always had difficulty distinguishing between the tragic situation and the writer's treatment of it and his mode of utterance. To western audiences, consequently, the most splendid and moving tragedies are those most splendidly and movingly written, whether the idiom be Shakespeare's high rhetoric or Hemingway's colloquial cadences, and in Dreiser we find neither the soaring magnificence nor purged intensity of language which strikes the reader as the proper vehicle for tragedy.

Here, too, there is the tendency toward an unjust appraisal of *An American Tragedy*; for although Dreiser fails to overwhelm us with his eloquence, he persuades us by means of his novel's exceedingly durable and tight structure and by his use of ironic parallels, juxtapositions, and foreshadowings, which effectively emphasize the tragic irony of its theme.

Structurally, An American Tragedy is by far the most carefully planned of Dreiser's novels, each "Book" of the novel's three-part division is deliberately matched to a major aspect of its situations and themes. Although the three "books" vary in length, they achieve considerable symmetry, the first two dealing with cause and the third with effect. Further, Books I and II together comprise about two-thirds of the novel, with Roberta's death occurring almost exactly at the two-thirds mark. to use an analogy from drama, Book I is like the first act of a three-act play. It is relatively short, quick in movement and action, and it sets out the main lines of characterization as well as the basis for the conflict. (Note: in Dreiser's original manuscript Book I was considerably longer, containing nine chapters detailing Clyde's boyhood and offering additional documentation for his sense of inferiority). In Book II the conflict between sex and ambition is established, intensified by complications which produce a crisis (Roberta's pregnancy) and which result in a climax, the "murder." Book III provides a long dénouement, the trial, imprisonment, and execution, in which matters are settled but, as we have already observed, not resolved. That is, *An American Tragedy* is an open-ended drama. Within this general framework Clyde's tragic career may be described as an arc rather than a rise and fall. Just at the midpoint of his climb, when he has become a member of the smart set, has accompanied Sondra home for a midnight snack and declared his love for her, and she responds—a scene which occurs almost exactly midway in the novel—Roberta tells Clyde she is pregnant. For a time his momentum continues to carry him forward to greater social prestige and romantic success with Sondra, but to the observer, if not to Clyde himself, it is clear that the only possible movement is downward.

This deliberateness in structure carries over into Dreiser's use of various devices for ironic emphasis, devices thickly but not obtrusively deployed throughout the novel. By far the most obvious is the similarity of scene with which the novel begins and ends. Despite the passage of twelve years, the disgrace of a daughter and the execution of a son, the Griffiths continue to loft their prayers and hymns to a just and merciful God against the tall, indifferent walls of a commercial city, as a symbolic darkness descends. Everything Mother Griffiths has learned can be summed up in the dime for ice cream she gives Esta's illegitimate child, Clyde's replacement in the group of street evangelists; it is her way of forestalling another American tragedy. And the door through which the group disappears into the mission house reminds us of the door through which Clyde had passed to the electric chair. Another such parallel concludes both Book I and Book II. At the close of Book I Clyde flees, in darkness, from an accident in which a girl has been killed; at the end of Book II Clyde flees, once more in darkness, from the scene of a second girl's death. A somewhat similar device is Dreiser's detailed reproduction of religious mottoes and fragments of scripture at just those moments when the bitter facts of life are most shockingly apparent, especially in Books I and III. Note, for example, the heavy irony in the last few pages of Chapter xvii of Book III, where each stage of Mother Griffiths' anguish at hearing of Clyde's indictment for murder is interlined with fragments from the Psalms.

There are still other ironic techniques, only a few of which will be set down here. One of the more subtle is Dreiser's use of season and weather. Clyde's job at the Green-Davidson Hotel, a crucial experience in the shaping of his desires for sex, money, and position, begins in the fall (a better season for endings than beginnings; that, too, is intentional). Likewise, Clyde's sexual intimacy with Roberta begins in the fall, and his trial for murder takes place in the fall. Winter is an even gloomier Dreiserian season, for Clyde runs away from Kansas City in the winter, Roberta announces her pregnancy to Clyde in the winter, the judge passes sentence on Clyde in the winter, and Clyde's execution is carried out in the winter—and in darkness.

Finally, Dreiser stages a series of suggestive word-plays and scene-parallels which serve both to foreshadow and intensify the action. Just after coming to Lycurgus Clyde admires the Griffiths' stately home, which has as its lawn decorations a fountain in which a boy holds a swan (would Clyde have let Sondra drown?), and an arrangement of statuary in which dogs pursue a fleeing stag. Soon after this Clyde finds himself in the company of an all-too-willing girl named Rita (whom he has met at a church social), and in his efforts to remain on his feet and avoid risky sexual entanglements he dances with her to a tune called "The Love Boat." When, a few months later the lonely and now less cautious Clyde encounters Roberta on the shores of a nearby lake, he persuades her to come into his canoe, assuring her, "You won't be in any danger. . . . It's perfectly safe. . . . It won't tip over." Shortly after this, when they meet on the street (in darkness) for their first rendezvous, Clyde says presciently, "We have so little time." Later still, just after Roberta has determined that Clyde must either arrange an abortion or marry her, Dreiser shifts focus momentarily to Sondra, whose romantic daydreams of Clyde include fancied episodes in which she and Clyde are alone in a canoe on some remote, idyllic lake. And after Roberta's death, when an inwardly hysterical Clyde has rejoined the gay vacation group at Twelfth Lake, Sondra says to a boy steering a boat in which she, Clyde, and others are riding, "O, say, what do you want to do? Drown us all?"

Is it now not obvious that any judgment of *An American Tragedy* which has been made solely or largely on the basis of its "style" (always the same word) must be a narrow and capricious judgment? This is too big, too significant, too serious a book to permit an assessment of the writer's diction and command of sentence structure to stand as the last word; the strength and dimensions of its architecture tower over whatever defects may appear in the facing. In any case, *An American Tragedy* has already survived virtually a half-century of critical winnowing. It seems safe to predict that it will continue to grow in our esteem, and that in time it will join that all-too-small group of permanent books we call American classics.

The Bulwark

Theodore Dreiser's
The Bulwark:
A Final Resolution

Sidney Richman*

One of the more vexing problems in modern American literature surrounds Theodore Dreiser's activities in the final year of his life. In that year, 1945, the pre-eminent naturalist in America completed *The Bulwark*, a novel which in content and tone sits squarely in the transcendental tradition—owing nothing at all to Herbert Spencer and everything to Thoreau and John Woolman. And as if this were not startling enough, a few months later he joined the Communist party. Taken together the two acts are so strikingly opposed to the popular image of Dreiser the naturalist, and are in themselves so paradoxical, that even now they await a coherent explanation.

To be sure, some light has been cast upon the problem by those critics who have recognized in Dreiser a much more complex figure than the terms "naturalist" or "materialist" would allow. And in this area no one has done better service than Charles Walcutt. In a pioneer but still sound essay, Mr. Walcutt clearly perceived that Dreiser's thought was remarkably unscientific and incomplete; that despite his grounding in Spencer or the theoretical implications of Jacques Loeb's mechanistic materialism, Dreiser lacked the ability or the will to utilize materialist doctrine in a way that would dispel his involvement with super-naturalism. And it was an ambivalence that Mr. Walcutt found reflected in all of Dreiser's early novels.[1]

But if Dreiser's inconsistencies as a thinker anticipate his actions in 1945, they do not explain those actions. Aside from *The Bulwark*, Dreiser left no coherent statement of his final beliefs. And even if we admit that his thought had always been torn between the claims of Spencer and an impulsive or native idealism, Lionel Trilling also seemed correct when he said of Dreiser that "these rifts in his nearly monolithic materialism cannot quite prepare us for the blank pietism of *The Bulwark*."[2]

Actually, it is only in the last few years that the possibility of a real

*Reprinted from *American Literature*, 34 (May, 1962), 229–45. Reprinted by permission of Duke University Press.

understanding of Dreiser's later philosophy has arisen. With the recent publication of the author's letters it has finally become possible to fill in the major outlines of his life and interests in the later years of his life. And what is more important, the sudden availability of his private papers, and in particular the large collection of philosophical notes which he willed to the University of Pennsylvania, allow us to see his philosophy in the making. Though disjointed and frequently incoherent, the notes reflect that search for understanding which was to culminate in *The Bulwark*.

But it must be said that in each area the record is as familiar as it is strange. What has always touched Dreiser's activities with grandeur was his unceasing concern for the significance of life; and in the years following the publication of *An American Tragedy* the search seemed, if anything, to take on renewed vigor. If would seem, in fact, that Dreiser was himself consciously seeking for an end to his intellectual perplexity; and in the twenty years that intervened between the story of Clyde Griffiths and *The Bulwark*, Dreiser to a large extent abandoned literature in order to achieve philosophical and political certainty.

The form of this quest, however, was clearly indicated in the closing years of the twenties. In the few works of fiction which he produced in these years, Dreiser offered numerous hints that the theoretical framework of his greatest novel could no longer answer for some basic beliefs that had already survived a quarter-century study of naturalist theory. In fact in *A Gallery of Women*, which appeared in 1929, he called into doubt the whole concept of a fortuitous universe which had animated *An American Tragedy*. As a preface to the story "Giff," an account of a spiritualist he had known, he wrote:

> In the face of all inductive science and the strange yet narrow walls of all naturalistic philosophies . . . I hold that behind the seemingly foolish predictions which "came true" moves something which is . . . solidly real . . . an all pervasive intention or plan.

It was in search of this "intention or plan" that Dreiser began in these years a new course of study. But it was perhaps inevitable that he should seek to enlarge his concept of reality within the framework of beliefs he had already derived from naturalism. From 1928 on he was a frequent visitor at a number of institutions for advanced scientific research in the East; and when in the early thirties he established residence on the West coast, he began a rather striking correspondence with such scientists as Flexner, Langmuir, Millikan, and Crile. Dreiser was particularly interested in those advances in science which could at once be interpreted as supporting and developing the materialist doctrines he had received from Jacques Loeb, the University of Chicago biologist who had perfected the theory of chemical determinism and had supplied him with the guiding concept in his characterization of Frank Algernon Cowperwood. And in the twenties and thirties, despite the sudden ascendancy of the so-called Vitalist school of biology, Dreiser found support for his Loebian view in a number of diverse but reputable quarters. Upon reading George Crile's *The Phenomena of Life*, he wrote to congratulate that scientist for having produced a work which "seemed to be exactly in line with the mechanistic reality we call life."[3] And when in September of 1936 he read an account of Clark Hull's attempt to build a mechanical model of the human brain in order to prove that mind could be explained on purely physical grounds, Dreiser requested a full explanation, adding in his letter: "I am very much inclined to believe in a mechanistic conception of things in general."[4]

But it should be stressed that in any full-blown mechanistic analysis of life Dreiser found at best only a description of the physical world, not the final explanation he sought. In truth, the philosophy raised for the author the problem of ultimate causation; and in doing so involved him again in the very mysteries he sought to dispel.

Dreiser's bewilderment about the matter of individual freedom is perhaps the best illustration of the difficulties he was facing at this time. Throughout the twenties and early thirties Dreiser's studies both of mechanism and Freudian psychology had convinced him that a belief in human freedom was highly suspect. And it was only a short step from this to a repudiation of all individuality. Writing in "The Myth of Individuality" in 1934, he stated that "man is not really and truly living and thinking, but, on the contrary, is being lived and thought by that which has produced [him]. Apart from it . . . he has no existence."[5] Such a thesis had some curious effects on Dreiser. On the one hand, it helped support a lingering strain of skepticism, for it followed that if all thought was simply "tropistic" or motivated from without, then all thought was limited; there were barriers beyond which the mind, even the best scientific mind, could not proceed. But on the other hand, the theory evoked as never before the mysticism that had always been an essential aspect of his personality, for it seemed another revelation of that "plan" or ordination which he had written of in the preface to "Giff." Indeed, what it finally amounted to was a need to celebrate a universe as logically and beautifully patterned as his studies of mechanistic theory had led him to believe it was. And in this regard, Loeb's mechanism had for Dreiser something of the spiritual content that the Celestial Mechanics had for Cotton Mather. It diverted him not away from God but toward Him. In the same year in which "The Myth of Individuality" was written, for instance, Dreiser could suggest that the planners of the Chicago Fair build a monument to "the helpful spirit of religion . . . something which will awaken thought and awe and perhaps reverence in man in regard to the universe as a whole."[6]

It was to formulate this new attitude toward life and life's mysterious order that Dreiser began, sometime in the mid-thirties, to gather notes for a philosophical volume he intended calling "The Formulae Called Life." Though never finished, the work comprises some eleven manuscript boxes of assorted essays, fragments of essays, and newspaper clippings. Unfortunately most of the material is undated. But it would seem that Dreiser's permanent plan was to complete a study which would embody a description of the purely mechanistic structure of life, and at the same time elaborate his belief that the Mind or Spirit which animated and ordered that life was, if incalculable, more benign than otherwise, and was in most essentials indistinguishable from the God of Eastern philosophy.

But taken as a testament of belief, the work is bewilderingly shapeless. Aside from two or three obviously early essays, most of the material consists of notes which were to serve as illustrations for various chapters. And as often as not, the really valuable revelations of Dreiser's mind occur not in the more developed sections but in the various preliminary notations. In the collection of materials he proposed calling "The Mechanism Called Man," for instance, there is a series of notes which elucidate the book's initial problem:

> The secrets of energies that make the plants and animals grow . . . Energy—electrical energy—passing along the nerve cells to the veins and arteries provide the command or pressure which holds them normally controlled, giving the same rate and quantity of flow throughout the entire body. Is this mental or a mechanical procedure? If it is mechanical what is the nature of the force that controls electricity and causes it to serve, as it does?[7]

The form of the question arises of course out of the answer, for in a later note Dreiser states that

> —the laws of compulsion of physics and chemistry—appear to indicate something that is not so much matter or energy (matter-energy) as a super something immaterial and imponderable that throughout all man-recorded time operates and directs all to such ends as man can register or see. . . .[8]

The final conclusion is that it is indeed Mind which directs the world and the universe, and Dreiser completes the argument with the statement that the mechanical forces we witness all about us are simply a revelation of higher force:

> The word mechanistic, deriving as it does from our crude machinery and used in connection with the stupendous and baffling and beautiful thing we call the universe, is, of course, nothing more than a very crude and inadequate attempt to emphasize the idea of regularity in nature as well as form in connection with all the forms of nature we call life. . . . The nature of God, or the creative force that appears to operate directly through matter-energy as well as the laws and spatial

conditions environing the same is, in fact, the one reality—universal creative reality.[9]

What the particular nature of this "creative reality" might be is never decisively answered. But there are some suggestive hints in the materials that were to comprise the chapter "Mind in Nature." Here Dreiser maintained that "The Mind, the Being, the Creator, the Will, is the *latent* possibilities of any atom, which are enhanced, brought out, and act, through combination and interaction, and never through any individual acting as such."[10]

But such a conclusion was bound to appear "too mechanistic" and Dreiser drops it in favor of a more human force—in particular, an aesthetic force. Contemplating the structure of a snowflake, he wrote that "Unless we are ready to presuppose an artistic form-designing force in nature or the Universe . . . how are we to explain their appearance—and more, their mathematical exactness and beauty?"[11]

More often than not, it is precisely the aesthetic sense which compels Dreiser to celebrate nature. "When one realizes the wonderful mechanism of life," he wrote, "one can, without religious or dogmatic delusion, experience awe, reverence, gratitude, and more, love for so wondrous a process or spirit. . . ."[12]

But fragments such as these, undated and probably written over a long period of time, serve only to indicate the direction of Dreiser's thought. Perhaps the only comprehensive statement in the collection is the essay "My Creator" which Dreiser completed in 1943 and intended using as the book's concluding chapter. Though more impressionistic than philosophic, the essay does chart the outlines of Dreiser's later thought, and does so with a revealing degree of self-consciousness. In it he wrote that when people in the past had asked for his opinion for life his "brash and certainly most unpremeditated reply was that I took no meaning from all that I saw." But he added that since then many things had revealed to him "the evidence of plan and design in all things everywhere from time immemorial." And he went on to discuss the evidence for purposeful design in the universe, first in conjunction with the avocado tree that grew in his yard and then in respect to the farthest stars:

> I am moved not only to awe but to reverence for the creator of the same whom—his presence in all things from worm to star to thought—I meditate constantly. . . . Awe I have. And, at long last, profound reverence for so amazing and esthetic and wondrous a process.[13]

But despite its suggestiveness, "The Formulae Called Life" represents only a preliminary to the completion of Dreiser's philosophy. Soon after he finished "My Creator," Dreiser underwent a prolonged period of anxiety and apparently never returned to the work. Instead, in the summer of 1944 he took up the manuscript of *The Bulwark* and in the following months rewrote and finished the novel. And it is to this book that one must turn for a consideration of Dreiser's final philosophy.

On the surface, however, this is no easier task than deciphering "The Formulae Called Life." For one thing, it is extremely hard to credit the work to the same author who had written *An American Tragedy* or the Cowperwood series. Of the fictional techniques that Dreiser had been evolving for over forty years—almost all are gone.

Perhaps the most striking departure from his older ways lies in the spareness of *The Bulwark*, its lack of detail. What so distinguished Dreiser's method in his earlier books was his patient regard for details, his tendency to linger over particularities. But in *The Bulwark* there is hardly a trace of that vision which could evoke the compulsions of an age through a pair of patent-leather shoes. In a way, Dreiser was simply illustrating in his new style and conception of the novel the major distinction between the naturalist and the literary mystic. To the naturalist the sources of inspiration are inevitably linked to the environment and the things of the environment—to the world as an extension of personality. But for the mystic matter is always threatening to break down into its spiritual counterpart; it has no life except in relation to the force or design which brings it into being. As Matthiessen said of *The Bulwark*, and it can be said of no other of Dreiser's books, it reads not so much like a naturalist tract as a simple parable, symbolic to the core.[14]

The most obvious symptom of this lies in the handling of setting. *The Bulwark* is Dreiser's only novel to depart completely from the big-city background. The major action occurs in the rural countryside just outside Philadelphia—primarily in the house of Solon Barnes; and even though passing scenes are set not only in Philadelphia but in New York as well, there are none of those impressionistic evocations of social force that Dreiser had traditionally written into these backgrounds. In the same sense as the city was the dramatic corollary to Dreiser's naturalism, nature had now become an extension of his mysticism.

Perhaps the only familiar Dreiserian theme in *The Bulwark* is the social one, for the major conflict in the novel surrounds Solon Barnes's inability to understand or cope with social change. Indeed, the book not only incorporates Dreiser's favorite subject of the individual's efforts to preserve his identity in a world in revolt, but it intensifies it as well. For unlike Old Gerhardt or Asa Griffiths, Solon Barnes is not only victimized by his world, but he is consciously aware of it. In a sense, in fact, *The Bulwark* embodies the old parable of an education for sainthood, complete with rigorous tests and preliminary misjudgments.

The child of Quakers of the "old school," there is about Solon Barnes in his youth a curiously spiritual and sensitive manner. But as the book progresses, Solon's spiritual nature loses its original fire. In fact his development appears to reflect the transcendental concept of maturity being tantamount to a loss of vision. Originally Solon's responses to nature and to men had been of a spontaneous religious order. But in early manhood it became evident that his religion was as much a matter of precept as of innate compulsion. And the change, as Dreiser records it, represents a dramatic adjustment to the social forces at work in society. For by the last quarter of the nineteenth century (the period in which the novel opens), the Quakers had fallen partial victim to "the enormous spirit of change and modernism" that had overtaken America; and the forms of their faith were gradually changing in response to newer impulses. Solon, while he continues to retain as many symbols of pure faith as possible, is sharply aware of the demands of the day. And throughout the novel the internalized conflict between success and simplicity, between primitive faith and material luxury, is the cornerstone of his development.

The tensions in Solon's character are a major symptom of Dreiser's own political and spiritual ambivalence. Not only a bulwark of the faith, Solon also represents a bulwark of sound business sense, and his success as a director of the Traders and Builders Bank of Philadelphia is almost as resounding as his success in the meetinghouse. Indeed, Solon cannot separate the two activities. Success in life, he would have argued, was simply the adjunct of goodness. In Solon's mind, therefore, the operations of the banks and the laws of commerce were "directly connected with Divine Will," and control of money was a kind of stewardship under God. It is because of this that Solon's ultimate resignation from the bank, his refusal to benefit from schemes he thought immoral, serves as the climax to one of the novel's major themes.

Far the larger section of the narrative, however, deals with Solon's painful inability to understand his children, particularly Etta and Stewart. The issue of his middle years, the two represent the kind of young people that, as Matthiessen has said, "Dreiser has always treated with perfect sympathy."[15] And indeed, the author's analysis of Etta's character is in most essentials identical to that of his favorite heroine, Jennie Gerhardt, a character who had survived all the accidents of a naturalist world by virtue of some mysterious and mystic personality. If Etta differs from Jennie, it is perhaps only in regard to her intellectual prowess—for her search for life leads her to an acquaintance with books, to summer courses at the University of Wisconsin, and ultimately to Greenwich Village and an unhappy love affair with a painter.

Stewart Barnes, the youngest of the children, rounds off the cast of Dreiserian types. In most respects he represents an abrupt transition to the modernism which has invaded Solon's life. In revolt against his father's moral inflexibility, Stewart yearns for immediate self-fulfilment; and like Clyde Griffiths before him, his search for sexual gratification leads to disaster. One evening, in the company of two school friends, Stewart picks up a working-class girl and drives her to the country. One of the boys puts an opiate in the girl's coffee, and as a result of drinking it she dies. For his role in the crime Stewart is arrested; but so overcome is he with shame and panic that he kills himself in his cell.

Stewart's death serves as the final catalyst in Solon Barnes's development. Torn by the tragedy, he retires to his home and there ensues a prolonged period of mental recovery. And it is in this final section of the book that Dreiser completes the essential outlines of his philosophy.

In the course of his search after meaning, Solon spends more and more time in the gardens that surround his home, and in time he regains the sensitivity that had been his as a child—the feeling that in nature God moves close to the surface. It was a discovery that Dreiser himself had made in the middle thirties and had developed in "My Creator," where in contemplating the form of a tree in his back yard he had decided that the forces of creation were purposive and constructive.

For Solon, too, the close attention to the forms of flowers and trees—to all of vegetative life—confirms in him the belief that the Creative Divinity moves purposefully throughout nature. But one day he encounters a scene that thirty years before would have supplied Dreiser's naturalistic theory with a positive illustration. Perched on a bud was a fly; and as Solon watched, he saw suddenly that the insect was busily engaged in devouring the plant. In a way, it is an almost perfect re-enactment of young Cowperwood's experience in *The Financier* with the squid and the lobster, the scene—and the image—which was to supply the youthful tycoon with his first comprehensive look at society, the world, and the universe. And for Solon, too, the experience is significant. But his reactions are totally different than Cowperwood's:

> After bending down and examining a blade of grass here, a climbing vine there, a minute flower, as lovely and yet as inexplicable as his green fly, Solon turned in a kind of religious awe and wonder. Surely there must be a Creative Divinity, and so a purpose, behind all this variety and beauty and tragedy of life.

If Solon's response is reminiscent of anyone, it is of Thoreau's emotionalizing over the natural struggle he saw about Walden Pond. And in truth, there is little doubt that Dreiser was here taking over and incorporating into his own philosophy some of the essential insights of transcendental theory. In *Walden*, for instance, Thoreau at one point makes much of a lone and dignified fisherman:

> Such a man has some right to fish, and I love to see nature carried out in him. The perch swallows the grub-worm, the pickerel swallows the perch, and the fisherman swallows the pickerel; and so all the chinks in the scale of being are filled.[16]

In the late thirties Dreiser undertook an edition of Thoreau's writings for the Living Thoughts Library and wrote a lengthy introduction which illustrates the kinship between his own thought and Thoreau's. What Dreiser especially appreciated in the transcendentalist was his delight in the "mechanics" of nature but his refusal to let the apparent processes of life explain life. As Dreiser wrote in the introduction, "The philosopher and dreamer or poet, while profiting and on occasion being identical with the scientist, has never ceased to concern himself with the . . . mystery of why."[17]

If he is describing anyone, Dreiser is describing himself. Like Thoreau, he had found in science the means of framing certain insights into the world. But above and beyond the realm of scientific applicability the mysteries, the "Unknown," remained inviolable but penetrating. In fact, Dreiser managed to smuggle into the introduction a clear statement of his own attitudes:

> Nowadays the scientists insist that philosophical generalizations must be founded on scientific results. All talk of any supreme regulating and hence, legal or directing force or spirit is *out*. . . . Hence the unconscious confession of scientific defeat. . . . For all its knowledge of *how*, science cannot say *why*.[18]

Something of the nature of this "directing force" Dreiser describes a few lines later in an almost direct paraphrase of some of his notes for "The Formulae Called Life": "There are these various laws by which the different forms of matter-energy are regulated. . . . In other words they are regulated by something (God is one word . . . also Spirit, Brahma, Divine Essence, or Force)."[19]

But perhaps the most revealing section of Dreiser's essay on Thoreau is that which, by implication, answers for the riddle of savagery which both Cowperwood and Solon Barnes had witnessed:

> At no point [Dreiser writes] is Thoreau willing to imply, let alone admit the absence, even for any fraction of time, of a universal and apparently beneficent control, which, however dark and savage its results or expressions may seem to us . . . is none-the-less, in some larger and realer sense, the substance of something that in its infinite breadth and allness and duration is good—and more, artistically beautiful and satisfying, and so, well intended for all.[20]

In a sense, the passage is a restatement of the guiding principle Dreiser had been moving toward in "The Formulae Called Life." Thoreau could "rejoice to see a contest between two Indian tribes for the possession of a hunting ground," Dreiser wrote, without losing sight of the ultimate order of the universe.[21] All that Thoreau would object to is the struggle which arises from the unnatural exertions of the human will, from the perversions of commercialism.[22] That is why Dreiser declares that Thoreau "would have despised our recent world war as a commercial enterprise."[23]

All of this is made clear in *The Bulwark*. Solon can witness the savagery of life destroying life without questioning his belief in the ultimate harmony of things; indeed, the harmony is glorified by the savagery. But when the directors of his bank stoop to brutal but not unlawful machinations, Solon is horrified and forced to resign his lucrative post as treasurer. In succumbing to the "artificial" motives of a commercial society, man was foregoing his proper and natural role. Or as Dreiser said of Thoreau, he "did not consider man as a social organism or part of one. He was a universal organism."[24]

Elsewhere in his introduction, Dreiser calls attention to Thoreau's kinship with John Woolman. Ultimately, Dreiser saw this resemblance in the major beliefs which both held and which could be summed up in two principles: "(1) that solitary contemplation of nature brought about a harmony with spiritual forces which created the world, and (2) that what is right is so by reference to intuition."[25] Both principles are illustrated in Solon's development, for its is only when he wanders alone through the countryside that Solon comes into harmony with Creative Divinity. And further, he cannot communicate his experience to Etta except by recourse to vague mystical images.

And in this regard, Solon's experiences with nature may again be related to those which Dreiser underwent in his later years. Solon, for one thing, believed he could communicate with animals. Dreiser frequently believed the same thing. Elias writes that one day in the late thirties, while walking near his home on Mount Kisco, Dreiser encountered a puff adder coiled to strike:

> Dreiser had attempted to speak to it reassuringly, saying he intended no harm. As it had lowered its head and begun to slip away, Dreiser had followed after, to observe its movements, whereupon the snake had coiled and puffed out its neck again. Again Dreiser had spoken to it, promising he would not harm it, and having stepped back . . . he observed the snake . . . uncoil and come toward him, passing by the toe of his shoe as it had crawled away. . . . Dreiser had been sure the snake had understood—indeed, Dreiser had soon decided that man could talk with animals or birds, perhaps even with the grass and the flowers.[26]

In the concluding pages of *The Bulwark*, Solon Barnes undergoes an experience with a puff adder which is at every point identical with Dreiser's. And he explains it to his daughter in the following fashion:

> "I mean that good intent is of itself a universal language, and if our intention is good, all creatures in their particular way understand, and so it was that this puff adder understood me just as I understood it. It had no ill intent, but was only afraid. And then, my intent being not only good but loving, it understood me and had no fear, but came back to me. . . . And now I thank God for this revelation of His universal

presence and His good intent toward all things—all of His created world. For otherwise how would it understand me, and I it, if we were not both a part of Himself?"

The history of such a concept is as old as philosophy itself; but in *The Bulwark* the form of Dreiser's belief in the inner principle of God and its expression in communal life appears to have been taken directly from the Quaker concept of the Inner Light—a concept which he describes in the novel as "the indwelling consciousness of the Divine Spirit, the true union of God with human beings."

Dreiser's interest in Quaker thought, however, is apparently a late development. As Gerhard Friedrich points out, it was through a chance meeting with Rufus Jones, while the latter headed a committee for the relief of Spanish Civil War refugees, that Dreiser was first introduced to the subject.[27] But soon after the meeting Dreiser acquired a copy of Woolman's *Journal* and was deeply impressed by it. In 1939, for instance, he wrote to the Dean of Whittier College to urge that the book be placed on the required reading list for students as it "will be the greatest service and encouragement for all seeking an intelligible faith."[28]

In many ways Dreiser found in Woolman a speculative system ideally suited to his own philosophical and political needs. It brought into clear equilibrium both the reforming zeal that had been developing during the depression and the philosophical idealism that marked his deeper thinking. Needless to say, in the light of *The Bulwark* it would be nonsense to argue that Dresier's participation in the Marxian world-view was unequivocal. His metaphysic stands to dialectical materialism like day to night, and in letter after letter in the thirties,[29] in comments to friends, in marginal asides in such books as *Dreiser Looks at Russia* or *Tragic America*, there is full and eloquent support for James T. Farrell's remark that Dreiser found in Communism only "a half-way house."[30] What Communism offered Dreiser was a system of reform that seemed efficacious and humane. He felt in fact that what animated the Russian "experiment" was the very Creative Divinity or spirit of "good intent" that transcended all "commercial" motives. As he wrote in a letter of 1934 to Warren Clark: "I find very little difference between what the Friends are seeking to do here and what the communists are seeking to do in Russia. Both are laying aside the profit motive in order to help mankind to a better level and a happier life."[31]

And in truth, Solon Barnes's success in old age, indeed his very perfection, resides not only in his acceptance of an immanent and benign Divinity, but in his renunciation of social evil as well. Ultimately there can be no separation between the two. "To help mankind to a better level" was a religious imperative.

It was from just such a compulsion that Solon Barnes renounced his position at the bank. But it should be added that throughout the novel he had always been sympathetic to the cause of the underdog, a fact which he owed "to his training and membership in that faith which he believed sought, more than any other, to achieve and maintain a happy balance and equity in all human affairs." In the final analysis, in fact, it is the Quaker concept of brotherhood which rounds out both Dreiser's philosophical and social interests. In his last days, Solon has Etta read to him that section of Woolman's *Journal* which sums up the Quaker principle of interdependence:

> "A principle placed in the human mind, which in different places and ages hath had different names; it is, however, pure and proceeds from God. It is deep and inward, confined to no forms of religion nor excluded from any, when the heart stands in perfect sincerity. In whomsoever this takes root and grows, they become brethren."

It was therefore not the form or forms of religion that gave truth, but the truth behind all such forms. And it was with this knowledge in mind that Dreiser frequented with impartial enthusiasm all churches just before his death.[32] If the rituals of worship differed, true religion wiped out all distinctions. Whether it be the passion of the Communist, the Quaker, or the writer, the effort to improve man's condition was simply an extension of that principle of God awakened in the human soul. Shortly after he completed *The Bulwark*, Dreiser framed the thesis in a long poem which states that in a period of war and misery many men are moved by a Divine Force to the *religious* task of bettering the world—the "small-town editor," the "worker's friend," the "educator" and the "minister:"

> And so from the heart comes the answer
> Of him who does and serves
> That by degrees
> A new and better world
> May be made.

In essence, the poem conveys the same message as Solon's remark to Etta that "good intent is of itself a universal language," and a "revelation of His universal presence."

By and large, *The Bulwark* is thus the clearest statement of Dreiser's final philosophy. In the few months that yet remained to him before his death, the author attempted to apply the same system of thought to the final volume of the Cowperwood trilogy, *The Stoic*. But *The Stoic* is both too sketchy and too dependent upon the lines of development already charted by *The Financier* and *The Titan* to serve so clearly as *The Bulwark* as a model of Dreiser's philosophy. In Solon Barnes's life, no matter how refracted, Dreiser's entire career as a thinker is recapitulated and decisively reordered.

And yet, beyond this talk of philosophy, one is tempted to draw some conclusions in regard to the literary relationship of *The Bulwark* to

Dreiser's earlier and, as most critics have pointed out, better work. Matthiessen has suggested that *The Bulwark* is as far from the literary modes of its day—the modes which Dreiser himself is partially responsible for—as *Sister Carrie* was from its day; and he concluded that it simply lacked the force of Dreiser's best work.[33] And it is true that *The Bulwark* is deficient in many of the qualities we have come to appreciate as Dreiser's unique gifts to American literature. To perhaps a fatal degree, the novel lacks that solidity of presentation, the giant massing of detail, that made *Sister Carrie* or *An American Tragedy* so memorable. And if closer in technique to Dreiser's second novel, it still has little of *Jennie Gerhardt's* tragic dimension. And this is not only a result of *The Bulwark's* affirmative conclusion, but rather of the form of that affirmation—which is after all too traditional to be exciting.

But a great deal of the book is still unmistakably Dreiser. It has in fact a breadth of sensitivity that given the spareness of the style appears almost unaccountable. Perhaps it is the sense of actual pain one feels for Solon in his crises or Etta and Stewart in their desperation. Or perhaps it is just a function of what is so good about all of Dreiser's work—the compassion he feels for his characters and his patient understanding of their pretensions. And in this regard, it is well to remember that Solon's death is not quite the end of the book. The last word belongs to Etta, who has remained at her father's side and has received through him a new appreciation for life and spirit. But despite the affirmative nature of *her* final view, Etta is still the emotional sister of Jennie Gerhardt. When her brother Orville finds her weeping over Solon's coffin he expresses surprise that she should be so shaken by their father's death. And Etta's reply must be Dreiser's own—for it sounds a note that through all his work, through fifty years of changing philosophies and shifting attitudes, had remained the sum of his dramatic vision, as true for him as it was moving for his readers:

"Oh," she says, "I am not crying for myself, or for father—I am crying for *life*."

Notes

1. Charles C. Walcutt, "The Three Stages of Theodore Dreiser's Naturalism," *PMLA*, 55, 266–289 (March, 1940). Revised and reprinted in Walcutt's *American Literary Naturalism, A Divided Stream* (Minneapolis, 1956), pp. 180–221.

2. Lionel Trilling, *The Liberal Imagination* (New York, 1953), p. 21.

3. *The Collected Letters of Theodore Dreiser*, ed. Robert H. Elias (Philadelphia, 1959), III, 776.

4. *Ibid.*, p. 779.

5. Theodore Dreiser, "The Myth of Individuality," *American Mercury*, 31, 341 (March, 1934).

6. Quoted in Robert H. Elias, *Theodore Dreiser: Apostle of Nature* (New York, 1946), p. 284.

7. Theodore Dreiser, "The Mechanism Called Man," typewritten MS (n.d., the Dreiser Papers, University of Pennsylvania Library).

8. *Ibid.*

9. *Ibid.*

10. Theodore Dreiser, "The Mind in Nature," typewritten MS (n.d., the Dreiser Papers, University of Pennsylvania Library).

11. Theodore Dreiser, "Form in Nature," typewritten MS (n.d., the Dreiser Papers, University of Pennsylvania Library).

12. Theodore Dreiser, "Equation Inevitable," typewritten MS (n.d., the Dreiser Papers, University of Pennsylvania Library).

13. Theodore Dreiser, "My Creator," typewritten MS (November, 1943, the Dreiser Papers, University of Pennsylvania Library).

14. F. O. Matthiessen, *Theodore Dreiser* (New York, 1951), p. 243.

15. *Ibid.*, p. 244.

16. Henry David Thoreau, *Walden and Other Writings* (New York, 1934), p. 254.

17. Introduction to *The Living Thoughts of Thoreau* (New York, 1939), p. 2.

18. *Ibid.*, pp. 2–3.

19. *Ibid.*

20. *Ibid.*, p. 16.

21. *Ibid.*, p. 32.

22. *Ibid.*, p. 26.

23. *Ibid.*, p. 32.

24. *Ibid.*, p. 24.

25. *Ibid.*, p. 8.

26. Elias, *Theodore Dreiser*, p. 288.

27. Gerhard Friedrich, "Theodore Dreiser's Debt to Woolman's *Journal*," *American Quarterly*, 7, 386 (Winter, 1955).

28. *Letters*, III, 834.

29. The reader should consult the following letters: II, 586–587, 718; III, 980.

30. James T. Farrell, *Literature and Morality* (New York, 1947), p. 33.

31. *Letters*, III, 679.

32. Matthiessen, *Theodore Dreiser*, p. 249.

33. *Ibid.*

INDEX